FOR REFERENCE

Do Not Take From This Room

Around the World with Historical Fiction and Folktales

Highly Recommended and Award-Winning Books, Grades K–8

Beth Bartleson Zarian

The Scarecrow Press, Inc.
Lanham, Maryland • Toronto • Oxford
2004

SCARECROW PRESS, INC.

Published in the United States of America
by Scarecrow Press, Inc.
A wholly owned subsidary of
The Rowman & Littlefield Publishing Group, Inc.
4501 Forbes Boulevard, Suite 200, Lanham, Maryland 20706
www.scarecrowpress.com

PO Box 317
Oxford
OX2 9RU, UK

British Library Cataloguing in Publication Information Available

Library of Congress Cataloging-in-Publication Data

Zarian, Beth Bartleson, 1960–
  Around the world with historical fiction and folktales : highly recommended and award-
winning books, grades K–8 / Beth Bartleson Zarian.
      p. cm.
   Includes index.
   ISBN 0-8108-4816-3 (pbk. : alk. paper)
   1. Historical fiction—Bibliography. 2. Tales—Bibliography. 3. Children's stories—
Bibliography. 4. Children—Books and reading—United States. 5. Best books—United
States. I. Title.
   Z1037.A2Z37 2004
   [PN1009.A1]
   809.3'81—dc22
                                                                        2004004427

⊖™ The paper used in this publication meets the minimum requirements of
American National Standard for Information Sciences—Permanence of
Paper for Printed Library Materials, ANSI/NISO Z39.48-1992.
Manufactured in the United States of America.

This book is inspired by and dedicated to
Larry, Paul, Steven, Adam, and Michael

Contents

Part III: Myths and Folktales

Acknowledgments

The production of any book requires the expertise of a number of individuals, and this book is no exception.

I would like to thank my family for providing me with the inspiration and emotional support that enabled me to complete this project. They generously allowed me time away from tasks while tolerating mediocre meals during periods of writing intensity. In addition, I am thankful to my wonderful neighbor and friend, Pam Johnson, and her family for providing helpful encouragement during the production process.

Several professionals at Lake Forest School District 67 provided various levels of assistance. I am thankful to Rosemary Ferche and Sherri Randolph for their materials and insight. I feel compelled to make special mention of Sandra George, whose expert librarianship skills were a source of inspiration, and who encouraged me to promote this book at a professional level.

Some of my most productive hours of research and writing occurred while listening to the rhythmic sound made by competitive swimmers swimming their early morning practice laps. I am grateful to Coach Maureen Sheehan and the Lake Forest Swim Club for generously providing space and tolerating my continuous presence during my son's morning swim practices.

The assistance of my professional editor, Kathe Gustafson, was absolutely invaluable. Her outstanding editorial skills, keen eye for details, and organizational ability helped shape and form my research into this finished product. Kathe's questions and opinions provided a delightful source for intellectual debate, and her creative insight was responsible for the wonderful title of this book.

I am grateful to all the professionals at Scarecrow Press, who enthusiastically accepted and promoted this book. I would like to give special mention to Acquisitions Editor Sue Easun, and Editorial Assistant Nicole Carty. Their professional expertise and patience with my multitude of questions is greatly appreciated. In addition, the indexing provided by Kathy Little will assist users of this book in finding the materials they are seeking.

Introduction

When a child becomes emotionally connected to a historical period of time through literature, important educational advantages result. His awareness of the social context expands, and his desire to obtain more factual information increases. This awareness and desire builds an emotional bridge between fact and fiction for the young student.

Several experiences prompted me to compile this bibliography. First, as a mother of four children, I seek opportunities to ignite my children's educational passion with quality literature that allows them to approach the educational curriculum with heightened interest. Second, my background in library reference gives me the expertise to accomplish the necessary research to compile this bibliography. Third, my current position on the curriculum committee of my local school district allows me insight into the conflicts that ensue when teachers attempt to integrate their curricula. Observing their struggle prompted the creation of this bibliography to complement the teaching of social studies and language arts. The intended audience for this publication, therefore, includes parents, librarians, and professional educators who want to offer their young readers more than facts when teaching history.

This is an easily used reference source of award-winning fiction books in the areas of American and world history as well as myths and folktales from around the world. It also includes lists and descriptions of the awards that the nearly eight hundred books have received. Similar reference books on the market tend to focus on only one area of historical fiction, either American history or world history, not both. The beautifully illustrated books of myths and folktales are a complement to any curriculum that focuses on cultural studies.

This bibliography is limited to the elementary school years of kindergarten through eighth grade. The books selected must have won awards or been highly recommended by professional journals specializing in reviewing this type of literature. Books were chosen for inclusion by reviewing recommended reading lists, scrutinizing professional trade journals, and searching literature award data bases.

Current publisher information was obtained from the Books in Print data base through the publication year 2003.

The bibliographic entries are divided into three sections. The books in section I pertain to American history and are grouped into major chronological periods. Section II focuses on world history, beginning with prehistoric times and moving forward to the present through the chronological stages of European history first. Then literature from the world's remaining geographic regions is presented, arranged by geographic proximity. Section III contains myths and folktales, with books representing different American cultures listed first and then those from countries in the remainder of the world arranged in alphabetical order. Please refer to the table of contents for the subheadings within sections I, II, and III.

Within each historical division, the books are separated into grade levels and grouped together so that redundancy between the grade levels is reduced. Each entry is listed alphabetically by the author's last name with complete bibliographic information and grade level recommendations. It also indicates the format the book has been published in, including hardcover, paperback, audio versions, and a VHS or VHS/DVD notation if the book has been made into a movie. As an additional source of information for school districts that primarily use the Lexile reading scale, a Lexile measure is provided when available to indicate the reading demand of the text in terms of semantic difficulty (vocabulary) and syntactic complexity (sentence length). More information about this scale can be found at www.lexile.com. Following the reference data is a brief summary of the story. These succinct annotations are based on reviews written by professional trade publications such as *Booklist, Publishers Weekly, Kirkus Reviews, School Library Journal, Riverbank Review,* and book descriptions distributed by individual publishers. The awards the book has received are listed alphabetically after the summary.

The appendixes contain additional sources of reference information. "A Guide to the Awards" is an alphabetical listing of the awards received by the books included in the bibliography with information about their background, eligibility requirements, publications, etc. The inclusion of award descriptions allows the user of this bibliography to evaluate book selections more thoroughly. "Sources" lists the original data used to research and compile this bibliography.

The bibliography culminates in an index that allows the books to be located by title, author, illustrator, or subject.

It is my hope that educators will find this material helpful in making history come to life and creating more interest in the subject for their students while exposing them to a higher level of literature. The awards these books have won validate these selections to the parents, librarians, and teachers who use them.

I

AMERICAN HISTORY

Chapter 1

Prior to 1600

Grades Kindergarten to 2

No award winning books were found.

Grades 3 to 6

Dorris, Michael. *Sees Behind Trees.*
First copyright 1945. New York: Hyperion, 1996. 96 pages. ISBN 0-7868-2215-5.
New York: Disney Press, 1999. 128 pages. ISBN 0-7868-1357-1pbk.
Lexile 840. Grades 3 to 6.

In pre-Colonial America, a young Native American boy, Walnut, has disabling vision problems that prevent him from undergoing a ceremony to receive a new name and become an adult. After his sympathetic uncle invents a new contest to "see what can't be seen," the boy's other senses bring success and earn him the name Sees Behind Trees.

Minnesota Book Awards, Publishers Weekly Best Books of the Year, and *School Library Journal Best Book.*

Garland, Sherry. *Indio.*
San Diego, CA: Harcourt Children's Books, 1995. 304 pages. ISBN 0-15-38631-9 and 0-15-20021-6pbk. Lexile 960. Grades 6 to 10.

In the early 16th century, Apache raiders take her brother prisoner and kill her grandmother when Ipa-tah-chi is ten years old. On the day she is to marry, Ipa is captured by Spanish conquistadors, sold into slavery, and forced to work in a Mexican silver mine. A Spanish soldier's kindness is the only relief from the exploitation of Ipa and her family.

American Bookseller Pick of the Lists and American Library Association Best Books for Young Adults.

Grades 7 and 8

Garland, Sherry. *Indio.*
Refer to complete information under Grades 3 to 6.

O'Dell, Scott. *The King's Fifth.*
Samuel Bryant, illustrator. New York: Houghton Mifflin Co., 1966. 272 pages. ISBN 0-395-06963-7. Lexile 840. Grades 7 to 10.

In 1541, seventeen-year-old Esteban waits in a California prison to be tried for throwing a fifth of the king's gold into a desert sinkhole after seeing how the Conquistadors' desire for gold was corrupting them.

Newbery Honor Book.

Vick, Helen Hughes. *Walker of Time.*
Niwot, CO: Roberts Rinehart Publishers, 1993. 212 pages. ISBN 0-943173-84-1 and 0-943173-80-9pbk. Grades 7 to 10.

Two fifteen-year-old Hopi Indian boys are propelled eight hundred years back in time to the Sinagua culture. In 1250 A.D., they assist in saving their ancestors.

American Library Association Best Books for Young Adults.

Vick, Helen Hughes. *Walker's Journey Home.*
Niwot, CO: Roberts Rinehart Publishers, 1995. 192 pages. ISBN 1-57140-000-1 and 1-57140-001-Xpbk. Grades 7 to 10.

In this sequel to *Walker of Time*, the 20th century Hopi teenager named Walker who traveled eight hundred years back in time to rescue his people leads his Sinagua Indian tribe from its contaminated water supply across the desert to the land of the Hopi. Joining old enemies with new makes the journey treacherous and teaches Walker lessons about human greed and jealousy.

New York City School District Best Books for Teens.

Chapter 2

American Colonial Experience: 1600 to 1774

Grades Kindergarten to 2

Bruchac, Joseph. *Squanto's Journey.*
Greg Shed, illustrator. San Diego, CA: Harcourt Children's Books, 2000. 32 pages. ISBN 0-15-201817-4.
New York: Raintree Steck-Vaughn Publishers, 2000. 32 pages. ISBN 0-7398-3072-4. Lexile 560. Grades K to 4.

Native American Squanto welcomes the English people on the Mayflower when it lands in Plymouth in 1620. Told with respect and dignity in first-person narrative.

National Council for the Social Studies Notable Children's Trade Books in the Field of Social Studies.

Kay, Verla. *Tattered Sails.*
Dan Andreasen, illustrator. New York: Putnam, 2001. 32 pages. ISBN 0-399-23345-8. Grades K to 3.

Rythmic text describes one family's difficult voyage from London to the Massachusetts Bay Colony in 1635.

National Council for the Social Studies Notable Children's Trade Books in the Field of Social Studies.

McGill, Alice. *Molly Bannaky.*
New York: Houghton Mifflin Co., 1999. 32 pages. ISBN 0-395-72287-X. Lexile AD720. Grades K to 3.

A young dairymaid is exiled from England and sentenced to work as an indentured servant in colonial Maryland for seven years. After her servitude, she purchases an African slave whom she frees, falls in love with, and eventually marries.

American Library Association Notable Children's Books and *International Reading Association Notable Books for a Global Society.*

Stanley, Diane. *Joining the Boston Tea Party.*
Holly Berry, illustrator. New York: HarperCollins Children's Book Group, 2001. 48 pages. ISBN 0-06-027067-5. Lexile 380. Grades 1 to 4.

A magical hat helps twins journey back in time to experience the Boston Tea Party.

International Reading Association Children's Choices.

Sewall, Marcia. *The Pilgrims of Plimouth.*
New York: Atheneum Books for Young Readers, 1996. 48 pages. ISBN 0-689-31250-4.
New York: Aladdin Paperbacks, 1996. 48 pages. ISBN 0-689-80861-5pbk. Lexile 910. Grades 2 to 5.

Illustrated by the author, this is an introduction to the life and times of the Pilgrims in their new land in 1620. It chronicles their daily chores, struggles, and relationships with Native Americans.

Boston Globe-Horn Book Award, Horn Book Fanfare Honor List, International Reading Association Children's Choices, National Council for the Social Studies Notable Children's Trade Books in the Field of Social Studies, and *School Library Journal Best Book.*

Grades 3 to 6

Avi. *Night Journeys.*
First copyright 1979. New York: Avon Books, 2000. 160 pages. ISBN 0-380-73242-4pbk. Grades 5 to 8.

An exciting colonial adventure set on the Pennsylvania-New Jersey border in 1768, it concerns the young orphan Peter Cook and his efforts to help two indentured servants escape from the authorities while he contemplates escaping from his strict Quaker guardian.

Scott O'Dell Award for Historical Fiction.

Bruchac, Joseph. *Squanto's Journey.*
Refer to complete information under Grades Kindergarten to 2.

Bruchac, Joseph. *The Winter People.*
New York: Dial Books for Young Readers, 2002. 176 pages. ISBN 0-8037-2694-5. Grades 5 to 9.

A fourteen-year-old Abenaki boy pursues British soldiers after they kidnap his mother and sisters during a massacre raid on his Canadian village during the French and Indian war.

Children's Literature Choices, International Reading Association Notable Books for a Global Society, National Council for the Social Studies Notable Social Studies Trade Books for Young People, School Library Journal Best Book, and *Smithsonian Magazine Notable Books for Children.*

Bulla, Clyde Robert. *A Lion to Guard Us.*
Michele Chessare, illustrator. New York: HarperCollins Children's Book Group, 1981. 118 pages. ISBN 0-690-04097-0.
New York: HarperTrophy, 1989. 116 pages. ISBN 0-06-440333-5pbk.
Lexile 360. Grades 3 to 6.

In 1609 London, three poverty-stricken children draw upon all their inner resources to stay together and make their way to the Virginia colony, Jamestown, in search of their father.

National Council for the Social Studies Notable Children's Trade Books in the Field of Social Studies.

Clapp, Patricia. *Witches' Children.*
First copyright 1982. Magnolia, MA: Peter Smith Publishers, 1992. 160 pages. ISBN 0-8446-6572-X. (Out of print). Grades 5 to 9.

During the winter of 1692 when several young girls of Salem suddenly experience fits of screaming and strange visions, many believe that they have seen the devil and are the victims of witches.

American Library Association Best Books for Young Adults and *Jefferson Cup Award.*

Cooney, Caroline. *The Ransom of Mercy Carter.*
New York: Delacorte, 2001. 249 pages. ISBN 0-385-32615-7.
New York: Laurel Leaf Library, 2002. 256 pages. ISBN 0-440-22775-5.
Lexile 730. Grades 6 to 8.

Kahnawake Mohawk Indians raid a Deerfield, Massachusetts village and kidnap 100 settlers, forcing them on a difficult winter trek to Canada. Eleven-year-old Mercy learns to appreciate the Kahnawake way of life while waiting to be ransomed.

International Reading Association Notable Books for a Global Society.

Edmonds, Walter. *The Matchlock Gun.*
Paul Lantz, illustrator. First copyright 1941. New York: Penguin Putnam,

1989. 64 pages. ISBN 0-399-21911-0.
New York: Papstar, 1998. 63 pages. ISBN 0-399-21911-0pbk. Lexile 860. Grades 3 to 6.

In 1756 during the French and Indian War in upper New York state, ten-year-old Edward is determined to protect his home and family with the ancient, and much too heavy, Spanish gun that his father gave him before leaving home to fight the enemy. Based on a true story.

Newbery Medal.

Field, Rachel. *Calico Bush.*
Allen Lewis, illustrator. First copyright 1931. New York: Macmillan Publishing Co., 1987. 224 pages. ISBN 0-02-734610-2.
New York: Aladdin Paperbacks, 1998. 201 pages. ISBN 0-689-82285-5pbk and 0-689-82968-Xpbk. Lexile 1060. Grades 4 to 7.

Marguerite, a young French orphan in the New World, promises to serve the Sargent family for six long years in exchange for shelter, food, and clothing in 1740.

Newbery Honor Book.

Forbes, Esther. *Johnny Tremain.*
Lynd War, illustrator. New York: Houghton Mifflin Co., 1943. 272 pages. ISBN 0-395-06766-9 and 0-395-95447-9.
New York: Yearling, 1987. 256 pages. ISBN 0-440-44250-8pbk. (VHS). Lexile 840. Grades 5 to 8.

Fourteen-year-old Johnny Tremain is injured while apprenticing as a silversmith and gets caught up in the events of the Boston Tea Party, which eventually leads to the American Revolution.

Newbery Medal.

Hermes, Patricia. *Our Strange New Land: Elizabeth's Diary, James-town, Virginia, 1609. ("Dear America Series").*
New York: Scholastic Trade, 2000. 109 pages. ISBN 0-439-11208-7. Lexile 350. Grades 3 to 6.

Nine-year-old Elizabeth travels from England to Jamestown and be-friends Captain John Smith and Pocahontas while learning about the strange new land.

National Council for the Social Studies Notable Children's Trade Books in the Field of Social Studies.

Kay, Verla. *Tattered Sails.*
Refer to complete information under Grades Kindergarten to 2.

Koller, Jackie French. *The Primrose Way.*
San Diego, CA: Harcourt Children's Books, 1995. 272 pages. ISBN 0-15-256745-3.
Topeka, KS: Econo-Clad Books, 1999. 334 pages, ISBN 0-7857-6725-8.
San Diego, CA: Gulliver Books, 1995. 334 pages. ISBN 0-15-200372-Xpbk. Lexile 890. Grades 6 to Young Adult.

Living in a Puritan settlement that borders an Indian village in 1633, Rebekah befriends the Pawtucket people. She falls in love with a Pawtucket medicine man, resulting in a difficult choice.

American Library Association Best Books for Young Adults and *New York Public Library Books for the Teen Age.*

Lasky, Kathryn. *Beyond the Burning Time.*
Topeka, KS: Econo-Clad Books, 1999. 272 pages. ISBN 0-613-00260-1.
New York: Point, 1996. 288 pages. ISBN 0-590-47332-8pbk. Lexile 970. Grades 5 to 9.

In 1691, twelve-year-old Mary Chase desperately tries to rescue her mother, Virginia, who has been accused of witchcraft and sentenced to hang. This novel about the Salem witch trials captures the mass hysteria, ignorance, and violence that drove the New England community to execute two dozen people as devil advocates.

American Library Association Best Books for Young Adults.

McGill, Alice. *Molly Bannaky.*
Refer to complete information under Grades Kindergarten to 2.

Moore, Robin. *The Man with the Silver Oar.*
New York: HarperCollins Children's Book Group, 2002. 192 pages. ISBN 0-06-000048-1. Grades 5 to 8.

In 1718, a fifteen-year-old Quaker boy from Philadelphia stows away aboard a ship whose goal is to hunt down and eliminate a famous pirate.

National Council for the Social Studies Notable Social Studies Trade Books for Young People.

Sewall, Marcia. *The Pilgrims of Plimouth.*
Refer to complete description under Grades Kindergarten to 2.

Sewall, Marcia. *Thunder from the Clear Sky.*
Topeka, KS: Econo-Clad Books, 1999. 56 pages. ISBN 0-613-11163-X.
New York: Aladdin Paperbacks, 1998. 64 pages. ISBN 0-689-82176-Xpbk. Grades 3 to 5.

Told from the opposite perspectives of a Wampanoag brave and a Pilgrim settler, the story relates what transpires when their cultures first meet and describes the misunderstandings and cultural clashes that eventually ignite King Phillip's War.

National Council for the Social Studies Notable Children's Trade Books in the Field of Social Studies.

Speare, Elizabeth George. *The Sign of the Beaver.*
Boston: Houghton Mifflin Co., 1983. 144 pages. ISBN 0-395-33890-5.
New York: Scholastic Trade, 1998. 144 pages. ISBN 0-439-04475-8pbk.
New York: Bantam Books unabridged audio, 1998. ISBN 0-8072-7975-7.
Old Greenwich, CT: Listening Library abridged audio, 2000. ISBN 0-8072-0875-2. (VHS/DVD). Lexile 770. Grades 4 to 7.

Thirteen-year-old Matt is left alone to guard his family's wilderness home in 18th century Maine. He finds it difficult to survive until local Indians assist him and teach him wilderness skills.

American Library Association Notable Children's Books, The Child Study Committee Children's Book Award, Christopher Award, Newbery Honor Book, School Library Journal Best Book, and *Scott O'Dell Award for Historical Fiction.*

Speare, Elizabeth George. *The Witch of Blackbird Pond.*
Boston: Houghton Mifflin Co., 1958. 256 pages. ISBN 0-395-07114-3.
New York: Laurel Leaf Library, 1978. 223 pages. ISBN 0-440-99577-9pbk.
New York: American School Publishers unabridged audio, 1979. ISBN 0-394-7741-9.
Old Greenwich, CT: Listening Library abridged audio, 2002. ISBN 0-8072-0748-9. Lexile 850. Grades 5 to 8.

In 1687 Connecticut, spirited orphan Kit Tyler befriends an old Quaker woman she meets in the meadow. The association leads to an accusation of witchcraft against Kit.

International Board on Books for Young People and *Newbery Medal.*

Stanley, Diane. *Joining the Boston Tea Party.*
Refer to complete information under Grades Kindergarten to 2.

Grades 7 and 8

Avi. *Night Journeys.*
Refer to complete information under Grades 3 to 6.

Bruchac, Joseph. *The Winter People.*
Refer to complete information under Grades 3 to 6.

Clapp, Patricia. *Constance: A Story of Early Plymouth.*
First copyright 1968. Magnolia, MA: Peter Smith Publishers, 1993. 256 pages. ISBN 0-8446-6647-5.
New York: Morrow, 1993. 255 pages. ISBN 0-8446-6647-5 and ISBN 0-688-10976-4pbk. Lexile 1060. Grades 7 to Young Adult.
    Fifteen-year-old Constance keeps a journal of her experiences in the early Plymouth Colony, chronicling her experiences with the Indians and first Thanksgiving dinner while observing difficulties between people and cultures.
American Book Award finalist.

Clapp, Patricia. *Witches' Children.*
Refer to complete information under Grades 3 to 6.

Cooney, Caroline. *The Ransom of Mercy Carter.*
Refer to complete information under Grades 3 to 6.

Field, Rachel. *Calico Bush.*
Refer to complete information under Grades 3 to 6.

Fleischman, Paul. *Saturnalia.*
New York: HarperTrophy, 1992. 128 pages. ISBN 0-06-447089-Xpbk.
Topeka, KS: Econo-Clad Books, 1999. 128 pages. ISBN 0-8335-9095-2.
Lexile 1030. Grades 7 to Young Adult.
    William is a Narraganset Native American boy working as a Boston printer's apprentice in 1681. At night, he searches for his lost relatives, hoping to find them as the celebration of Saturnalia nears.
American Library Association Notable Children's Books, Booklist Editors' Choice, Boston Globe-Horn Book Award, The Bulletin of the Center for Children's Books Blue Ribbon Award, Horn Book Fanfare Honor List, International Reading Association Teachers' Choices, National Council for the Social Studies Notable Children's Trade Books in the Field of Social Studies, National Council of Teachers of English Notable Trade Books in the Language Arts, New York Public Library Books

for the Teen Age, Publishers Weekly "Critic's Choice," and *School Library Journal Best Book.*

Forbes, Esther. *Johnny Tremain.*
Refer to complete information under Grades 3 to 6.

Koller, Jackie French. *The Primrose Way.*
Refer to complete information under Grades 3 to 6.

Lasky, Kathryn. *Beyond the Burning Time.*
Refer to complete information under Grades 3 to 6.

Moore, Robin. *The Man with the Silver Oar.*
Refer to complete information under Grades 3 to 6.

Myers, Walter Dean. *The Glory Field.*
Topeka, KS: Econo-Clad Books, 1999. 333 pages. ISBN 0-7857-8741-0.
New York: Point, 1996. 375 pages. ISBN 0-590-45898-1pbk. Lexile 800.
Grades 7 to Young Adult.
Follows five generations of an African American family spanning two hundred and fifty years, from the capture and enslavement of the first ancestor in 1750, through the Civil War and the end of segregation, to a final reunion of relatives.
American Library Association Best Books for Young Adults.

Rinaldi, Ann. *A Break with Charity.*
San Diego, CA: Harcourt Children's Books, 1992. 257 pages. ISBN 0-15-200353-3 and 0-15-200101-8pbk. Lexile 730. Grades 7 to Young Adult.
While waiting for a church meeting in 1706, Susanna English recalls with regret her participation in a group led by deceitful Ann Putnam that instigated the imprisonment and deaths of twenty-two innocent people in a witch hunt in 1692.
American Library Association Best Books for Young Adults and *New York Public Library Books for the Teen Age.*

Rinaldi, Ann. *The Fifth of March: A Story of the Boston Massacre.*
San Diego, CA: Gulliver Books, 1993. 335 pages. ISBN 0-15-200343-6 and 0-15-227517-7pbk. Lexile 600. Grades 7 to 9.
In the years preceding the Revolutionary War, fourteen-year-old Rachel Marsh, an indentured servant in the John and Abigail Adams household, is torn between loyalties when she falls in love with a British sol-

dier and is caught up in the colonists' unrest that eventually escalates into the Boston Massacre of 1770.
New York Public Library Books for the Teen Age.

Rinaldi, Ann. *Hang a Thousand Trees with Ribbons: The Story of Phyllis Wheatley.*
San Diego, CA: Gulliver Books, 1996. 352 pages. ISBN 0-15-200876-4 and 0-15-200877-2pbk. Lexile 560. Grades 7 to 10.

Tutored by her master's son, African-American Phyllis develops her poetry skills and meets famous historical figures in pre-Revolutionary Boston.
International Reading Association Notable Books for a Global Society.

Speare, Elizabeth George. *The Sign of the Beaver.*
Refer to complete information under Grades 3 to 6.

Speare, Elizabeth George. *The Witch of Blackbird Pond.*
Refer to complete information under Grades 3 to 6.

Wibberley, Leonard. *John Treegate's Musket.*
First copyright 1959. Magnolia, MA: Peter Smith Publishers, 1993. 188 pages. ISBN 0-8446-6655-6. (Out of print). Lexile 1120. Grades 7 to 10.

During 1769 in South Carolina, Peter Treegate shipwrecks after escaping from a murderer. Peter's amnesia prevents him from telling an exiled Scot about his background. Six years later, he returns to Boston to find his father.
Southern California Council on Literature for Children.

Chapter 3

American Revolution: 1775 to 1783

Grades Kindergarten to 2

Fleming, Candace. *The Hatmaker's Sign: A Story.*
Robert Andrew Parker, illustrator. New York: Orchard Books, 1998. 32 pages. ISBN 0-531-30075-7 and 0-531-07174-Xpbk. Lexile 410. Grades K to 5.

This tale is based on a parable Benjamin Franklin told Thomas Jefferson while Congress was demanding that Jefferson rewrite sections of the Declaration of Independence. Upon consultation with others, a Boston hatmaker eliminates words from his store sign until it is finally blank.

Aesop Accolade and *Storytelling World Award Honor Book.*

Grades 3 to 6

Avi. *The Fighting Ground.*
Ellen Thompson, illustrator. New York: HarperCollins Children's Book Group, 1984. 160 pages. ISBN 0-397-32074-4.
New York: HarperTrophy, 1987. 157 pages. ISBN 0-06-440185-5pbk. Lexile 580. Grades 5 to 8.

Thirteen-year-old Jonathan goes off to fight in the Revolutionary War near Trenton, New Jersey, and discovers that the real war is being fought within himself.

American Library Association Notable Children's Books, American Library Association Recommended Books for Reluctant Young Adult Readers, Horn Book Fanfare Honor List, Lesbian and Gay Children's/

Young Adult Award, and *New York Public Library Books for the Teen Age.*

Blackwood, Gary L. *Year of the Hangman.*
New York: Dutton Children's Books, 2002. 196 pages. ISBN 0-525-46921-4. Lexile 820. Grades 6 to 9.

In this alternative novel that shows what would happen if the British won the Revolutionary War, fifteen-year-old Creighton is kidnapped from London and becomes part of the political unrest after he is forced to spy on Benjamin Franklin.

American Library Association Best Books for Young Adults and *School Library Journal Best Book.*

Caudill, Rebecca. *Tree of Freedom.*
Dorothy Bayley, illustrator. First copyright 1949. New York: Peter Smith Publishers, 1988. 284 pages. ISBN 0-8446-6401-4. (Out of print). Lexile 1030. Grades 5 to 8.

Stephanie's father moves her family from Kentucky to North Carolina in 1780 to escape taxes. Stephanie plants an apple tree she names "Tree of Freedom" as a symbol of their experiences.

Newbery Honor Book and *New York Herald Tribune Award.*

Fleming, Candace. *The Hatmaker's Sign: A Story.*
Refer to complete information under Grades Kindergarten to 2.

Leeuwen, Jean Van. *Hannah's Winter of Hope.*
Donna Diamond, illustrator. New York: Phyllis Fogelman Books, 2000. 96 pages. ISBN 0-8037-2492-6.
New York: Puffin Books, 2001. 96 pages. ISBN 0-14-130950-4pbk. Lexile 530. Grades 3 to 6.

During the winter of 1780 in the midst of the American Revolution, the six-member Perley family is worried about their captured son and brother as they are forced to survive in a one-room shed after the British burn down their house. Eleven-year-old Hannah describes their lifestyle as she struggles to help rebuild their home.

National Council for the Social Studies Notable Children's Trade Books in the Field of Social Studies.

Rinaldi, Ann. *Cast Two Shadows: The American Revolution in the South.*
San Diego, CA: Gulliver Books, 1998. 288 pages. ISBN 0-15-200881-0 and 0-15-200882-9pbk. Lexile 610. Grades 5 to 9.

Fourteen-year-old Caroline observes the impact of the Revolutionary War on her family and friends in 1780 South Carolina.
International Reading Association Notable Books for a Global Society.

Rinaldi, Ann. *Or Give Me Death: A Novel of Patrick Henry's Family.*
San Diego, CA: Gulliver Books, 2003. 240 pages. ISBN 0-15-216687-4. Grades 5 to 9.

Related from the perspective of Patrick Henry's children, this novel explores the impact this famous American had on his mentally ill wife and the rest of his family.
Parent's Choice Gold Award.

Rinaldi, Ann. *The Secret of Sarah Revere.*
San Diego, CA: Gulliver Books, 1995. 320 pages. ISBN 0-15-200393-2 and 0-15-200392-4pbk. Lexile 530. Grades 6 to 9.

When Dr. Warren comes to conduct an interview with her father, Paul Revere, thirteen-year-old Sarah fears that Dr. Warren has dishonorable feelings for her mother. She witnesses her father's fight for independence during the early years of the American Revolution.
American Bookseller Pick of the Lists.

Grades 7 and 8

Avi. *The Fighting Ground.*
Refer to complete information under Grades 3 to 6.

Blackwood, Gary L. *Year of the Hangman.*
Refer to complete information under Grades 3 to 6.

Caudill, Rebecca. *Tree of Freedom.*
Refer to complete information under Grades 3 to 6.

Collier, Christopher and James Collier. *My Brother Sam is Dead.*
New York: Simon & Schuster, 1984. 216 pages. ISBN 0-02-722980-7.
New York: Scholastic, 1989. 224 pages. ISBN 0-590-42792-Xpbk.
Northport, ME: Audio Bookshelf unabridged audio, 1996. ISBN 1-883332-19-2. (VHS). Lexile 770. Grades 7 to Young Adult.

Describes the tragedy that strikes the Meeker family during the American Revolution when one son joins the rebel forces while the rest

of the family tries to stay neutral in a Tory town.
Newbery Honor Book and *Phoenix Award Honor Book.*

Pope, Elizabeth. *The Sherwood Ring.*
First copyright 1958. New York: Houghton Mifflin Co., 2001. 256
pages. ISBN 0-618-16968-7 and 0-618-15074-9pbk. Grades 7 to Young
Adult.

In this historical fantasy, newly-orphaned Peggy is transported back
in time to the year 1773 during the American Revolution.
American Library Association Notable Children's Books and *New-bery Honor Book.*

Rinaldi, Ann. *Cast Two Shadows: The American Revolution in the South.*
Refer to complete information under Grades 3 to 6.

Rinaldi, Ann. *Or Give Me Death: A Novel of Patrick Henry's Family.*
Refer to complete information under Grades 3 to 6.

Rinaldi, Ann. *The Secret of Sarah Revere.*
Refer to complete information under Grades 3 to 6.

Wibberley, Leonard. *John Treegate's Musket.*
First copyright 1959. Magnolia, MA: Peter Smith Publishers, 1993. 188
pages. ISBN 0-8446-6655-6. (Out of print). Lexile 1120. Grades 7 to 10.

During 1769 in South Carolina, Peter Treegate shipwrecks after escaping from a murderer. Peter's amnesia prevents him from telling an
exiled Scot about his background. Six years later, he returns to Boston to
find his father.
Southern California Council on Literature for Children.

Chapter 4

Westward Expansion and Settlement, Including Native Americans: 1784 to 1916

Grades Kindergarten to 2

Brenner, Barbara. *Wagon Wheels.*
Don Bolobnese, illustrator. New York: HarperCollins Children's Book Group, 1993. 64 pages. ISBN 0-06-020668-3 and 0-06-444052-4pbk. (An "I Can Read" book). Lexile 380. Grades K to 3.

Based on the true story of a widowed African American man and his three young sons who learn to care for one another while traveling west in 1878 to find free Kansas land.

American Library Association Notable Children's Books and *National Council for the Social Studies Notable Children's Trade Books in the Field of Social Studies.*

Bruchac, Joseph. *Crazy Horse's Vision.*
S.D. Nelson, illustrator. New York: Lee & Low Books, 2000. 40 pages. ISBN 1-880000-94-6. Lexile 420. Grades K to 4.

A young Lakota boy seeks a vision in hopes of saving his people. He grows into the fierce warrior Crazy Horse who leads the Lakota people in the Battle of the Little Bighorn.

American Library Association Notable Children's Books, National Council for the Social Studies Notable Children's Trade Books in the Field of Social Studies, and *Parent's Choice Gold Award.*

Bunting, Eve. *Dandelions.*
Greg Shed, illustrator. San Diego, CA: Harcourt Children's Books, 1995. 48 pages. ISBN 0-15-200050-X.
San Diego, CA: Voyager, 2001. 32 pages. ISBN 0-15-202407-7pbk.

Lexile 580. Grades 2 to 4.

The chronicle of a family's journey from Illinois to the Nebraska territory in the 1800s. When the Boltons arrive on the prairie, Papa looks forward to the challenges, but Mama fears the loneliness and hardships while being preoccupied with sad memories of those left behind. As a surprise for Mama, Zoe finds dandelions and brings them home to plant on their soddie's roof.

National Council for the Social Studies Notable Children's Trade Books in the Field of Social Studies.

Gerrard, Roy. *Wagons West!*
New York: Farrar, Straus & Giroux, 1996. 32 pages. ISBN 0-374-38249-2. Grades K to 3.

A rhyming text picture book about some eastern farmers and their families who take a wagon train west to find more fertile ground. They encounter geographic difficulties, Indians, and cattle rustlers.

School Library Journal Best Book.

Hancock, Sibyl. *Old Blue.*
Erick Ingraham, illustrator. New York: Penguin Putnam Books for Young Readers, 1980. 48 pages, ISBN 0-399-61141-X. Grades K to 3.

A child rides the leading steer with pride during a cattle drive in 1878.

American Library Association Notable Children's Books.

Harvey, Brett. *My Prairie Year.*
Deborah Kogan Ray, illustrator. New York: Holiday House, 1986. 40 pages. ISBN 0-8234-0604-0. (Out of print). Lexile 1000. Grades K to 3.

Based on the diary of Elenore Plaisted, a nine-year-old girl moves from Maine to homestead in the Dakotas. Recounts details of natural disasters and daily chores.

American Library Association Notable Children's Books.

Howard, Ellen. *The Log Cabin Quilt.*
Ronald Himler, illustrator. New York: Holiday House, 1996. 32 pages. ISBN 0-8234-1247-4 and 0-8234-1136-5pbk. Lexile 580. Grades K to 3.

A pioneer family moves into a log cabin in the Michigan woods after the mother dies. The daughter stuffs the cracks in the walls of the cabin with fabric strips when the mud caulking falls out, thus making a "log cabin quilt."

Christopher Award.

Levinson, Nancy Smiler. *Snowshoe Thompson.*
Joan Sandin, illustrator. Topeka, KS: Econo-Clad Books, 1999. 32 pages. ISBN 0-7857-7598-6.
New York: HarperTrophy, 1996. 32 pages. ISBN 0-06-444206-3pbk. (An "I Can Read" book). Lexile 330. Grades K to 3.

In an adventure that introduces skiing to the new world, Scandinavian immigrant John Thompson (1827 to 1876) earns a place in American folklore by making a treacherous journey over the Sierra Nevada Mountains to deliver the mail.

National Council for the Social Studies Notable Children's Trade Books in the Field of Social Studies.

MacLachlan, Patricia. *Three Names.*
Alexander Pertzoff, illustrator. New York: HarperCollins Children's Book Group, 1991. 32 pages. ISBN 0-06-024036-9 and 0-06-443360-9pbk.
New York: Scholastic, 1991. 26 pages. ISBN 0-590-46405-1. Lexile AD690. Grades K to 4.

The story of a little boy and his dog, Three Names, who travel to his one-room schoolhouse on the prairie in a wagon drawn by horses.

School Library Journal Best Book.

Martin, Jacqueline Briggs. *The Lamp, the Ice, and the Boat Called Fish.*
Beth Krommes, illustrator. New York: Houghton Mifflin Co., 2001. 48 pages. ISBN 0-618-00341-X. Lexile 810. Grades 2 to 4.

In 1913, a Canadian research boat becomes trapped in ice during an Arctic expedition, and the men learn to survive by using Inupiat cultural traditions.

American Library Association Notable Children's Books, Golden Kite Award, and *National Council for the Social Studies Notable Children's Trade Books in the Field of Social Studies.*

Sorensen, Henri. *New Hope.*
New York: Lothrop, Lee & Shepard Books, 1995. 32 pages. ISBN 0-688-13925-6.
New York: Penguin Putnam, 1998. 32 pages. ISBN 0-14-056359-8pbk. Grades 1 to 4.

Visiting New Hope with Grandpa, Jimmy asks about the statue in the park which pays tribute to his great-great-great grandfather from Denmark, the founder of the town who set down roots when his wagon axle broke.

National Council for the Social Studies Notable Children's Trade Books in the Field of Social Studies.

Stanley, Diane. *Saving Sweetness.*
G. Brian Karas, illustrator. New York: Putnam, 1996. 32 pages. ISBN 0-399-22645-1.
New York: Puffin Books, 2001. 32 pages. ISBN 0-698-11767-0pbk.
Pine Plains, NY: Live Oak Media audio, 2002. ISBN 0-87499-900-6. Lexile AD660. Grades K to 3.

Sweetness, a little orphan in mean old Mrs. Sump's orphanage, runs away, so the kind-hearted sheriff sets out to find her before she meets up with nasty Coyote Pete. An offbeat tall tale full of laughs.
School Library Journal Best Book.

Thomas, Joyce Carol. *I Have Heard of a Land.*
Floyd Cooper, illustrator. New York: HarperCollins Children's Book Group, 1998. 32 pages. ISBN 0-06-023477-6.
New York: HarperTrophy, 2000. 32 pages. ISBN 0-06-443617-9. Lexile NP. Grades 2 to 5.

A lyrical introduction to the race for land in the Oklahoma Territory by African Americans in the late 1880s.
American Library Association Notable Children's Books.

Turner, Ann. *Dakota Dugout.*
Ronald Himler, illustrator. Topeka, KS: Econo-Clad Books, 1999. 32 pages. ISBN 0-8335-2793-2.
New York: Aladdin Paperbacks, 1989. 32 pages. ISBN 0-689-971296-0pbk. Lexile AD 1040. Grades K to 3.

A woman describes her experiences living with her husband in a sod house on the Dakota prairie.
American Library Association Notable Children's Books.

Welch, Catherine A. *Clouds of Terror.*
Laurie K. Johnson, illustrator. Minneapolis, MN: Carolrhoda Books, 1994. 48 pages. ISBN 0-87614-771-6 and 0-87614-639-6pbk. Lexile 450. Grades 2 to 4.

Living on a Minnesota farm in the 1870s, a Swedish immigrant brother and sister try to help their family cope with swarms of locusts.
National Council for the Social Studies Notable Children's Trade Books in the Field of Social Studies.

Grades 3 to 6

Alder, Elizabeth. *Crossing the Panther's Path.*
New York: Farrar, Straus & Giroux, 2002. 272 pages. ISBN 0-525-46268-6. Grades 6 to 8.

Based on a true story, fifteen-year-old Billy Calder assists Shawnee Chief Tecumseh during the war of 1812. Half Mohawk and half Irish, Billy's proficiencies in several languages aids the chief during negotiations with the British Army in addition to assisting him in battle.

National Council for the Social Studies Notable Social Studies Trade Books for Young People.

Anderson, Laurie Halse. *Fever 1793.*
New York: Simon & Schuster, 2000. 251 pages. ISBN 0-689-83858-1 and 0-689-84891-9pbk.
New York: Bantam Books unabridged audio, 2000. ISBN 0-8072-658-0. Lexile 580. Grades 6 to 10.

Spirited sixteen-year-old Matilda becomes an orphan and struggles to survive after her mother and a friend die of yellow fever. The novel is based on an actual epidemic of yellow fever that killed ten percent of the population of Philadelphia in three months.

American Library Association Top Ten Historical Fiction for Youth.

Arrington, Frances. *Bluestem.*
New York: Philomel Books, 2000. 144 pages. ISBN 0-399-23564-7.
New York: Puffin Books, 2001. 144 pages. ISBN 0-698-11911-8pbk. Lexile 570. Grades 4 to 6.

A novel depicting the pioneering courage of two young girls who try to survive the harsh life of the open prairie in 1878 after their mother loses her mind while their father is away.

National Council for the Social Studies Notable Children's Trade Books in the Field of Social Studies.

Brenner, Barbara. *Wagon Wheels.*
Refer to complete information under Grades Kindergarten to 2.

Brink, Carol Ryre. *Caddie Woodlawn.*
Trina S. Hyman, illustrator. First copyright 1935. New York: Simon & Schuster, 1983. 275 pages. ISBN 0-02-713670-1.
New York: Aladdin Paperbacks, 1990. 275 pages. ISBN 0-689-71370-3pbk.
Prince Frederick, MD: Recorded Books unabridged audio, 1994. ISBN

1-4025-0470-5cd. Lexile 890. Grades 3 to 6.

An eleven-year-old tomboy grows up as a pioneer on the Wisconsin frontier in the mid-19th century. Based on the adventures of the author's grandmother.

Newbery Medal.

Bruchac, Joseph. *Crazy Horse's Vision.*
Refer to complete information under Grades Kindergarten to 2.

Bunting, Eve. *Dandelions.*
Refer to complete information under Grades Kindergarten to 2.

Calabro, Marian. *The Perilous Journey of the Donner Party.*
New York: Clarion Books, 1999. 192 pages. ISBN 0-395-86610-3. Lexile 1020. Grades 5 to 8.

The Donner Party leaves Springfield, Illinois, in search of a better life in California and is forced to camp in impassable snow in the Sierra Nevada Mountains. The tragic story is told by twelve-year-old Virginia Reed.

American Library Association Notable Children's Books.

Conrad, Pam. *Prairie Songs.*
Darryl Zudeck, illustrator. New York: HarperCollins Children's Book Group, 1987. 167 pages. ISBN 0-06-021337-X and 0-06-440206-1pbk. Lexile 780. Grades 5 to 9.

Louisa's life in a loving pioneer family on the Nebraska prairie is altered by the arrival of a new doctor and his beautiful frail wife, who succumbs to madness.

American Library Association Best Books for Young Adults, Booklist Best of the 1980s, Boston Globe-Horn Book Award, Golden Kite Award Honor Book, Judy Lopez Children's Book Award, New York Public Library Books for the Teen Age, Society of Midlands Authors Award, Western Heritage Award, and *Western Writers of America Golden Spur Award.*

Cushman, Karen. *The Ballad of Lucy Whipple.*
New York: Houghton Mifflin Co., 1996. 195 pages. ISBN 0-395-72806-1.
New York: HarperTrophy, 1998. 218 pages. ISBN 0-06-440684-9pbk.
Prince Frederick, MD: Recorded Books unabridged audio, 1997. ISBN 0-7887-0892-9. Lexile 1030. Grades 5 to 7.

Twelve-year-old Lucy Whipple lives in Lucky Diggins, California, where her mother runs a boarding house in a large tent. Through first-person narrative and her letters to relatives, Lucy gives a child's perspective on that historical period.

School Library Journal Best Book.

Cushman, Karen. *Rodzina.*
New York: Clarion Books, 2003. 215 pages. ISBN 0-618-13351-8.
Old Greenwich, CT: Listening Library Unabridged audio, 2003. ISBN 0-8072-1576-7.
Old Greenwich, CT: Random House Abriged Audio, 2003. ISBN 0-8072-1577-5. Grades 5 to 9.

A twelve-year-old Polish-American orphan struggles to find a place of acceptance while traveling on an 1881 orphan train traveling from Chicago to California.

Parent's Choice Gold Award.

Demers, Barbara. *Willa's New World.*
Regina, Saskatchewan Canada: Coteau Books, 1999. 303 pages. ISBN 1-55050-150-Xpbk. Lexile 1030. Grades 5 to 8.

At the turn of the 19th century, a fifteen-year-old orphan is roughly cast aside by a relative and transported from Canada to a trading post on Hudson's Bay where she befriends a Native American girl named Amelia. She learns strength and independence through her hardships.

American Library Association Top Ten Historical Fiction for Youth.

Erdrich, Louise. *The Birchbark House.*
New York: Hyperion, 1999. 244 pages. ISBN 0-786-82241-4 and 0-786-81454-3pbk.
Northport, ME: Audio Bookshelf unabridged audio, 2002. ISBN 1-883332-79-6 and 1-88332-83-4cd. Lexile 970. Grades 4 to 6.

A young Ojibwa girl named Omakyas lives on an island in Lake Superior in 1847.

American Library Association Notable Children's Books, International Reading Association Notable Books for a Global Society, Parent's Choice Gold Award, and *Western Heritage Award.*

Field, Rachel. *Hitty: Her First Hundred Years.*
Dorothy Lathrop, illustrator. First copyright 1929. New York: Simon & Schuster, 1991. 207 pages. ISBN 0-02-734840-7.
New York: Aladdin Paperbacks, 1998. 256 pages. ISBN 0-689-82284-7pbk.
Cedar Knolls, NJ: MediaBay Audio Publishing unabridged audio, 2000.

ISBN 0-9668567-6-7. Lexile 1180. Grades 3 to 6.

The story of the first one hundred years of a doll's life during the late 18th to early 19th centuries.

Newbery Medal.

Fleischman, Sid. *Bandit's Moon.*
Joseph A. Smith, illustrator. New York: Greenwillow Books, 1998. 144 pages. ISBN 0-688-15830-7.
New York: Yearling Books, 2000. 136 pages. ISBN 0-440-41586-1pbk.
Prince Frederick, MD: Recorded Books unabridged audio, 2002. ISBN 1-4025-0736-4 and 1-4025-2291-6cd. Lexile 690. Grades 3 to 6.

Tricking them into believing she is a boy, twelve-year-old Annyrose unites with Joaquin Murieta and his band of outlaws in the California gold-mining region during the mid-1800s.

American Library Association Notable Children's Books and *Friends of Children and Literature Award.*

Fleischman, Sid. *Humbug Mountain.*
First copyright 1978. New York: Peter Smith Publishers, 1999. 149 pages. ISBN 0-8446-7005-7.
New York: Yearling, 1998. 133 pages. ISBN 0-440-41403-2pbk. Lexile 670. Grades 3 to 7.

A young boy and his wandering family thwart evil villains as they make a home for themselves in a beached boat on the banks of the Missouri River.

American Library Association Best Books for Young Adults and *Boston Globe-Horn Book Award.*

Garland, Sherry. *In the Shadow of the Alamo.*
San Diego, CA: Gulliver Books, 2001. 282 pages. ISBN 0-15-201744-5. Grades 6 to 8.

Fifteen-year-old Lorenzo is forced to march and fight at the Alamo after the Mexican army captures his village.

National Council for the Social Studies Notable Children's Trade Books in the Field of Social Studies.

Garland, Sherry. *Voices of the Alamo.*
Ronald Himler, illustrator. New York: Scholastic Trade, 2000. 40 pages. ISBN 0-590-98833-6. Lexile 970. Grades 4 to 8.

A picture book for older readers, it describes events leading up to the

thirteen-day siege of the Alamo as told by sixteen different people.
National Council for the Social Studies Notable Children's Trade Books in the Field of Social Studies.

Gerrard, Roy. *Wagons West!*
Refer to complete information under Grades Kindergarten to 2.

Gipson, Fred. *Old Yeller.*
New York: HarperCollins Children's Book Group, 1956. 184 pages. ISBN 0-06-011545-9 and 0-06-440382-3pbk.
New York: Scholastic, 1988. 117 pages. ISBN 0-590-02310-1pbk.
Los Angeles, CA: Audio Renaissance Tapes abridged audio, 1995. ISBN 1-55927-357-X. (VHS/DVD). Lexile 910. Grades 4 to 7.
The moving story of a boy and his dog during the wild Texas frontier days of the 1860s.
American Library Association Notable Children's Books of 1940 to 1970, Newbery Honor Book, and *Sequoyah Children's Book Award.*

Gregory, Kristiana. *Earthquake at Dawn.*
San Diego, CA: Harcourt Children's Books, 1992. 192 pages. ISBN 0-15-200446-7 and 0-15-200099-2pbk. (A "Great Episodes" book). Lexile 840. Grades 5 to 7.
On April 18, 1906, a powerful earthquake rocked San Francisco, California. Based on a thirty-page letter written by Mary Exa Atkins Campbell and actual photographs taken by Edith Irvine, fifteen-year-old Daisy gives an exciting fictionalized account of the devastation suffered by the city and the courage of its citizens.
American Library Association Best Books for Young Adults, National Council for the Social Studies Notable Children's Trade Books in the Field of Social Studies, and *New York Public Library Books for the Teen Age.*

Gregory, Kristiana. *Jenny of the Tetons.*
San Diego, CA: Harcourt Children's Books, 1989. 120 pages. ISBN 0-15-200480-7 and 0-15-200481-5pbk. Lexile 680. Grades 5 to 7.
Orphaned by an Indian raid while traveling west with a wagon train in 1857, fifteen-year-old Carrie Hill is befriended by the English trapper Beaver Dick and taken to live with his Shoshone Indian wife, Jenny, and their six children.
Golden Kite Award.

Harrell, Beatrice O. *Longwalker's Journey.*
Tony Meers, illustrator. New York: Dial Books for Young Readers, 1999. 144 pages. ISBN 0-8037-2380-6. Lexile 840. Grades 3 to 6.

In 1831, ten-year-old Minko and his father suffer terrible hardships when the government forces the Choctaw Indians to relocate from Mississippi to Oklahoma.

International Reading Association Notable Books for a Global Society.

Hancock, Sibyl. *Old Blue.*
Refer to complete information under Grades Kindergarten to 2.

Harvey, Brett. *My Prairie Year.*
Refer to complete information under Grades Kindergarten to 2.

Hill, Kirkpatrick. *Minuk: Ashes in the Pathway. ("Girls of Many Lands Series").*
Middleton, WI: Pleasant Company Publications, 2002. 210 pages. ISBN 1-58485-596-7 and 1-58485-520-7pbk. Lexile 940. Grades 5 to 8.

The 1892 arrival of Christian Missionaries brings cultural changes as well as devastating diseases to a twelve-year-old girl's Yupik Eskimo village in Alaska.

School Library Journal Best Book.

Holm, Jennifer. *Boston Jane: An Adventure.*
New York: HarperCollins Children's Book Group, 2001. 288 pages. ISBN 0-06-028738-1 and 0-06-440849-3pbk.
Old Greenwich, CT: Listening Library unabridged audio, 2001. ISBN 0-8072-0465-X. Lexile 690. Grades 4 to 7.

Sixteen-year-old Jane sails from Philadelphia to Oregon in 1854 and sheds some of the lessons learned at a Boston finishing school while searching for her fiancé.

American Library Association Best Books for Young Adults.

Holm, Jennifer L. *Our Only May Amelia.*
New York: HarperCollins Children's Book Group, 1999. 251 pages. ISBN 0-06-027822-6 and 0-06-440856-6pbk.
New York: Bantam Books unabridged audio, 2000.
ISBN 0-8072-8234-0.
New York: Listening Library audio, 2000. ISBN 0-8072-8234-0. Lexile 900. Grades 3 to 6.

A twelve-year-old Finnish American pioneer girl describes her life with seven brothers in 1899 Washington state.

American Library Association Notable Children's Books, Dorothy Canfield Fisher Award, National Council for the Social Studies Notable Children's Trade Books in the Field of Social Studies, Newbery Honor Book, Parent's Choice Silver Award, and *Utah Children's Book Award.*

Hotze, Sollace. *A Circle Unbroken.*
New York: Houghton Mifflin Co., 1988. 224 pages. ISBN 0-89919-733-7 and 0-395-59702-1pbk. Lexile 920. Grades 6 to 10.

In 1838, Rachel Porter is captured by Sioux Indians and raised as the chief's daughter. Her minister father recaptures Rachel when she is seventeen years old. Longing to return to the Sioux tribe, she finds it difficult to adjust to her old life.

Carl Sandburg Award.

Howard, Ellen. *The Log Cabin Quilt.*
Refer to complete information under Grades Kindergarten to 2.

Ingold, Jeanette. *The Big Burn.*
San Diego, CA: Harcourt Children's Books, 2002. 304 pages. ISBN 0-15-216470-7 and 0-15-204924-Xpbk.
Old Greenwich, CT: Listening Library Unabridged Audio, 2002. ISBN 0-8072-0814-0. Lexile 860. Grades 5 to 8.

Three teens and their companions battle to survive one of the worst wildfires of the century that raced across Idaho and Montana during a hot and dry summer in 1910.

Western Writers of America Spur Award.

Kimmel, Elizabeth Cody. *One Sky Above Us. ("The Adventures of Young Buffalo Bill Series").*
Scott Snow, illustrator. New York: HarperCollins Children's Book Group, 2002. 192 pages. ISBN 0-06-029119-2 and 0-06-029120-6pbk. Grades 3 to 6.

Young Buffalo Bill and his family fight to protect their land from pro-slavery forces determined to drive them off their Kansas property.

National Council for the Social Studies Notable Social Studies Trade Books for Young People.

Lenski, Lois. *Indian Captive: The Story of Mary Jemison.*
First copyright 1941. New York: HarperCollins Children's Book Group, 1994. 304 pages. ISBN 0-397-3076-X and 0-06-446162-9pbk. Lexile 800. Grades 5 to 8.

The story of twelve-year-old Mary Jemison's capture in 1758 and early years with the Seneca Indians. Despite finding it difficult to adjust to the Seneca way of life, she decides not to return to the white world when given the chance. Based on a true story.
Newbery Honor Book.

Levinson, Nancy Smiler. *Snowshoe Thompson.*
Refer to complete information under Grades Kindergarten to 2.

Levitin, Sonia. *Clem's Chances.*
New York: Orchard Books, 2001. 208 pages. ISBN 0-439-29314-6. Lexile 770. Grades 4 to 7.

Abused and motherless, fourteen-year-old Clem travels the 1860 Overland Trail from Missouri to California in search of his father. He encounters seedy characters, a kidnapped slave, and kindness when he least expects it.
National Council for the Social Studies Notable Children's Trade Books in the Field of Social Studies.

MacLachlan, Patricia. *Sarah, Plain and Tall.*
New York: HarperCollins Children's Book Group, 1985. 58 pages. ISBN 0-06-024102-0 and 0-06-440205-3pbk.
New York: Caedmon unabridged audio, 1995. ISBN 0-89845-635-5.
New York: HarperAudio unabridged audio, 2001. ISBN 0-694-52602-9cd. (VHS/DVD). Lexile 560. Grades 3 to 6.

A story that gently explores the themes of love and loss in the late 19th century. A widowed Midwestern farmer with two children advertises for a wife. Sarah is homesick for Maine after she joins the family, but she explains to Anna and Caleb that she would miss them even more than the ocean if she returned home.
American Library Association Notable Children's Books, Booklist Editors' Choice, Christopher Award, Golden Kite Award, Horn Book Fanfare Honor List, International Board on Books for Young People, International Reading Association Children's Choices, Jefferson Cup Award, National Council of Teachers of English Notable Trade Books in the Language Arts, Newbery Medal, New York Times Outstanding Children's Books, School Library Journal Best Book, and *Scott O'Dell Award for Historical Fiction.*

MacLachlan, Patricia. *Three Names.*
Refer to complete information under Grades Kindergarten to 2.

Martin, Jacqueline Briggs. *The Lamp, the Ice, and the Boat Called Fish.*
Refer to complete information under Grades Kindergarten to 2.

McGraw, Eloise Jarvis. *Moccasin Trail.*
First copyright 1952. New York: Peter Smith Publishers, 1988. 256 pages. ISBN 0-8446-6346-8.
New York: Penguin Putnam, 1986. 247 pages. ISBN 0-14-032170-5pbk. Lexile 960. Grades 6 to 9.
Young Jim follows his uncle, a trapper, until he is mauled by a bear and subsequently brought up by Crow Indians. After he is reunited with his family, Jim attempts to readjust to the white man's culture.
Junior Literary Guild Selection, Lewis Carroll Shelf Award, and *Newbery Honor Book.*

Myers, Walter Dean. *The Righteous Revenge of Artemis Bonner.*
First copyright 1992. Topeka, KS: Econo-Clad Books, 1999. 144 pages. ISBN 0-7857-5609-4.
New York: HarperTrophy. 1994. 144 pages. ISBN 0-06-440462-5pbk. Lexile 980. Grades 5 to 9.
Fifteen-year-old Artemis journeys from New York City to Tombstone, Arizona, in 1882 to avenge the murder of his uncle and locate the uncle's gold stake.
American Library Association Best Books for Young Adults and *New York Public Library Books for the Teen Age.*

Nixon, Joan. *A Family Apart.*
First copyright 1987. Topeka, KS: Econo-Clad Books, 1999. 162 pages. ISBN 0-8335-1833-X.
New York: Bantam Dell Publishing Group, 1996. 162 pages. ISBN 0-440-22676-7pbk.
Prince Frederick, MD: Recorded Books unabridged audio, 2000. ISBN 0-7887-4235-3. Lexile 820. Grades 5 to 7.
In 1860, six siblings are sent by the Children's Aid Society of New York City to live with farm families in Missouri after their mother can no longer support them. Frances cuts her hair and pretends to be a boy so she can be placed with her little brother. When the family that adopts them finds out Frances is a girl, they are impressed by her courage and hard work as she helps them transport slaves along the Underground Railroad.
Western Writers of America Spur Award.

O'Dell, Scott. *Island of the Blue Dolphins.*
Ted Lewin, illustrator. First copyright 1960. Boston: Houghton Mifflin
Co., 1990. 192 pages. ISBN 0-395-53680-4.
New York: Bantam Dell Publishing Group, 1987. 184 pages. ISBN 0-
440-43988-4pbk.
New York: Bantam Books unabridged audio, 1995. ISBN 0-553-4705-7.
(VHS). Lexile 1000. Grades 5 to 10.

This book is based on the life of a remarkable young American Indian woman who, during the evacuation of Ghalas-at (an island off the
coast of California), jumps ship to stay with her young brother who has
been abandoned on the island. He dies shortly thereafter, and Karana
fends for herself for eighteen years.

*American Library Association Notable Children's Books, Friends of
Children and Literature Award, International Board on Books for Young
People, Newbery Medal, School Library Journal Best Book, Southern
California Council on Literature for Children,* and *Young People's
Awards.*

O'Dell, Scott. *Sing Down the Moon.*
First copyright 1970. Boston: Houghton Mifflin Co., 1990. 181 pages.
ISBN 0-395-53680-4.
New York: Bantam Dell Publishing Group, 1987. 184 pages. ISBN 0-
440-43988-4pbk.
Prince Frederick, MD: Recorded Books unabridged audio, 1994. ISBN
0-7887-0006-5. Lexile 820. Grades 5 to 8.

In 1864, a young Navajo girl is kidnapped by Spanish slavers and
rescued by a young man who becomes her husband.

Newbery Honor Book and *New York Times Notable Books of the
Year.*

O'Dell, Scott and Elizabeth Hall. *Thunder Rolling in the Mountains.*
Boston: Houghton Mifflin Co., 1992. 128 pages. ISBN 0-395-59966-0.
New York: Bantam Dell Publishing Group, 1993. 128 pages. ISBN 0-
440-40879-2pbk.
Prince Frederick, MD: Recorded Books unabridged audio, 1995. ISBN
0-7887-0453-4. Lexile 680. Grades 6 to 9.

In the winter of 1877, Chief Joseph of the Nez Perce tribe prepares
his people to leave their home peacefully for the reservation. However,
the U.S. army attacks the Indians, who try to flee to safety in Canada and
are attacked along the way. This tale of genocide is narrated by Chief

Joseph's daughter.
National Council for the Social Studies Notable Children's Trade Books in the Field of Social Studies.

Osborne, Mary Pope. *Adaline Falling Star.*
New York: Scholastic Trade, 2000. 170 pages. ISBN 0-439-05947-X and 0-439-05948-8pbk.
New York: Bantam Books unabridged audio, 2001. ISBN 0-8072-9430-7.
New York: Listening Library unabridged audio, 2001. ISBN 0-8072-0430-7. Lexile 720. Grades 6 to Young Adult.

Adaline Falling Star is the daughter of the legendary frontier scout Kit Carson. After her Arapahoe Indian mother dies, Adaline is cruelly treated by the racist relatives she is left with. She disguises herself as a boy and runs away to find work on a steamboat while trying to locate her father.

International Reading Association Notable Books for a Global Society and *National Council for the Social Studies Notable Children's Trade Books in the Field of Social Studies.*

Reichart, George. *A Bag of Lucky Rice.*
Mark Mitchell, illustrator. Boston, MA: David R. Godine, 2002. 224 pages. ISBN 1-56792-166-3. Grades 4 to 6.

An old Chinese prospector deceives the populace of a Nevada Mining town after he discovers a strongbox full of gold.

Smithsonian Magazine Notable Books for Children.

Rice, Bebe Faas. *The Place at the Edge of the Earth.*
New York: Clarion Books, 2002. 192 pages. ISBN 0-618-15978-9. Grades 5 to 8.

The suffering endured by Lakota children at a boarding school in the 1880's is discovered through the relationship a present-day girl has with the ghost of an Indian boy.

National Council for the Social Studies Notable Social Studies Trade Books for Young People.

Seely, Debra. *Grasslands.*
New York: Holiday House, 2002. 128 pages. ISBN 0-8234-1731-X. Grades 5 to 8.

A thirteen-year-old Virginia boy finds 1880s Kansas farm life difficult after he moves in with his father and stepfamily.

Society of Midlands Author Award and *Western Writers of America Spur Award.*

Sorensen, Henri. *New Hope.*
Refer to complete information under Grades Kindergarten to 2.

Stanley, Diane. *Saving Sweetness.*
Refer to complete information under Grades Kindergarten to 2.

Stanley, Diane. *The True Adventure of Daniel Hall.*
New York: Dial Books for Young Readers, 1995. 40 pages. ISBN 0-8037-1468-8.
New York: Puffin Books, 1999. 40 pages. ISBN 0-14-056674-0pbk.
Grades 4 to 6.

A story illustrated in pastels about a fourteen-year-old seaman who leaves his New Bedford, Massachusetts, home in 1856 on a whaling voyage that lasts four years. He survives an abusive captain and the Siberian wilderness before being rescued.

National Council for the Social Studies Notable Children's Trade Books in the Field of Social Studies.

Tate, Nikki. *Jo's Triumph.*
Custer, WA: Orca Book Publishers, 2002. 139 pages. ISBN 1-55143-199-8. Grades 3 to 6.

A young girl disguises herself as a boy to escape an orphanage and finds a job riding on the pony express in the 1850s West.

Western Writers of America Spur Award.

Thomas, Joyce Carol. *I Have Heard of a Land.*
Refer to complete information under Grades Kindergarten to 2.

Tunbo, Frances G. *Stay Put, Robbie McAmis.*
Charles Shaw, illustrator. Texas Christian University Press, 1988. 158 pages. ISBN 0-87565-025-2. Grades 5 to 7.

In this story of survival in the Texas wilderness of 1848, a wagon train accident separates five helpless children and Grammie from the parents. They depend on twelve-year-old Robbie to find food and shelter.

Western Heritage Award.

Turner, Ann. *Dakota Dugout.*
Refer to complete information under Grades Kindergarten to 2.

Wangerin, Walter, Jr. *The Crying for a Vision.*
New York: Simon & Schuster, 1994. 278 pages. ISBN 0-671-7911-8.
(Out of print). Lexile 760. Grades 6 to 10.
  A Lakota Indian orphan named Move Walking finds himself confronting a fierce warrior after being outcast by his own tribe.
  Publishers Weekly Starred Review and *School Library Journal Starred Review.*

Welch, Catherine A. *Clouds of Terror.*
Refer to complete information under Grades Kindergarten to 2.

Wilder, Laura Ingalls. *By the Shores of Silver Lake.*
Garth Williams, illustrator. First copyright 1939. New York: Harper-Collins Children's Book Group, 1953. 292 pages. ISBN 0-06-026416-0
and 0-06-440005-0pbk. Lexile 820. Grades 3 to 7.
  In 1880, Ma and the girls follow Pa west by train where they make their home in a rough railroad camp and plan for their own homestead.
  American Library Association Notable Children's Books of 1940 to 1954 and *Newbery Medal.*

Wilder, Laura Ingalls. *Farmer Boy.*
Garth Williams, illustrator. First copyright 1933. New York: Harper-Collins Children's Book Group, 1961. 384 pages. ISBN 0-06-026425-X
and 0-06-440003-4pbk. Lexile 820. Grades 3 to 7.
  The third Little House book describes Almanzo Wilder's boyhood on his father's farm in upper New York State around 1875.
  American Library Association Notable Children's Books of 1940 to 1954.

Wilder, Laura Ingalls. *The First Four Years.*
Garth Williams, illustrator. New York: HarperCollins Children's Book Group, 1971. 134 pages. ISBN 0-06-026426-8 and 0-06-440031-Xpbk.
Lexile 1030. Grades 3 to 7.
  The ninth Little House book tells of the hardships Laura and Almanzo face and the birth of their daughter Rose while Dakota homesteading in the 1880s during their first four years of marriage.
  National Council for the Social Studies Notable Children's Trade Books in the Field of Social Studies.

Wilder, Laura Ingalls. *Little House in the Big Woods.*
Garth Williams, illustrator. New York: HarperCollins Children's Book Group, 1953. 256 pages. ISBN 0-06-026445-4 and 0-06-440001-8pbk.

New York: HarperAudio unabridged audio, 2002. ISBN 0-06-001241-2. Lexile 930. Grades 3 to 7.

A year in the life of two young girls growing up on the Wisconsin frontier in 1872. They help their mother with daily chores, enjoy their father's stories and singing, and share special occasions with relatives and neighbors.

American Booksellers Choices, American Library Association Notable Children's Books of 1940 to 1970, and *Lewis Carroll Shelf Award.*

Wilder, Laura Ingalls. *Little House on the Prairie.*
Garth Williams, illustrator. New York: HarperCollins Children's Book Group, 1953. 352 pages. ISBN 0-06-025445-4 and 0-06-44002-6pbk.
New York: HarperAudio unabridged audio, 2002. ISBN 0-06-001242-0. (VHS/DVD). Lexile 760. Grades 3 to 7.

After the little house in the big woods becomes crowded, Laura and her family travel from Wisconsin to Kansas and build a house on the prairie.

American Library Association Notable Children's Books 1940 to 1954 and *Horn Book Children's Classics.*

Wilder, Laura Ingalls. *Little Town on the Prairie.*
Garth Williams, illustrator. New York: HarperCollins Children's Book Group, 1953. 308 pages. ISBN 0-06-026450-0 and 0-06-440007-7pbk. Lexile 850. Grades 3 to 7.

The little settlement of *The Long Winter* becomes a frontier town. Fifteen-year-old Laura receives a certificate to teach school, and Almanzo Wilder asks permission to walk her home from church.

American Library Association Notable Children's Books of 1940 to 1954 and *Newbery Honor Book.*

Wilder, Laura Ingalls. *The Long Winter.*
Garth Williams, illustrator. First copyright 1940. New York: HarperCollins Children's Book Group, 1953. 352 pages. ISBN 0-06-026460-8 and 0-06-440006-9pbk. Lexile 790. Grades 3 to 7.

Almanzo Wilder risks his life to make a dangerous trip to secure wheat and save the village from starvation during the terrible winter of 1880 to 1881.

American Library Association Notable Children's Books of 1940 to 1954 and *Newbery Honor Book.*

Wilder, Laura Ingalls. *On the Banks of Plum Creek.*
Garth Williams, illustrator. First copyright 1937. New York: Harper-

Collins Children's Book Group, 1953. 340 pages. ISBN 0-06-026470-5 and 0-06-440004-2pbk.
New York: HarperAudio unabridged audio, 2002. ISBN 0-06-001243-9. Lexile 720. Grades 3 to 7.

After moving to Minnesota, the Ingalls family lives in a sod house by Plum Creek and encounters a terrible blizzard as well as a grasshopper plague.

American Library Association Notable Children's Books of 1940 to 1954 and *Newbery Honor Book.*

Wilder, Laura Ingalls. *These Happy Golden Years.*
Garth Williams, illustrator. First copyright 1953. New York: Harper-Collins Children's Book Group, 1971. 289 pages. ISBN 0-06-026480-5 and 0-06-440008-5pbk. Lexile 840. Grades 5 to 9.

This volume tells about Laura's school teaching experiences as a fifteen-year-old in a claim shanty twelve miles from home. After they marry, Laura and Almanzo move into their own little house on a home-stead claim.

American Library Association Notable Children's Books of 1940 to 1970 and *Newbery Honor Book.*

Yep, Laurence. *When the Circus Came to Town.*
New York: HarperCollins Children's Book Group, 2002. 128 pages. ISBN 0-06-029325-X and 0-06-440965-1pbk. Lexile 530. Grades 3 to 6.

A Chinese cook at a Montana stagecoach station helps coax a ten-year-old girl out of self-imposed isolation after a bout with smallpox scars her face.

National Council for the Social Studies Notable Social Studies Trade Books for Young People.

Grades 7 and 8

Alder, Elizabeth. *Crossing the Panther's Path.*
Refer to complete information under Grades 3 to 6.

Anderson, Laurie Halse. *Fever 1793.*
Refer to complete information under Grades 3 to 6.

Bruchac, Joseph. *Sacajawea: The Story of Bird Woman and the Lewis and Clark Expedition.*
San Diego, CA: Silver Whistle, 2000. 128 pages. ISBN 0-15-202234-1.

New York: Scholastic, 2001. 208 pages. ISBN 0-439-28068-0pbk. Lexile 840. Grades 7 to Young Adult.

A novel about the life of young Sacajawea, the famous interpreter and guide for Lewis and Clark, told in alternating points of view by Sacajawea and Clark. Includes parts of Clark's original diaries.

National Council for the Social Studies Notable Children's Trade Books in the Field of Social Studies.

Calabro, Marian. *The Perilous Journey of the Donner Party.*
Refer to complete information under Grades 3 to 6.

Conrad, Pam. *Prairie Songs.*
Refer to complete information under Grades 3 to 6.

Cushman, Karen. *The Ballad of Lucy Whipple.*
Refer to complete information under Grades 3 to 6.

Cushman, Karen. *Rodzina.*
Refer to complete information under Grades 3 to 6.

Demers, Barbara. *Willa's New World.*
Refer to complete information under Grades 3 to 6.

Durham, David Anthony. *Gabriel's Story.*
New York: Doubleday Broadway Publishing Group, 2001. 288 pages. ISBN 0-385-49814-4 and 0-385-72033-5pbk. Grades 7 to Young Adult.

A fifteen-year-old African American boy leaves his pioneering family and joins a brutal gang of cowboys in the 1870s American West.

Alex Award.

Fleischman, Sid. *Humbug Mountain.*
Refer to complete information under Grades 3 to 6.

Garland, Sherry. *In the Shadow of the Alamo.*
Refer to complete information under Grades 3 to 6.

Garland, Sherry. *Voices of the Alamo.*
Refer to complete information under Grades 3 to 6.

Gipson, Fred. *Old Yeller.*
Refer to complete information under Grades 3 to 6.

Gregory, Kristiana. *Earthquake at Dawn.*
Refer to complete information under Grades 3 to 6.

Gregory, Kristiana. *Jenny of the Tetons.*
Refer to complete information under Grades 3 to 6.

Hill, Kirkpatrick. *Minuk: Ashes in the Pathway. ("Girls of Many Lands Series").*
Refer to complete information under Grades 3 to 6.

Holm, Jennifer. *Boston Jane: An Adventure.*
Refer to complete information under Grades 3 to 6.

Hotze, Sollace. *A Circle Unbroken.*
Refer to complete information under Grades 3 to 6.

Ingold, Jeanette. *The Big Burn.*
Refer to complete information under Grades 3 to 6.

Lasky, Katheryn. *Beyond the Divide.*
New York: Simon & Schuster, 1983. 264 pages. ISBN 0-02-751670-9.
New York: Aladdin Paperbacks, 1995. 297 pages. ISBN 0-689-80163-7pbk. Lexile 900. Grades 7 to Young Adult.
    In 1849, a fourteen-year-old Amish girl named Mariah chooses to leave her Pennsylvania home to accompany her shunned father across the continent by wagon train. During the journey, some men rape her new friend and her father dies of gangrene. The Yani (Mill Creek) Indians help her survive.
    American Library Association Best Book for Young Adults, American Library Association Notable Children's Books, and *National Council of Teachers of English Recommended Books.*

Lenski, Lois. *Indian Captive: The Story of Mary Jemison.*
Refer to complete information under Grades 3 to 6.

Levitin, Sonia. *Clem's Chances.*
Refer to complete information under Grades 3 to 6.

McGraw, Eloise Jarvis. *Moccasin Trail.*
Refer to complete information under Grades 3 to 6.

Myers, Walter Dean. *The Righteous Revenge of Artemis Bonner.*
Refer to complete information under Grades 3 to 6.

Nixon, Joan. *A Family Apart.*
Refer to complete information under Grades 3 to 6.

Nixon, Joan. *In the Face of Danger: The Orphan Train Quartet Three.*
Topeka, KS: Econo-Clad Books, 1999. 152 pages. ISBN 0-8335-3222-7.
New York: Bantam Books, 1988. 151 pages. ISBN 0-553-28196-8pbk
and ISBN 0-440-222705-4pbk. Lexile 850. Grades 7 to 10.
The Orphan Train Quartet follows the story of the six Kelly children,
whose widowed mother has sent them west from New York City in 1856
because she is unable to support them. Megan is happy when a loving
young couple living in the rugged Kansas territory adopts her. But during
the first trying months, a blizzard, a pack of prairie wolves, and an armed
fugitive bring disaster to her new family.
Western Writers of America Spur Award.

O'Dell, Scott. *Island of the Blue Dolphins.*
Refer to complete information under Grades 3 to 6.

O'Dell, Scott. *Sing Down the Moon.*
Refer to complete information under Grades 3 to 6.

O'Dell, Scott. *Streams to the River, River to the Sea.*
New York: Houghton Mifflin Co., 1986. 191 pages. ISBN 0-395-40430-
4.
New York: Fawcett, 1987. 163 pages. ISBN 0-449-70244-8pbk. Lexile
740. Grades 8 to Young Adult.
A young Indian woman named Sacajawea is accompanied by her
infant and cruel husband when she joins Lewis and Clark on their famous
journey. Sacajawea narrates the story, describing the land and Indian life,
sharing joy and heartbreak, and telling of her growing feelings for Captain Clark.
Scott O'Dell Award for Historical Fiction.

O'Dell, Scott and Elizabeth Hall. *Thunder Rolling in the Mountains.*
Refer to complete information under Grades 3 to 6.

Osborne, Mary Pope. *Adaline Falling Star.*
Refer to complete information under Grades 3 to 6.

Rice, Bebe Faas. *The Place at the Edge of the Earth.*
Refer to complete information under Grades 3 to 6.

Seely, Debra. *Grasslands.*
Refer to complete information under Grades 3 to 6.

Tunbo, Frances G. *Stay Put, Robbie McAmis.*
Refer to complete information under Grades 3 to 6.

Wangerin, Walter Jr. *The Crying for a Vision.*
Refer to complete information under Grades 3 to 6.

Wilder, Laura Ingalls. *By the Shores of Silver Lake.*
Refer to complete information under Grades 3 to 6.

Wilder, Laura Ingalls. *Farmer Boy.*
Refer to complete information under Grades 3 to 6.

Wilder, Laura Ingalls. *The First Four Years.*
Refer to complete information under Grades 3 to 6.

Wilder, Laura Ingalls. *Little House in the Big Woods.*
Refer to complete information under Grades 3 to 6.

Wilder, Laura Ingalls. *Little House on the Prairie.*
Refer to complete information under Grades 3 to 6.

Wilder, Laura Ingalls. *Little Town on the Prairie.*
Refer to complete information under Grades 3 to 6.

Wilder, Laura Ingalls. *The Long Winter.*
Refer to complete information under Grades 3 to 6.

Wilder, Laura Ingalls. *On the Banks of Plum Creek.*
Refer to complete information under Grades 3 to 6.

Wilder, Laura Ingalls. *These Happy Golden Years.*
Refer to complete information under Grades 3 to 6.

Chapter 5

Slavery and Abolitionists: 1814 to 1865

Grades Kindergarten to 2

Altman, Linda Jacobs. *The Legend of Freedom Hill.*
Ying-Hwa Hu and Cornelius Van Wright, illustrators. New York: Lee &
Low Books, 2000. 32 pages. ISBN 1-58430-003-5. Lexile 680. Grades 2
to 4.

Two young girls buy freedom for the African American girl's mother
and four other slaves by panning for gold during California's Gold Rush
of the 1850s.

Storytelling World Award Honor Book.

Monjo, F. N. *The Drinking Gourd.*
Fred Brenner, illustrator. First copyright 1970. New York: HarperCollins
Children's Book Group, 1993. 64 pages. ISBN 0-06-024329-5 and 0-06-
444042-7pbk.
Prince Frederick, MD: Recorded Books unabridged audio, 1995. ISBN
0-7887-0213-0. (An "I Can Read" book). Lexile 370. Grades 2 to 4.

When he is sent home alone for misbehaving in church, Tommy
discovers that his house is a station on the Underground Railroad.
Tommy and his father help an escaping slave family follow the "drinking
gourd," or North Star, to Canada.

American Library Association Notable Children's Books.

Olson, Arielle. *The Lighthouse Keeper's Daughter.*
Elaine Wentworth, illustrator. Boston: Little, Brown & Company, 1987.
32 pages. ISBN 0-316-65053-6. (Out of print). Grades K to 3.

Miranda struggles to keep the fourteen lamps of the lighthouse burning during an 1850s blizzard off the coast of Maine while her father is stranded ashore.

Friends of American Writers Juvenile Book Merit Award.

Smalls-Hector, Irene. *Irene Jennie and the Christmas Masquerade.*
Melodye Rosales, illustrator. Boston: Little, Brown & Company, 1996. 32 pages. ISBN 0-316-79878-9. (Out of print). Grades K to 3.

On a North Carolina plantation, a young slave girl's Christmas is brightened by the Johnkankus parade she witnesses while waiting for her parents to come home after being on loan to another plantation master.

International Reading Association Notable Books for a Global Society.

Vaughan, Marcia K. *The Secret to Freedom.*
Larry Johnson, illustrator. New York: Lee & Low Books, 2001. 32 pages. ISBN 1-58430-021-3. Grades K to 3.

A young girl listens while her great aunt tells stories of escape from slavery through the use of patchwork quilt patterns.

Society of School Librarians International Book Award.

Grades 3 to 6

Altman, Linda Jacobs. *The Legend of Freedom Hill.*
Refer to complete information under Grades Kindergarten to 2.

Avi. *The Barn.*
New York: Orchard Books, 1994. 106 pages. ISBN 0-531-06861-7.
New York: Scholastic, 1996. 106 pages. ISBN 0-380-72562-2pbk.
Prince Frederick, MD: Recorded Books unabridged audio, 1995. ISBN 0-7887-0213-0. Lexile 670. Grades 4 to 6.

Ben is summoned home from boarding school in 1855 to care for his father, who has suffered a stroke. Ben becomes convinced that his father will recover if the family fulfills his dream of building a barn.

ABC Children's Booksellers Choices Award, American Library Association Notable Children's Books, Booklist Editors' Choice, and *International Reading Association Teachers' Choices.*

Avi. *The True Confessions of Charlotte Doyle.*
New York: Orchard Books, 1990. 215 pages. ISBN 0-531-05893-X.
New York: Avon Books, 1992. 232 pages. ISBN 0-380-71475-2pbk.
Prince Frederick, MD: Recorded Books unabridged audio, 1992.

ISBN 1-55690-593-9. Lexile 740. Grades 5 to 8.

After being accused and convicted of murder, thirteen-year-old Charlotte Doyle finds that she is the only passenger aboard the "Seahawk," which is piloted by a murderous captain and crewed by mutinous seamen during the summer of 1832.

Boston Globe-Horn Book Award, Golden Kite Award, Judy Lopez Children's Book Award, and *Newbery Honor Book.*

Beatty, Patricia. *Jayhawker.*
New York: Morrow, 1991. 214 pages. ISBN 0-688-09850-9 and 0-688-14422-5pbk. Lexile 780. Grades 5 to 9.

After his father dies in 1858, Kansas farm boy Lije Tulley becomes a Jayhawker, an abolitionist spy who frees slaves from the neighboring state of Missouri.

School Library Journal Best Book.

DeFelice, Cynthia. *The Apprenticeship of Lucas Whitaker.*
New York: Farrar, Straus & Giroux, 1996. 160 pages. ISBN 0-374-34669-0.
New York: Morrow, 1998. 160 pages. ISBN 0-380-72920-2pbk.
Prince Frederick, MD: Recorded Books unabridged audio, 1997. ISBN 0-7887-0885-6. Lexile 830. Grades 5 to 7.

After twelve-year-old Lucas Whitaker loses his whole family to tuberculosis in 1849, he learns of a bizarre cure. He takes a job as apprentice to the town doctor and learns the difference between superstition and science.

National Council for the Social Studies Notable Children's Trade Books in the Field of Social Studies and *School Library Journal Best Book.*

Fleischman, Paul. *The Borning Room.*
Topeka, KS: Econo-Clad Books, 1999. 112 pages. ISBN 0-7857-0798-0.
New York: HarperTrophy, 1993. 101 pages. ISBN 0-06-447099-7pbk. Lexile 800. Grades 6 to Young Adult.

Lying at the end of her life in the room where she was born in 1851, Georgina Lott remembers what it was like to grow up on the Ohio frontier and witness the Civil War, slavery, and the beginning uses of electricity.

American Library Association Best Books for Young Adults, American Library Association Notable Children's Books, Booklist Editors' Choices, The Bulletin of the Center for Children's Books Blue Ribbon Award, Golden Kite Award Honor Book, Horn Book Fanfare Honor List,

International Reading Association Teachers' Choices, National Council for the Social Studies Notable Children's Trade Books in the Field of Social Studies, National Council of Teachers of English Notable Trade Books in the Language Arts, New York Public Library Books for the Teen Age, Publishers Weekly Best Books of the Year, and *School Library Journal Best Book.*

Fox, Paula. *The Slave Dancer.*
Eros Keith, illustrator. New York: Simon & Schuster, 1973. 192 pages. ISBN 0-689-84505-7.
New York: Laurel Leaf Library, 1996. 127 pages. ISBN 0-440-96132-7pbk.
New York: Bantam Books unabridged audio, 1996. ISBN 0-553-47696-3. Lexile 970. Grades 5 to 8.

Kidnapped from the docks of New Orleans by the crew of a ship bound for Africa, a thirteen-year-old boy discovers to his horror that his job is to play his fife so that captured slaves will "dance" to keep their muscles strong and their bodies profitable.
Newbery Medal.

Guccione, Leslie Davis. *Come Morning.*
Minneapolis, MN: The Lerner Publishing Group, 1995. 120 pages. ISBN 0-87614-892-5 and 1-57505-228-8pbk. (An "Adventures in Time" book). Lexile 670. Grades 4 to 7.

A twelve-year-old African American boy gets drawn into the danger and drama of helping to transport slaves on the Underground Railroad in 1850 after his father is caught by slavers from the South and their home is burned.
Society of School Librarians International Book Award.

Hamilton, Virginia. *The House of Dies Drear.*
Eros Keith, illustrator. New York: Macmillan Publishing Co., 1968. 247 pages. ISBN 0-02-742500-2 and 0-02-043520-7pbk.
Prince Frederick, MD: Recorded Books unabridged audio, 1995. ISBN 0-7887-0329-3. (VHS). Lexile 670. Grades 5 to 7.

An African American family tries to unravel the secrets of their new home, which was once a stop on the Underground Railroad. Thirteen-year-old Thomas explores the hidden passageways in and under the house.
Edgar Award.

Hansen, Joyce. *The Captive.*
New York: Scholastic, 1994. 195 pages. ISBN 0-590-41625-1.
New York: Scholastic, 1995. 195 pages. ISBN 0-590-41624-3pbk. Lexile 810. Grades 5 to Young Adult.

In a story based on an actual slave narrative, Kofi, the prince of a West African village, is betrayed, kidnapped, and sold into slavery in Massachusetts. While working for a New England family of Puritans, he studies the English language and a shipbuilder gives him the chance to return home.

Coretta Scott King Award Honor Book and *National Council for the Social Studies Notable Children's Trade Books in the Field of Social Studies.*

Hurmence, Belinda. *A Girl Called Boy.*
First copyright 1982. Topeka, KS: Econo-Clad Books, 1999. 168 pages. ISBN 0-8335-5952-4.
New York: Clarion Books, 1990. 180 pages. ISBN 0-395-55698-8pbk. Lexile 860. Grades 3 to 6.

A historical fantasy where a young African American girl finds herself mysteriously transported back into the times of slavery.
Parent's Choice Award.

Myers, Walter Dean. *Amistad: A Long Road to Freedom.*
New York: Dutton Children's Books, 1998. 96 pages. ISBN 0-525-4970-7.
New York: Penguin Putnam, 2001. 99 pages. ISBN 0-14-130004-3pbk. Lexile 1050. Grades 5 to 9.

The dramatic story of the 1839 rebellion of captured Africans against their Spanish kidnappers aboard the slave ship, Amistad. The subsequent arrest and trial of the Africans led to their acquittal by the Supreme Court.
International Reading Association Notable Books for a Global Society.

Monjo, F. N. *The Drinking Gourd.*
Refer to complete information under Grades Kindergarten to 2.

Nixon, Joan. *A Family Apart.*
First copyright 1987. Topeka, KS: Econo-Clad Books, 1999. 162 pages. ISBN 0-8335-1833-X.
New York: Bantam Dell Publishing Group, 1996. 162 pages. ISBN 0-440-22676-7pbk.

Prince Frederick, MD: Recorded Books unabridged audio, 2000. ISBN 0-7887-4235-3. Lexile 820. Grades 5 to 7.

In 1860, six siblings are sent by the Children's Aid Society of New York City to live with farm families in Missouri after their mother can no longer support them. Frances cuts her hair and pretends to be a boy so she can be placed with her little brother. When the family that adopts them finds out Frances is a girl, they are impressed by her courage and hard work as she helps them transport slaves along the Underground Railroad.

Western Writers of America Spur Award.

Olson, Arielle. *The Lighthouse Keeper's Daughter.*
Refer to complete information under Grades Kindergarten to 2.

Paterson, Katherine. *Jip: His Story.*
New York: Lodestar, 1996. 181 pages. ISBN 0-525-67543-4.
New York: Puffin Books, 1998. 181 pages. ISBN 0-14-038674-2pbk.
Prince Frederick, MD: Recorded Books unabridged audio, 1997. ISBN 0-7887-1345-0 and 0-7887-4967-6cd. Lexile 860. Grades 5 to 9.

Raised on a poor Vermont farm after tumbling off the back of a wagon as a small child, Jip is astonished when he learns in the late 1850s that he is the property of a slave owner. Jip's teacher Lyddie and her Quaker sweetheart help Jip escape to Canada.

School Library Journal Best Book.

Paterson, Katherine. *Lyddie.*
New York: Lodestar, 1991. 192 pages. ISBN 0-525-67338-5.
New York: Puffin Books, 1994. 182 pages. ISBN 0-14-034981-2.
Prince Frederick, MD: Recorded Books unabridged audio, 1993. ISBN 1-55690-851-2. Lexile 860. Grades 6 to 9.

Impoverished Vermont farm girl Lyddie Worthen is determined to gain her independence by becoming a factory worker in Lowell, Massachusetts, in the 1840s.

The Bulletin of the Center for Children's Books Blue Ribbon Award.

Pearsall, Shelley. *Trouble Don't Last.*
New York: Random House, 2002. 160 pages. ISBN 0-375-81490-6. Grades 5 to 8.

In 1859 Kentucky, an eleven-year-old African American slave and his elderly companion flee their tyrannical master via the Underground

Railroad.
Booklist Editors' Choice, Booklist Top Ten Historical Fiction for Youth, and Scott O'Dell Award for Historical Fiction.

Rinaldi, Ann. *An Acquaintance With Darkness.*
San Diego, CA: Harcourt Children's Books, 1997. 356 pages. ISBN 0-15-201294-X and 0-15-202197-3pbk. Lexile 520. Grades 6 to Young Adult.

In 1865, fourteen-year-old Emily is forced to live with a despised uncle in Washington, D.C. who is both a physician and a body snatcher. He forbids Emily to see her best friend, whose family is implicated in President Lincoln's assassination.
American Library Association Best Books for Young Adults and New York Public Library Books for the Teen Age.

Rosen, Michael J. *A School for Pompey Walker.*
Aminah Brenda Lynn Robinson, illustrator. San Diego, CA: Harcourt Children's Books, 1995. 48 pages. ISBN 0-15-200114-X. Lexile AD1170. Grades 3 to 7.

In this story based on fact, Pompey Walker is born into slavery and dreams of going to school, but he cannot escape from the brutalities of plantation life. The slavery-hating son-in-law of the plantation owner comes up with a daring scheme of helping Pompey, and he voluntarily returns to the auction block thirty-nine times, after which his white friend helps Pompey obtain his freedom. The auction profits are used to build a school for African Americans.
American Library Association Notable Children's Books.

Schwartz, Virginia Frances. *If I Just Had Two Wings.*
Toronto, Canada: Stoddart Kids, 2001. 221 pages. ISBN 0-7737-3302-7. Lexile 520. Grades 6 to 8.

A thirteen-year-old African American slave girl works on an Alabama plantation in 1861 and befriends another girl who helps her escape via the Underground Railroad to a boat bound for Canada.
Canadian Library Association Notable Children's Book and Geoffrey Bilson Award for Historical Fiction for Young People.

Smalls-Hector, Irene. *Irene Jennie and the Christmas Masquerade.*
Refer to complete information under Grades Kindergarten to 2.

Smucker, Barbara. *Runaway to Freedom.*
First copyright 1977. New York: Peter Smith Publishers, 1992. 154

pages. ISBN 0-8446-6585-1.
New York: HarperTrophy, 1979. 152 pages. ISBN 0-06-440106-5pbk.
Lexile 770. Grades 4 to 8.

With the help of a white man, two young slave girls escape from a plantation in Mississippi and travel a hazardous route toward freedom in Canada via the Underground Railroad.

International Reading Association Children's Choices and *National Council for the Social Studies Notable Children's Trade Books in the Field of Social Studies.*

Stolz, Mary. *Cezzane Pinto: A Memoir.*
New York: Alfred A. Knopf, 1994. 252 pages. ISBN 0-679-84917-3 and 0-679-88933-7pbk. Lexile 1020. Grades 5 to 9.

In his old age, Cezanne Pinto recalls his youth as a slave on a Virginia plantation, the painful forced separation from his mother, his love of horses, and his escape to a new life in the North.

Jane Addams Children's Book Award Honor Book.

Vaughan, Marcia K. *The Secret to Freedom.*
Refer to complete information under Grades Kindergarten to 2.

Grades 7 and 8

Avi. *The True Confessions of Charlotte Doyle.*
Refer to complete information under Grades 3 to 6.

Beatty, Patricia. *Jayhawker.*
Refer to complete information under Grades 3 to 6.

DeFelice, Cynthia. *The Apprenticeship of Lucas Whitaker.*
Refer to complete information under Grades 3 to 6.

Fleischman, Paul. *The Borning Room.*
Refer to complete information under Grades 3 to 6.

Fox, Paula. *The Slave Dancer.*
Refer to complete information under Grades 3 to 6.

Guccione, Leslie Davis. *Come Morning.*
Refer to complete information under Grades 3 to 6.

Hamilton, Virginia. *The House of Dies Drear.*
Refer to complete information under Grades 3 to 6.

Hansen, Joyce. *The Captive.*
Refer to complete information under Grades 3 to 6.

Lyons, Mary E. *Letters from a Slave Girl: The Story of Harriet Jacobs.*
New York: Atheneum Books for Young Readers, 1992. 146 pages. ISBN 0-684-19446-5.
New York: Atheneum Books for Young Readers, 1996. 160 pages. ISBN 0-689-80015-0pbk. Lexile 880. Grades 7 to 10.
The life of Harriet Jacobs as told in the form of fictionalized letters that she might have written during her slavery in North Carolina and as she prepared for escape to the North in 1842. She later became a published author and abolitionist.
American Library Association Best Books for Young Adults, American Library Association Notable Children's Books, Horn Book Fanfare Honor List, and *School Library Journal Starred Review.*

Myers, Walter Dean. *Amistad: A Long Road to Freedom.*
Refer to complete information under Grades 3 to 6.

Nixon, Joan. *A Family Apart.*
Refer to complete information under Grades 3 to 6.

Paterson, Katherine. *Jip: His Story.*
Refer to complete information under Grades 3 to 6.

Paterson, Katherine. *Lyddie.*
Refer to complete information under Grades 3 to 6.

Pearsall, Shelley. *Trouble Don't Last.*
Refer to complete information under Grades 3 to 6.

Rinaldi, Ann. *An Acquaintance With Darkness.*
Refer to complete information under Grades 3 to 6.

Rinaldi, Ann. *Wolf by the Ears.*
Topeka, KS: Econo-Clad Books, 1999. 252 pages. ISBN 0-7857-0587-2.
New York: Scholastic, 1993. 252 pages. ISBN 0-590-43412-8. Lexile 580. Grades 7 to Young Adult.
Harriet Hemmings, rumored to be the daughter of Thomas Jefferson

and Sally Hemmings, one of his slaves, keeps a diary as she struggles with difficult decisions facing her as a young adult.

American Library Association Best Books for Young Adults and *American Library Association Best of the Best Books, 1966 to 1992.*

Rosen, Michael J. *A School for Pompey Walker.*
Refer to complete information under Grades 3 to 6.

Schwartz, Virginia Frances. *If I Just Had Two Wings.*
Refer to complete information under Grades 3 to 6.

Smucker, Barbara. *Runaway to Freedom.*
Refer to complete information under Grades 3 to 6.

Stolz, Mary. *Cezzane Pinto: A Memoir.*
Refer to complete information under Grades 3 to 6.

Chapter 6

The Civil War: 1861 to 1865

Grades Kindergarten to 2

Turner, Ann Warren. *Abe Lincoln Remembers.*
Wendell Minor, illustrator. New York: HarperCollins Children's Book
Group, 2000. 32 pages. ISBN 0-06-027577-4. New York: HarperTrophy,
2003. ISBN 0-06-051107-9pbk. Lexile 790. Grades K to 3.
    A fictional biography picture book that shows Abe Lincoln reflecting
on his life one evening in 1865 after the Civil War is over.
    *National Council for the Social Studies Notable Children's Trade
Books in the Field of Social Studies.*

Grades 3 to 6

Armstrong, Jennifer. *The Dreams of Mairhe Mehan: A Novel of the
Civil War.*
New York: Alfred A. Knopf, 1996. 119 pages. ISBN 0-679-88152-2.
New York: Random House, 1997. 119 pages. ISBN 0-679-88557-9pbk.
Lexile 1060. Grades 6 to 8.
    The impact of the Civil War is terrible on Mairhe's family living in
an Irish slum in Washington, D.C. during the 1860s. While struggling to
understand her brother's enlistment in the Union army, Mairhe meets and
is encouraged by Walt Whitman.
    The Bulletin of the Center for Children's Books Blue Ribbon Award.

Beatty, Patricia. *Charley Skedaddle.*
New York: Morrow, 1987. 192 pages. ISBN 0-688-06687-9.

Mahwah, NJ: Troll Communications, 1989. 186 pages. ISBN 0-8167-1317-0pbk.

Prince Frederick, MD: Recorded Books unabridged audio, 1987. ISBN 0-7887-3823-2. Lexile 870. Grades 5 to 9.

During the Civil War in 1864, twelve-year-old Charley from New York City joins the Union army as a drummer boy, deserts during a battle in Virginia, and encounters a hostile old mountain woman.

Scott O'Dell Award for Historical Fiction.

Blos, Joan. *A Gathering of Days: A New England Girl's Journal, 1830 to 1832.*

New York: Atheneum Books for Young Readers, 1980. 144 pages. ISBN 0-684-16340-3.

New York: Aladdin Paperbacks, 1990. 144 pages. ISBN 0-689-71419-Xpbk.

Prince Frederick, MD: Recorded Books unabridged audio, 1979. ISBN 1-55690-646-3. Lexile 960. Grades 4 to 7.

The journal a fourteen-year-old girl kept the last year she lived on the family farm records daily events in her small New Hampshire town, including her father's remarriage and the death of her best friend. She gives this journal to her fourteen-year-old great-granddaughter in 1899.

Newbery Medal.

Donahue, John. *An Island Far from Home.*

Minneapolis, MN: The Lerner Publishing Group, 1995. 180 pages. ISBN 0-87614-859-3 and 1-57505-076-5pbk. (An "Adventures in Time" book). Lexile 690. Grades 4 to 7.

Twelve-year-old Joshua expresses a desire to join the army to avenge his father's death. Joshua's uncle encourages him to write to an imprisoned rebel soldier, after which he gains insight as well as a deep friendship.

International Reading Association Children's Choices, National Council for the Social Studies Notable Children's Trade Books in the Field of Social Studies, and *Society of School Librarians International Book Award.*

Fleischman, Paul. *Bull Run.*

New York: HarperCollins Children's Book Group, 1993. 104 pages. ISBN 0-06-021446-5 and 0-06-440588-5pbk.

Northport, ME: Audio Bookshelf abridged audio, 1999. ISBN 1-883332-37-0 and 1-883332-58-3cd. Lexile 810. Grades 5 to 9.

Eight Southern and eight Northern characters, including slaves, soldiers, and citizens, offer sixteen different perspectives about their involvement in the 1861 Battle of Bull Run, the first great battle of the Civil War.

American Library Association Best Books for Young Adults, American Library Association Notable Children's Books, Anne Izard Storytellers' Choice Award, Booklist Editors' Choice, Horn Book Fanfare Honor List, International Reading Association Teachers' Choices, National Council for the Social Studies Notable Children's Trade Books in the Field of Social Studies, New York Public Library Books for the Teen Age, Publishers Weekly Best Books of the Year, School Library Journal Best Book, and *Scott O'Dell Award for Historical Fiction.*

Forrester, Sandra. *Sound the Jubilee.*
New York: Lodestar, 1995. 184 pages. ISBN 0-525-67486-1.
New York: Puffin Books, 1997. 192 pages. ISBN 0-14-037930-4pbk.
Lexile 790. Grades 6 to 9.

In 1861, an eleven-year-old slave and her family find refuge on Roanoke Island, North Carolina, during the Civil War.

National Council for the Social Studies Notable Children's Trade Books in the Field of Social Studies.

Hunt, Irene. *Across Five Aprils.*
First copyright 1965. Topeka, KS: Econo-Clad Books, 1999. 190 pages. ISBN 0-88103-002-3.
New York: Berkley Publishing Group, 2002. 224 pages. ISBN 0-425-18278-9pbk.
Audio Bookshelf unabridged audio, 2002. ISBN 1-883332-48-6 and 1-883332-75-3cd. Lexile 1100. Grades 6 to Young Adult.

With his relatives fighting on opposite sides, young Jethro Creighton grows into a man when he is left to take care of the family farm in Illinois during the difficult years of the Civil War.

Newbery Honor Book and *Society of Midlands Authors Award.*

Osborne, Mary Pope. *My Brother's Keeper: Virginia's Diary, Gettysburg, Pennsylvania, 1863.*
New York: Scholastic Trade, 2000. 109 pages. ISBN 0-439-15307-7. *(A "Dear America" book).* Lexile 590. Grades 3 to 6.

Nine-year-old Virginia is left behind in 1863 Gettysburg when her father tries to hide horses from the Confederate soldiers. Her experiences while witnessing the bloody Civil War battle and President Lincoln's

Gettysburg Address are recorded in diary format.

National Council for the Social Studies Notable Children's Trade Books in the Field of Social Studies.

Polacco, Patricia. *Pink and Say.*
New York: Philomel Books, 1994. 48 pages. ISBN 0-399-22671-0.
New York: Spoken Arts audio, 1996. ISBN 0-8045-6835-4. (VHS). Lexile 590. Grades 4 to 8.

Based on the true story of a remarkable wartime friendship, a young white Union soldier and a young African American Union soldier are captured by the Confederate army and sent to Andersonville Prison, where one is hanged.

Jefferson Cup Award.

Reeder, Carolyn. *Shades of Gray.*
New York: Simon & Schuster, 1989. 152 pages. ISBN 0-02-775810-9.
New York: Aladdin Paperbacks, 1999. 152 pages. ISBN 0-689-82696-6pbk. Lexile 800. Grades 5 to 7.

At the end of the Civil War, twelve-year-old Will, the only surviving member of his immediate family, reluctantly leaves his city home to live in the Virginia countryside with his aunt and the uncle he considers a traitor because of his refusal to take part in the war.

American Library Association Notable Children's Books, The Child Study Committee Children's Book Award, Jefferson Cup Award, and *Scott O'Dell Award for Historical Fiction.*

Rinaldi, Ann. *An Acquaintance With Darkness.*
San Diego, CA: Harcourt Children's Books, 1997. 356 pages. ISBN 0-15-201294-X and 0-15-202197-3pbk. Lexile 520. Grades 6 to Young Adult.

In 1865, fourteen-year-old Emily is forced to live with a despised uncle in Washington, D.C. who is both a physician and a body snatcher. He forbids Emily to see her best friend, whose family is implicated in President Lincoln's assassination.

American Library Association Best Books for Young Adults and *New York Public Library Books for the Teen Age.*

Rinaldi, Ann. *Numbering All the Bones.*
New York: Hyperion Books for Children, 2002. 176 pages. ISBN 0-7868-0533-1. Lexile 600. Grades 6 to 8.

A thirteen-year-old African American girl joins the efforts of Clara Barton to search for her brother, incarcerated in the horrendous Ander-

sonville prison during the Civil War.
National Council for the Social Studies Notable Social Studies Trade Books for Young People.

Steele, William O. *The Perilous Road.*
First copyright 1958. New York: Peter Smith Publishers, 1991. 156 pages. ISBN 0-8446-6507-X.
San Diego, CA: Harcourt Children's Books, 1990. 156 pages. ISBN 0-15-260647-5pbk. Lexile 750. Grades 3 to 7.

Union troops raid Chris's home in Tennessee, taking all his family's stored food and only horse. His hatred compels Chris to tell the Rebels that a Union wagon train has moved into the region, but he is unaware that his brother has joined the Union army and is among them.
Jane Addams Children's Book Award and *Newbery Honor Book.*

Turner, Ann Warren. *Abe Lincoln Remembers.*
Refer to complete information under Grades Kindergarten to 2.

Wisler, G. Clifton. *Run the Blockade.*
New York: HarperCollins Children's Book Group, 2000. 128 pages. ISBN 0-06-029208-3 and 0-688-16538-9.
Prince Frederick, MD: Recorded Books unabridged audio, 2002. ISBN 1-4025-1333-X. Lexile 800. Grades 5 to 8.

Twelve-year-old Henry from Ireland signs on to be a ship's boy and has many adventures trying to break through the Union ships blockading Confederate ports in America with needed supplies. After being captured by the Union Navy, he languishes in a New York prison until a relative rescues him.
National Council for the Social Studies Notable Children's Trade Books in the Field of Social Studies.

Grades 7 and 8

Armstrong, Jennifer. *The Dreams of Mairhe Mehan: A Novel of the Civil War.*
Refer to complete information under Grades 3 to 6.

Beatty, Patricia. *Charley Skedaddle.*
Refer to complete information under Grades 3 to 6.

Blos, Joan. *A Gathering of Days: A New England Girl's Journal, 1830 to 1832.*
Refer to complete information under Grades 3 to 6.

Donahue, John. *An Island Far from Home.*
Refer to complete information under Grades 3 to 6.

Fleischman, Paul. *Bull Run.*
Refer to complete information under Grades 3 to 6.

Forrester, Sandra. *Sound the Jubilee.*
Refer to complete information under Grades 3 to 6.

Hunt, Irene. *Across Five Aprils.*
Refer to complete information under Grades 3 to 6.

Keith, Harold. *Rifles for Watie.*
First copyright 1957. HarperCollins Children's Book Group, 1991. 334 pages. ISBN 0-690-04907-2 and 0-06-447030-Xpbk.
Prince Frederick, MD: Recorded Books unabridged audio, 1999. ISBN 0-7887-3209-9 and 0-7887-3732-5cd. Lexile 910. Grades 7 to 10.

Jeff fights for the Union and watches his friends die in a Civil War battle against Stand Watie, a Cherokee Indian Rebel leader. After the battle, he becomes a spy and discovers that the enemy is not necessarily on the Confederate side.

American Library Association Notable Children's Books, Lewis Carroll Shelf Award, and *Newbery Medal.*

Myers, Walter Dean. *The Glory Field.*
Topeka, KS: Econo-Clad Books, 1999. 334 pages. ISBN 0-7857-8741-0.
New York: Point, 1996. 375 pages. ISBN 0-590-45898-1pbk. Lexile 800. Grades 7 to Young Adult.

Follows five generations of an African American family spanning two hundred and fifty years, from the capture and enslavement of the first ancestor in 1750, through the Civil War and the end of segregation, to a final reunion of relatives.

American Library Association Best Books for Young Adults.

Paulsen, Gary. *Soldier's Heart: Being the Story of the Enlistment and Due Service of the Boy Charley Goddard in the First Minnesota Volunteers.*
New York: Doubleday Broadway Publishing Group, 1998. 106 pages.

ISBN 0-385-32498-7.
New York: Laurel Leaf Library, 2000. 106 pages. ISBN 0-440-33838-7pbk.
New York: Bantam Books unabridged audio, 1999. ISBN 0-553-52611-1. Lexile 1000. Grades 7 to Young Adult.

Based on the life of a fifteen-year-old boy who lies his way into the Union army because he thinks the war will be a great adventure. Wounded and sent home before reaching the age of twenty, the war has destroyed his will to live and leaves him with a "soldier's heart."
Booklist Editors' Choice and *Jefferson Cup Award.*

Polacco, Patricia. *Pink and Say.*
Refer to complete information under Grades 3 to 6.

Reeder, Carolyn. *Shades of Gray.*
Refer to complete information under Grades 3 to 6.

Rinaldi, Ann. *An Acquaintance With Darkness.*
Refer to complete information under Grades 3 to 6.

Rinaldi, Ann. *In My Father's House.*
Topeka, KS: Econo-Clad Books, 1999. 323 pages. ISBN 0-7858-5475-X.
New York: Point, 1996. 323 pages. ISBN 0-590-44731-9pbk. Lexile 640. Grades 7 to Young Adult.

Based on the real McLean family on whose property the Civil War began and in whose parlor it ended when Lee surrendered in 1865, Oscie grows up with Southern views and finds it difficult to change her beliefs about slavery.
American Library Association Best Books for Young Adults.

Rinaldi, Ann. *Numbering All the Bones.*
Refer to complete information under Grades 3 to 6.

Steele, William O. *The Perilous Road.*
Refer to complete information under Grades 3 to 6.

Wisler, G. Clifton. *Run the Blockade.*
Refer to complete information under Grades 3 to 6.

Chapter 7

Immigration, Ethnicity, and American Assimilation: 1800 to the Modern Era

Grades Kindergarten to 2

Broyles, Anne. *Shy Mama's Halloween.*
Leane Morin, illustrator. Gardiner, ME: Tilbury House Publishers, 2000. 40 pages. ISBN 0-88448-218-9. Lexile AD580. Grades K to 4.

When their father becomes ill and cannot go with them, the children of recent Russian immigrants take shy Mama trick-or-treating on Halloween

National Council for the Social Studies Notable Children's Trade Books in the Field of Social Studies.

Bunting, Eve. *Dreaming of America: An Ellis Island Story.*
Ben F. Stahl, illustrator. Mahwah, NJ: Troll Communications, 2000. 32 pages. ISBN 0-8167-6520-0 and 0-8167-6521-9pbk. Lexile 320. Grades K to 3.

A picture book based on the story of fifteen-year-old Annie Moore, the first Irish immigrant to be processed on Ellis Island in 1892.

International Reading Association Teachers' Choices and *Storytelling World Award Honor Book.*

Coerr, Eleanor. *Chang's Paper Pony.*
Deborah Kogan Ray, illustrator. New York: HarperCollins Children's Book Group, 1988. 63 pages. ISBN 0-06-021329-9 and 0-06-444163-6pbk.
Prince Frederick, MD: Recorded Books unabridged audio, 2000. ISBN 0-787-4016-4. (An "I Can Read" book). Lexile 440. Grades 2 to 4.

In San Francisco during the 1850s gold rush, Chang, the son of Chinese immigrants, and his grandfather run a hotel for the miners. Chang wants a pony but cannot afford one until his friend Big Pete finds a solution.

John and Patricia Beatty Award.

Hest, Amy. *When Jessie Came Across the Sea.*
P. J. Lynch, illustrator. Cambridge, MA: Candlewick Press, 1997. 40 pages. ISBN 0-7636-0094-6. Lexile 470. Grades 2 to 4.

The brother of an Eastern European rabbi dies and leaves one ticket to America, which the rabbi gives to Jessie. Upon arrival, Jessie follows her grandmother's trade and becomes a dressmaker while saving to purchase a ticket for her grandmother to join her. Conveys the emotions of loss, hope, and love while illustrating the struggles of immigrants.

Caldecott Honor Book, Children's Literature Choices, Christopher Award, International Reading Association Notable Books for a Global Society, National Council for the Social Studies Notable Children's Trade Books in the Field of Social Studies, and *Parent's Choice Gold Award.*

Oberman, Sheldon. *The Always Prayer Shawl.*
Ted Lewin, illustrator. Honesdale, PA: Boyds Mills Press, 1994. 32 pages. ISBN 1-878093-22-3.
New York: Penguin Putnam, 1997. 40 pages. ISBN 0-14-056157-9pbk. Lexile 460. Grades K to 3.

An ancient prayer shawl teaches Adam the importance of tradition and change in a story that spans six generations, from czarist Russia, when his grandfather gave him the shawl, to the present day.

ABC Children's Bookseller Choices Award, American Bookseller Pick of the Lists, International Reading Association Teachers' Choices, National Council for the Social Studies Notable Children's Trade Books in the Field of Social Studies, National Jewish Book Award, Reading Rainbow Review Book, Storytelling World Award Honor Book, and *Sydney Taylor Book Award.*

Partridge, Elizabeth. *Oranges on Golden Mountain.*
Aki Sogabe, illustrator. New York: Dutton's Children's Books, 2001. 40 pages. ISBN 0-525-46453-0.
New York: Puffin Books, 2003. 40 pages. ISBN 0-14-250033-Xpbk. Lexile AD690. Grades K to 3.

Accompanied by branches from his mother's Orange Tree, a young Chinese boy is sent from his drought-stricken village to work with his

Uncle, a fisherman, in San Francisco.
International Reading Association Notable Books for a Global Society.

Sandin, Joan. *The Long Way to a New Land.*
New York: HarperCollins Children's Book Group, 1981. 64 pages. ISBN 0-06-025194-8 and 0-06-444100-8pbk.
New York: Caedmon Audio, 1991. ISBN 1-55994-494-3. (An "I Can Read" book). Lexile 340. Grades 2 to 4.
    Carl Erik journeys with his family from Sweden to America during the famine of 1868.
    American Library Association Notable Children's Books, Booklist Editors' Choice, and *National Council for the Social Studies Notable Children's Trade Books in the Field of Social Studies.*

Sandin, Joan. *The Long Way Westward.*
New York: HarperCollins Children's Book Group, 1989. 64 pages. ISBN 0-06-025207-3 and 0-06-444198-9pbk. (An "I Can Read" book). Lexile 320. Grades 2 to 4.
    Relates the experiences of two young brothers and their family, immigrants from Sweden, from their arrival in New York through the journey to their new home in Minnesota. Sequel to *The Long Way to a New Land.*
    American Library Association Notable Children's Books, New York Public Library Children's Books, and *USA Through Children's Books.*

Say, Allen. *El Chino.*
New York: Houghton Mifflin Co., 1990. 32 pages. ISBN 0-395-52023-1 and 0-395-77875-1pbk. Lexile 600. Grades 2 to 5.
    The true story of a Chinese boy who becomes a famous bullfighter in Spain after growing up in the Southwestern United States.
    The Bulletin of the Center for Children's Books Blue Ribbon Award.

Say, Allen. *Grandfather's Journey.*
New York: Houghton Mifflin Co., 1993. 32 pages. ISBN 0-395-57035-2. Lexile AD650. Grades K to 3.
    A Japanese American man recounts his grandfather's journey to America, which he also undertakes in the early 20th century, and the feelings of being torn by his love for two different countries.
    Booklist Editors' Choice, Boston Globe-Horn Book Award, The Bulletin of the Center for Children's Books Blue Ribbon Award, Caldecott Medal, and *School Library Journal Best Book.*

Say, Allen. *Tea With Milk.*
New York: Houghton Mifflin Co., 1999. 32 pages. ISBN 0-395-90495-1.
Lexile AD450. Grades K to 3.

A young Japanese American girl is caught between two cultures in San Francisco. Her family moves back to Japan, which creates new problems for her.

American Library Association Notable Children's Books and *International Reading Association Notable Books for a Global Society.*

Sorensen, Henri. *New Hope.*
New York: Lothrop, Lee & Shepard Books, 1995. 32 pages. ISBN 0-688-13925-6.
New York: Penguin Putnam, 1998. 32 pages. ISBN 0-14-056359-8pbk.
Grades 1 to 4.

Visiting New Hope with Grandpa, Jimmy asks about the statue in the park which pays tribute to his great-great-great grandfather from Denmark, the founder of the town who set down roots when his wagon axle broke.

National Council for the Social Studies Notable Children's Trade Books in the Field of Social Studies.

Woodruff, Elvira. *The Memory Coat.*
Michael Dooling, illustrator. New York: Scholastic, 1999. 32 pages. ISBN 0-590-67717-9. Lexile AD650. Grades K to 3.

Quick thinking by a Russian family saves a cousin's passage through Ellis Island Inspection Station at the turn of the century.

International Reading Association Notable Books for a Global Society.

Yin, Rosanna Yin Lau. *Coolies.*
Chris Soentpiet, illustrator. New York: Philomel Books, 2001. 40 pages. ISBN 0-399-23227-3. Lexile AD660. Grades 2 to 4.

Two Chinese immigrant brothers working on the Transcontinental Railroad in the mid-1800s endure prejudice and dangerous working conditions in California.

American Library Association Notable Children's Books, Children's Literature Choices, International Reading Association Children's Book Award, and *Parent's Choice Gold Award.*

Grades 3 to 6

Broyles, Anne. *Shy Mama's Halloween.*
Refer to complete information under Grades Kindergarten to 2.

Bunting, Eve. *Dreaming of America: An Ellis Island Story.*
Refer to complete information under Grades Kindergarten to 2.

Coerr, Eleanor. *Chang's Paper Pony.*
Refer to complete information under Grades Kindergarten to 2.

Fletcher, Susan. *Walk Across the Sea.*
New York: Atheneum Books for Young Readers, 2001. 214 pages. ISBN
0-689-84133-7. Lexile 600. Grades 6 to 9.

A fifteen-year-old girl living in a lighthouse examines the prejudices
against Chinese immigrant workers after a young Chinese boy saves her
from drowning. She later challenges her community to protect him during a period of racial violence.

Booklist Top Ten Historical Fiction for Youth and *Children's Literature Choices.*

Gundisch, Karin. *How I Became an American.*
James Skofield, translator. Chicago: Cricket Books, 2001. 144 pages.
ISBN 0-8126-4875-7. Lexile 870. Grades 4 to 6.

The author draws from information in the personal letters of real
German American immigrants to create the story of a fictional ten-year-
old boy and his family who immigrate to America from Austria in 1902.

American Library Association Notable Children's Books and *Mildred L. Batchelder Award.*

Herman, Charlotte. *The House on Walenska Street.*
Susan Avishai, illustrator. Topeka, KS: Econo-Clad Books, 1999. 80
pages. ISBN 0-613-07997-3. (Out of print). Grades 3 to 5.

Set in 1913 Russia, after an eight-year-old girl's father dies, she
writes to Minnesota relatives and describes her life spent helping her
mother and sisters.

Carl Sandburg Award.

Hest, Amy. *When Jessie Came Across the Sea.*
Refer to complete information under Grades Kindergarten to 2.

Holm, Jennifer L. *Our Only May Amelia.*
New York: HarperCollins Children's Book Group, 1999. 251 pages. ISBN 0-06-027822-6 and 0-06-440856-6pbk.
New York: Bantam Books unabridged audio, 2000. ISBN 0-8072-8234-0.
New York: Listening Library audio, 2000. ISBN 0-8072-8234-0. Lexile 900. Grades 3 to 6.

A twelve-year-old Finnish American pioneer girl describes her life with seven brothers in 1899 Washington state.

American Library Association Notable Children's Books, Dorothy Canfield Fisher Award Masterlist, National Council for the Social Studies Notable Children's Trade Books in the Field of Social Studies, Newbery Honor Book, Parent's Choice Silver Award, and *Utah Children's Book Award.*

Howard, Ellen. *Sister.*
New York: Atheneum Books for Young Readers, 1990. 148 pages. ISBN 0-689-31653-4. (Out of print). Grades 5 to 7.

Alena's mother becomes depressed after the death of her baby in 1886 Midwestern America. Alena leaves school to stay home and help her, so a teacher assists Alena in getting her diploma.

American Library Association Notable Children's Books.

Karr, Kathleen. *Man of the Family.*
New York: Farrar, Straus & Giroux, 1999. 178 pages. ISBN 0-374-34764-6. Lexile 600. Grades 3 to 6.

A Hungarian immigrant family tries to make a home in America in the 1920s.

American Library Association Notable Children's Books.

Lasky, Kathryn. *The Night Journey.*
Trina S. Hyman, illustrator. First copyright 1986. Topeka, KS: Econo-Clad Books, 1999. 152 pages. ISBN 0-8085-8472-3.
New York: Penguin Putnam, 1986. 150 pages. ISBN 0-14-032048-2pbk. Lexile 860. Grades 5 to 7.

A young girl ignores her parents' wishes and persuades her great-grandmother to relate the story of her escape from czarist Russia after hiding the family gold in cookies.

American Library Association Notable Children's Books, Association of Jewish Libraries Award, National Jewish Book Award, and *Sydney Taylor Book Award.*

Latham, Jean Lee. *Carry On, Mr. Bowditch.*
John O'Hara Cosgrave II, illustrator. New York: Houghton Mifflin Co.,
1955. 256 pages. ISBN 0-395-06881-9 and 0-395-13713-6pbk. Lexile
570. Grades 5 to 8.

A fictionalized biography of the mathematician and astronomer who,
after bad family fortune and being an indentured servant for nine years,
was able to realize his childhood dream to become a ship's captain. Na-
thaniel Bowditch taught himself several languages and used his naviga-
tional skills to author *The American Practical Navigator* in 1802.
Newbery Medal.

Lord, Bette Bao. *In the Year of the Boar and Jackie Robinson.*
New York: HarperCollins Children's Book Group, 1984. 176 pages.
ISBN 0-06-024004-0 and 0-06-440175-8pbk.
Prince Frederick, MD: Recorded Books unabridged audio, 1997. ISBN
0-7887-1794-4 and 0-7887-4220-5cd. Lexile 730. Grades 4 to 7.

In 1947, a Chinese child comes to Brooklyn where she becomes
Americanized by her school, apartment building neighbors, and love for
baseball and the Brooklyn Dodgers.
*American Library Association Notable Children's Books, Jefferson
Cup Award, National Council for the Social Studies Notable Children's
Trade Books in the Field of Social Studies, New York Public Library
Children's Books*, and *School Library Journal Best Book.*

Moss, Marissa. *Hannah's Journal: The Story of an Immigrant Girl.*
San Diego, CA: Silver Whistle, 2000. 56 pages. ISBN 0-15-202155-8.
Lexile 730. Grades 3 to 5.

Ten-year-old Hannah immigrates to America from Lithuania in
1901. She survives traveling in the steerage section of a ship with the
help of her cousin and an orphaned boy. Her experiences are recorded in
this fictional diary that is illustrated with watercolors.
*National Council for the Social Studies Notable Children's Trade
Books in the Field of Social Studies.*

Oberman, Sheldon. *The Always Prayer Shawl.*
Refer to complete information under Grades Kindergarten to 2.

Partridge, Elizabeth. *Oranges on Golden Mountain.*
Refer to complete information under Grades Kindergarten to 2.

Rocklin, Joanne. *Strudel Stories.*
New York: Delacorte, 1999. 144 pages. ISBN 0-385-32602-5.

New York: Yearling, 2000. 144 pages. ISBN 0-440-41509-8pbk. Lexile 540. Grades 3 to 6.

The stories of seven generations of a Jewish family are told while making strudel.

American Library Association Notable Children's Books and *School Library Journal Best Book of the Year.*

Sandin, Joan. *The Long Way to a New Land.*
Refer to complete information under Grades Kindergarten to 2.

Sandin, Joan. *The Long Way Westward.*
Refer to complete information under Grades Kindergarten to 2.

Say, Allen. *El Chino.*
Refer to complete information under Grades Kindergarten to 2.

Say, Allen. *Grandfather's Journey.*
Refer to complete information under Grades Kindergarten to 2.

Say, Allen. *Tea With Milk.*
Refer to complete information under Grades Kindergarten to 2.

Sorensen, Henri. *New Hope.*
Refer to complete information under Grades Kindergarten to 2.

Woodruff, Elvira. *The Memory Coat.*
Refer to complete information under Grades Kindergarten to 2.

Yep, Laurence. *Dragon's Gate.*
New York: HarperCollins Children's Book Group, 1993. 273 pages. ISBN 0-06-022972-1 and 0-06-440489-7pbk.
Prince Frederick, MD: Recorded Books unabridged audio, 1994. ISBN 0-7887-0132-0. Lexile 730. Grades 5 to 9.

When he accidentally kills a Manchu, a fifteen-year-old Chinese boy is sent to America to join his father, an uncle, and other Chinese immigrants working to build a tunnel for the Transcontinental Railroad through the Sierra Nevada mountains in 1867.

American Bookseller Pick of the Lists, American Library Association Notable Children's Books, Commonwealth Club of California Silver Medal Book Award, John and Patricia Beatty Award, Newbery Honor Book, and *New York Public Library Books for the Teen Age.*

Yep, Laurence. *Dragonwings.*
New York: HarperCollins Children's Book Group, 1987. 256 pages.
ISBN 0-06-026738-0 and 0-06-440085-9pbk.
New York: HarperAudio unabridged audio, 2001. ISBN 0-694-52561-8.
Lexile 870. Grades 4 to 7.
    In 1903, a young Chinese boy joins his father in San Francisco and
helps him realize his dream of making a flying machine. Both endure the
San Francisco earthquake in April 1906.
    *American Library Association Notable Children's Books of 1971 to
1975, Boston Globe-Horn Book Award Honor Book, Carter G. Woodson
Book Award, Friends of Children and Literature Award, Horn Book
Fanfare Honor List, International Reading Association Children's Book
Award, Lewis Carroll Shelf Award, National Council for the Social Studies Notable Children's Trade Books in the Field of Social Studies, New-
bery Honor Book, New York Public Library Books for the Teen Age,
Phoenix Award,* and *School Library Journal "Best of the Best" Children's Books 1966 to 1978.*

Yin, Rosanna Yin Lau. *Coolies.*
Refer to complete information under Grades Kindergarten to 2.

Grades 7 and 8

Auch, Mary Jane. *Ashes of Roses.*
New York: Henry Holt & Co., 2002. 256 pages. ISBN 0-8050-6686-1.
Grades 7 to 10.
    Sixteen-year-old Rose is filled with hope when her family immi-
grates from Ireland to New York City. The hardships she faces culminates in the tragic Triangle Shirtwaist Factory Fire in 1911.
    Booklist Top Ten Historical Fiction for Youth.

Fletcher, Susan. *Walk Across the Sea.*
Refer to complete information under Grades 3 to 6.

Howard, Ellen. *Sister.*
Refer to complete information under Grades 3 to 6.

Lasky, Kathryn. *The Night Journey.*
Refer to complete information under Grades 3 to 6.

Latham, Jean Lee. *Carry On, Mr. Bowditch.*
Refer to complete information under Grades 3 to 6.

Lord, Bette Bao. *In the Year of the Boar and Jackie Robinson.*
Refer to complete information under Grades 3 to 6.

Na, An. *A Step from Heaven.*
Asheville, NC: Front Street, 2001. 156 pages. ISBN 1-886910-58-8.
New York: Listening Library unabridged audio, 2002. ISBN 0-8072-0721-7. Lexile 670. Grades 7 to Young Adult.

A story which chronicles the immigration experiences of a young girl and her family, starting with her plane ride from Korea to California when she was four years old, through her childhood, and culminating in her adolescence. Her adjustment is complicated by an alcoholic and abusive father.

American Library Association Notable Children's Books, Bay Area Book Reviewers Association Award, Children's Literature Choices, International Reading Association Children's Book Award, Michael L. Printz Award, National Book Award for Young People's Literature Finalist, National Council of Teachers of English Notable Children's Books in the English Language Arts, and *School Library Journal Best Book.*

Tan, Amy. *Joy Luck Club.*
New York: Putnam, 1989. 288 pages. ISBN 0-399-13420-4.
New York: Random House, 1991. 288 pages. ISBN 0-679-72768-Xpbk.
Los Angeles, CA: Dove Audio, 1989. ISBN 1-55800-206-5.
(VHS/DVD). Lexile 930. Grades 8 to Young Adult.

In 1949, four Chinese women from different families that recently immigrated to San Francisco begin to meet and share their stories. Forty years and two generations later, they continue their gathering called the Joy Luck Club.

American Library Association Best Books for Young Adults.

Yep, Laurence. *Dragon's Gate.*
Refer to complete information under Grades 3 to 6.

Yep, Laurence. *Dragonwings.*
Refer to complete information under Grades 3 to 6.

Chapter 8

Reconstruction to Pre-World War I: 1866 to 1916

Grades Kindergarten to 2

Bartone, Elisa. *Peppe the Lamplighter.*
Ted Lewin, illustrator. New York: Lothrop, Lee & Shepard Books, 1993.
32 pages. ISBN 0-688-10268-9 and 0-688-15469-7pbk. Lexile AD570.
Grades K to 3.
   Living in Little Italy in New York City, a young immigrant boy
named Peppe takes a job as a lamplighter to help support his impoverished family. This is not what his father has envisioned for him, but one
night when the lamps are not lit, Peppe's father realizes how important
his job is.
   Caldecott Honor Book.

Bradby, Marie. *More Than Anything Else.*
Chris K. Soentpiet, illustrator. New York: Orchard Books, 1995. 32
pages. ISBN 0-531-09464-2. Lexile 660. Grades K to 3.
   Based on the childhood of Booker T. Washington, a young and determined African American boy responds with joy after someone helps
him learn to read.
   *International Reading Association Notable Books for a Global Soci-
ety.*

Cooney, Barbara. *Hattie and the Wild Waves.*
New York: Viking, 1990. 40 pages. ISBN 0-670-83056-9 and 0-14-
054193-4pbk. Lexile AD730. Grades K to 3.
   A young girl from Brooklyn, New York, enjoys her summer at the
beach where she can paint and listen to the rhythmic waves of the sea.

Set in the 19th century.
Lupine Award.

Cooney, Barbara. *Island Boy.*
New York: Viking, 1988. 32 pages. ISBN 0-670-81749-X and 0-14-0507566-7pbk. Lexile AD660. Grades K to 3.

The youngest of twelve children, Matthias becomes fond of Tibbets Island, Maine, while learning its secrets. He sails to faraway places through the years, but he always returns to the island he loves. Set in the 19th century.
School Library Journal Best Book.

Howard, Elizabeth Fitzgerald. *Chita's Christmas Tree.*
Floyd Cooper, illustrator. Topeka, KS: Econo-Clad Books, 1999. 32 pages. ISBN 0-7857-1393-X. Lexile AD440. Grades K to 3.

Papa and Chita leave downtown Baltimore in a buggy at the turn of the 20th century to find a Christmas tree in the deep woods.
American Library Association Notable Children's Books.

Howard, Elizabeth Fitzgerald. *Virgie Goes to School with Us Boys.*
Earl B. Lewis, illustrator. New York: Simon & Schuster, 2000. 32 pages. ISBN 0-689-80076-2. Lexile 190. Grades K to 3.

A young African American girl wants to accompany her five brothers on the seven-mile walk to school in post-Civil War Tennessee. She gets her wish and learns to read.
National Council for the Social Studies Notable Children's Trade Books in the Field of Social Studies.

Martin, Jacqueline Briggs. *Snowflake Bentley.*
Mary Azarian, illustrator. New York: Houghton Mifflin Co., 1998. 32 pages. ISBN 0-395-86162-4. Lexile AD830. Grades 2 to 4.

A historical biography of how a Vermont boy grew up to become an expert on snowflakes.
American Library Association Notable Children's Books, Booklist Editors' Choice, The Bulletin of the Center for Children's Books Blue Ribbon Award, Caldecott Medal, Lupine Award, and *Outstanding Science Trade Books for Children.*

McKenzie, Ellen Kindt. *Stargone John.*
William Low, illustrator. New York: Henry Holt & Co., 1990. 67 pages. ISBN 0-8050-1451-9 and 0-8050-1451-9. Lexile 780. Grades 2 to 4.

Six-year-old John, emotionally withdrawn and resistant to traditional teaching methods, experiences ridicule and punishment in his one-room schoolhouse until an old and blind retired teacher teaches him to read using Braille.

The Bulletin of the Center for Children's Books Blue Ribbon Award.

Medearis, Michael and Angela Shelf Medearis. *Daisy and the Doll.* Larry Johnson, illustrator. Middlebury, VT: Vermont Folklife Center, 2000. 32 pages. ISBN 0-916718-15-8. Lexile 450. Grades 2 to 4.

An eight-year-old African American girl shows courage and fortitude when ridiculed by classmates in 1890s rural Vermont.

Aesop Accolade.

Nobisso, Josephine. *John Blair and the Great Hinckley Fire.* Ted Rose, illustrator. New York: Houghton Mifflin Co., 2000. 32 pages. ISBN 0-618-01560-4. Lexile 860. Grades K to 5.

An African American porter saves people from a raging fire by pulling them onto a train in 1894 Minnesota.

Storytelling World Award.

Rael, Elsa Okon. *Rivka's First Thanksgiving.* Maryann Kovalski, illustrator. New York: Simon & Schuster, 2001. 32 pages. ISBN 0-689-83901-4. Grades K to 3.

Nine-year-old Rivka persuades her rabbi and Jewish immigrant family to celebrate Thanksgiving in 1910 Manhattan, New York.

National Council for the Social Studies Notable Children's Trade Books in the Field of Social Studies and *Sydney Taylor Book Award.*

Rand, Gloria. *Sailing Home: A Story of a Childhood at Sea.* Ted Rand, illustrator. New York: North-South Books, 2001. 32 pages. ISBN 0-7358-1539-9. Grades K to 3.

The description of life on board the ship "John Ena" for the family of the seafaring Captain Madsen between 1896 and 1910 while trading to the Hawaiian Islands. Based on Captain Madsen's journal.

National Council for the Social Studies Notable Children's Trade Books in the Field of Social Studies.

Ray, Mary Lyn. *Shaker Boy.* Jeanette Winter, illustrator. San Diego, CA: Harcourt Children's Books, 1994. 46 pages. ISBN 0-15-276921-8. (Out of print). Grades 1 to 4.

After his widowed mother places six-year-old Caleb in a Shaker colony after the Civil War, he spends the rest of his life learning their songs and ways.

National Council for the Social Studies Notable Children's Trade Books in the Field of Social Studies.

Yezerski, Thomas F. *A Full Hand.*
New York: Farrar, Straus & Giroux, 2002. 32 pages. ISBN 0-374-42502-7. Grades K to 3.

Nine-year-old Asa helps his father by leading mules that pull a canal boat down a 19th century Pennsylvania waterway.

National Council for the Social Studies Notable Social Studies Trade Books for Young People.

Grades 3 to 6

Bartoletti, Susan Campbell. *A Coal Miner's Bride: The Diary of Anetka Kaminska, Lattimer, Pennsylvania, 1896.*
New York: Scholastic Trade, 2000. 219 pages. ISBN 0-439-05386-2. Lexile 800. Grades 6 to 8.

In 1896, thirteen-year-old Anetka leaves her Polish village for an arranged marriage to an American coal miner after his wife dies. This loveless marriage lasts only a few months before her husband is killed in an accident, and Anetka is forced to take in boarders while caring for his three small daughters. A growing romance with a young union organizer adds dimension to this story that is written in diary format.

National Council for the Social Studies Notable Children's Trade Books in the Field of Social Studies.

Bartone, Elisa. *Peppe the Lamplighter.*
Refer to complete information under Grades Kindergarten to 2.

Bradby, Marie. *More Than Anything Else.*
Refer to complete information under Grades Kindergarten to 2.

Carbone, Elisa. *Storm Warriors.*
New York: Alfred A. Knopf, 2001. 168 pages. ISBN 0-375-80664-4. New York: Yearling, 2002. 176 pages. ISBN 0-440-41879-8pbk. Lexile 890. Grades 5 to 7.

Off the North Carolina coast in 1895, twelve-year-old Nathan wishes to become a surfman with the only African American lifesaving crew on Pea Island. When he discovers his personal limitations, he finds a better way to contribute.

American Library Association Notable Children's Books and *Jefferson Cup Award.*

Collier, James Lincoln. *Chipper.*
Tarrytown, NY: Marshall Cavendish, 2001. 144 pages. ISBN 0-7614-5084-X. Lexile 790. Grades 6 to 8.

Homeless twelve-year-old Chipper must decide to be loyal to his gang members or true to himself when he is asked to pretend to be a wealthy family's long-lost nephew in 1890s New York.

National Council for the Social Studies Notable Children's Trade Books in the Field of Social Studies.

Conrad, Pam. *My Daniel.*
New York: HarperCollins Children's Book Group, 1989. 137 pages. ISBN 0-06-021314-0 and 0-06-440309-2pbk.
Prince Frederick, MD: Recorded Books unabridged audio, 1995. ISBN 0-7887-048903. Lexile 780. Grades 5 to 8.

Ellie and Stevie learn about a family legacy when their grandmother tells them stories about her brother's quest for dinosaur bones on their Nebraska farm, his wonderful find, and the terrible tragedy that changed their lives.

American Library Association Best Books for Young Adults, Booklist Editors' Choice, International Reading Association Teachers' Choices, National Council for the Social Studies Notable Children's Trade Books in the Field of Social Studies, New York Public Library Books for the Teen Age, New York Public Library Children's Books, and *Western Writers of America Silver Spur Award.*

Cooney, Barbara. *Hattie and the Wild Waves.*
Refer to complete information under Grades Kindergarten to 2.

Cooney, Barbara. *Island Boy.*
Refer to complete information under Grades Kindergarten to 2.

Fleischman, Sid. *The Midnight Horse.*
Peter Sis, illustrator. New York: Greenwillow Books, 1990. 96 pages. ISBN 0-688-09441-4.
New York: Bantam Dell Publishing Group, 1992. 84 pages. ISBN 0-440-40614-5pbk. Lexile 630. Grades 3 to 6.

Touch enlists the help of The Great Chaffalo, a ghostly magician, to ruin his great-uncle's plans to put Touch into an orphanage and swindle the Red Raven Inn away from Miss Sally. Set in New Hampshire during the 1870s.

Edgar Award and *School Library Journal Best Book.*

Hamilton, Virginia. *The Bells of Christmas.*
Lambert Davis, illustrator. San Diego, CA: Harcourt Children's Books, 1989. 64 pages. ISBN 0-15-206450-8 and 0-15-201550-7pbk. Lexile 570. Grades 4 to 6.

Twelve-year-old Jason describes the wonderful Christmas of 1890 that he and his family celebrate with relatives in their home in Springfield, Ohio.

American Library Association Notable Children's Books and *Coretta Scott King Award Honor Book.*

Hill, Donna. *Shipwreck Season.*
New York: Houghton Mifflin Co., 1998. 224 pages. ISBN 0-395-86614-6. Lexile 670. Grades 3 to 7.

In the late 19th century, Daniel's mother sends him to live with an uncle, who is in charge of the lifesavers' station on Cape Cod. Through trials and rescues, Daniel learns to become a confident young man.

Christopher Award.

Hill, Kirkpatrick. *Minuk: Ashes in the Pathway. ("Girls of Many Lands Series").*
Middleton, WI: Pleasant Company Publications, 2002. 210 pages. ISBN 1-58485-596-7 and 1-58485-520-7pbk. Lexile 940. Grades 5 to 8.

The 1892 arrival of Christian Missionaries brings cultural changes as well as devastating diseases to a twelve-year-old girl's Yupik Eskimo village in Alaska.

School Library Journal Best Book.

Howard, Elizabeth Fitzgerald. *Chita's Christmas Tree.*
Refer to complete information under Grades Kindergarten to 2.

Howard, Elizabeth Fitzgerald. *Virgie Goes to School With Us Boys.*
Refer to complete information under Grades Kindergarten to 2.

Howard, Ellen. *Edith Herself.*
Ronald Himler, illustrator. New York: Atheneum Books for Young Readers, 1987. 132 pages. ISBN 0-689-31314-4. (Out of print). Lexile 740. Grades 5 to 7.

Orphaned by her mother's death, Edith goes to live with her older

sister and her stern husband on their Christian farm in 1890. The strain of her new living arrangements aggravates Edith's epileptic seizures.
School Library Journal Best Book.

Kline, Lisa Williams. *Eleanor Hill.*
Chicago, IL: Cricket Books, 2000. 224 pages. ISBN 0-8126-2715-6. Lexile 850. Grades 4 to 7.

A twelve-year-old girl yearns for independence from her small and isolated North Carolina fishing village in 1912. She leaves to escape the drudgery and live with her aunt and uncle in a nearby town.
American Association of University Women Award for Juvenile Literature.

Lenski, Lois. *Strawberry Girl.*
First copyright 1945. New York: HarperCollins Children's Book Group, 1964. 208 pages. ISBN 0-397-30109-X and 0-06-440585-0pbk. (VHS). Lexile 650. Grades 5 to 8.

Two families have to learn to work together in Florida in the early 1900s.
American Library Association Notable Children's Books and *Newbery Medal.*

Martin, Jacqueline Briggs. *Snowflake Bentley.*
Refer to complete information under Grades Kindergarten to 2.

McKenzie, Ellen Kindt. *Stargone John.*
Refer to complete information under Grades Kindergarten to 2.

Medearis, Michael and Angela Shelf Medearis. *Daisy and the Doll.*
Refer to complete information under Grades Kindergarten to 2.

Moss, Marissa. *Hannah's Journal: The Story of an Immigrant Girl.*
San Diego, CA: Silver Whistle, 2000. 56 pages. ISBN 0-15-202155-8. Lexile 730. Grades 3 to 5.

Ten-year-old Hannah immigrates to America from Lithuania in 1901. She survives traveling in the steerage section of a ship with the help of her cousin and an orphaned boy. Her experiences are recorded in this fictional diary that is illustrated with watercolors.
National Council for the Social Studies Notable Children's Trade Books in the Field of Social Studies.

Nobisso, Josephine. *John Blair and the Great Hinckley Fire.*
Refer to complete information under Grades Kindergarten to 2.

Paterson, Katherine. *Preacher's Boy.*
New York: Houghton Mifflin Co., 1999. 168 pages. ISBN 0-395-83897-5.
New York: HarperTrophy, 2001. 186 pages. ISBN 0-06-447233-7pbk.
Prince Frederick, MD: Recorded Books unabridged audio, 2001. ISBN 0-7887-9789-1 and 1-4025-1495-6cd. Lexile 860. Grades 3 to 6.

At the end of the 19th century in Vermont, ten-year-old Robbie defies his preacher father by becoming an atheist, getting into trouble, and facing a moral dilemma that results in a reevaluation of his beliefs.

Booklist Editors' Choice, Jefferson Cup Award, and *Parent's Choice Gold Award.*

Peck, Richard. *Fair Weather.*
New York: Dial Books for Young Readers, 2001. 160 pages. ISBN 0-8037-2516-7. Lexile 670. Grades 4 to 7.

The author transports readers first to rural Illinois in 1893 where thirteen-year-old Rosie lives on a farm, then on to Chicago after Rosie and her siblings have been invited by their aunt to the World's Columbia Exposition. The fair opens Rosie's eyes to a different world in a story that is full of humor and history.

American Library Association Best Books for Young Adults, Booklist Editors' Choice, Booklist Top Ten Historical Fiction for Youth, Children's Literature Choices, National Council for the Social Studies Notable Children's Trade Books in the Field of Social Studies, National Council of Teachers of English Notable Children's Books in the English Language Arts, and *School Library Journal Best Book.*

Rael, Elsa Okon. *Rivka's First Thanksgiving.*
Refer to complete information under Grades Kindergarten to 2.

Rand, Gloria. *Sailing Home: A Story of a Childhood at Sea.*
Refer to complete information under Grades Kindergarten to 2.

Ray, Mary Lyn. *Shaker Boy.*
Refer to complete information under Grades Kindergarten to 2.

Riskind, Mary. *Apple Is My Sign.*
New York: Peter Smith Publishers, 1999. 146 pages. ISBN 0-8446-7004-9.

New York: Houghton Mifflin Co., 1993. 160 pages. ISBN 0-395-65747-4pbk. Lexile 630. Grades 4 to 6.

A ten-year-old boy returns to his parents' apple farm for the 1899 holidays with newfound confidence after his first term at a school for the deaf in Philadelphia.

American Library Association Notable Children's Books.

San Souci, Robert D. *Kate Shelley: Bound for Legend.*
Max Ginsburg, illustrator. New York: Dial Books for Young Readers, 1995. 32 pages. ISBN 0-8037-1289-8. Lexile 1050. Grades 3 to 6.

After a terrible storm, an Iowa teenager risks her life to rescue the survivors of an 1881 train wreck.

National Council for the Social Studies Notable Children's Trade Books in the Field of Social Studies.

Sebestyen, Ouida. *Words By Heart.*
New York: Bantam Books, 1981. 135 pages. ISBN 0-440-22688-0pbk. Lexile 750. Grades 6 to 9.

Twelve-year-old Lena Sills struggles to fulfill her papa's dream of a better future for their family in the Southwestern town where they are the only African Americans in 1910. Vowing to gain her father's approval and her white classmates' respect by winning a Bible-quoting contest, Lena is horrified when her success brings violence and death to her home.

American Book Award and *International Reading Association Children's Book Award.*

Skurzynski, Gloria. *Rockbuster.*
New York: Atheneum Books for Young Readers, 2001. 253 pages. ISBN 0-689-83391-X. Lexile 860. Grades 6 to 9.

Ten-year-old Tommy inadvertently exposes his union-supporting uncle to Pinkerton detectives, and his uncle is later found dead. Tommy blames himself for his uncle's death while he grows from boy to man, forms a romance with the mine owner's daughter, and ultimately is forced to choose where his loyalties lie.

Western Writers of America Spur Award.

Winter, Jeanette. *The Christmas Tree Ship.*
New York: Philomel Books, 1994. 32 pages. ISBN 0-399-22693-1. Grades 3 to 6.

The tale of a young schooner captain who sails treacherous Lake Michigan each year at Christmastime to supply Chicagoans with spruce trees for their holiday celebrations. In 1912, he does not return after a fierce storm and the trees never arrive in Chicago. After grieving for a year, his family takes over the tradition to continue his legacy.

The Bulletin of the Center for Children's Books Blue Ribbon Award.

Yezerski, Thomas F. *A Full Hand.*
Refer to complete information under Grades Kindergarten to 2.

Grades 7 and 8

Auch, Mary Jane. *Ashes of Roses.*
New York: Henry Holt & Co., 2002. 256 pages. ISBN 0-8050-6686-1. Grades 7 to 10.

Sixteen-year-old Rose is filled with hope when her family emigrates from Ireland to New York City. The hardships she faces culminates in the tragic Triangle Shirtwaist Factory Fire in 1911.

American Library Association Best Books for Young Adults, Booklist Top Ten Historical Fiction for Youth, Children's Literature Choices, and *National Council for the Social Studies Notable Social Studies Trade Books for Young People.*

Bartoletti, Susan Campbell. *A Coal Miner's Bride: The Diary of Anetka Kaminska, Lattimer, Pennsylvania, 1896.*
Refer to complete information under Grades 3 to 6.

Carbone, Elisa. *Storm Warriors.*
Refer to complete information under Grades 3 to 6.

Collier, James Lincoln. *Chipper.*
Refer to complete information under Grades 3 to 6.

Conrad, Pam. *My Daniel.*
Refer to complete information under Grades 3 to 6.

Edmonds, Walter. *Bert Breen's Barn.*
Boston: Little, Brown & Company. 1975. 270 pages. ISBN 0-316-21166-4.
New York: Syracuse University Press, 1991. 270 pages. ISBN 0-8156-0255-3pbk. Grades 7 to Young Adult

A young man attempts to claim ownership of an old barn rumored to contain a hidden treasure.

Christopher Award and *National Book Award for Young People's Literature.*

Hamm, Diane Johnston. *Bunkhouse Journal.*
New York: Atheneum Books for Young Readers, 1990. 89 pages. ISBN 0-684-19206-3. (Out of print). Lexile 800. Grades 7 to 10.

A young man leaves home and college to escape an alcoholic father in 1911 to live with a cousin's family in Wyoming.

Western Heritage Award.

Hill, Donna. *Shipwreck Season.*
Refer to complete information under Grades 3 to 6.

Hill, Kirkpatrick. *Minuk: Ashes in the Pathway. ("Girls of Many Lands Series").*
Refer to complete information under Grades 3 to 6.

Howard, Ellen. *Edith Herself.*
Refer to complete information under Grades 3 to 6.

Hurmence, Belinda. *Tancy.*
New York: Houghton Mifflin Co., 1984. 224 pages. ISBN 0-89919-228-9. (Out of print). Grades 8 to 10.

At the end of the Civil War, sixteen-year-old Tancy gains her freedom and sets off to search for her mother, who was sold when she was two, as well as the mother of the young child currently in her care.

American Association of University Women Award for Juvenile Literature, Golden Kite Award, and *School Library Journal Best Book.*

Karr, Kathleen. *The Boxer.*
New York: Farrar, Straus & Giroux, 2000. 144 pages. ISBN 0-374-30921-3. Lexile 640. Grades 7 to Young Adult.

Fifteen-year-old Johnny takes up boxing to help support his fatherless family in 1885 New York City. Johnny meets former lightweight champion Michael O'Shaunnessey, who begins training Johnny to fight while Johnny serves time in jail. At the same time, Johnny also tries to improve his education.

American Library Association Best Books for Young Adults, Golden Kite Award, and *National Council for the Social Studies Notable Children's Trade Books in the Field of Social Studies.*

Kline, Lisa Williams. *Eleanor Hill.*
Refer to complete information under Grades 3 to 6.

Lenski, Lois. *Strawberry Girl.*
Refer to complete information under Grades 3 to 6.

Meyer, Carolyn. *Gideon's People.*
San Diego, CA: Harcourt Children's Books, 1996. 297 pages. ISBN 0-15-200303-7 and 0-15-200304-5pbk. Lexile 900. Grades 7 to 10.

When a wagon accident leaves twelve-year-old Isaac Litsky too bruised to travel, he is forced to stay with an Amish family whose sixteen-year-old son is considering running away.
American Bookseller Pick of the Lists.

Peck, Richard. *Fair Weather.*
Refer to complete information under Grades 3 to 6.

Sebestyen, Ouida. *Words By Heart.*
Refer to complete information under Grades 3 to 6.

Skurzynski, Gloria. *Rockbuster.*
Refer to complete information under Grades 3 to 6.

Taylor, Mildred D. *The Land.*
New York: Phyllis Fogelman Books, 2001. 375 pages. ISBN 0-8037-1950-7.
Old Greenwich, CT: Listening Library unabridged audio, 2001. ISBN 0-8072-0618-0. Lexile 760. Grades 7 to Young Adult.

This prequel to Taylor's *Roll of Thunder, Hear My Cry* goes back to the time of Reconstruction to tell a story of cruelty, racism, and betrayal. It is also a coming-of-age tale about friendship, hope, and family strength.
American Library Association Notable Children's Books, American Library Association Top Ten Best Books for Young Adults, Booklist Editors' Choice, Booklist Top Ten Historical Fiction for Youth, The Bulletin of the Center for Children's Books Blue Ribbon Award, Children's Literature Choices, Coretta Scott King Award, International Reading Association Notable Books for a Global Society, National Council for the Social Studies Notable Children's Trade Books in the Field of Social Studies, National Council of Teachers of English Notable Children's Books in the English Language Arts, and *Scott O'Dell Award for Historical Fiction.*

Chapter 9

World War I, Roaring Twenties, and the Great Depression: 1917 to 1940

Grades Kindergarten to 2

Bartoletti, Susan Campbell. *The Christmas Promise.*
David Christiana, illustrator. New York: Blue Sky Press, 2001. 40 pages. ISBN 0-59098451-9. Lexile AD470. Grades 2 to 4.

A young girl is placed in a kindly home after she and her homeless father are jailed in this Depression-era story. Her father finds work and returns to retrieve her in time for Christmas.

National Council for the Social Studies Notable Children's Trade Books in the Field of Social Studies.

Lasky, Kathryn. *Marven of the Great North Woods.*
Kevin Hawkes, illustrator. San Diego, CA: Harcourt Children's Books, 1997. 48 pages. ISBN 0-152-00104-2. Lexile AD620. Grades 2 to 4.

Ten-year-old Marven is sent away to stay with a family friend at a logging camp in Minnesota to escape the influenza outbreak that plagues his community in 1918.

American Library Association Notable Children's Books and *Lupine Award.*

McDonald, Megan. *The Potato Man.*
Ted Lewin, illustrator. New York: Orchard Books, 1991. 32 pages. ISBN 0-531-05914-6 and 0-531-07053-0pbk. Grades K to 2.

Grampa entertains his grandchildren with a story about his fear of and eventual friendship with a fruit and vegetable peddler who was disfigured in World War I.

School Library Journal Best Book.

Mitchell, Margaree King. *Uncle Jed's Barbershop.*
James Ransome, illustrator. New York: Simon & Schuster, 1993. 46
pages. ISBN 0-671-76969-3.
New York: Aladdin Paperbacks, 1998. 32 pages. ISBN 0-689-81913-
7pbk. (VHS). Lexile AD710. Grades K to 3.

Sarah's Uncle Jed has saved every penny he can spare to open a new
barbershop during segregated times in the 1920s, but he uses most of the
money to give Sarah an operation that saves her life. He then loses his
remaining savings during a Depression bank failure. On his seventy-
ninth birthday, Uncle Jed finally realizes his dream.
Coretta Scott King Award.

Rabin, Staton. *Casey Over There.*
Greg Shed, illustrator. San Diego, CA: Harcourt Children's Books, 1994.
32 pages. ISBN 0-15-253186-6. (Out of print). Grades 1 to 3.

Seven-year-old Aubrey writes to his brother, Casey, who is fighting
in France in 1917, and Woodrow Wilson responds.
Marion Bannett Ridgway Award and *National Council for the Social
Studies Notable Children's Trade Books in the Field of Social Studies.*

Rael, Elsa Okon. *What Zeesie Saw on Delancey Street.*
Marjorie Priceman, illustrator. New York: Simon & Schuster, 1996. 40
pages. ISBN 0-689-80549-7 and 0-689-83535-3pbk. Lexile 490. Grades
1 to 3.

In 1930s New York, Zeesie goes to her first "package party," a feast
where funds are raised for immigrants in the Jewish community. She
quickly learns a valuable lesson in sharing after sneaking into a special
"money room" and observing an exchange of money between those who
can give and those in need who receive.
The Bulletin of the Center for Children's Books Blue Ribbon Award.

Ringold, Faith. *Tar Beach.*
New York: Crown, 1991. 32 pages. ISBN 0-517-58030-6 and 0-517-
88544-1pbk. (VHS). Lexile AD790. Grades K to 3.

An eight-year-old girl dreams of flying above her Harlem home in
1939 to claim all she sees for herself and her family. Based on the au-
thor's quilt painting of the same name.
*American Library Association Notable Children's Books; Caldecott
Honor Book; California Children's Book, Video, and Software Award;
Coretta Scott King Award; New York Times Best Illustrated Book of the
Year, Parent's Choice Award;* and *School Library Journal Best Book.*

Rylant, Cynthia. *When I Was Young in the Mountains.*
Diane Goode, illustrator. New York: Dutton Children's Books, 1982. 32 pages. ISBN 0-525-42525-X. (VHS). Lexile AD980. Grades K to 3.

Reminiscences of the pleasures of life in the mountains without modern conveniences.
American Library Association Notable Children's Books.

Santiago, Chiori. *Home to Medicine Mountain.*
Judith Lowry, illustrator. San Francisco, CA: Children's Book Press, 1998. 32 pages. ISBN 0-89239-155-3. Lexile 520. Grades K to 3.

Tells the story of the illustrator's relatives, two Native American brothers, who are sent to a severe California boarding school in the 1930s. They find a way to escape and make it back home.
American Library Association Notable Children's Books.

Wells, Rosemary and Tom Wells. *The House in the Mail.*
Dan Andreasen, illustrator. New York: Viking Penguin, 2002. 48 pages. ISBN 0-670-03545-9. Grades K to 4.

Twelve-year-old Emily keeps a scrapbook that documents the construction of a 1927 Kentucky house ordered through the mail.
National Council for the Social Studies Notable Social Studies Trade Books for Young People.

Grades 3 to 6

Ames, Mildred. *Grandpa Jake and the Grand Christmas.*
New York: Scribner, 1990. 96 pages. ISBN 0-684-19241-1. Grades 4 to 7.

Lizzie's family suffers hard times during the Depression until long-lost Grandpa Jake appears on their doorstep, resulting in some positive changes.
School Library Journal Best Book.

Armstrong, William O. *Sounder.*
New York: HarperCollins Children's Book Group, 1969. 128 pages. ISBN 0-06-020143-6 and 0-06-440020-4pbk.
New York: Caedmon Audio, 1995. ISBN 1-55994-671-7. (VHS). Lexile 900. Grades 5 to 10.

Angry and humiliated when his sharecropper father is jailed for stealing food for his family, a young black boy grows in courage and understanding with the help of his devoted dog Sounder.

American Library Association Notable Children's Books of 1940 to 1970, Horn Book Fanfare Honor List, Lewis Carroll Shelf Award, Newbery Medal, New York Times Outstanding Children's Books, Publishers Weekly Select Children's Books, and *School Library Journal "Best of the Best" Children's Books 1966 to 1978*.

Avi. *The Secret School.*
San Diego, CA: Harcourt Children's Books, 2001. 153 pages. ISBN 0-15-216375-1 and 0-15-204699-2pbk. Lexile 540. Grades 3 to 6.

An early instructor departure forces fourteen-year-old Ida to take things into her own hands and become the teacher of a one-room schoolhouse in 1925 rural Colorado.
International Reading Association Children's Choices.

Bartoletti, Susan Campbell. *The Christmas Promise.*
Refer to complete information under Grades Kindergarten to 2.

Beard, Darleen Bailey. *The Babbs Switch Story.*
New York: Farrar, Straus & Giroux, 2002. 176 pages. ISBN 0-374-30475-0. Grades 5 to 8.

Inspired by a real tragedy, an adolescent Oklahoma girl appreciates the value of her mentally disabled sister during a 1924 schoolhouse fire.
Oklahoma Book Award.

Curtis, Christopher Paul. *Bud, Not Buddy.*
New York: Delacorte, 1999. 245 pages. ISBN 0-385-32306-9.
New York: Yearling, 2002. 256 pages. ISBN 0-440-41328-1pbk.
New York: Bantam Books unabridged audio, 2000. ISBN 0-553-52675-8. Lexile 950. Grades 5 to 7.

An orphan on the run from abusive foster homes in 1930s Michigan, ten-year-old Buddy is in pursuit of his long-lost father.
Booklist Editors' Choice, Coretta Scott King Award, International Reading Association Notable Books for a Global Society, Newbery Medal, Parent's Choice Gold Award, and *Volunteer State Book Award.*

English, Karen. *Francie.*
New York: Farrar, Straus & Giroux, 1999. 208 pages. ISBN 0-374-32456-5.
Prince Frederick, MD: Recorded Books unabridged audio, 2002. ISBN 1-4025-2131-6. Lexile 660. Grades 3 to 6.

Thirteen years old and poor, African American Francie struggles with the culture of pre-Civil Rights Alabama while waiting for her father to get settled in Chicago so he can move his family up North. She displays courage in attempting to teach a framed young African American man to read and assisting him to escape.

American Library Association Notable Children's Books, International Reading Association Notable Books for a Global Society, and *Parent's Choice Award.*

Fuqua, Jonathon Scott. *Darby.*
Cambridge, MA: Candlewick Press, 2002. 242 pages. ISBN 0-7636-1417-3 and 0-7445-9056-6pbk. Grades 4 to 6.

A nine-year-old girl becomes the target for hatred and violence after she writes a controversial article that promotes racial equality for a local newspaper in 1926 South Carolina.

Children's Literature Choices and *National Council for the Social Studies Notable Social Studies Trade Books for Young People.*

Hesse, Karen. *Out of the Dust.*
New York: Scholastic Trade, 1997. 227 pages. ISBN 0-590-36080-9 and 0-590-3725-8pbk.
New York: Bantam Books unabridged audio, 1999. ISBN 0-8072-8050-X. Lexile NP. Grades 5 to 8.

Set in the Oklahoma Dust Bowl during the Great Depression, this poetic novel about a fourteen-year-old girl's endurance of family hardships chronicles her mother's death and her father's emotional demise.

American Library Association Notable Children's Books, Booklinks Best Book of the Year, Newbery Medal, Publishers Weekly Best Books of the Year, School Library Journal Best Book, and *Scott O'Dell Award for Historical Fiction.*

Koller, Jackie French. *Nothing to Fear.*
San Diego, CA: Harcourt Children's Books, 1991. 279 pages. ISBN 0-15-200544-7 and 0-15-257582-0pbk. Lexile 730. Grades 5 to 7.

During the Great Depression, an Irish immigrant family struggles when the mother becomes ill and the father has to move away to find work.

International Reading Association Young Adults' Choices.

Lafaye, A. *The Strength of Saints.*
New York: Simon & Schuster, 2002. 192 pages. ISBN 0-689-83200-1. Grades 5 to 8.

A fourteen-year-old girl develops two separate but equal libraries in response to the 1936 escalation of racial tension in her small Louisiana

town.
Smithsonian Magazine Notable Books for Children.

Lasky, Kathryn. *Marven of the Great North Woods.*
Refer to complete information under Grades Kindergarten to 2.

Lyon, George Ella. *Borrowed Children.*
New York: Orchard Books, 1988. 154 pages. ISBN 0-531-05751-8.
Lexington, KY: University Press of Kentucky, 1999. 176 pages. ISBN 0-8131-0972-8pbk. Lexile 510. Grades 5 to 7.

Twelve-year-old Amanda's mother becomes ill after childbirth, and Amanda takes care of her. Finally, during a holiday in Memphis that is far removed from the Depression drudgery of her Kentucky mountain family, Amanda finds her world expanding as she reflects on her own culture and experiences.
Golden Kite Award and *School Library Journal Best Book.*

Mitchell, Margaree King. *Uncle Jed's Barbershop.*
Refer to complete information under Grades Kindergarten to 2.

Moss, Marissa. *Rose's Journal: The Story of a Girl in the Great Depression.*
San Diego, CA: Silver Whistle, 2001. 56 pages. ISBN 0-15-202423-9. Lexile 820. Grades 3 to 5.

A young Midwestern farm girl keeps a diary over a six-month period in 1935.
National Council for the Social Studies Notable Children's Trade Books in the Field of Social Studies.

Myers, Anna. *Red-Dirt Jessie.*
Topeka, KS: Econo-Clad Books, 1999. ISBN 0-7857-5732-5.
New York: Puffin Books, 1997. 128 pages. ISBN 0-14-038734-Xpbk. Lexile 720. Grades 6 to 9.

Jessie, a young girl living in the Oklahoma Dust Bowl during the Depression, tries to tame a wild dog and help her father recover from a nervous breakdown after her baby sister dies in 1930.
Land of Enchantment Children's Book Award Masterlist, Oklahoma Book Award, Parent's Choice Award, Sequoyah Children's Book Award Masterlist, and *Volunteer State Book Award Masterlist.*

Olsen, Violet. *The View from the Pighouse Roof.*
New York: Atheneum Books for Young Readers, 1987. 176 pages. ISBN

0-689-31324-1. (Out of print). Grades 5 to 7.

Marie looks after her sister Rosie's two-year-old child after her sister dies in an accident during the Depression.

Society of Midlands Authors Award.

Peck, Richard. *A Long Way from Chicago: A Novel in Stories.*
New York: Dial Books for Young Readers, 1998. 148 pages. ISBN 0-8037-2290-7.
New York: Puffin Books, 2000. 148 pages. ISBN 0-14-130352-2pbk.
New York: Bantam Books unabridged audio, 2001. ISBN 0-8072-6162-9. Lexile 750. Grades 4 to 7.

The antics of a feisty grandmother and her two grandchildren from Chicago are covered within eight short stories spanning several summers in a rural Illinois town during the Depression.

American Library Association Notable Children's Books and *Newbery Honor Book.*

Peck, Richard. *A Year Down Yonder.*
Steve Cleslawski, illustrator. New York: Dial Books for Young Readers, 2000. 130 pages. ISBN 0-8037-2518-3.
New York: Bantam Books unabridged audio, 2000. ISBN 0-8072-6167-X. Lexile 610. Grades 4 to 8.

Fifteen-year-old Mary Alice is sent from Chicago to a small Illinois town to live with her feisty grandmother in 1937. The sequel to *A Long Way from Chicago.*

Newbery Medal.

Rabin, Staton. *Casey Over There.*
Refer to complete information under Grades Kindergarten to 2.

Rael, Elsa Okon. *What Zeesie Saw on Delancey Street.*
Refer to complete information under Grades Kindergarten to 2.

Raven, Margot Theis. *Angels in the Dust.*
Roger Essley, illustrator. Topeka, KS: Econo-Clad Books, 1999. 32 pages. ISBN 0-613-18233-2.
Mahwah, NJ: Troll Communications, 1997. 32 pages. ISBN 0-8167-3806-8pbk. Lexile AD650. Grades 3 to 6.

A picture book that illustrates the struggle for survival of an Oklahoma family living on a wheat farm during the dust storms of the 1930s.

Storytelling World Award Honor Book.

Ringold, Faith. *Tar Beach.*
Refer to complete information under Grades Kindergarten to 2.

Robinet, Harriette Gillem. *Mississippi Chariot.*
New York: Simon & Schuster, 1994. 128 pages. ISBN 0-689-31960-6 and 0-689-80632-9pbk. Lexile 640. Grades 5 to 7.

In 1936 Mississippi, twelve-year-old Shortening Bread Jackson saves a white boy from drowning. In gratitude, the father helps to free Shortening Bread's father from the chain gang to which he was sentenced for a crime he did not commit.

National Council for the Social Studies Notable Children's Trade Books in the Field of Social Studies and *New York Public Library Books for the Teen Age.*

Rostowski, Margaret. *After the Dancing Days.*
New York: HarperCollins Children's Book Group, 1986. 217 pages. ISBN 0-06-025078-X and 0-06-440248-7pbk. Lexile 650. Grades 6 to 9.

After Annie's father returns from the war, she begins a forbidden friendship with a badly disfigured soldier. The aftermath of World War I forces thirteen-year-old Annie to redefine the word "hero" and to question conventional ideas of patriotism.

American Library Association Best Books for Young Adults, American Library Association Notable Children's Books, Booklist Editors' Choice, Golden Kite Award, International Reading Association Children's Book Award, International Reading Association Young Adults' Choices, Jefferson Cup Award, Judy Lopez Children's Book Award Certificate of Merit, National Council for the Social Studies Notable Children's Trade Books in the Field of Social Studies, National Council of Teachers of English Recommended Books, and *USA Through Children's Books.*

Ryan, Pam Munoz. *Esperanza Rising.*
New York: Scholastic Trade, 2000. 262 pages. ISBN 0-439-12041-1 and 0-439-12042-Xpbk.
New York: Bantam Books unabridged audio, 2001. ISBN 0-8072-6207-2. Lexile 750. Grades 5 to 8.

Privileged fourteen-year-old Esperanza is forced to move from Mexico to the United States to work in an agricultural labor camp after her father dies and her mother falls ill. Her transition is made even more difficult when she witnesses the injustices economic difficulties impose upon others during the Depression.

American Library Association Notable Children's Books, Interna-

tional Reading Association Notable Books for a Global Society, Jane Addams Children's Book Award, National Council for the Social Studies Notable Children's Trade Books in the Field of Social Studies, and *Pura Belpre Award*.

Rylant, Cynthia. *When I Was Young in the Mountains.*
Refer to complete information under Grades Kindergarten to 2.

Santiago, Chiori. *Home to Medicine Mountain.*
Refer to complete information under Grades Kindergarten to 2.

Skurzynski, Gloria. *Good-bye, Billy Radish.*
Topeka, KS: Econo-Clad Books, 1999. 137 pages. ISBN 0-613-00470-1.
New York: Aladdin Paperbacks, 1996. 144 pages. ISBN 0-689-80443-1pbk. Lexile 840. Grades 5 to 8.
In 1917 as the United States enters World War I, ten-year-old Hank sees change all around him in his western Pennsylvania steel mill town. His older Ukrainian friend, Billy, suffers a tragedy that changes Hank.
Jefferson Cup Award Honor Book, New York Public Library Books for the Teen Age, and *School Library Journal Best Book*.

Taylor, Mildred. *The Friendship.*
Max Ginsburg, illustrator. New York: Dial Books for Young Readers, 1987. 53 pages. ISBN 0-8037-0417-8.
New York: Puffin Books, 1998. 56 pages. ISBN 0-14-038964-4pbk. Lexile 750. Grades 3 to 6.
Four children sent to retrieve medicine witness a prejudicial confrontation between an elderly black man and a white storekeeper in rural Mississippi in the 1930s.
American Library Association Notable Children's Books, Boston Globe-Horn Book Award, and *Coretta Scott King Award*.

Taylor, Mildred. *Mississippi Bridge.*
Topeka, KS: Econo-Clad Books, 2000. 64 pages. ISBN 0-8335-9262-9.
New York: Bantam Books, 1992. 62 pages. ISBN 0-553-15992-5pbk. Lexile 810. Grades 4 to 7.
During a heavy rainstorm in 1930s rural Mississippi, a ten-year-old white boy watches as a bus driver orders all the black passengers off a crowded bus to make room for late-arriving white passengers. In a cruel twist of fate, the bus plunges over the side of the bridge close to town.
Christopher Award.

Taylor, Mildred. *Roll of Thunder, Hear My Cry.*
Jerry Pinkney, illustrator. First copyright 1976. New York: Phyllis
Fogelman Books, 2001. 276 pages. ISBN 0-8037-2647-3.
New York: Puffin Books, 1997. 276 pages. ISBN 0-14-038451-0pbk.
New York: Bantam Books unabridged audio, 2001. ISBN 0-8072-0621-
0. (VHS) Lexile 920. Grades 5 to 9.

An African American family living in the South during the 1930s is
faced with prejudice and discrimination while trying to hold on to their
land.

*American Library Association Notable Children's Books, Boston
Globe-Horn Book Award Honor Book, Buxtehude Bulla Prize, George C.
Stone Center for Children's Books Recognition of Merit Award, Jane
Addams Children's Book Award Honor Citation, National Book Award
for Young People's Literature Finalist,* and *Newbery Medal.*

Taylor, Mildred. *Song of the Trees.*
New York: Dial Books for Young Readers, 1975. 48 pages. ISBN 0-
8037-5452-3.
New York: Skylark, 1996. 48 pages. ISBN 0-440-41396-6pbk. Lexile
710. Grades 3 to 5.

A rural black family tries to prevent the removal of their beloved
trees by an unscrupulous white man during the Great Depression.

*The Council on Interracial Books for Children First Prize, Jane Ad-
dams Children's Book Award Honor Citation,* and *New York Times Outstanding Children's Books.*

Taylor, Mildred. *The Well: David's Story.*
New York: Dial Books for Young Readers, 1995. 92 pages. ISBN 0-
8037-1803-9.
New York: Penguin Putnam, 1998. 96 pages. ISBN 0-14-038642-4pbk.
Lexile 760. Grades 4 to 7.

During a drought, the Logan family shares its well water with all its
neighbors, black and white alike, until some mean-spirited white teenagers poison it.

*American Library Association Notable Children's Books, Interna-
tional Reading Association Notable Books for a Global Society,* and *Jane
Addams Children's Book Award.*

Uchida, Yoshiko. *The Best Bad Thing.*
New York: Atheneum Books for Young Readers, 1983. 120 pages. ISBN
0-689-50290-7 and 0-689-71745-8pbk. (VHS). Lexile 870. Grades 3 to
6.

Japanese American Rinko discovers that there are pleasant surprises for her, but then bad things start to happen while she is helping out, at the request of her mother, in the household of recently widowed Mrs. Hata. The sequel to *A Jar of Dreams.*
American Library Association Notable Children's Books and *School Library Journal Best Book.*

Uchida, Yoshiko. *The Happiest Ending.*
New York: Atheneum Books for Young Readers, 1985. 120 pages. ISBN 0-689-50326-1. (Out of print). Lexile 890. Grades 4 to 6.

The last book of the trilogy with *A Jar of Dreams* and *The Best Bad Thing*, Rinko revolts against another girl's arranged marriage until she begins to see the other side of things.
Bay Area Book Reviewers Association Award.

Uchida, Yoshiko. *A Jar of Dreams.*
New York: Atheneum Books for Young Readers, 1981. 131 pages. ISBN 0-689-50210-9.
New York: Aladdin Paperbacks, 1993. 144 pages. ISBN 0-689-71672-9pbk. Lexile 970. Grades 3 to 6.

A young girl grows up in a closely-knit Japanese American family in California during the 1930s, a time of great prejudice. When an aunt comes to visit, she influences everyone to start working on their goals.
Commonwealth Club of California Book Award and *Friends of Children and Literature Award.*

Wells, Rosemary and Tom Wells. *The House in the Mail.*
Refer to complete information under Grades Kindergarten to 2.

Wells, Rosemary. *Mary on Horseback: Three Mountain Stories.*
New York: Viking, 1999. 54 pages. ISBN 0-670-88923-7.
New York: Puffin Books, 2000. 53 pages. ISBN 0-14-130815-Xpbk. Lexile 660. Grades 3 to 6.

Three stories illustrate the life of Mary Breckenridge, founder of the Frontier Nursing Service in 1925 that provided medical care to rural Appalachian Kentucky.
Christopher Award, Horn Book Fanfare Honor List, School Library Journal Best Book of the Year, and *Smithsonian Magazine Notable Books for Children.*

Wells, Rosemary. *Wingwalker.*
New York: Hyperion, 2002. 80 pages. ISBN 0-7868-0397-5. Grades 3 to

6.

Second-grader Reuben worries when his father takes a dangerous carnival job walking on the wings of an airplane in order to survive during the Depression.

Booklist Top Ten Historical Fiction for Youth.

Whelan, Gloria. *That Wild Berries Should Grow: The Story of a Summer.*
Grand Rapids, MI: William B. Eerdmans Publishing Company, 1994. 122 pages. ISBN 0-8028-3754-9 and 0-8028-5091-Xpbk. Grades 4 to 7.

Twelve-year-old Elsa spends the last few months of the 1933 school year ill. In order to recuperate, her parents send her to stay with her grandparents in rural Michigan near Lake Huron. Although initially convinced she will hate it, Elsa slowly grows to love it.

American Bookseller Pick of the Lists.

Grades 7 and 8

Ames, Mildred. *Grandpa Jake and the Grand Christmas.*
Refer to complete information under Grades 3 to 6.

Armstrong, William O. *Sounder.*
Refer to complete information under Grades 3 to 6.

Beard, Darleen Bailey. *The Babbs Switch Story.*
Refer to complete information under Grades 3 to 6.

Curtis, Christopher Paul. *Bud, Not Buddy.*
Refer to complete information under Grades 3 to 6.

Hesse, Karen. *Out of the Dust.*
Refer to complete information under Grades 3 to 6.

Hesse, Karen. *Witness.*
New York: Scholastic, 2001. 161 pages. ISBN 0-439-27199-1.
New York: Bantam Books unabridged audio, 2001. ISBN 0-8072-0592-3. Lexile NP. Grades 7 to Young Adult.

Eleven townspeople from a 1920s small Vermont town tell in free verse the story of dealing with an infiltration of the Ku Klux Klan.

American Library Association Notable Children's Books, Christopher Award, International Reading Association Notable Books for a

Global Society, National Council of Teachers of English Notable Children's Books in the English Language Arts, and *School Library Journal Best Book.*

Koller, Jackie French. *Nothing to Fear.*
Refer to complete information under Grades 3 to 6.

Lafaye, A. *The Strength of Saints.*
Refer to complete information under Grades 3 to 6.

Lyon, George Ella. *Borrowed Children.*
Refer to complete information under Grades 3 to 6.

Meyer, Carolyn. *White Lilacs.*
San Diego, CA: Harcourt Children's Books, 1996. 320 pages. ISBN 0-15-200614-9 and 0-15-295876-2pbk. Lexile 990. Grades 7 to 10.

In a story based on the actual events that occurred in Quakertown, Texas, in 1921, twelve-year-old Rose Lee sees trouble emerge in her African American community known as Freedomtown. The white leaders decide to take the Freedomtown land for a park and forcibly relocate the families who live there to an ugly stretch of territory outside the town.

American Library Association Best Books for Young Adults, International Reading Association Young Adults' Choices, and *New York Public Library Books for the Teen Age.*

Myers, Walter Dean. *The Glory Field.*
Topeka, KS: Econo-Clad Books, 1999. 333 pages. ISBN 0-7857-8741-0. New York: Point, 1996. 375 pages. ISBN 0-590-45898-1pbk. Lexile 800. Grades 7 to Young Adult.

Follows five generations of an African American family spanning two hundred and fifty years, from the capture and enslavement of the first ancestor in 1750, through the Civil War and the end of segregation, to a final reunion of relatives.

American Library Association Best Books for Young Adults.

Myers, Anna. *Red-Dirt Jessie.*
Refer to complete information under Grades 3 to 6.

Olsen, Violet. *The View from the Pighouse Roof.*
Refer to complete information under Grades 3 to 6.

Peck, Richard. *A Long Way from Chicago: A Novel in Stories.*
Refer to complete information under Grades 3 to 6.

Peck, Richard. *A Year Down Yonder.*
Refer to complete information under Grades 3 to 6.

Rostowski, Margaret. *After the Dancing Days.*
Refer to complete information under Grades 3 to 6.

Ryan, Pam Munoz. *Esperanza Rising.*
Refer to complete information under Grades 3 to 6.

Sebestyen, Ouida. *Far from Home.*
Boston: Little, Brown & Company, 1980. 191 pages. ISBN 0-316-77932-6. (Out of print). Grades 7 to 10.
A thirteen-year-old boy lives and works in a boardinghouse and learns about his father after his mother dies during the Depression.
School Library Journal Best Book.

Skurzynski, Gloria. *Good-bye, Billy Radish.*
Refer to complete information under Grades 3 to 6.

Taylor, Mildred. *Let the Circle Be Unbroken.*
New York: Dial Books for Young Readers, 1982. 432 pages. ISBN 0-8037-4748-9.
New York: Puffin Books, 1991. 394 pages. ISBN 0-14-034892-1pbk. Lexile 850. Grades 7 to 9.
Four black children growing up in rural Mississippi in 1934 during the Depression experience racial antagonisms and hard times, but they learn from their parents the pride and self-respect they need to survive. The sequel to *A Song of the Trees*, and *Roll of Thunder, Hear My Cry.*
American Library Association Notable Children's Books, Coretta Scott King Award, and *George C. Stone Center for Children's Books Recognition of Merit Award.*

Taylor, Mildred. *Mississippi Bridge.*
Refer to complete information under Grades 3 to 6.

Taylor, Mildred. *Roll of Thunder, Hear My Cry.*
Refer to complete information under Grades 3 to 6.

Taylor, Mildred. *Song of the Trees.*
Refer to complete information under Grades 3 to 6.

Taylor, Mildred. *The Well: David's Story.*
Refer to complete information under Grades 3 to 6.

Whelan, Gloria. *That Wild Berries Should Grow: The Story of a Summer.*
Refer to complete information under Grades 3 to 6.

Chapter 10

World War II: 1941 to 1945

Grades Kindergarten to 2

Adler, David A. *One Yellow Daffodil: A Hanukkah Story.*
Lloyd Bloom, illustrator. San Diego, CA: Gulliver Books, 1995. 32 pages. ISBN 0-15-200537-4 and 0-15-202094-2pbk. Lexile 440. Grades K to 3.

Holocaust survivor Morris Kaplan is invited by his favorite flower shop customers to spend Hanukkah with their family, which results in giving him the courage to face his past.

International Reading Association Notable Books for a Global Society and *National Council for the Social Studies Notable Children's Trade Books in the Field of Social Studies.*

Bunting, Eve. *So Far from the Sea.*
New York: Clarion Books, 1998. 32 pages. ISBN 0-395-72095-8. Prince Frederick, MD: Recorded Books Unabridged Audio, 1998. ISBN 0-7887-2332-4. Lexile 590. Grades 2 to 5.

A seven-year-old Japanese American child leaves behind a special momento while visiting the Eastern California Manzanar War Relocation Center grave of her grandfather.

International Reading Association Notable Books for a Global Society.

Lee, Milly. *Nim and the War Effort.*
Yangsook Choi, illustrator. New York: Farrar, Straus & Giroux, 1997. 40 pages. ISBN 0-374-35523-1 and 0-374-45506-6pbk. Lexile AD510. Grades 1 to 3.

A Chinese American schoolgirl collects the most newspapers for a war-effort paper drive in her school.

American Library Association Notable Children's Books, International Reading Association Notable Books for a Global Society, and *National Council for the Social Studies Notable Children's Trade Books in the Field of Social Studies.*

Grades 3 to 6

Adler, David A. *One Yellow Daffodil: A Hanukkah Story.*
Refer to complete information under Grades Kindergarten to 2.

Bauer, Marian. *Rain of Fire.*
New York: Clarion Books, 1983. 160 pages. ISBN 0-89919-190-8. (Out of Print). Grades 4 to 8.

After Steve's brother returns from World War II, he is unable to discuss it until he finally reveals to Steve the horrors of his Hiroshima experience.

Jane Addams Children's Book Award.

Bunting, Eve. *So Far from the Sea.*
Refer to complete information under Grades Kindergarten to 2.

Davies, Jacqueline. *Where the Ground Meets the Sky.*
Tarrytown, NY: Marshall Canvendish Corporation, 2002. 224 pages. ISBN 0-7614-5105-6. Grades 5 to 8.

Twelve-year-old Hazel tries to cope with her mother's emotional retreat and the physical absence of her father, who is secretly assisting in the construction of the atomic bomb.

National Council for the Social Studies Notable Social Studies Trade Books for Young People.

Elliott, Laura. *Under a War-Torn Sky.*
New York: Hyperion, 2001. 284 pages. ISBN 0-7868-0755-5 and 0-7868-2485-9. Lexile 640. Grades 6 to 9.

Based on the author's father's World War II experiences, this novel chronicles the attempt of a nineteen-year-old pilot to escape the Nazis with the help of French citizens and return to the American Front after being shot down in occupied France.

Jefferson Cup Award Honor Book and *National Council for the So cial Studies Notable Children's Trade Books in the Field of Social Studies.*

Giff, Patricia Reilly. *Lily's Crossing.*
New York: Delacorte, 1997. 180 pages. ISBN 0-385-32142-2.
New York: Yearling, 1999. 180 pages. ISBN 0-440-41453-9pbk.
New York: Bantam Books unabridged audio, 1998. ISBN 0-553-52529-8.
Old Greenwich, CT: Listening Library abridged audio, 2000. ISBN 0-8072-0878-7. Lexile 720. Grades 3 to 6.

In the summer of 1944, ten-year-old Lily's father enlists in the army while Lily befriends a Hungarian refugee named Albert who lost his family in the war. This friendship causes her to see the war differently.

American Library Association Notable Children's Books, Boston Globe-Horn Book Award Honor Book, and *Newbery Honor Book.*

Griese, Arnold A. *The Wind Is Not a River.*
Glo Coalson, illustrator. First copyright 1978. Topeka, KS: Econo-Clad Books, 1999. 113 pages. ISBN 0-7857-9740-8. Lexile 780. Grades 3 to 6.

Sasan and Sidak are Aleutian siblings living on the island of Attu in 1942. When they see Japanese soldiers invading their island, they escape to the hills and must forage for food. While there, they decide to help a wounded soldier.

National Council for the Social Studies Notable Children's Trade Books in the Field of Social Studies.

Hahn, Mary Downing. *Stepping on the Cracks.*
New York: Clarion Books, 1991. 216 pages. ISBN 0-395-58507-4.
New York: Camelot, 1992. 176 pages. ISBN 0-380-71900-2pbk. Lexile 780. Grades 5 to 7.

In 1944 while her brother is overseas fighting in World War II, eleven-year-old Margaret decides to help school bully Gordy when she finds him hiding his own brother, an army deserter, because his abusive father will beat him if he returns home.

American Library Association Notable Children's Books, The Bulletin of the Center for Children's Books Blue Ribbon Award, Joan G. Sugarman Children's Book Award, School Library Journal Best Book, and *Scott O'Dell Award for Historical Fiction.*

Lee, Milly. *Nim and the War Effort.*
Refer to complete information under Grades Kindergarten to 2.

Lisle, Janet Taylor. *The Art of Keeping Cool.*
New York: Atheneum Books for Young Readers, 2000. 216 pages. ISBN 0-689-837887-9 and 0-689-83788-7pbk. Lexile 730. Grades 5 to 8.

A complex novel narrated by thirteen-year-old Robert, who tries to deal with the tensions inside his family against the backdrop of World War II.

American Library Association Top Ten Historical Fiction for Youth and *Scott O'Dell Award for Historical Fiction.*

Mazer, Harry. *A Boy at War: A Novel of Pearl Harbor.*
New York: Simon & Schuster, 2001. 104 pages. ISBN 0-689-84161-2. Lexile 530. Grades 6 to 9.

After being mistaken for a Navy man, fourteen-year-old Adam is thrown into the sea to help save lives during the bombing of Pearl Harbor in 1941.

Children's Literature Choices.

Mochizuki, Ken. *Baseball Saved Us.*
Dom Lee, illustrator. New York: Lee & Low Books, 1993. 32 pages. ISBN 1-880000-01-6 and 1-880000-19-9pbk. Lexile AD550. Grades 3 to 6.

A Japanese American boy learns to play baseball while he and his family are forced to live in an internment camp during World War II. His ability to play helps him after the war is over.

American Bookseller Pick of the Lists, Parent's Choice Award, and *Publishers Weekly Editor's Choice.*

Paterson, Katherine. *Jacob Have I Loved.*
New York: HarperCollins Children's Book Group, 1980. 256 pages. ISBN 0-690-04078-4 and 0-06-440368-8pbk.
New York: Caedmon unabridged audio, 1995. ISBN 1-55994-611-3. (VHS). Lexile 880. Grades 6 to Young Adult.

Not until Louise leaves the Chesapeake Island she grew up on in the early 1940s does she realize that the things she experienced as an adolescent and the intense jealousy she felt toward her twin sister have assisted her in finding her own identity.

American Book Award Nominee, American Library Association Best Books for Young Adults, American Library Association Notable Children's Books of 1976 to 1980, Booklist Editors' Choice, Horn Book Fanfare Honor List, Newbery Medal, New York Times Outstanding Children's Books of 1980, New York Public Library Children's Books, and *School Library Journal Best Book.*

Paulsen, Gary. *The Cookcamp.*
New York: Orchard Books, 1991. 116 pages. ISBN 0-531-05927-8.
New York: Bantam Books, 1992. 128 pages. ISBN 0-440-40704-4pbk.
Lexile 1070. Grades 3 to 6.

During World War II, a little boy is sent to live with his grandmother, who is a cook in a camp for workers building a road through the wilderness from Minnesota to Canada, while his father fights in the war and his mother remains in Chicago.
School Library Journal Best Book.

Rinaldi, Ann. *Keep Smiling Through.*
San Diego, CA: Harcourt Children's Books, 1996. 208 pages. ISBN 0-15-200768-7. Lexile 570. Grades 4 to 6.

Ten-year-old Kay tries to deal with the hardships of living with her abusive stepmother, detached father, and siblings against the backdrop of World War II.
National Council for the Social Studies Notable Children's Trade Books in the Field of Social Studies.

Salisbury, Graham. *Under the Blood-Red Sun.*
New York: Delacorte, 1994. 246 pages. ISBN 0-385-32099-X.
New York: Yearling, 1995. 246 pages. ISBN 0-440-41139-4pbk.
Prince Frederick, MD: Recorded Books unabridged audio, 1995. ISBN 0-7887-0427-3 and 1-4025-2348-3cd. Lexile 640. Grades 5 to 8.

Growing up in Oahu, Tomikazu's world is destroyed when the Japanese attack Pearl Harbor. Tomi's Japan-born father and grandfather are arrested, and Tomi must help his mother and sister to survive.
American Library Association Best Books for Young Adults and *Scott O'Dell Award for Historical Fiction.*

Taylor, Theodore. *The Cay.*
First copyright 1969. New York: Random House, 1987. 138 pages. ISBN 0-385-07906-0.
New York: Avon Books, 1995. 144 pages. ISBN 0-380-00142-Xpbk.
New York: Bantam Books abridged audio, 1992. ISBN 0-553-47038-3. Lexile 860. Grades 6 to 9.

When the freighter on which they are traveling is torpedoed by a German submarine in 1942 during World War II, an adolescent white boy, blinded by a head injury he sustained during the ship's explosion, and an old black man are stranded on a tiny Caribbean island. The boy acquires an appreciation for the vision, courage, and love of his old com panion.

American Library Association Notable Children's Book, Child Study Children's Book Committee Children's Book of the Year, Children's Literature Council of Southern California Book Award, Commonwealth Club of California Book Award, Cooperative Children's Book Center Children's Book of the Year, Jane Addams Children's Book Award, and *Lewis Carroll Shelf Award.*

Uchida, Yoshiko. *Journey to Topaz.*
Donald Carrick, illustrator. First copyright 1971. Creative Arts Books, 1985. 160 pages. ISBN 0-916870-85-5pbk. Lexile 970. Grades 4 to 8.

In 1941, eleven-year-old Yuki Sakane is looking forward to Christmas when her peaceful world is suddenly shattered by the bombing of Pearl Harbor. After her father is arrested, Yuki is uprooted from her home and shipped with thousands of West Coast Japanese Americans to the desert concentration camp in Utah called Topaz.

American Library Association Notable Children's Books.

Yep, Laurence. *Hiroshima: A Novella.*
New York: Scholastic, 1995. 56 pages. ISBN 0-590-29832-2 and 0-590-20833-0pbk.
Prince Frederick, MD: Recorded Books unabridged audio, 1997. ISBN 0-7887-1111-3. Lexile 660. Grades 5 to 7.

Chronicles the bombing of Hiroshima in 1945 and its citizens' struggles to survive despite death and devastation as seen through the eyes of a twelve-year-old Japanese girl.

Booklist Editors' Choice and National Council for the Social Studies Notable Children's Trade Books in the Field of Social Studies.

Grades 7 and 8

Bat-Ami, Miriam. *Two Suns in the Sky.*
Chicago, IL: Cricket Books, 1999. 208 pages. ISBN 0-8126-2900-0. Lexile 550. Grades 8 to Young Adult.

A fenced-in refugee shelter in Oswego, New York, was home to one thousand Jewish refugees from liberated Italy in the fall of 1944. Fifteen-year-old Yugoslav refugee Adam forms a forbidden romance with Chris, a fifteen-year-old Oswego native.

American Library Association Best Books for Young Adults, Booklist Editors' Choice, and *Scott O'Dell Award for Historical Fiction.*

Bauer, Marian. *Rain of Fire.*
Refer to complete information under Grades 3 to 6.

Davies, Jacqueline. *Where the Ground Meets the Sky.*
Refer to complete information under Grades 3 to 6.

Elliott, Laura. *Under a War-Torn Sky.*
Refer to complete information under Grades 3 to 6.

Greene, Bette. *Summer of My German Soldier.*
First copyright 1973. New York: Peter Smith Publishers, 2000. 224 pages. ISBN 0-8446-7144-4.
New York: Puffin Books, 1999. 230 pages. ISBN 0-14-130636-Xpbk.
Prince Frederick, MD: Recorded Books unabridged audio, 1995. ISBN 0-7887-0365-X and 1-4025-2339-4cd. Lexile 800. Grades 7 to 10.
    Sheltering an escaped German prisoner of war is the beginning of some shattering experiences for a twelve-year-old Jewish girl in Arkansas in the summer of 1944.
    American Library Association Notable Children's Books, Golden Kite Award, National Book Award for Young People's Literature Finalist, and *New York Times Outstanding Children's Books.*

Hahn, Mary Downing. *Stepping on the Cracks.*
Refer to complete information under Grades 3 to 6.

Kerr, M. E. *Slap Your Sides.*
New York: HarperCollins Children's Book Group, 2001. ISBN 0-06-029481-7. Lexile 700. Grades 7 to 10.
    The story of a Quaker teenager who is a pacifist during World War II.
    Booklist Editors' Choice.

Lisle, Janet Taylor. *The Art of Keeping Cool.*
Refer to complete information under Grades 3 to 6.

Mazer, Harry. *A Boy at War: A Novel of Pearl Harbor.*
Refer to complete information under Grades 3 to 6.

Otsuka, Julie. *When the Emperor Was Divine.*
New York: The Knopf Publishing Group, 2002. 160 pages. ISBN 0-375-41429-0 and 0-375-2181-1pbk.
New York: Random House Unabridged Audio, 2003. ISBN 0-739-

30791-6CD. Grades 8 to 12.

A Japanese family suffers after being sent to an internment camp during World War II only to be humiliated by the vandalization of their Berkeley home upon return.

Alex Award, Booklist Editors' Choice, and *New York Times Notable Books of the Year.*

Paterson, Katherine. *Jacob Have I Loved.*
Refer to complete information under Grades 3 to 6.

Paulsen, Gary. *The Cookcamp.*
Refer to complete information under Grades 3 to 6.

Rylant, Cynthia. *I Had Seen Castles.*
San Diego, CA: Harcourt Children's Books, 1993. 97 pages. ISBN 0-15-238003-5 and 0-15-200374-6pbk. Lexile 950. Grades 7 to Young Adult.

Now an old retired professor in Canada, John is haunted by memories of enlisting to fight in World War II despite the urging of his girlfriend to become a conscientious objector, a decision which forced him to face the horrors of war, lose his girlfriend, and change his life forever.

New York Public Library Books for the Teen Age.

Salisbury, Graham. *Under the Blood-Red Sun.*
Refer to complete information under Grades 3 to 6.

Spiegelman, Art. *Maus: A Survivor's Tale.*
New York: Pantheon Books, 1997. 340 pages. ISBN 0-394-0641-7 and 0-679-74840-7pbk. Lexile NP. Grades 7 to Young Adult.

The author interviews his father, a Holocaust survivor, and portrays his story into comic form throughout this novel, causing the reader to look at the Holocaust in a different way.

American Library Association 100 Best Books for Teens and *Pulitzer Prize.*

Taylor, Theodore. *The Cay.*
Refer to complete information under Grades 3 to 6.

Uchida, Yoshiko. *Journey to Topaz.*
Refer to complete information under Grades 3 to 6.

Yep, Laurence. *Hiroshima: A Novella.*
Refer to complete information under Grades 3 to 6.

Chapter 11

Mid-20th Century to the Present

Grades Kindergarten to 2

Crews, Donald. *Bigmama's.*
New York: Greenwillow Books, 1991. 32 pages. ISBN 0-688-09950-5
and 0-688-15842-0pbk. Lexile 550. Grades K to 3.

The author reflects nostalgically on his childhood and his grandmother, "Bigmama," and sees that the old place and its surroundings are
just the same as before.

American Library Association Notable Children's Books.

Evans, Freddi Williams. *A Bus of Our Own.*
Shawn Costello, illustrator. Morton Grove, IL: Albert Whitman & Co.,
2001. 32 pages. ISBN 0-8075-0970-1. Lexile AD460. Grades K to 3.

Based on true events, a community of African Americans raises
money to refurbish an old school bus when their children are not allowed
to ride on the white kids' bus in post-World War II Mississippi.

*National Council for the Social Studies Notable Children's Trade
Books in the Field of Social Studies.*

Kinsey-Warnock, Natalie. *The Canada Geese Quilt.*
Leslie W. Bowman, illustrator. New York: Dutton Children's Books,
1989. 64 pages. ISBN 0-525-65004-0.
New York: Puffin Books, 2000. 64 pages. ISBN 0-14-130462-6pbk.
Prince Frederick, MD: Recorded Books unabridged audio, 1998. ISBN
0-7887-1906-8. Lexile 680. Grades 2 to 5.

Worried that the coming of a new baby and her grandmother's serious illness will change things on her family's Vermont farm in 1946, ten-

year-old Ariel combines her artistic talent with her grandmother's knowledge to make a very special quilt.

American Library Association Notable Children's Books, Booklist Editors' Choice, and *National Council for the Social Studies Notable Children's Trade Books in the Field of Social Studies.*

Littlesugar, Amy. *Freedom School, Yes.*
New York: Philomel Books, 2001. 40 pages. ISBN 0-399-23006-8. Lexile 390. Grades K to 3.

The frightening violence of the 1960s South is revealed through this story where a young white woman withstands harassment to teach African-American children their heritage.

International Reading Association Notable Books for a Global Society.

McKissack, Patricia C. *Goin' Someplace Special.*
Jerry Pinkney, illustrator. New York: Atheneum Books for Young Readers, 2001. 40 pages. ISBN 0-689-81885-8. Lexile AD550. Grades 2 to 4.

A young African American girl endures indignities as she makes her way to the town's public library, one of the few public places where she is welcome in 1950s Nashville, Tennessee.

American Library Association Notable Children's Books, Children's Literature Choices, Coretta Scott King Illustrator Award, International Reading Association Notable Books for a Global Society, National Council of Teachers of English Notable Children's Books in the English Language Arts, Parent's Choice Gold Award, and *Storytelling World Award.*

Taylor, Mildred. *The Gold Cadillac.*
New York: Dial Books for Young Readers, 1987. 43 pages. ISBN 0-8037-0342-2.
New York: Puffin Books, 1998. 48 pages. ISBN 0-14-038963-6pbk. Lexile 650. Grades 2 to 5.

Two African American girls living in the North are proud of their family's beautiful new Cadillac until they take it on a visit to the South and encounter racial prejudice for the first time.

Christopher Award.

Wiles, Deborah. *Freedom Summer.*
Jerome Lagarrigue, illustrator. New York: Atheneum Books for Young Readers, 2001. 32 pages. ISBN 0-689-83016-5. Lexile AD460. Grades K to 3.

The friendship between an African American boy and a white boy reflects the turmoil of 1964 Mississippi after the passage of the Civil Rights Act.

Children's Literature Choices, Coretta Scott King/John Steptoe Award for New Talent, Jefferson Cup Award Honor Book, and *National Council for the Social Studies Notable Children's Trade Books in the Field of Social Studies.*

Grades 3 to 6

Boutis, Victoria. *Looking Out.*
New York: Atheneum Books for Young Readers, 1988. 139 pages. ISBN 0-02-711830-4. (Out of print). Grades 6 to 9.

An adolescent girl attempts to hide the fact that her parents are Communists in 1953.

Jane Addams Children's Book Award.

Crews, Donald. *Bigmama's.*
Refer to complete information under Grades Kindergarten to 2.

Crowe, Chris. *Mississippi Trial, 1955.*
New York: Phyllis Fogelman Books, 2002. 231 pages. ISBN 0-8037-2745-3. Grades 6 to 9.

A white teenager visiting Mississippi in the 1950's clashes with his racist grandfather over the lynching of a black teenager from Chicago.

American Library Association Best Books for Young Adults, Children's Literature Choices, and *International Reading Association Notable Books for a Global Society.*

Curtis, Christopher Paul. *The Watsons Go to Birmingham–1963.*
New York: Delacorte, 1995. 210 pages. ISBN 0-385-32175-9.
New York: Bantam Books, 1997. 210 pages. ISBN 0-440-41412-1pbk.
New York: Bantam Books unabridged audio, 1996. ISBN 0-553-347786-2.
Greenwich, CT: Listening Library abridged audio, 2000. ISBN 0-8072-0880-9. Lexile 1000. Grades 5 to 8.

An African American family from Flint, Michigan, visits Grandmother in Birmingham, Alabama, and witnesses a church bombing.

American Library Association Best Books for Young Adults, American Library Association Notable Children's Books, The Bulletin of the Center for Children's Books Blue Ribbon Award, Children's Book Com-

mittee at the Bank Street College of Education Award, Coretta Scott King Award Honor Book, Horn Book Fanfare Honor List, International Reading Association Notable Books for a Global Society, Land of Enchantment Children's Books Award, and *Newbery Honor Book.*

Enger, Leif. *Peace Like a River.*
New York: Atlantic Monthly Press, 2001. 320 pages. ISBN 0-87113-795-X.
New York: HarperAudio unabridged audio, 2001. ISBN 0-694-52583-9.
Newport Beach, CA: Books On Tape unabridged audio, 2001. ISBN 0-7366-7636-8cd. Lexile 900. Grades 6 to Young Adult.
   An asthmatic eleven-year-old boy experiences despair and an adventure with his family after his brother is convicted for shooting two bullies who break into their 1962 Minnesota home.
   Alex Award and *Book Sense Book of the Year Award.*

Evans, Freddi Williams. *A Bus of Our Own.*
   Refer to complete information under Grades Kindergarten to 2.

Herschler, Mildred Barger. *The Darkest Corner.*
Asheville, NC: Front Street, 2000. 224 pages. ISBN 1-886910-54-5.
Grades 5 to 8.
   Ten-year-old Teddy is horrified by her father's participation in the lynching of her best friend's parent. The next five years of Teddy's life witness the internal family conflicts and rise of the civil rights movement that result from racial tensions.
   Children's Literature Choices and *International Reading Association Notable Books for a Global Society.*

Holt, Kimberly Willis. *When Zachary Beaver Came to Town.*
New York: Henry Holt & Co., 1999. 227 pages. ISBN 0-8050-6116-9.
New York: Yearling, 2001. 227 pages. ISBN 0-440-22904-9pbk.
New York: Bantam Books unabridged audio, 2000. ISBN 0-8072-8247-2. Lexile 700. Grades 5 to 8.
   In 1971 in the small town of Antler, Texas, thirteen-year-old Toby is struggling with the departure of his mother, the death of his best friend's brother in the Vietnam War, and the arrival of Zachary Beaver, the self-proclaimed "fattest boy in the world."
   Booklist Editors' Choice and *National Book Award for Young People's Literature.*

Kinsey-Warnock, Natalie. *The Canada Geese Quilt.*
Refer to complete information under Grades Kindergarten to 2.

Layden, Joseph and Virginia Euwer Wolff. *Bat 6.*
New York: Scholastic Trade, 1998. 256 pages. ISBN 0-590-89799-3 and 0-590-89800-0pbk.
New York: Bantam Books unabridged audio, 2000. ISBN 0-553-52663-4.
Old Greenwich, CT: Listening Library abridged audio, 2000. ISBN 0-8072-8223-5. Lexile 930. Grades 5 to 8.
During a post-war, small-town softball game, a girl whose father was killed at Pearl Harbor slams her elbow into the face of Aki, a Japanese American. Issues of prejudice are discussed as the event is related by each of the team members.
American Library Association Notable Children's Books.

Levitin, Sonia. *Dream Freedom.*
San Diego, CA: Silver Whistle, 2000. 288 pages. ISBN 0-15-202404-2. Lexile 670. Grades 5 to 8.
Based on a true story of contemporary enslavement in Sudan where thousands of members of the Dinka and Nuba tribes are captured and forced into hard labor. A group of students in Denver, Colorado, raises money to free slaves and educate others of their plight.
International Reading Association Notable Books for a Global Society and *National Council for the Social Studies Notable Children's Trade Books in the Field of Social Studies.*

Littlesugar, Amy. *Freedom School, Yes.*
Refer to complete information under Grades Kindergarten to 2.

Marino, Jan. *The Day That Elvis Came to Town.*
Boston: Little, Brown & Company, 1991. 204 pages. ISBN 0-316-54618-6. (Out of print). Lexile 600. Grades 5 to 8.
Thirteen-year-old Wanda befriends and then becomes disillusioned by a singer who moves into her boardinghouse.
The Bulletin of the Center for Children's Books Blue Ribbon Award and *School Library Journal Best Book.*

Martin, Ann M. *Belle Teal.*
New York: Scholastic, 2001. 214 pages. ISBN 0-439-09823-8. Lexile 870. Grades 4 to 6.
Relates the experiences of a poor, white, fifth-grade girl in the rural

South during the era of the Civil Rights Movement and school integration.

National Council for the Social Studies Notable Children's Trade-Books in the Field of Social Studies.

McKissack, Patricia C. *Goin' Someplace Special.*
Refer to complete information under Grades Kindergarten to 2.

Myers, Walter Dean. *Patrol: An American Soldier in Vietnam.*
Ann Grifalconi, illustrator. New York: HarperCollins Children's Book Group, 2002. 40 pages. ISBN 0-06-028363-7. Lexile 280. Grades 3 to 8.

The emotions of a frightened young American soldier fighting in the Vietnam War are demonstrated in this picture book for older readers.

The Bulletin for the Center for Children's Books Blue Ribbon Award, Children's Literature Choices, Jane Addams Children's Book Award, and *National Council for the Social Studies Notable Social Studies Trade Books for Young People.*

Murphy, Rita. *Black Angels.*
New York: Delacorte, 2001. 176 pages. ISBN 0-385-32776-5.
New York: Bantam Doubleday Dell Books for Young Readers, 2002. 176 pages. ISBN 0-440-22934-0pbk. Grades 5 to 7.

The actions of a small segregated southern town are examined through the life of a racially mixed eleven-year-old girl living in 1960s Georgia.

International Reading Association Notable Books for a Global Society.

Paulsen, Gary. *The Rifle.*
San Diego, CA: Harcourt Children's Books, 1995. 105 pages. ISBN 0-15-292880-4.
New York: Laurel Leaf Library, 1997. 105 pages. ISBN 0-440-21920-5pbk.
Prince Frederick, MD: Recorded Books unabridged audio, 1996. ISBN 0-7887-0529-6. Lexile 1480. Grades 5 to 9.

After building a handsome rifle, his greatest piece of work in 1768, gunsmith Cornish McManus is forced to sell it in order to support his family. The rifle becomes a testament to history as it passes from owner to owner, until it has a fatal impact in modern times.

National Council for the Social Studies Notable Children's Trade Books in the Field of Social Studies, and *New York Public Library Books for the Teen Age.*

Robinet, Harriette Gillem. *Walking to the Bus-Rider Blues.*
New York: Aladdin Paperbacks, 2002. 146 pages. ISBN 0-689-83886-7pbk. Lexile 550. Grades 3 to 6.

A mystery set during the 1956 Montgomery bus boycott encourages an adventurous twelve-year-old African American boy to prove his innocence after being accused of stealing.
Jane Addams Children's Book Award.

Slepian, Jan. *Risk n' Roses.*
New York: Philomel Books, 1990. 175 pages. ISBN 0-399-22219-7. (Out of print). Lexile 630. Grades 5 to 7.

In 1948, an eleven-year-old girl finally chooses to reject a manipulative friend after the friend hurts a kind man who is seeking family survivors of a World War II concentration camp.
The Bulletin of the Center for Children's Books Blue Ribbon Award.

Smucker, Anna Egan. *No Star Nights.*
Steve Johnson, illustrator. New York: Alfred A. Knopf, 1989. 48 pages. ISBN 0-394-99925-8 and 0-679-86724-4pbk. Lexile 980. Grades 3 to 6.

A young girl growing up within the shadows of a great steel mill in a coalmining area of Pennsylvania remembers red fires that lit the night sky.
American Library Association Notable Children's Books and *International Reading Association Children's Book Award.*

Taylor, Mildred. *The Gold Cadillac.*
Refer to complete information under Grades Kindergarten to 2.

Veciana-Suarez, Ana. *Flight to Freedom. ("First Person Fiction Series").*
New York: Orchard Books, 2002. 208 pages. ISBN 0-439-38199-1. Grades 6 to 9.

Thirteen-year-old Yara keeps a diary where she describes her transition through immigration from 1967 Havana, Cuba to her new life in Miami, Florida.
National Council for the Social Studies Notable Social Studies Trade Books for Young People.

White, Ruth. *Belle Prater's Boy.*
New York: Farrar, Straus & Giroux, 1996. 208 pages. ISBN 0-374-30668-0.
New York: Yearling, 1998. 196 pages. ISBN 0-440-41372-9.

New York: Bantam Books unabridged audio, 1998. ISBN 0-553-47898-2. Lexile 760. Grades 5 to 8.

When Belle Prater disappears, her boy Woodrow goes to live with his grandparents in Coal Station, Virginia. Woodrow's cousin Gypsy lives next door, and the two children find they have much in common. But unlike Woodrow, who has accepted his mother's disappearance, Gypsy cannot get over her father's suicide until Woodrow tells Gypsy the truth about his mother.

Boston Globe-Horn Book Award, International Reading Association Notable Books for a Global Society, Newbery Honor Book, and *School Library Journal Best Book.*

White, Ruth. *Sweet Creek Holler.*
First copyright, 1948. Topeka, KS: Econo-Clad Books, 1999. 215 pages. ISBN 0-8335-9157-6.
New York: Farrar, Straus & Giroux, 1992. ISBN 0-374-47375-7pbk. Lexile 790. Grades 5 to 8.

The story of a young girl's life in an Appalachian community after her father dies.

American Library Association Notable Children's Books.

Wiles, Deborah. *Freedom Summer.*
Refer to complete information under Grades Kindergarten to 2.

Woods, Brenda. *The Red Rose Box.*
New York: Penguin Putnam Books for Young Readers, 2002. 160 pages. ISBN 0-399-23702-X. Grades 4 to 6.

A ten-year-old girl experiences a taste of freedom when she is given the opportunity to leave the segregated South for a visit to California.

Coretta Scott King Award Honor Book and *International Reading Association Notable Books for a Global Society.*

Grades 7 and 8

Boutis, Victoria. *Looking Out.*
Refer to complete information under Grades 3 to 6.

Brooks, Bruce. *The Moves Make the Man.*
New York: HarperCollins Children's Book Group, 1984. 280 pages. ISBN 0-06-020698-5 and 0-06-440564-8pbk.
Prince Frederick, MD: Recorded Books unabridged audio, 1996. ISBN

0-7887-0829-5. Lexile 1150. Grades 7 to Young Adult.

The only African American boy in his North Carolina high school and an emotionally troubled white boy form a precarious friendship in the 1960s.

American Library Association Best of the Best Books, 1966 to 1992; American Library Association Notable Children's Books; Boston Globe-Horn Book Award; Newbery Honor Book; and *School Library Journal Best Book.*

Curtis, Christopher Paul. *The Watsons Go to Birmingham–1963.*
Refer to complete information under Grades 3 to 6.

Crowe, Chris. *Mississippi Trial, 1955.*
Refer to complete information under Grades 3 to 6.

Easton, Kelly. *The Life History of a Star.*
New York: Simon & Schuster, 2001. 208 pages. ISBN 0-689-83134-X and 0-689-85270-3pbk. Lexile 650. Grades 7 to Young Adult.

In diary entries, fourteen-year-old Kristin records the events of a tumultuous year in 1973. She chronicles her mother's struggle with alcoholism, while her brother who was severely wounded in Vietnam spends most of his time in the attic.

Golden Kite Award Honor Book.

Enger, Leif. *Peace Like a River.*
Refer to complete information under Grades 3 to 6.

Herschler, Mildred Barger. *The Darkest Corner.*
Refer to complete information under Grades 3 to 6.

Hobbs, Valerie. *Sonny's War.*
New York: Frances Foster Books, 2002. 224 pages. ISBN 0-374-37136-9. Grades 7 to 10.

Societal conflicts over the Vietnam War and the emotional damage of soldiers who participated is examined in this novel where a teenage girl watches her brother be forever changed from his tour of duty.

Children's Literature Choices.

Holt, Kimberly Willis. *When Zachary Beaver Came to Town.*
Refer to complete information under Grades 3 to 6.

Jones, Adrienne. *Long Time Passing.*
New York: HarperCollins Children's Book Group, 1990. 245 pages.
ISBN 0-06-023056-8. (Out of print). Grades 7 to Young Adult.

Jonas makes the difficult decision to enroll in the army in 1969 in an attempt to find his father who is missing in action in Vietnam.
New York Public Library Books for the Teen Age.

Layden, Joseph and Virginia Euwer Wolff. *Bat 6.*
Refer to complete information under Grades 3 to 6.

Les Becquets, Diane. *The Stones of Mourning Creek.*
New York: Winslow Press, 2001. 250 pages. ISBN 1-58837-004-6. Lexile 670. Grades 7 to 10.

In 1960s rural Alabama, fourteen-year-old Francie's mother is murdered while trying to save an African American girl from rape. Francie befriends the young girl while she suffers neglect from her alcoholic father and persecution from the town's most evil and powerful man.
American Library Association Best Books for Young Adults and *Children's Literature Choices.*

Levitin, Sonia. *Dream Freedom.*
Refer to complete information under Grades 3 to 6.

Marino, Jan. *The Day That Elvis Came to Town.*
Refer to complete information under Grades 3 to 6.

Myers, Walter Dean. *Patrol: An American Soldier in Vietnam.*
Refer to complete information under Grades 3 to 6.

Murphy, Rita. *Black Angels.*
Refer to complete information under Grades 3 to 6.

Nelson, Theresa. *And One For All.*
New York: Orchard Books, 1989. 182 pages. ISBN 0-531-05804-2.
New York: Yearling, 1991. 182 pages. 0-440-40456-8pbk. Lexile 850.
Grades 7 to Young Adult.

Geraldine's close relationship with her older brother Wing and his friend Sam changes when Wing joins the Marines and Sam leaves for Washington to join a peace march. Geraldine attempts to keep their pledge of friendship intact.
American Library Association Notable Children's Books and *School Library Journal Best Book.*

O'Brien, Tim. *The Things They Carried.*
New York: Houghton Mifflin Co., 1990. 273 pages. ISBN 0-395-51598-X.
New York: Broadway Books, 1999. 246 pages. ISBN 0-7679-0289-0pbk.
Lexile 880. Grades 8 to Young Adult.
A collection of short stories reflecting the author's experiences in Vietnam.
American Library Association 100 Best Books for Teens and Pulitzer Prize Finalist.

Paulsen, Gary. *The Rifle.*
Refer to complete information under Grades 3 to 6.

Slepian, Jan. *Risk n' Roses.*
Refer to complete information under Grades 3 to 6.

Veciana-Suarez, Ana. *Flight to Freedom. ("First Person Fiction Series").*
Refer to complete information under Grades 3 to 6.

Weaver, Will. *Farm Team.*
New York: HarperCollins Children's Book Group, 1995. 283 pages. ISBN 0-06-023589-6 and 0-06-447118-7pbk. Lexile 700. Grades 8 to Young Adult.
After his father is jailed for bulldozing the used-car lot that cheated him, fourteen-year-old Billy Baggs and his mother fashion a baseball field on their Minnesota farm and build an unusual team with unexpected results.
American Library Association Best Books for Young Adults.

Weaver, Will. *Striking Out.*
Topeka, KS: Econo-Clad Books, 1999. 272 pages. ISBN 0-7857-6156-X.
New York: HarperTrophy, 1999. 288 pages. ISBN 0-06-447113-6pbk.
Lexile 540. Grades 7 to Young Adult.
Ever since the death of his older brother, thirteen-year-old Billy Baggs has had a distant relationship with his father, but life on their farm in northern Minnesota begins to change when he starts to play baseball in 1970.
American Bookseller Pick of the Lists, American Library Association Best Books for Young Adults, and *New York Public Library Books for the Teen Age.*

White, Ellen. *The Road Home.*
New York: Scholastic, 1995. 469 pages. ISBN 0-590-46737-9. (Out of print). Lexile 850. Grades 8 to Young Adult.

Twenty-two-year-old Rebecca Phillips is a nurse who has seen bloodshed, horror, and suffering in Vietnam. When her helicopter crashes in the jungle, she faces a brutal showdown for survival that changes her and makes it difficult to cope once she returns to Boston, so she travels to Colorado to locate a fellow survivor.

American Library Association Best Books for Young Adults.

White, Ruth. *Belle Prater's Boy.*
Refer to complete information under Grades 3 to 6.

White, Ruth. *Sweet Creek Holler.*
Refer to complete information under Grades 3 to 6.

II

WORLD HISTORY

Chapter 12

Prehistory and the Ancient World
to the 5th Century

Grades Kindergarten to 2

Demi. *The Donkey and the Rock.*
New York: Henry Holt & Co., 1999. 32 pages. ISBN 0-8050-5959-8.
Lexile AD750. Grades K to 3.

A Tibetan King ruling a town full of foolish people puts a donkey and a rock on trial to settle a dispute between two honest men in 550 B.C.

Aesop Accolade.

Zeman, Ludmila. *The Last Quest of Gilgamesh.*
Plattsburgh, New York: Tundra Books of Northern New York, 1995. 22 pages. ISBN 0-88776-328-6 and 0-88776-380-4pbk. Grades K to 6.

An intricately illustrated retelling of the Epic of Gilgamesh that was first carved onto clay tablets in Mesopotamia five thousand years ago.

Governor General's Award for Children's Literature.

Grades 3 to 6

Chaikin, Miriam. *Alexandra's Scroll: The Story of the First Hanukkah.*
New York: Henry Holt & Co., 2002. 115 pages. ISBN 0-8050-6384-6.
Grades 4 to 7.

A young Jewish girl keeps a diary that describes the events of the Maccabee-led Jewish rebellion that is remembered with the celebration of Hanukkah.

Association of Jewish Libraries Award Notable Book.

Cooney, Caroline. *Goddess of Yesterday.*
New York: Delacorte, 2002. 264 pages. ISBN 0-385-72945-6.
New York: Laurel Leaf Library, 2003. 272 pages. ISBN 0-440-22930-8pbk. Lexile 730. Grades 6 to 9.

A young hostage survives a brutal attack by pirates and assumes a different identity to assure her safety. Rescued by King Menalaus, she watches as events in ancient Sparta lead to the bloody siege of Troy.

American Library Association Notable Children's Books, Child Study Children's Book Committee at Bank Street College of Education Award, and *Josette Frank Award.*

Demi. *The Donkey and the Rock.*
Refer to complete information under Grades Kindergarten to 2.

Geras, Adele. *Troy.*
San Diego, CA: Harcourt Children's Books, 2001. 352 pages. ISBN 0-15-216492-8. Lexile 670. Grades 6 to 9.

The classic struggle between Greece and Troy as seen through the eyes of two sisters.

American Library Association Best Books for Young Adults and *Boston Globe-Horn Book Award Honor Book.*

Kindl, Patrice. *Lost in the Labyrinth.*
New York: Houghton Mifflin Company, 2002. 194 pages. ISBN 0-618-16684-X. Grades 5 to 9.

The ancient Greek legend of Theseus and the Minotaur is told through the eyes of the kind fourteen-year-old, Xenodice, the younger sister of ruthless Ariadne.

National Council for the Social Studies Notable Social Studies Trade Books for Young People.

Lawrence, Caroline. *The Thieves of Ostia.*
Brookfield, CT: Roaring Book Press, 2002. 160 pages. ISBN 0-7613-1582-9.
London: Orion Publishing, 2002. 160 pages. ISBN 1-84255-020-9. Grades 3 to 6.

A group of young children solve a local mystery in this novel that is rich with descriptions of ancient Roman life.

Children's Literature Choices.

Lester, Julius. *Pharaoh's Daughter: A Novel of Ancient Egypt.*
San Diego, CA: Silver Whistle, 2000. 192 pages. ISBN 0-15-201826-3.

New York: HarperTrophy, 2002. 192 pages. ISBN 0-06-440469-4. Lexile 720. Grades 4 to 6.

The Biblical story of Moses as seen through the eyes of a brother and sister.

International Reading Association Children's Choices.

McGraw, Eloise. *The Golden Goblet.*
First copyright 1961. Magnolia, MA: Peter Smith Publishers, 1988. 248 pages. ISBN 0-8446-6342-5. Lexile 930. Grades 5 to 9.

In this ancient Egyptian mystery, a young boy named Ranofer thwarts his evil half-brother's attempt to steal a golden goblet and assures himself a place as a goldsmith's apprentice because of his courage.

Newbery Honor Book.

Moss, Marissa. *Galen: My Life in Imperial Rome. ("Ancient World Journals Series").*
San Diego, CA: Silver Whistle, 2002. 56 pages. ISBN 0-15-21635-5. Grades 3 to 6.

Ancient Roman life is depicted through the life of a twelve-year-old slave boy living in Augustus Caesar's household.

National Council for the Social Studies Notable Social Studies Trade Books for Young People.

Osborne, Mary Pope. *The Land of the Dead. ("Tales from the Odyssey, 2").*
New York: Hyperion, 2002. 105 pages. ISBN 0-7868-0771-7 and 0-7868-0929-9pbk. Grades 4 to 8.

This second book based on the ancient tales by Homer retells the continuous trials that occur to Odysseus and his men after they defeat the one-eyed giant and continue towards home.

Publishers Weekly Best Children's Books.

Osborne, Mary Pope. *The One-Eyed Giant. ("Tales from the Odyssey, 1").*
New York: Hyperion, 2002. 105 pages. ISBN 0-7868-07709 and 0-7868-0928-0pbk. Lexile 700. Grades 4 to 8.

First in a series of books based on the ancient tales of Homer. Odysseus fights in the Trojan War and encounters many dangerous, mythological creatures on his perilous journey home.

Publishers Weekly Best Children's Books.

Spinner, Stephanie. *Quiver.*
New York: The Knopf Publishing Group, 2002. 176 pages. ISBN 0-375-81489-2. Lexile 730. Grades 6 to 10.

A retelling of the classic legend of Atalanta, the fleet-footed female warrior who could outrun any man in ancient Greece.

National Council for the Social Studies Notable Social Studies Trade Books for Young People.

Sutcliff, Rosemary. *The Lantern Bearers.*
New York: Peter Smith Publishers, 1994. 248 pages.
ISBN 0-8446-6837-0.
New York: Farrar, Straus & Giroux, 1994. 281 pages. ISBN 0-374-44302-5pbk.
Ashland, OR: Blackstone Audio Books unabridged audio, 2001. ISBN 0-7861-1991-8 and 0-7861-9733-1cd. Lexile 1210. Grades 5 to 8.

Describing the end of the Roman Empire and the creation of Anglo-Saxon Britain, a young soldier fights to keep a lantern lit during the dark days of the barbarian invasions of Rome in 450 A.D.

American Library Association Notable Children's Books.

Sutcliff, Rosemary. *Warrior Scarlet.*
Charles Keeping, illustrator. First copyright 1958. Topeka, KS: Econo-Clad Books, 1999. 240 pages. ISBN 0-7857-5713-9.
New York: Farrar, Straus & Giroux, 1995. 207 pages. ISBN 0-374-48244-6pbk. Grades 5 to 9.

In Bronze Age Britain, a young boy must kill a wolf to earn the right to wear a scarlet cloak and obtain the status of tribal warrior. Drem fails because of his disabled arm and is outcast by his tribe, which later reconsiders the law when Drem succeeds in killing three wolves while protecting another outcast.

Carnegie Medal Commendation and *International Board on Books for Young People.*

Zeman, Ludmila. *The Last Quest of Gilgamesh.*
Refer to complete information under Grades Kindergarten to 2.

Grades 7 and 8

Bradshaw, Gillian. *The Sand-Reckoner.*
New York: Forge, 2000. 352 pages. ISBN 0-312-87340-9 and 0-312-87581-9pbk. Lexile 840. Grades 7 to 10.
   Young Archimedes is called away from a delightful three years of study at the museum of Ptolemy in Alexandria to help defend his ailing father and hometown of Syracuse from the invading Romans. There he finds fame as the royal engineer as well as love and betrayal.
   Alex Award.

Chaikin, Miriam. *Alexandra's Scroll: The Story of the First Hanukkah.*
   Refer to complete information under Grades 3 to 6.

Cooney, Caroline. *Goddess of Yesterday.*
   Refer to complete information under Grades 3 to 6.

Geras, Adele. *Troy.*
   Refer to complete information under Grades 3 to 6.

Haugaard, Erik. *The Rider and His Horse.*
Leo Dillon and Diane Dillon, illustrators. New York: Houghton Mifflin Co., 1968. 243 pages. ISBN 0-395-06801-0. (Out of print.) Grades 7 to 10.
   A young Jewish man battles at Masada against the Romans and lives to create a true historical record of events.
   Phoenix Award.

Kindl, Patrice. *Lost in the Labyrinth.*
   Refer to complete information under Grades 3 to 6.

McGraw, Eloise. *The Golden Goblet.*
   Refer to complete information under Grades 3 to 6.

Osborne, Mary Pope. *The Land of the Dead. ("Tales from the Odyssey, 2").*
   Refer to complete information under Grades 3 to 6.

Osborne, Mary Pope. *The One-Eyed Giant. ("Tales from the Odyssey, 1").*
   Refer to complete information under Grades 3 to 6.

Speare, Elizabeth George. *The Bronze Bow.*
First copyright 1961. Topeka, KS: Econo-Clad Books, 1999. 256 pages. ISBN 0-8085-3900-0.
New York: Houghton Mifflin Co., 1997. 254 pages. ISBN 0-395-13719-5pbk.
Prince Frederick, MD: Recorded Books unabridged audio, 2001. ISBN 0-7887-5363-9. Lexile 760. Grades 7 to Young Adult.

Eighteen-year-old Daniel resents the Palestinian Romans after they crucify his father and uncle. He is sold to a blacksmith who leaves his work to follow Jesus of Galilee. Daniel is slowly won over by the teachings of the gentle man.

International Board on Books for Young People and *Newbery Medal.*

Spinner, Stephanie. *Quiver.*
Refer to complete information under Grades 3 to 6.

Sutcliff, Rosemary. *The Lantern Bearers.*
Refer to complete information under Grades 3 to 6.

Sutcliff, Rosemary. *The Mark of the Horse Lord.*
First copyright 1965. New York: Bantam Dell Publishing Group, 1989. 276 pages. ISBN 0-440-40161-5pbk. (Out of print). Lexile 1240. Grades 7 to 10.

A Roman slave gladiator kills his opponent and wins his freedom to pose as his twin brother, King Midir of Dalardian, in order to help save his people from the enemy.

Phoenix Award.

Sutcliff, Rosemary. *Warrior Scarlet.*
Refer to complete information under Grades 3 to 6.

Chapter 13

Europe–5th to 15th Centuries: Dark Ages, Middle Ages, and Renaissance

Grades Kindergarten to 2

DePaola, Tomie. *Strega Nona.*
New York: Simon & Schuster, 1989. 40 pages. ISBN 0-671-66283-X and 0-671-66606-1pbk.
Prince Frederick, MD: Recorded Books unabridged audio, 1999. ISBN 0-7887-2621-8. Lexile 800. Grades K to 3.

When Strega Nona leaves Big Anthony alone with her magic pot, he is determined to show the townspeople how it works in this ancient tale set in a Medieval village.

American Library Association Notable Children's Books, Caldecott Silver Medal, and *Horn Book Fanfare Honor List.*

Grades 3 to 6

Alder, Elizabeth. *The King's Shadow.*
New York: Farrar, Straus & Giroux, 1995. 259 pages. ISBN 0-374-34182-6.
New York: Bantam Books, 1997. 259 pages. ISBN 0-440-22011-4pbk.
Prince Frederick, MD: Recorded Books unabridged audio, 1998. ISBN 0-7887-1782-0. Lexile 940. Grades 6 to 9.

The story of a young Welsh surf, Evyn, who is rendered mute after an attack and sold to the wife of Harold Godwinson, who eventually becomes Britain's last Saxon King. Evyn follows King Harold loyally until Harold is killed at the Battle of Hastings in 1066. Evyn's dream of becoming a storyteller is realized when he chronicles King Harold's life in writing.

American Library Association Best Books for Young Adults.

Avi. *Crispin: The Cross of Lead.*
New York: Hyperion, 2002. 262 pages. ISBN 0-7868-0828-4 and 0-7868-1658-9pbk.
Prince Frederick, MD: Recorded Books unabridged audio, 2002. ISBN 1-4025-2202-9. Lexile 780. Grades 5 to 9.

Falsely accused of a crime, thirteen-year-old Crispin is aided by a tenderhearted traveling juggler during a terrifying journey across the English countryside while carrying mother's lead cross. Revealed throughout are the motivations for the peasant uprising of 1381.

American Library Association Notable Children's Books, Children's Literature Choices, National Council for the Social Studies Notable Social Studies Trade Books for Young People, and *Newbery Medal.*

Buff, Conrad and Mary. *The Apple and the Arrow.*
New York: Houghton Mifflin Co., 2001. 80 pages. ISBN 0-618-12807-7 and 0-618-12809-3pbk. Lexile 750. Grades 3 to 6.

The legend of William Tell and the 1291 Swiss struggle for freedom from the Austrians is retold from the point of view of William Tell's twelve-year-old son.

Newbery Honor Book.

Cadnum, Michael. *The Book of the Lion.*
New York: Viking, 2000. 220 pages. ISBN 0-670-88386-7.
New York: Puffin Books, 2001. 208 pages. ISBN 0-14-230034-9pbk. Lexile 980. Grades 6 to 9.

After a knight rescues him while he is awaiting trial for a counterfeiting charge, a teenage boy named Edmund finds himself fighting in the 12th century Crusades. Through his experiences, Edmund learns courage and compassion while experiencing storms at sea and the brutality of hand-to-hand combat at the Battle of Arsuf.

National Book Award for Young People's Literature Finalist.

Crossley-Holland, Kevin. *At the Crossing Places. ("Arthur Trilogy 2").*
Michael Maloney, narrator. New York: Scholastic, 2002. 352 pages. ISBN 0-439-26598-3 and 0-439-26599-1pbk.
Old Greenwich, CT: Listening Library unabridged audio, 2002. ISBN 0-8072-0540-0.
Old Greenwich, CT: Listening Library abridged audio, 2002. ISBN 0-8072-0548-6. Lexile 650. Grades 6 to 9.

Thirteen-year-old Arthur lives with Lord Stephen at Holt to begin his training as squire while preparing to become a Crusader.
Smithsonian Magazine Notable Books for Children.

Crossley-Holland, Kevin. *The Seeing Stone. ("Arthur Trilogy 1").*
New York: Scholastic, 2001. 340 pages. ISBN 0-439-26326-3 and 0-439-26327-1pbk.
New York: Bantam Books unabridged audio, 2001. ISBN 0-8072-0538-9. Lexile 640. Grades 5 to 7.

Thirteen-year-old Arthur lives in 12th century Medieval England. His friend Merlin gives him a magical obsidian that allows him to travel back to the time of the legendary King Arthur.
American Library Association Notable Children's Books, Booklist Editors' Choice, and *National Council for the Social Studies Notable Children's Trade Books in the Field of Social Studies.*

Cushman, Karen. *The Midwife's Apprentice.*
New York: Clarion Books, 1995. 122 pages. ISBN 0-395-69229-6.
New York: HarperTrophy, 1996. 122 pages. ISBN 0-06-440630-Xpbk.
New York: Bantam Books abridged audio, 1996. ISBN 0-553-47798-6.
Old Greenwich, CT: Listening Library audio, 2000. ISBN 0-8072-8281-2. Lexile 1240. Grades 5 to 9.

In 13th to 14th century Medieval England, a midwife finds a twelve-year-old homeless girl named Brat burrowing into a dung heap to keep herself warm. The midwife apprentices her and renames her Beetle. Beetle renames herself Alyce as she gains proficiency in her skill as a midwife and survives her employer's harsh treatment.
American Bookseller Pick of the Lists, American Library Association Best Books for Young Adults, American Library Association Notable Children's Books, Booklist Editors' Choice, Horn Book Fanfare Honor List, Newbery Medal, and *School Library Journal Best Book.*

Czarnota, Lorna MacDonald. *Medieval Tales: That Kids Can Read and Tell.*
New York: August House, 2000. 96 pages. ISBN 0-87483-589-5 and 0-87483-588-7pbk. Grades 3 to 6.

Simplified versions of many Medieval tales arranged by country and accompanied by suggested classroom activities.
Youth Storytelling Pegasus Award.

De Angeli, Marguerite. *The Door in the Wall: A Story of Medieval London.*
First copyright 1949. New York: Doubleday Broadway Publishing Group, 1989. 129 pages. ISBN 0-385-07283-X.
New York: Yearling, 1990. 121 pages. ISBN 0-440-40283-2pbk.
New York: Bantam Books unabridged audio, 1998. ISBN 0-553-52522-0.
Old Greenwich, CT: Listening Library abridged audio, 2002. ISBN 0-8072-0872-8. Lexile 990. Grades 3 to 7.

A 14th century story of a boy's triumph over his handicap that results in knighthood. After his legs are rendered useless by the plague, Robin is taken to a monastery to recover where he is educated, taught woodcarving, and physically strengthened by swimming. While waiting for his parents, his castle is attacked and Robin becomes a hero.
Lewis Carroll Shelf Award and *Newbery Medal.*

DePaola, Tomie. *Strega Nona.*
Refer to complete information under Grades Kindergarten to 2.

Ellis, Deborah, Celia Godkin, and Shirley Woods. *A Company of Fools.*
Ontario, Canada: Fitzhenry & Whiteside, 2002. 180 pages. ISBN 1-55041-719-3. Lexile 740. Grades 6 to 8.

The effects of the Black Plague are revealed through the experiences of a choir student and a newly arrived street boy in a 1348 Paris Abbey.
Canadian Library Association Book of the Year for Children Award Honor Book.

Harnett, Cynthia. *The Cargo of the Madalena.*
First copyright 1959. Minneapolis, MN: The Lerner Publishing Group, 1984. 236 pages. ISBN 0-8225-0890-7. (Out of print). Grades 5 to 9.

In 1492, William Caxton hires Benny, despite his scrivener brother's resistance, and brings the printing press to England. This advancement supports an attempt to dethrone Edward IV.
Carnegie Medal Commendation.

Harnett, Cynthia. *The Merchant's Mark.*
First copyright 1951. Minneapolis, MN: The Lerner Publishing Group, 1984. 192 pages. ISBN 0-8225-0891-5. (Out of print). Grades 5 to 10.

In 1493 England, fifteen-year-old Nicholas, the son of a wealthy wool merchant, manages to unmask a plot designed to ruin his father's business.

Carnegie Medal.

Harris, Robert J. and Jane Yolen. *Girl in a Cage.*
New York: Philomel Books, 2002. 240 pages. ISBN 0-399-23627-9.
Lexile 690. Grades 5 to 9.

An eleven-year-old Princess, daughter of king of Scotland Robert the
Bruce, is kidnapped and put on display in a cage by the ruthless rival
king of England in 1306.

American Library Association Best Books for Young Adults, Children's Literature Choices, National Council for the Social Studies Notable Social Studies Trade Books for Young People, and *School Library Journal Best Book.*

Hendry, Frances Mary. *Quest for a Maid.*
New York: Farrar, Straus & Giroux, 1992. 273 pages. ISBN 0-374-36162-2 and 0-374-46155-4pbk. Lexile 930. Grades 5 to 9.

In 13th century Scotland, nine-year-old Meg tries to protect a young
Norwegian princess, the rightful heir to the Scottish throne, after King
Alexander of Scotland dies from suspected sorcery.

American Library Association Notable Children's Book and *The Bulletin of the Center for Children's Books Blue Ribbon Award.*

Konigsburg, E. L. *A Proud Taste for Scarlet and Miniver.*
New York: Atheneum Books for Young Readers, 1973. 201 pages. ISBN 0-689-3011-1.
New York: Yearling, 1985. 208 pages. ISBN 0-440-47201-6pbk. Lexile 770. Grades 6 to 9.

Eleanor of Aquitaine (1122 to 1204) tells stories of her life with
three others who remember her while she waits for her husband, Henry
II, to join her in heaven. Eleanor recalls her roles as the mother of two
kings and the wife of two others while living in Medieval France and
England.

Phoenix Award Honor Book.

Llorente, Pilar Molina. *The Apprentice.*
Juan Ramon Alonso, translator. First copyright, 1989. New York: Farrar, Straus & Giroux, 1993. 101 pages. ISBN 0-374-30389-4 and 0-374-40432-1pbk. Lexile 730. Grades 6 to 9.

Living in Florence, Italy, during the Renaissance, thirteen-year-old
Arduino dreams of becoming a painter and apprentices himself to a cruel
master. He finds another talented apprentice chained in the attic and frees

him to finish a commitment during their master's illness.
Mildred L. Batchelder Award.

Llywelyn, Morgan. *Brian Boru: Emperor of the Irish.*
New York: Tor Books, 1995. 160 pages. ISBN 0-312-85623-7 and 0-8125-4461-7pbk. Grades 6 to 9.

Brian Boru witnessed the murder of his mother and two of his brothers at the hands of Viking invaders as a child. He vows to avenge their deaths as he studies to become a great leader of United Ireland.
Irish Children's Book Trust Book of the Year.

Morpurgo, Michael. *Arthur, High King of Britain.*
Michael Foreman, illustrator. San Diego, CA: Harcourt Children's Books, 1995. 144 pages. ISBN 0-15-200080-1. Lexile 760. Grades 4 to 7.

King Arthur tells his legends to a twelve-year-old boy who lies in a cave recovering from a near-drowning.
Storytelling World Award Honor Book.

Skurzynski, Gloria. *What Happened in Hamelin.*
First copyright 1979. New York: Peter Smith Publishers, 1993. 192 pages. ISBN 0-8446-6828-1.
New York: Random House, 1993. 192 pages. ISBN 0-679-83645-3pbk. Grades 5 to 9.

In a chilling version of the classic Pied Piper story, a gypsy piper named Gast frees a town from a rat infestation but does not receive his final payment, so he leads the children away from the town, and plans to sell them back for a piece of silver each.
Booklist Reviewer's Choice, Christopher Award, and *Horn Book Fanfare Honor List.*

Sutcliff, Rosemary. *The Shining Company.*
New York: Farrar, Straus & Giroux, 1990. 304 pages. ISBN 0-374-36807-4 and 0-374-46616-5pbk.
Prince Frederick, MD: Recorded Books unabridged audio, 1994. ISBN 0-7887-0133-9. Lexile 1240. Grades 6 to 10.

Set in 600 A.D. Britain, a young shield bearer witnesses a devastating battle against the Saxons near York. He travels to Constantinople with another survivor to escape his loneliness.
American Library Association Notable Children's Books.

Vining, Elizabeth Gray and Elizabeth Janet Gray. *Adam of the Road.*
Robert Lawson, illustrator. First copyright 1942. New York: Viking, 1984. 320 pages. ISBN 0-670-10435-3 and 0-14-032464-Xpbk.
Pine Plains, NY: Live Oak Media audio, 1980. ISBN 0-670-10437-X.
Lexile 1030. Grades 4 to 7.

Eleven-year-old Adam loses his minstrel father at a fair and spends the next year wandering 13th century England looking for him and their dog.
Newbery Medal.

Grades 7 and 8

Alder, Elizabeth. *The King's Shadow.*
Refer to complete information under Grades 3 to 6.

Avi. *Crispin: The Cross of Lead.*
Refer to complete information under Grades 3 to 6.

Cadnum, Michael. *The Book of the Lion.*
Refer to complete information under Grades 3 to 6.

Cadnum, Michael. *Forbidden Forest: The Story of Little John and Robin Hood.*
New York: Orchard Books, 2002. 218 pages. ISBN 0-439-31774-6. Lexile 960. Grades 7 to 10.

Little John escapes the Sheriff of Nottingham's men after an accidental killing, joins Robin Hood, and protects a beautiful lady wrongfully accused of murder.
Smithsonian Magazine Notable Books for Children.

Crichton, Michael. *Timeline.*
New York: Random House, 1999. 449 pages. ISBN 0-679-44481-5.
New York: Ballantine Books, 2000. 496 pages. ISBN 0-345-41762-3pbk.
New York: Bantam Books unabridged audio, 1999. ISBN 0-375-40437-6.
New York: Bantam Books abridged audio, 1999. ISBN 0-375-40435-X and 0-375-40436-8cd. Lexile 620. Grades 7 to Adult.

Modern historians use scientific advances to travel back in time to 1357 Medieval France. They find danger in this era ruled by cruel lords, power-hungry abbots, scheming ladies, and ferocious knights.
American Library Association Best Books for Young Adults.

Crossley-Holland, Kevin. *At the Crossing Places. ("Arthur Trilogy 2").*
Refer to complete information under Grades 3 to 6.

Crossley-Holland, Kevin. *The Seeing Stone.*
Refer to complete information under Grades 3 to 6.

Cushman, Karen. *Catherine Called Birdy.*
New York: Clarion Books, 1994. 169 pages. ISBN 0-395-68186-3.
New York: HarperTrophy, 1995. 224 pages. ISBN 0-06-440584-2pbk.
New York: Bantam Books unabridged audio, 1996. ISBN 0-553-47669-6.
Old Greenwich, CT: Listening Library abridged audio, 2002. ISBN 0-8072-0870-1. Lexile 1170. Grades 7 to 10.
Fourteen-year-old Catherine details Medieval life in 1290 England through her diary. She expresses courage and tenacity at trying to evade the suitors her father is arranging for her betrothal as a way to pay off his debts.
American Library Association Best Books for Young Adults, American Library Association Notable Children's Books, Booklist Editors' Choice, Carl Sandburg Award, Golden Kite Award, Newbery Honor Book, Parenting Magazine Ten Best, and *School Library Journal Best Book.*

Cushman, Karen. *The Midwife's Apprentice.*
Refer to complete information under Grades 3 to 6.

De Angeli, Marguerite. *Black Fox of Lorne.*
New York: Doubleday Broadway Publishing Group, 1956. 191 pages. ISBN 0-385-08300-9. (Out of print). Grades 7 to 10.
Scottish twins go to live with their father, Harald Redbeard, in 950 A.D., but one of them is captured after their father is killed. The twins exchange places, deal with adversity, are exposed to Christianity, and are eventually reunited with their mother.
Newbery Honor Book.

De Angeli, Marguerite. *The Door in the Wall: A Story of Medieval London.*
Refer to complete information under Grades 3 to 6.

Ellis, Deborah, Celia Godkin, and Shirley Woods. *A Company of Fools.*
Refer to complete information under Grades 3 to 6.

Harnett, Cynthia. *The Cargo of the Madalena.*
Refer to complete information under Grades 3 to 6.

Harnett, Cynthia. *The Merchant's Mark.*
Refer to complete information under Grades 3 to 6.

Harris, Robert J. and Jane Yolen. *Girl in a Cage.*
Refer to complete information under Grades 3 to 6.

Hendry, Frances Mary. *Quest for a Maid.*
Refer to complete information under Grades 3 to 6.

Kelly, Eric. *The Trumpeter of Krakow.*
Janina Domanska, illustrator. First copyright 1928. New York: Simon & Schuster, 1968. 224 pages. ISBN 0-02-750140-X.
New York: Aladdin Paperbacks, 1992. 208 pages. ISBN 0-689-71571-4pbk.
New York: American School Publishers unabridged audio, 1985. ISBN 0-394-77134-6. Lexile 1200. Grades 7 to Young Adult.
The story of a destitute boy living in 1400s Krakow, Poland. Joseph and his family hide a treasure while living with an alchemist's family that is assisting them. At fifteen, Joseph becomes a trumpeter in a Krakow church and continues the tradition of a heroic young trumpeter who lived two centuries earlier.
Newbery Medal.

Konigsburg, E. L. *A Proud Taste for Scarlet and Miniver.*
Refer to complete information under Grades 3 to 6.

Llorente, Pilar Molina. *The Apprentice.*
Refer to complete information under Grades 3 to 6.

Llywelyn, Morgan. *Brian Boru: Emperor of the Irish.*
Refer to complete information under Grades 3 to 6.

Morpurgo, Michael. *Arthur, High King of Britain.*
Refer to complete information under Grades 3 to 6.

Skurzynski, Gloria. *What Happened in Hamelin.*
Refer to complete information under Grades 3 to 6.

Sutcliff, Rosemary. *The Shining Company.*
Refer to complete information under Grades 3 to 6.

Tingle, Rebecca. *The Edge on the Sword.*
New York: Penguin Putnam, 2001. 277 pages. ISBN 0-399-23580-9.
Prince Frederick, MD: Recorded Books unabridged audio, 2002. ISBN
1-4025-1457-3. Lexile 930. Grades 7 to 10.

Fifteen-year-old Aethelflaed, daughter of the 800s King Alfred of West Saxon, must fight off villains as she makes a journey to wed the King's friend, Ethelred. She later becomes the most renowned queen of the Saxons.

American Library Association Best Books for Young Adults and *Children's Literature Choices.*

Vining, Elizabeth Gray and Elizabeth Janet Gray. *Adam of the Road.*
Refer to complete information under Grades 3 to 6.

Chapter 14

Europe–16th to 18th Centuries: Discovery, Reformation, Enlightenment, and Liberty

Grades Kindergarten to 2

Hodges, Margaret. *Saint George and the Dragon: A Golden Legend.*
Trina Schart Hyman, illustrator. Boston: Little, Brown & Company, 1984. 32 pages. ISBN 0-316-36789-3 and 0-316-36795-8pbk. Lexile AD1080. Grades 1 to 5.
A beautifully illustrated retelling of Edmund Spenser's 16th century poem featuring a ferocious three-day battle between St. George and the dragon. The illustrations reflect the religious art of the Middle Ages.
Caldecott Medal.

Grades 3 to 6

Blackwood, Gary. *Shakespeare's Scribe.*
Lucia Monfried, editor. New York: Dutton Children's Books, 2000. 224 pages. ISBN 0-525-46444-1.
New York: Puffin Books, 2002. 272 pages. ISBN 0-14-230066-7pbk. Lexile 870. Grades 4 to 6.
Set in 1600s London just after the black plague, an orphaned actor transcribing for the injured Shakespeare wins a coveted role in the play.
American Library Association Best Books for Reluctant Young Readers.

Bulla, Clyde Robert. *A Lion to Guard Us.*
Michele Chessare, illustrator. New York: HarperCollins Children's Book Group, 1981. 118 pages. ISBN 0-690-04097-0.

New York: HarperTrophy, 1989. 116 pages. ISBN 0-06-440333-5pbk. Lexile 360. Grades 3 to 6.

In 1609 London, three poverty-stricken children draw upon all their inner resources to stay together and make their way to the Virginia colony, Jamestown, in search of their father.

National Council for the Social Studies Notable Children's Trade Books in the Field of Social Studies.

Cooper, Susan. *King of Shadows.*
New York: Simon & Schuster, 1999. 186 pages. ISBN 0-689-82817-9 and 0-689-84445-Xpbk.
New York: Bantam Books unabridged audio, 2000. ISBN 0-8072-8242-1. Lexile 1010. Grades 5 to 8.

A young actor travels back in time to 1599, saves William Shakespeare's life, and performs with him at the Globe Theatre, only to awaken in contemporary times.

Booklist Editors' Choice.

Garfield, Leon. *The December Rose.*
New York: Viking, 1987. 208 pages. ISBN 0-670-81054-1. (Out of print). Grades 6 to 9.

The story of a delinquent thief in 18th century London and his eventual reform.

School Library Journal Best Book.

Garfield, Leon. *Devil-in-the-Fog.*
First copyright 1966. Magnolia, MA: Peter Smith Publishers, 1991. 205 pages. ISBN 0-8446-6452-9. (Out of print). Grades 5 to 8.

Fourteen-year-old George Treet is sold to the Dexters to act as their heir.

Guardian Fiction Prize.

Garfield, Leon. *The Empty Sleeve.*
New York: Doubleday Broadway Publishing Group, 1988. 207 pages. ISBN 0-385-29817-X. (Out of print). Grades 6 to 8.

Twins in 18th century England receive identical carved ships encased in glass from an old man. After the ships are switched, one twin leaves home as a locksmith's apprentice and encounters difficulties, while the ship that was originally his decays.

School Library Journal Best Book.

Garfield, Leon. *Footsteps.*
New York: Delacorte, 1980. 192 pages. ISBN 0-385-28294-X. (Out of print). Grades 5 to 8.

A deathbed confession causes conflict between two English families. After twelve-year-old William resolves the conflict, he no longer hears the pacing footsteps he has heard each night since his father's death.

Whitbread Book of the Year.

Garfield, Leon. *Smith.*
First copyright 1967. New York: Farrar, Straus & Giroux, 2000. 195 pages. ISBN 0-374-37082-6 and 0-374-46762-5pbk.
Prince Frederick, MD: Recorded Books unabridged audio, 2001. ISBN 0-7887-5370-3. Lexile 920. Grades 6 to 9.

Twelve-year-old Smith survives by picking pockets in 18th century London. He steals a document from a man just before the man is murdered, which leads to a series of encounters and adventures.

Boston Globe-Horn Book Award Honor Book, Carnegie Medal Commendation, and *Phoenix Award.*

Gavin, Jamila. *Coram Boy.*
New York: Farrar, Straus & Giroux, 2000. 336 pages. ISBN 0-374-31544-2. Lexile 900. Grades 6 to 9.

In 18th century England, an unscrupulous peddlar and his simpleton son remove unwanted children from their mothers until the son falls in love with one of the mothers and rescues her baby. The child later discovers his aristocratic father in this complex, uplifting novel.

Children's Literature Choices.

Gilson, Jamie. *Stink Alley.*
New York: HarperCollins Children's Book Group, 2002. 192 pages. ISBN 0-688-17864-2. Grades 4 to 6.

A twelve-year-old orphan living in 1614 Holland breaks with Puritan tradition to find adventure with an eight-year-old boy named Rembrandt, who loves to draw.

Society of Midlands Authors Award.

Greene, Jaqueline Dembar. *One Foot Ashore.*
New York: Walker & Company, 1993. 144 pages. ISBN 0-8027-8281-7 and 0-8027-7601-9pbk. Grades 5 to 8.

Kidnapped from their parents during the Portuguese Inquisition in 1648 and sent to work as slaves at a monastery in Brazil, two Jewish sisters escape by stowing away on ships and make their way back to Europe

to find their parents. Maria is separated from her sister, ends up in Amsterdam, and is eventually reunited with her parents. A companion novel to *Out of Many Waters.*
Sydney Taylor Book Award Honor Book.

Greene, Jaqueline Dembar. *Out of Many Waters.*
New York: Walker & Company, 1988. 200 pages. ISBN 0-8027-6811-3 and 0-8027-7401-6pbk.
Topeka, KS: Econo-Clad Books, 1999. 200 pages. ISBN 0-613-14040-0.
Lexile 830. Grades 5 to 8.
Kidnapped from their parents during the Portuguese Inquisition in 1648 and sent to work as slaves at a monastery in Brazil, two Jewish sisters escape by stowing away on ships and make their way back to Europe to find their parents. Isobel becomes part of a group founding the first Jewish settlement in New Amsterdam. A companion novel to *One Foot Ashore.*
New York Public Library Books for the Teen Age and *Sydney Taylor Book Award Honor Book.*

Hautzig, Esther. *Riches.*
Donna Diamond, illustrator. New York: HarperCollins Children's Book Group, 1992. 44 pages. ISBN 0-06-022260-3. (Out of print). Lexile 670. Grades 4 to 8.
A Jewish man retires and spends three months driving around the countryside in a cart, leading to some personal revelations.
National Council for the Social Studies Notable Children's Trade Books in the Field of Social Studies and *National Jewish Book Award Finalist.*

Hodges, Margaret. *Saint George and the Dragon: A Golden Legend.*
Refer to complete information under Grades Kindergarten to 2.

Lawrence, Iain. *The Buccaneers.*
New York: Delacorte, 2001. 244 pages. ISBN 0-385-32736-6.
Prince Frederick, MD: Recorded Books unabridged audio, 2001. ISBN 1-4025-2768-3. Lexile 720. Grades 6 to Young Adult.
Seventeen-year-old John Spencer, now a seasoned sailor, pursues a dangerous game of cat and mouse with a ship full of malicious pirates in this sequel to *The Wreckers* and *The Smugglers.*
Children's Literature Choices.

Lawrence, Iain. *The Smugglers.*
New York: Delacorte, 1999. 224 pages. ISBN 0-385-32663-7.
New York: Yearling, 2000. 192 pages. ISBN 0-440-41596-9.
Prince Frederick, MD: Recorded Books unabridged audio, 2000. ISBN
0-7887-4242-6 and 0-7887-4734-7cd. Lexile 640. Grades 6 to Young
Adult.

John's father purchases a seafaring schooner and hires a captain to
navigate the ship off the Cornish coast in the 1700s. John is to accompany their wool cargo to London. As soon as they leave the port, the captain reveals himself to be a pirate, and a swashbuckling adventure begins.
Sequel to *The Wreckers.*
Booklist Editors' Choice.

Lawrence, Iain. *The Wreckers.*
New York: Delacorte, 1998. 196 pages. ISBN 0-385-32535-5.
New York: Laurel Leaf Library, 1999. 196 pages. ISBN 0-440-41545-
4pbk.
Prince Frederick, MD: Recorded Books unabridged audio, 2000. ISBN
0-7887-4008-3 and 0-7887-4654-5cd. Lexile 640. Grades 5 to 8.

Fourteen-year-old John thinks he is the only survivor of a shipwreck
on the rocky Cornwall coast in 1799. Then he realizes that his merchant
father is alive and being held prisoner by the ruthless pirate wreckers that
caused the accident.
Booklist Editors' Choice.

McCaughrean, Geraldine. *The Pirate's Son.*
New York: Scholastic, 1998. 224 pages. ISBN 0-590-20344-4 and 0-
590-20348-7pbk. Lexile 890. Grades 6 to 9.

Nathan and his sister find themselves orphaned and penniless in
1717 England. They become friends with the son of a pirate who travels
with them to Madagascar, and they live an adventurous life on the high
seas.
American Library Association Notable Children's Books.

Meyer, Carolyn. *Doomed Queen Anne. ("Young Royals Series").*
San Diego, CA: Gulliver Books, 2002. 240 pages. ISBN 0-15-216523-1.
Lexile 960. Grades 6 to 9.

Anne Boleyn's ambition to become Queen of England begins in her
teens, and ends with her tragic beheading in 16th century England.
*National Council for the Social Studies Notable Social Studies Trade
Books for Young People.*

Meyer, Louis. *Bloody Jack: Being an Account of the Curious Adventures of Mary "Jacky" Faber, Ship's Boy.*
San Diego, CA: Harcourt Children's Books, 2002. 336 pages. ISBN 0-15-216731-5. Lexile 1120. Grades 6 to 9.

In order to avoid begging and stealing in 18th century London, an orphaned thirteen-year-old girl disguises herself as a boy and becomes employed on a ship that encounters pirates.

Booklist Editors' Choice, The Bulletin for the Center for Children's Books Blue Ribbon Award, and *Lupine Award*.

Pope, Elizabeth Marie. *The Perilous Gard.*
Richard Cuffari, illustrator. Boston: Houghton Mifflin Co., 2001. 288 pages. ISBN 0-616-17736-1 and 0-618-15073-0pbk.
Prince Frederick, MD: Recorded Books unabridged audio, 1992. ISBN 1-55690-597-1. Lexile 1020. Grades 6 to 8.

In 1558 England, a young lady-in-waiting is exiled to an isolated castle in Derbyshire, a place known as the "perilous gard." There Kate encounters the legendary fairy folk who have chosen a young girl as a sacrifice. Kate and her friend Christopher trick the fairy folk to free the girl.

Newbery Honor Book.

Schmidt, Gary D. *Anson's Way.*
New York: Houghton Mifflin Co., 1999. 224 pages. ISBN 0-395-91529-5.
New York: Puffin Books, 2001. 213 pages. ISBN 0-14-131229-7pbk. Lexile 960. Grades 4 to 7.

A coming-of-age story in 18th century Ireland about a boy named Anson who seeks to be a drummer boy for the Fencibles in the service of King George II. Anson is forced to stand up to his father when he finds himself torn between suppressing Ireland's people and his growing love for the Irish.

Booklist Editors' Choice.

Sturtevant, Katherine. *At the Sign of the Star.*
New York: Farrar, Straus & Giroux, 2000. 140 pages. ISBN 0-374-30449-1. Lexile 860. Grades 4 to 7.

Twelve-year-old Meg is the child of a widowed bookseller in 17th century London. When her father remarries, her inheritance is at risk.

Booklist Editors' Choice.

Yolen, Jane. *The Ballad of the Pirate Queens.*
David Shannon, illustrator. San Diego, CA: Harcourt Children's Books, 1995. 32 pages. ISBN 0-15-200710-5 and 0-15-201885-9pbk.
Topeka, KS: Econo-Clad Books, 1999. 32 pages. ISBN 0-613-09936-2.
Grades 3 to 6.

The legendary story told in ballad form of two female pirates, Anne Bonney and Mary Reade, who defend their ship against the governor's men in 1720 while the male crew gamble below. They escape hanging on the gallows because they are pregnant, and both are set free.

American Library Association Notable Children's Books, The Bulletin of the Center for Children's Books Blue Ribbon Award, and *International Reading Association Children's Choices.*

Yolen, Jane. *Queen's Own Fool: A Novel of Mary Queen of Scots.*
Robert Harris and Cynthia von Buhler, illustrators. New York: Philomel Books, 2000. 448 pages. ISBN 0-399-23380-6.
New York: Puffin Books, 2001. 400 pages. ISBN 0-698-11918-5pbk.
Lexile 740. Grades 5 to 8.

Mary, Queen of Scots, asks eleven-year-old Nicola to stay at her court and be her eyes, ears, and "fool." Mary's rise, fall, and imprisonment in 1559 by her cousin Elizabeth are seen through Nicola's eyes.

American Library Association Top Ten Historical Fiction for Youth and *National Council for the Social Studies Notable Children's Trade Books in the Field of Social Studies.*

Grades 7 and 8

Brooks, Geraldine. *Year of Wonders: A Novel of the Plague.*
New York: Viking, 2001. 304 pages. ISBN 0-670-91021-X.
New York: Penguin Putnam, 2002. 320 pages. ISBN 0-14-200143-0.
St. Paul, MN: Highbridge Company abridged audio, 2001. ISBN 1-56511-488-4 and 1-56511-489-2cd. Grades 7 to Young Adult.

In the year 1666, the plague is carried from London to ravage a village's inhabitants with disease. This novel follows the experience through a housemaid named Anna Frith.

Alex Award.

Cooper, Susan. *King of Shadows.*
Refer to complete information under Grades 3 to 6.

De Trevino, Elizabeth. *I, Juan de Pareja.*
New York: Farrar, Straus & Giroux, 1965. 192 pages. ISBN 0-374-33531-1 and 0-374-43525-1pbk.
Ashland, OR: Blackstone Audio Books unabridged audio, 1998.
ISBN 0-7861-1422-3. Lexile 1100. Grades 7 to Young Adult.

Based on the true story of an African slave, Juan de Pareja, who is owned by and assists the great Spanish painter Diego Velasquez. Although slaves are prohibited from painting in 17th century Spain, he eventually becomes an accomplished artist.
Newbery Medal.

Garfield, Leon. *The December Rose.*
Refer to complete information under Grades 3 to 6.

Garfield, Leon. *Devil-in-the-Fog.*
Refer to complete information under Grades 3 to 6.

Garfield, Leon. *The Drummer Boy.*
Antony Mailand, illustrator. New York: Random House, 1969. 154 pages. ISBN 0-394-90855-4. (Out of print). Grades 7 to 9.

Charlie Sampson returns to England after battling in France and gets involved with a family having many problems.
Carnegie Medal.

Garfield, Leon. *The Empty Sleeve.*
Refer to complete information under Grades 3 to 6.

Garfield, Leon. *Footsteps.*
Refer to complete information under Grades 3 to 6.

Garfield, Leon. *Smith.*
Refer to complete information under Grades 3 to 6.

Gavin, Jamila. *Coram Boy.*
Refer to complete information under Grades 3 to 6.

Greene, Jaqueline Dembar. *One Foot Ashore.*
Refer to complete information under Grades 3 to 6.

Greene, Jaqueline Dembar. *Out of Many Waters.*
Refer to complete information under Grades 3 to 6.

Hautzig, Esther. *Riches.*
Refer to complete information under Grades 3 to 6.

Hawes, Charles Boardman. *The Dark Frigate.*
First copyright 1924. Boston: Little, Brown & Company, 1971. 264 pages. ISBN 0-316-35096-6 and 0-316-35009-5pbk.
Topeka, KS: Econo-Clad Books, 1999. ISBN 0-613-01326-3.
New York: Bantam Books unabridged audio, 2001. ISBN 0-8072-0447-1. Lexile 1230. Grades 7 to Young Adult.
    A terrible accident forces orphaned Philip Marsham to flee 17th century London in fear of his life, and he signs on with a frigate bound for Newfoundland. When pirates seize the ship, Philip is forced to join them on their murderous expeditions and become an outlaw.
    Newbery Medal.

Langenus, Ron. *Mission West.*
Willem Van Velzen, illustrator. Niesje C. Horsman-Delmonte, translator. Chester Springs, PA: Irish American Book Company, 1997. 144 pages. ISBN 0-86327-239-8pbk. Grades 7 to Young Adult.
    After the English supporting Cromwell brutally murder Rory's foster father, a priest, seventeen-year-old Rory walks across Ireland in 1649 to keep a parchment that contains vital information about Ireland safe.
    Belgian Book Prize.

Lawrence, Iain. *The Buccaneers.*
Refer to complete information under Grades 3 to 6.

Lawrence, Iain. *The Smugglers.*
Refer to complete information under Grades 3 to 6.

Lawrence, Iain. *The Wreckers.*
Refer to complete information under Grades 3 to 6.

McCaughrean, Geraldine. *The Pirate's Son.*
Refer to complete information under Grades 3 to 6.

Meyer, Carolyn. *Doomed Queen Anne. ("Young Royals Series").*
Refer to complete information under Grades 3 to 6.

Meyer, Louis. *Bloody Jack: Being an Account of the Curious Adventures of Mary "Jacky" Faber, Ship's Boy.*
Refer to complete information under Grades 3 to 6.

Pope, Elizabeth Marie. *The Perilous Gard.*
Refer to complete information under Grades 3 to 6.

Pressler, Mirjam. *Shylock's Daughter.*
Brian Murdoch, translator. New York: Penguin Putnam, 2001. 266
pages. ISBN 0-8037-2667-8. Grades 8 to 10.

A novel that expands upon Shakespeare's play, *The Merchant of Venice*, it examines the dilemma posed to sixteen-year-old Jessica and her Jewish father in 16th century Venice.

Booklist Top Ten Historical Fiction for Youth.

Schmidt, Gary D. *Anson's Way.*
Refer to complete information under Grades 3 to 6.

Sturtevant, Katherine. *At the Sign of the Star.*
Refer to complete information under Grades 3 to 6.

Yolen, Jane. *Queen's Own Fool: A Novel of Mary Queen of Scots.*
Refer to complete information under Grades 3 to 6.

Chapter 15

Europe–19th Century

Grades Kindergarten to 2

Sandin, Joan. *The Long Way to a New Land.*
New York: HarperCollins Children's Book Group, 1981. 64 pages. ISBN 0-06-025194-8 and 0-06-444100-8pbk.
New York: Caedmon Audio, 1991. ISBN 1-55994-494-3. (An "I Can Read" book). Lexile 340. Grades 2 to 4.

Carl Erik journeys with his family from Sweden to America during the famine of 1868.

American Library Association Notable Children's Books, Booklist Editors' Choice, and *National Council for the Social Studies Notable Children's Trade Books in the Field of Social Studies.*

Grades 3 to 6

Avi. *Beyond the Western Sea, Book One: The Escape from Home.*
New York: Orchard Books, 1996. 304 pages. ISBN 0-531-09513-4.
New York: Camelot, 1997. 336 pages. ISBN 0-380-72875-3pbk.
Prince Frederick, MD: Recorded Books unabridged audio, 1997. ISBN 0-7887-1160-1. Lexile 690. Grades 5 to 8.

In 1851, Maura and Patrick O'Connell are driven from their Irish home by a cruel English landlord. They join the landlord's abused son on a journey that takes them to the port of Liverpool to board a ship bound for America to search for their father.

American Library Association Best Books for Young Adults, Booklist

Starred Review, and *The Bulletin of the Center for Children's Books Blue Ribbon Award.*

Cameron, Eleanor. *The Court of the Stone Children.*
First copyright 1973. Magnolia, MA: Peter Smith Publishers, 1983. 208 pages. ISBN 0-8446-6757-9.
New York: Puffin Books, 1992. 191 pages. ISBN 0-14-034289-3pbk. Lexile 1110. Grades 4 to 7.

Nina, a girl fascinated by museums, meets Dominique, a figure from a 19th century painting. Dominique aids Nina in finding out what happened to her father and proving him innocent of the charges made against him by Napoleon's army.

American Book Award.

Conlon-McKenna, Marita. *Under the Hawthorn Tree.*
Donald Teskey, illustrator. New York: Holiday House, 1990. 153 pages. ISBN 0-8234-0838-8.
Dublin, Ireland: O'Brien Press, 2001. 160 pages. ISBN 0-86278-206-6pbk. Grades 5 to 8.

This survival story set during the Irish famine of the 1840s features a twelve-year-old girl and her two siblings who travel to a distant town to find relatives after their mother leaves to search for their working father. During their journey, they encounter many people who are surviving under worse conditions than theirs.

International Reading Association Teachers' Choices.

Dalokay, Vedat. *Sister Shako and Kolo the Goat: Memories of My Childhood in Turkey.*
Guner Ener, translator. New York: Lothrop, Lee & Shepard Books, 1994. 96 pages. ISBN 0-688-13271-5. Lexile 950. Grades 5 to 7.

A nostalgic memoir of growing up in eastern Turkey and a ten-year-old boy's transforming encounter with a remarkable woman. Left alone with her goats after her husband and sons are killed in a vendetta, Sister Shako survives by living in her father-in-law's old stable.

Mildred L. Batchelder Award Honor Book.

Giff, Patricia Reilly. *Nory Ryan's Song.*
New York: Bantam Books, 2000. 148 pages. ISBN 0-385-32141-4.
New York: Bantam Books unabridged audio, 2000. ISBN 0-8072-6163-7. Lexile 600. Grades 4 to 7.

The story of twelve-year-old Nory Ryan's struggle to assist her family during the Irish famine of 1845 to 1852 until they leave for a new life

in America.
   American Library Association Best Books for Middle Readers and
American Library Association Top Ten Historical Fiction for Youth.

Holub, Josef. *The Robber and Me.*
Elizabeth D. Crawford, translator. New York: Henry Holt & Co., 1997.
224 pages. ISBN 0-8050-5599-1.
New York: Yearling, 1999. 224 pages. ISBN 0-440-41540-3pbk. Lexile
650. Grades 4 to 7.
   Set in 1867 rural Germany, a young orphan is taken from an incom-
petent aunt and sent to live with his uncle who is mayor of the small village of Graab. The boy befriends the son of a suspected robber and fights
the town's prejudice. The persecuted man is found innocent, and the boy
cements his relationship with his uncle.
   Mildred L. Batchelder Award.

Lasky, Kathryn. *The Night Journey.*
Trina S. Hynam, illustrator. First copyright 1986. Topeka, KS: Econo-
Clad Books, 1999. 152 pages. ISBN 0-8085-8472-3.
New York: Penguin Putnam, 1986. 150 pages. ISBN 0-14-032048-2pbk.
Lexile 860. Grades 5 to 7.
   A young girl ignores her parents' wishes and persuades her great-
grandmother to relate the story of her escape from czarist Russia after
hiding the family gold in cookies.
   *American Library Association Notable Children's Books, Associa-
tion of Jewish Libraries Award, National Jewish Book Award,* and *Syd-
ney Taylor Book Award.*

Lunn, Janet. *Shadow in Hawthorn Bay.*
New York: Scribner, 1987. 192 pages. ISBN 0-684-18843-0. (Out of
print). Grades 5 to 9.
   In 1800 Scotland, Mairi "hears" her cousin's voice from Canada tell-
ing her to immigrate there. When she arrives, she learns that he recently
drowned. Despite this tragedy, she marries and begins a new life.
   *Canada Council Children's Literature Prize, Canadian Library
Association Book of the Year for Children Award,* and *International
Board on Books for Young People.*

Nichol, Barbara. *Beethoven Lives Upstairs.*
Scott Cameron, illustrator. New York: Orchard Books, 1994. 48 pages.
ISBN 0-531-06828-5 and 0-531-06828-5. (VHS).
Lexile 750. Grades 3 to 5.

Ten-year-old Christoph writes letters to his uncle about the "madman" who has moved into the upstairs of his Vienna home. After Christoph receives tickets to Beethoven's Ninth Symphony, he realizes that the deaf man isn't so crazy after all.

Booklist Editors' Choice.

Pullman, Philip. *Spring-Heeled Jack: A Story of Bravery and Evil.*
David Mostyn, illustrator. New York: Alfred A. Knopf, 2002. 112 pages. ISBN 0-375-81601-1 and 0-679-81057-9pbk. Lexile 770. Grades 4 to 8.

A 19th century historical fantasy about three orphan siblings who run away from their orphanage only to be caught and then released again when their father finally reappears to rescue them. The story is told in text and cartoons.

School Library Journal Best Book.

Sandin, Joan. *The Long Way to a New Land.*
Refer to complete information under Grades Kindergarten to 2.

Segal, Jerry. *The Place Where Nobody Stopped.*
Dav Pilkey, illustrator. New York: Orchard Books, 1991. 154 pages. ISBN 0-531-0897-2. (Out of print). Grades 5 to 8.

Yosif the baker hides Mordecai ben Yahbahbai from the Cossacks in Russia during the years 1895 to 1906.

The Bulletin of the Center for Children's Books Blue Ribbon Award.

Zei, Alki. *The Sound of Dragon's Feet.*
Edward Fenton, translator. New York: Dutton Children's Books, 1979. 113 pages. ISBN 0-525-39712-4. Grades 4 to 9.

In 1894 Russia, Sasha learns lessons of bravery and courage from her tutor.

Mildred L. Batchelder Award.

Grades 7 and 8

Avery, Gillian. *A Likely Lad.*
First copyright 1971. New York: Simon & Schuster, 1994. ISBN 0-671-79867-7. (Out of print). Grades 7 to Young Adult.

A story that spans Willy's childhood experiences from the age of six until twelve when he runs away to avoid being recruited into the family business.

Guardian First Book Award.

Avi. *Beyond the Western Sea, Book One: The Escape from Home.*
Refer to complete information under Grades 3 to 6.

Cameron, Eleanor. *The Court of the Stone Children.*
Refer to complete information under Grades 3 to 6.

Conlon-McKenna, Marita. *Under the Hawthorn Tree.*
Refer to complete information under Grades 3 to 6.

Dalokay, Vedat. *Sister Shako and Kolo the Goat: Memories of My Childhood in Turkey.*
Refer to complete information under Grades 3 to 6.

Giff, Patricia Reilly. *Nory Ryan's Song.*
Refer to complete information under Grades 3 to 6.

Heneghan, James. *The Grave.*
New York: Farrar, Straus & Giroux, 2000. 256 pages. ISBN 0-374-32765-3. Lexile 810. Grades 7 to 10.
Thirteen-year-old Tom falls through a hole in a construction site and travels back in time to 19th century Ireland to witness the effects of the potato famine.
American Library Association Best Books for Young Adults and *Sheila A. Egoff Prize.*

Holeman, Linda. *Search of the Moon King's Daughter.*
Plattsburgh, NY: Tundra Books, 2002. 304 pages. ISBN 0-88776-592-0 and 0-88776-609-9pbk. Grades 7 to 10.
After her father's death, fifteen-year-old Emmaline becomes employed as a maid in 1830 London to search for her deaf brother, who was sold into servitude by her drug-addicted mother.
American Library Association Best Books for Young Adults.

Holub, Josef. *The Robber and Me.*
Refer to complete information under Grades 3 to 6.

Lasky, Kathryn. *The Night Journey.*
Refer to complete information under Grades 3 to 6.

Lunn, Janet. *Shadow in Hawthorn Bay.*
Refer to complete information under Grades 3 to 6.

Pullman, Philip. *The Ruby in the Smoke.*
Topeka, KS: Econo-Clad Books, 1999. 230 pages. ISBN 0-8335-2603-0.
New York: Random House, 1994. 230 pages. ISBN 0-394-89589-4pbk.
Lexile 750. Grades 8 to Young Adult.

Determined and intelligent, sixteen-year-old Sally tries to discover the reason for her father's murder in Victorian London.

American Library Association Best Books for Young Adults and *International Reading Association Children's Book Award.*

Pullman, Philip. *Shadow in the North.*
New York: Alfred A. Knopf, 1988. 320 pages. ISBN 0-394-89453-7.
Lexile 740. Grades 7 to Young Adult.

Twenty-two-year-old Sally, working as a financial consultant in 1878 London, attempts to earn back the money a client loses because of her advice. After investigating his unscrupulous business, she destroys his factory without knowing that he is inside.

American Library Association Best Books for Young Adults, Booklist Editors' Choice, Edgar Award Nomination, and *International Reading Association Teachers' Choices.*

Pullman, Philip. *Spring-Heeled Jack: A Story of Bravery and Evil.*
Refer to complete information under Grades 3 to 6.

Segal, Jerry. *The Place Where Nobody Stopped.*
Refer to complete information under Grades 3 to 6.

Zei, Alki. *The Sound of Dragon's Feet.*
Refer to complete information under Grades 3 to 6.

Chapter 16

Europe–First Half of the 20th Century: World War I, World War II, and the Holocaust

Grades Kindergarten to 2

Deedy, Carmen Agra. *The Yellow Star: The Legend of King Christian X of Denmark.*
Henri Sorenson, illustrator. Atlanta, GA: Peachtree Publishers, 2000. 32 pages. ISBN 1-56145-208-4. Lexile AD550. Grades 2 to 6.

The story of the heroic King of Denmark who wore a Jewish Star of David and defied the Nazis during the occupation of his country during World War II. More than 7,000 Jews were smuggled to safety under his leadership.

Christopher Award, International Reading Association Notable Books for a Global Society, International Reading Association Teachers' Choices, Jane Addams Children's Book Award, National Council for the Social Studies Notable Children's Trade Books in the Field of Social Studies, Parent's Choice Gold Award, and *Storytelling World Award Honor Book.*

Hoestlandt, Jo. *Star of Fear, Star of Hope.*
Johanna King, illustrator. Mark Polizzotti, translator. New York: Walker & Company, 1995. 32 pages. ISBN 0-8027-8373-2 and 0-802-77588-8pbk. Lexile 490. Grades 2 to 5.

A picture book that illustrates the relationship of a young girl and her Jewish friend, Lydia, who came to stay overnight in 1942. Lydia suddenly departed during the night, leaving a present behind for the girl. She never saw Lydia or her friend's family again.

American Library Association Notable Children's Books, Interna-

tional Reading Association Teachers' Choices, Mildred L. Batchelder Award Honor Book, and *Sydney Taylor Book Award.*

Oppenheim, Shulamith Levey. *The Lily Cupboard.*
Ronald Himler, illustrator. New York: HarperTrophy, 1995. 32 pages. ISBN 0-06-443393-5pbk. Lexile 420. Grades K to 3.

Five-year-old Miriam's parents send her to stay with a Dutch farm family to hide her from the Nazis. When the Nazis invade the Netherlands in 1940, the family hides her and her rabbit in a secret cupboard that opens when a lily is pressed.

National Council for the Social Studies Notable Children's Trade Books in the Field of Social Studies.

Patz, Nancy. *Who Was the Woman Who Wore the Hat?*
New York: Dutton Children's Books, 2003. 48 pages. ISBN 0-525-46999-0. Grades 2 to 5.

A poem written as a tribute to a fictitious woman who wore a hat the author observed exhibited in the Jewish Historical Museum in Amsterdam.

Parent's Choice Award Recommended Book.

Grades 3 to 6

Attema, Martha. *Daughter of Light.*
Stephen McCallum, illustrator. Custer, WA: Orca Book Publishers, 2001. 144 pages. ISBN 1-55143-179-3pbk. Lexile 450. Grades 3 to 6.

Nine-year-old Ria and her family struggle to survive during World War II Nazi-occupied Holland, but Ria successfully petitions the mayor to turn on the electricity during her mother's labor and delivery of her third child.

Children's Literature Choices.

Bawden, Nina. *Carrie's War.*
Colleen Browning, illustrator. First copyright 1973. New York: HarperCollins Children's Book Group, 1992. 159 pages. ISBN 0-397-31450-7. (Out of print). Lexile 760. Grades 4 to 7.

A woman's guilt and fear control her life for thirty years until her son finds out that she had nothing to do with a house fire during an evacuation from London in 1939.

Carnegie Medal Commendation and *Phoenix Award.*

Bawden, Nina. *Henry.*
Joyce Powzyk, illustrator. New York: Lothrop, Lee & Shepard Books, 1988. 119 pages. ISBN 0-688-07894-X. (Out of print). Grades 3 to 6.

A family that is forced to evacuate from England to rural Wales takes in and raises a squirrel named Henry.
American Library Association Notable Children's Books.

Bawden, Nina. *The Peppermint Pig.*
First copyright 1975. New York: HarperCollins Children's Book Group, 1987. 192 pages. ISBN 0-397-31618-6. (Out of print). Grades 3 to 6.

A young girl buys and raises a runt pig that the family is forced to slaughter later to pay bills in the 1920s.
Guardian Fiction Prize and *Yorkshire Post Book Award.*

Bennett, Cherie and Jeff Gottesfeld. *Anne Frank and Me.*
New York: Penguin Putnam Books for Young Readers, 2001. 291 pages. ISBN 0-399-23329-6 0-698-11973-8pbk. Lexile 550. Grades 6 to 8.

During a class visit to a museum, tenth-grader Nicole suffers an identity change and finds herself transported back to Nazi occupied Paris to live the life of a Jewish teenager.
International Reading Association Children's Choices.

Bergman, Tamar. *Along the Tracks.*
Michael Swirdly, translator. Boston: Houghton Mifflin Co., 1991. 245 pages. ISBN 0-395-55328-8 and 0-395-74513-6pbk. Lexile 650. Grades 5 to 9.

Based on a true story, an eight-year-old Jewish boy from Poland is forced to evacuate to Russia during World War II. He loses his family on the train during an air raid and spends the next four years wandering and trying to survive, eventually to be reunited with his family.
American Library Association Notable Children's Books and *The Bulletin of the Center for Children's Books Blue Ribbon Award.*

Bishop, Claire Huchet. *Twenty and Ten.*
William Pene du Bois, illustrator. First copyright 1952. Topeka, KS: Econo-Clad Books, 1999. 76 pages. ISBN 0-8085-4743-7.
New York: Puffin Books, 1991. 76 pages. ISBN 0-14-031076-2pbk. Lexile 630. Grades 4 to 8.

Janet and twenty of her classmates hide ten Jewish children in a cave, feed them, and keep them secret during World War II Nazi-occupied France.
Child Study Committee Children's Book Award.

Cheng, Andrea. *Marika.*
Ashville, NC: Front Street, 2002. 163 pages. ISBN 1-886910-78-2.
Grades 4 to 7.

A young Hungarian Christian girl of Jewish descent experiences the impact of anti-semitism during World War II in this novel that spans ten years.

Association of Jewish Libraries Award Notable Book.

Deedy, Carmen Agra. *The Yellow Star: The Legend of King Christian X of Denmark.*
Refer to complete information under Grades Kindergarten to 2.

Gallaz, Christophe. *Rose Blanche.*
Roberto Innocenti, illustrator. Martha Coventry, translator. First copyright 1986. San Diego, CA: Harcourt Children's Books, 1996. 32 pages. ISBN 0-15-200918-3 and 0-15-200917-5pbk. Lexile 430. Grades 5 to 8.

Rose is a young girl whose curiosity compels her to follow a truck to a prison camp outside her German town during World War II where she discovers starving people. She feeds them her rations through the winter until her tragic death when foreign soldiers mistakenly shoot her, thinking she is the enemy.

American Library Association Notable Children's Books and Mildred L. Batchelder Award.

Hartling, Peter. *Crutches.*
Elizabeth Crawford, translator. New York: Lothrop, Lee & Shepard Books, 1988. 163 pages. ISBN 0-688-07991-1. (Out of print). Lexile 630. Grades 5 to 8.

A young boy looking for his mother is befriended and taken care of by a one-legged man called Crutches in post-war Vienna.

American Library Association Notable Children's Books and *Mildred L. Batchelder Award.*

Haugaard, Erik. *The Little Fishes.*
Milton Johnson, illustrator. Magnolia, MA: Peter Smith Publishers, 1967. 214 pages. ISBN 0-8446-6245-3. Grades 6 to 10.

Twelve-year-old Guido is forced to beg and steal in order to survive after his mother dies during World War II. He helps others in the same difficult position.

Boston Globe-Horn Book Award, Jane Addams Children's Book Award, and *New York Herald Tribune Award.*

Hoestlandt, Jo. *Star of Fear, Star of Hope.*
Refer to complete information under Grades Kindergarten to 2.

Holm, Ann. *North to Freedom.*
L.W. Kingsland, translator. First copyright 1965. Topeka, KS: Econo-
Clad Books, 1999. 239 pages. ISBN 0-8335-1289-7.
San Diego, CA: Harcourt Children's Books, 1990. 239 pages. ISBN 0-
15-257553-7pbk. Lexile 980. Grades 3 to 7.
    Twelve-year-old David escapes from a Soviet Union concentration
camp and travels through Italy on his way to Denmark. The many things
that exist in a free land amaze him.
    *American Library Association Notable Children's Books, Boy's Club
of America Award, Gyldendal Prize for Best Scandinavian Children's
Book,* and *Lewis Carroll Shelf Award.*

Holman, Felice. *The Wild Children.*
New York: Penguin Putnam, 1985. 152 pages. ISBN 0-14-031930-1pbk.
Lexile 820. Grades 6 to 9.
    Twelve-year-old Alex is the only member of his family not arrested
following the Bolshevik Revolution. He walks over a hundred miles to
Moscow, survives during the 1920s to reach Finland, and finally makes
his way to America.
    American Library Association Best Books for Young Adults.

Issacs, Anne. *Torn Thread.*
New York: Scholastic, 2000. 192 pages. ISBN 0-590-60363-9 and 0-
590-60364-7pbk. Lexile 880. Grades 6 to 8.
    Eva's father attempts to save the life of his twelve-year-old daughter
by sending Eva to be with her fourteen-year-old sister in a Czechoslova-
kian Concentration camp during World War II.
    *International Reading Association Notable Books for a Global Soci-
ety.*

Kacer, Kathy. *Clara's War.*
Toronto, Canada: Second Story Press, 2001. 189 pages. ISBN 1-895764-
42-8. Lexile 750. Grades 4 to 7.
    A thirteen-year-old girl and her brother befriend a street-wise boy
while struggling to survive the Terezin concentration camp in Czechoslovakia.
    Canadian Library Association Notable Book.

Levine, Ellen. *Darkness over Denmark: The Danish Resistance and the Rescue of the Jews.*
New York: Holiday House, 2002. 164 pages. ISBN 0-8234-1447-7 and 0-8234-1755-7pbk. Lexile 890. Grades 6 to 8.

The Danish people hide almost their entire Jewish population in an uprising against the Nazis during World War II. Their stories are chronicled along with accounts of the Jewish people who were not rescued.

Jane Addams Children's Book Award Honor Book and *Parent's Choice Award Recommended Book.*

Lowry, Lois. *Number the Stars.*
Boston: Houghton Mifflin Co., 1989. 169 pages. ISBN 0-395-51060-0.
New York: Laurel Leaf Library, 1998. 137 pages. ISBN 0-440-22753-4pbk.
Prince Frederick, MD: Recorded Books unabridged audio, 2000. ISBN 1-55690-856-3 and 0-7887-3454-7cd. Lexile 670. Grades 4 to 7.

In 1943 Denmark, Ellen and her family hide Ellen's Jewish friend and her family from the Nazis and smuggle them out of the country.

American Library Association Notable Children's Books, Association of Jewish Libraries Award, Booklist Editors' Choice, Boston Globe-Horn Book Award, Horn Book Fanfare Honor List, National Jewish Book Award, Newbery Medal, School Library Journal Best Book, and *Sydney Taylor Book Award.*

Maguire, Gregory. *The Good Liar.*
Boston: Houghton Mifflin Co., 1999. 144 pages. ISBN 0-395-90697-0.
New York: HarperCollins Children's Book Group, 2002. 144 pages. ISBN 0-06-440874-4pbk. Lexile 780. Grades 3 to 6.

During a school project interview, three students learn about the experiences of an elderly man, Marcel Delarue, and his life in a small French village during World War II. Marcel and his brother learn that their secret friendship with a German soldier cannot continue after their mother reveals that she is hiding a Jewish woman and her daughter in their house.

Booklist Editors' Choice.

Matas, Carol. *Daniel's Story.*
Topeka, KS: Econo-Clad Books, 1999. 136 pages. ISBN 0-7857-1060-4.
New York: Scholastic, 1993. 136 pages. ISBN 0-590-46588-0pbk. Lexile 720. Grades 4 to 8.

A fictional story, written in conjunction with the Children's Exhibit at the United States Holocaust Memorial Museum, about a fourteen-year-old boy and his family who are forced by the Nazis to travel by train in 1941 from Frankfurt, Germany, to a Jewish ghetto in Poland. Only he and his father survive.

National Council for the Social Studies Notable Children's Trade Books in the Field of Social Studies.

Morpurgo, Michael. *Waiting for Anya.*
Topeka, KS: Econo-Clad Books, 1999. 172 pages. ISBN 0-613-01690-4.
New York: Puffin Books, 1997. ISBN 0-14-038431-6pbk. Lexile 770. Grades 5 to 8.

During World War II in France, twelve-year-old Jo helps a neighbor smuggle Jewish children over the border into Spain.

School Library Journal Best Book.

Napoli, Donna Jo. *Stones in Water.*
New York: Dutton Children's Books, 1997. 154 pages. ISBN 0-525-45842-5.
New York: Puffin Books, 1999. 224 pages. ISBN 0-14-130600-9pbk. Lexile 630. Grades 6 to Young Adult.

Roberto is a Venetian boy about to graduate from middle school when he and his friend Samuele are rounded up by German soldiers and forced to provide labor in Nazi work camps inside German territory. They struggle to protect Samuele's secret in order to evade certain death.

American Library Association Best Books for Young Adults, American Library Association Notable Children's Books, and *National Council for the Social Studies Notable Children's Trade Books in the Field of Social Studies.*

Oppenheim, Shulamith Levey. *The Lily Cupboard.*
Refer to complete information under Grades Kindergarten to 2.

Orgel, Doris. *The Devil in Vienna.*
First copyright 1978. Magnolia, MA: Peter Smith Publishers, 1995. 246 pages. ISBN 0-8446-6797-8. Lexile 700. Grades 6 to 8.

The story of a thirteen-year-old Jewish girl and her best friend, whose father is a Nazi in 1938 Austria.

Association of Jewish Libraries Award, Child Study Committee Children's Book Award, Golden Kite Award Honor Book, and *Sydney Taylor Book Award.*

Orlev, Uri. *The Island on Bird Street.*
Hillel Halkin, translator. Boston: Houghton Mifflin Co., 1984. 162 pages. ISBN 0-395-33887-5 and 0-395-61623-9pbk. Lexile 690. Grades 5 to 8.

An eleven-year-old boy survives by hiding in an abandoned house in a Warsaw ghetto during World War II.

American Library Association Notable Children's Books, Association of Jewish Libraries Award, and *Sydney Taylor Book Award.*

Orlev, Uri. *The Lady with the Hat.*
Hillel Halkin, translator. New York: Houghton Mifflin Co., 1995. 183 pages. ISBN 0-395-69957-6.
New York: Puffin Books, 1997. 192 pages. ISBN 0-14-038571-1pbk. Lexile 840. Grades 6 to Young Adult.

Seventeen-year-old Yulek survives the Holocaust and in 1947 tries to return to his Polish home, only to confront more anti-Semitism. He flees to Palestine while his aunt, who is married to a Christian, tries to find him. He befriends a Jewish girl who hid from the Nazis in a convent and eventually becomes a nun.

American Library Association Best Books for Young Adults, American Library Association Notable Children's Books, and *Mildred L. Batchelder Award.*

Patz, Nancy. *Who Was the Woman Who Wore the Hat?*
Refer to complete information under Grades Kindergarten to 2.

Pelgrom, Els. *The Winter When Time Was Frozen.*
Maryka Rudnik and Raphel Rudnik, translators. New York: Morrow, 1980. 253 pages. ISBN 0-688-32247-6. (Out of print). Grades 6 to 10.

Eleven-year-old Noortje and her father stay on a Dutch farm whose owners are giving food to a Jewish family hiding in a nearby cave in 1944. After a baby is born in the cave, they take it in, only to find out from the baby's surviving uncle that the rest of the family died in a concentration camp.

Mildred L. Batchelder Award.

Polacco, Patricia. *The Butterfly.*
New York: Philomel Books, 2000. 48 pages. ISBN 0-399-23170-6. Lexile 430. Grades 3 to 5.

A young girl and her family befriend and hide a Jewish family until their secret is revealed to a neighbor. The freedom of butterflies is symbolically portrayed in this picture book introduction to Nazism, racism, and World War II.

International Reading Association Notable Books for a Global Society and *Storytelling World Award Honor Book.*

Propp, Vera W. *When the Soldiers Were Gone.*
New York: Penguin Putnam, 1999. 112 pages. ISBN 0-399-23325-3.
New York: Puffin Books, 2001. 112 pages. ISBN 0-698-11881-2pbk.
Lexile 540. Grades 4 to 9.

A loving Dutch farm couple hides a young Jewish boy from the Nazis and raise him for three years until his parents return to claim him. Based on a true story, the boy suffers survivor's trauma when he doesn't remember his parents and is forced to leave the only home he knows.

Booklist Editors' Choice and *Child Study Children's Book Committee Children's Book of the Year.*

Rees, David. *The Exeter Blitz.*
New York: Dutton Children's Books, 1980. 126 pages. ISBN 0-525-66683-4. (Out of print). Grades 5 to 9.

Set in 1942 England, Colin Lockwood and his family survive the bombing of the town of Exeter and help rebuild the town.

Carnegie Medal.

Reiss, Johanna. *The Upstairs Room.*
New York: HarperCollins Children's Book Group, 1972. 196 pages. ISBN 0-690-85127-8 and 0-06-440370-Xpbk.
Prince Frederick, MD: Recorded Books unabridged audio, 1999. ISBN 0-7887-3525-X and 0-7887-4219-1cd. Lexile 380. Grades 3 to 6.

Based on a true story, nine-year-old Annie and her sister are hidden from the Nazis for two years by a Dutch family in the upstairs room of their farmhouse during World War II.

American Library Association Notable Children's Books of 1971 to 1975, Buxtehude Bulla Prize, Jane Addams Children's Book Award Honor Citation, Jewish Book Council Children's Book Award, Newbery Honor Book, and *New York Times Outstanding Children's Books.*

Richter, Hans. *Friedrich.*
First copyright 1970. Topeka, KS: Econo-Clad Books, 1999. 149 pages. ISBN 0-8085-9302-1.
New York: Puffin Books, 1987. 149 pages. ISBN 0-14-032205-1pbk.
Lexile 650. Grades 5 to 9.

The story of a Jewish boy named Friedrich in Nazi Germany, as told by his non-Jewish friend who watches the family being persecuted for

their religious beliefs.
Mildred L. Batchelder Award.

Roth-Hano, Renee. *Touch Wood: A Girlhood in Occupied France.*
New York: Simon & Schuster, 1988. 297 pages. ISBN 0-02-777340-X.
(Out of print). Lexile 750. Grades 5 to 9.

A true story told in the form of a diary about a young girl and her
two sisters who are sent to a convent in Normandy to escape the Nazis.
The family eventually reunites in France.
American Library Association Notable Children's Books.

Schmidt, Gary D. *Mara's Stories: Glimmers in the Darkness.*
New York: Henry Holt & Co., 2001. 112 pages. ISBN 0-8050-6794-9.
Grades 5 to 8.

Mara tells twenty-two Jewish folktales to women and children in a
concentration camp during the Holocaust in order to distract them from
their suffering.
Storytelling World Award Honor Book.

Serraillier, Ian. *The Silver Sword.*
C. Walter Hodges, illustrator. Chatham, New York: S. G. Phillips, 1959.
187 pages. ISBN 0-87599-104-1.
Hampton, NH: Chivers Children's Audio Books unabridged audio, 1997.
ISBN 1-85549-753-0. Grades 6 to 9.

In 1940 Warsaw, Poland, the Nazis take Ruth's mother to a concentration camp and Ruth and her three siblings journey to Switzerland to
find their father. They narrowly escape persecution themselves while
relying on the assistance of strangers and a street urchin named Jan.
Boys Club of America Award and *Carnegie Medal Commendation.*

Sevela, Ephraim. *We Were Not Like Other People.*
Antonina Bouis, translator. New York: HarperCollins Children's Book
Group, 1989. 224 pages. ISBN 0-06-025508-0. Grades 6 to 10.

In 1937 Russia, a young Jewish boy is forcefully separated from his
family after his father, an army commander, is imprisoned by the Stalin
regime. He makes his way from Siberia to Germany to reunite with his
family at his grandfather's home.
International Board on Books for Young People.

Steiner, Connie Colker. *Shoes for Amelie.*
Denis Rodier, illustrator. Montreal, Canada: Lobster Press, 2001. 48
pages. ISBN 1-894222-37-7. Grades 3 to 6.

A young French boy helps his family hide Jews from their persecutors in France during World War II.
Canadian Library Association Notable Book.

Tunnell, Michael O. *Brothers in Valor: A Story of Resistance.*
New York: Holiday House, 2001. 214 pages. ISBN 0-8234-1541-4. Lexile 590. Grades 6 to 10.
Three Mormon teenagers living in Germany work together and risk their lives to resist the Nazi regime during World War II.
International Reading Association Notable Books for a Global Society.

Vos, Ida. *The Key Is Lost.*
Therese Edelstein, translator. New York: HarperCollins Children's Book Group, 2000. 272 pages. ISBN 0-688-16283-5. Lexile 500.
Grades 5 to 8.
A Holocaust survival story about a twelve-year-old Jewish girl living in Holland who is forced to flee and hide for five years during the Nazi occupation of World War II.
American Library Association Top Ten Historical Fiction for Youth.

Watts, Irene N. *Finding Sophie: A Search for Belonging in Postwar Britain.*
Toronto, Canada: Tundra Books, 2002. 136 pages. ISBN 0-88776-613-7pbk. Grades 5 to 8.
Raised for seven years by a family friend, fourteen-year-old Sophie experiences fear, pain, and hope when forced to return to parents she barely knows recently liberated from concentration camps.
Association of Jewish Libraries Award Notable Book.

Westall, Robert. *Blitzcat.*
Topeka, KS: Econo-Clad Books, 1999. 230 pages. ISBN 0-8335-5848-X.
New York: Point, 1994. 230 pages. ISBN 0-590-42771-7pbk.
Great Britain: Isis-Oasis audio, 1994. ISBN 1-85089-647-X. Lexile 760.
Grades 5 to 8.
In England during Hitler's World War II blitzkrieg, a courageous black cat named Lord Gort sets off to find her home and lost master.
American Library Association Best of the Books, 1966 to 1992 and *Horn Book Fanfare Honor List.*

Westall, Robert. *The Kingdom by the Sea.*
New York: Farrar, Straus & Giroux, 1990. 176 pages. ISBN 0-374-34205-9 and 0-374-44060-3pbk.
Hampton, NH: Chivers Children's Audio Books unabridged audio, 1994. ISBN 0-7451-2445-3. Lexile 680. Grades 6 to 9.

Twelve-year-old Harry escapes a bomb that destroys his family's house in 1942 England. Believing that his family is dead, Harry and a stray dog travel and survive together until they finally meet a kind schoolmaster who convinces Harry to return to his town, where he eventually reunites with his family.

Guardian Fiction Prize.

Whelan, Gloria. *Angel on the Square.*
New York: HarperCollins Children's Book Group, 2001. 304 pages. ISBN 0-06-029030-7 and 0-06-029031-5. Lexile 820. Grades 6 to 8.

Twelve-year-old Katya and her mother move into the household of Czar Nicholas II and witness Russia's descent into the first World War in 1913.

National Council for the Social Studies Notable Children's Trade Books in the Field of Social Studies.

Zei, Alki. *Petro's War.*
Edward Fenton, translator. New York: Dutton Children's Books, 1972. 240 pages. ISBN 0-525-36962-7. (Out of print). Grades 4 to 9.

Greece declares war on Italy in 1940, and a nine-year-old boy matures while fighting in the resistance with his family.

Mildred L. Batchelder Award.

Zei, Alki. *Wildcat Under Glass.*
Edward Fenton, translator. New York: Henry Holt & Co., 1968. 177 pages. ISBN 0-03-068005-0. (Out of print). Grades 5 to 9.

The story of two girls and their cousin in 1936 Greece that describes the impact of the Spanish Fascists on their family.

Mildred L. Batchelder Award.

Grades 7 and 8

Almond, David. *Kit's Wilderness.*
New York: Delacorte, 2000. 240 pages. ISBN 0-385-32665-3.
New York: Skylark, 2001. 240 pages. ISBN 0-440-41605-1pbk.
New York: Bantam Books unabridged audio, 2000. ISBN 0-553-50242-5. Lexile 470. Grades 8 to Young Adult.
A dark story of a thirteen-year-old boy and his adventures in an ancient English coal pit where the children play a game called "death" that connects them with their ghostly ancestors who were not properly buried.
Booklist Editors' Choice.

Bawden, Nina. *Carrie's War.*
Refer to complete information under Grades 3 to 6.

Bennett, Cherie and Jeff Gottesfeld. *Anne Frank and Me.*
Refer to complete information under Grades 3 to 6.

Bergman, Tamar. *Along the Tracks.*
Refer to complete information under Grades 3 to 6.

Bishop, Claire Huchet. *Twenty and Ten.*
Refer to complete information under Grades 3 to 6.

Breslin, Theresa. *Remembrance.*
New York: Delacorte, 2002. 304 pages. ISBN 0-385-73015-2. Grades 7 to 12.
The intertwined relationships, experiences, and romances of five teenagers from rural Scotland reveal the impact of World War I.
American Library Association Best Books for Young Adults.

Cheng, Andrea. *Marika.*
Refer to complete information under Grades 3 to 6.

Forman, James D. *Ceremony of Innocence.*
New York: Dutton Children's Books, 1970. 249 pages. ISBN 0-451-04647-1pbk. (Out of print). Grades 7 to Young Adult.
A twenty-four-year-old man in a 1943 Munich prison reflects on his life choices and the actions of others as he faces accusations of treason for distributing pamphlets condemning Hitler.
Lewis Carroll Shelf Award.

Frank, Rudolph. *No Hero for the Kaiser.*
Patricia Crampton, translator. Klaus Steffens, illustrator. New York: HarperCollins Children's Book Group, 1986. 222 pages. ISBN 0-688-06094-5. (Out of print). Grades 7 to 10.

In 1914, a fourteen-year-old Polish boy guides an invading German military unit through his country after his father leaves to join the Polish army, and his mother dies. His actions cause much internal distress, and he flees before receiving military honors and German citizenship from the Kaiser.

American Library Association Notable Children's Books and *Mildred L. Batchelder Award.*

Gallaz, Christophe. *Rose Blanche.*
Refer to complete information under Grades 3 to 6.

Gehrts, Barbara. *Don't Say a Word.*
New York: Macmillan Publishing Co., 1986. 170 pages. ISBN 0-689-50412-8. (Out of print). Grades 7 to 10.

The story of a German family during the war that shows the effects of Hitler's regime regardless of race or background.

American Library Association Notable Children's Books and *International Board on Books for Young People.*

Hartling, Peter. *Crutches.*
Refer to complete information under Grades 3 to 6.

Haugaard, Erik. *The Little Fishes.*
Refer to complete information under Grades 3 to 6.

Hautzig, Esther. *The Endless Steppe: Growing Up in Siberia.*
First copyright 1968. Topeka, KS: Econo-Clad Books, 1999. 243 pages. ISBN 0-8335-1754-6.
New York: HarperCollins Children's Book Group, 1995. 243 pages. ISBN 0-06-440577-Xpbk. Lexile 940. Grades 7 to Young Adult.

Taken as prisoners by the Russians in 1941, Esther, her mother, and her grandmother are forced to work in labor camps and help each other survive harsh winters and near starvation for five years. Based on the Polish author's personal experiences.

American Library Association Notable Children's Books, Boston Globe-Horn Book, Horn Book Fanfare Honor List, Jane Addams Children's Book Award, Lewis Carroll Shelf Award, National Book Award for Children's Literature Nominee, New York Times Outstanding Children's Books, and *Sydney Taylor Book Award.*

Holm, Ann. *North to Freedom.*
Refer to complete information under Grades 3 to 6.

Holman, Felice. *The Wild Children.*
Refer to complete information under Grades 3 to 6.

Hunter, Mollie. *A Sound of Chariots.*
New York: HarperCollins Children's Book Group, 1972. 241 pages. ISBN 0-06-022669-2. (Out of print). Grades 7 to 10.
 The story of a Scottish girl who loses her father at the age of nine and works to overcome her grief and attend college in the 1930s.
 American Library Association Notable Children's Books of 1971 to 1975, Child Study Committee Children's Book Award, Horn Book Fanfare Honor List, New York Times Outstanding Children's Books, and *Phoenix Award.*

Issacs, Anne. *Torn Thread.*
Refer to complete information under Grades 3 to 6.

Kacer, Kathy. *Clara's War.*
Refer to complete information under Grades 3 to 6.

Levine, Ellen. *Darkness over Denmark: The Danish Resistance and the Rescue of the Jews.*
Refer to complete information under Grades 3 to 6.

Lowry, Lois. *Number the Stars.*
Refer to complete information under Grades 3 to 6.

Magorian, Michelle. *Good Night, Mr. Tom.*
New York: HarperCollins Children's Book Group, 1982. 318 pages. ISBN 0-06-024079-2 and 0-06-440174-Xpbk. (VHS). Lexile 760. Grades 7 to Young Adult.
 Willie, a young boy from an abusive home, is evacuated from London to live with an older man, Mr. Tom, who grows to love the boy. After Willie is forced to return to his mother and Mr. Tom does not hear from him, he goes to London to find Willie.
 American Library Association Best Books for Young Adults, American Library Association Notable Children's Books, Booklist Editors'

Choice, Horn Book Fanfare Honor List, International Reading Association Children's Book Award, and *National Council for the Social Studies Notable Children's Trade Books in the Field of Social Studies.*

Matas, Carol. *Code Name Kris.*
New York: Atheneum Books for Young Readers, 1990. 152 pages. ISBN 0-684-19208-X. (Out of print). Grades 7 to 10.

Seventeen-year-old Jesper continues his work in the underground resistance movement after the Nazi occupation of Denmark forces his Jewish friends to flee the country. He is imprisoned, but he regains his freedom on May 4, Liberation Day. The sequel to *Lisa's War.*

Lester and Orpen Dennys Award.

Matas, Carol. *Daniel's Story.*
Refer to complete information under Grades 3 to 6.

Matas, Carol. *Lisa's War.*
New York: Atheneum Books for Young Readers, 1989. 111 pages. ISBN 0-684-19010-9. (Out of print). Lexile 600. Grades 7 to 10.

During World War II in Denmark, twelve-year-old Lisa and her brother must flee for their lives after helping other Jewish teenagers in an underground movement.

Geoffrey Bilson Award for Historical Fiction for Young People.

McKay, Sharon. *Charlie Wilcox.*
Toronto, Canada: Stoddart Kids, 2000. 221 pages. ISBN 0-7737-6093-8. Grades 7 to 10.

Fourteen-year-old Charlie accidentally boards a boat in Canada that is bound for England with soldiers to fight in World War I. While there, he fights in the war and cares for the wounded.

Geoffrey Bilson Award for Historical Fiction for Young People.

Morpurgo, Michael. *Waiting for Anya.*
Refer to complete information under Grades 3 to 6.

Napoli, Donna Jo. *Stones in Water.*
Refer to complete information under Grades 3 to 6.

Orgel, Doris. *The Devil in Vienna.*
Refer to complete information under Grades 3 to 6.

Orlev, Uri. *The Island on Bird Street.*
Refer to complete information under Grades 3 to 6.

Orlev, Uri. *The Lady with the Hat.*
Refer to complete information under Grades 3 to 6.

Orlev, Uri. *The Man from the Other Side.*
Hillel Halkin, translator. New York: Houghton Mifflin Co., 1991. 186 pages. ISBN 0-395-53808-4.
New York: Puffin Books, 1995. 185 pages. ISBN 0-14-037088-9pbk.
Lexile 930. Grades 7 to 10.
Set in Poland during World War II, fourteen-year-old Marek is anti-Semitic until he realizes that his own father is Jewish, leading him to help a Jewish man just days before the ghetto uprising.
American Library Association Notable Children's Books, The Bulletin of the Center for Children's Books Blue Ribbon Award, Mildred L. Batchelder Award, National Jewish Book Award, and *School Library Journal Best Book.*

Pausewang, Gudrun. *The Final Journey.*
Topeka, KS: Econo-Clad Books, 1999. 160 pages. ISBN 0-613-11536-8.
New York: Puffin Books, 1998. 160 pages. ISBN 0-14-130104-Xpbk.
Grades 8 to 12.
An eleven-year-old Jewish girl experiences the horrors of the Holocaust while traveling with her grandfather on a train bound for Auschwitz.
International Reading Association Notable Books for a Global Society.

Pelgrom, Els. *The Winter When Time Was Frozen.*
Refer to complete information under Grades 3 to 6.

Propp, Vera W. *When the Soldiers Were Gone.*
Refer to complete information under Grades 3 to 6.

Rees, David. *The Exeter Blitz.*
Refer to complete information under Grades 3 to 6.

Reuter, Bjarne. *The Boys from St. Petri.*
Anthea Bell, translator. New York: Dutton Children's Books, 1994. 192 pages. ISBN 0-525-45121-8. Lexile 720. Grades 7 to 10.
Set in Denmark under Nazi occupation in 1942, Lars and his brother

join their friends as resistance fighters. Initially ridiculing the Nazis with their pranks and then escalating into full-scale sabotage, they are finally arrested.
Mildred L. Batchelder Award.

Richter, Hans. *Friedrich.*
Refer to complete information under Grades 3 to 6.

Roth-Hano, Renee. *Touch Wood: A Girlhood in Occupied France.*
Refer to complete information under Grades 3 to 6.

Schmidt, Gary D. *Mara's Stories: Glimmers in the Darkness.*
Refer to complete information under Grades 3 to 6.

Serraillier, Ian. *The Silver Sword.*
Refer to complete information under Grades 3 to 6.

Sevela, Ephraim. *We Were Not Like Other People.*
Refer to complete information under Grades 3 to 6.

Tunnell, Michael O. *Brothers in Valor: A Story of Resistance.*
Refer to complete information under Grades 3 to 6.

Vos, Ida. *The Key Is Lost.*
Refer to complete information under Grades 3 to 6.

Watts, Irene N. *Finding Sophie: A Search for Belonging in Postwar Britain.*
Refer to complete information under Grades 3 to 6.

Westall, Robert. *Blitzcat.*
Refer to complete information under Grades 3 to 6.

Westall, Robert. *The Kingdom by the Sea.*
Refer to complete information under Grades 3 to 6.

Westall, Robert. *The Machine Gunners.*
Topeka, KS: Econo-Clad Books, 1999. 186 pages. ISBN 0-8335-4266-4. New York: Beech Tree, 1997. 192 pages. ISBN 0-688-15498-0pbk. Lexile 670. Grades 7 to 10.

Fourteen-year-old Chas and his friend remove a machine gun from a downed German fighter plane during World War II and hide it in a

nearby bomb shelter.
  Carnegie Medal.

Whelan, Gloria. *Angel on the Square.*
  Refer to complete information under Grades 3 to 6.

Wulffson, Don L. *Soldier X.*
New York: Viking, 2001. 244 pages. ISBN 0-670-88863-X. Lexile 740.
Grades 7 to Young Adult.
  During World War II, a seriously wounded sixteen-year-old German
boy switches uniforms with a dead Russian soldier and feigns amnesia as
he tries to escape the horrible fighting.
  The Bulletin of the Center for Children's Books Blue Ribbon Award,
Christopher Award, and *National Council for the Social Studies Notable*
Children's Trade Books in the Field of Social Studies.

Zei, Alki. *Petro's War.*
  Refer to complete information under Grades 3 to 6.

Zei, Alki. *Wildcat Under Glass.*
  Refer to complete information under Grades 3 to 6.

Chapter 17

Europe–Mid-20th Century to the Present

Grades Kindergarten to 2

Adler, David A. *One Yellow Daffodil: A Hanukkah Story.*
Lloyd Bloom, illustrator. San Diego, CA: Gulliver Books, 1995. 32 pages. ISBN 0-15-200537-4 and 0-15-202094-2pbk. Lexile 440. Grades K to 3.

Holocaust survivor Morris Kaplan is invited by his favorite flower shop customers to spend Hanukkah with their family, which results in giving him the courage to face his past.

International Reading Association Notable Books for a Global Society and *National Council for the Social Studies Notable Children's Trade Books in the Field of Social Studies.*

Bunting, Eve. *Gleam and Glow.*
San Diego, CA: Harcourt Children's Books, 2001. 40 pages. ISBN 0-15-202596-0. Lexile 450. Grades 2 to 4.

After a refugee leaves a pair of goldfish with a family who are trying to escape the civil war in Bosnia, the fish are released into the family pond. When the family returns, they find their home devastated but the pond teeming with beautiful golden fish.

International Reading Association Notable Books for a Global Society.

Zeifert, Harriet. *A New Coat for Anna.*
Anita Lobel, illustrator. First copyright 1986. Topeka, KS: Econo-Clad Books, 1999. 40 pages. ISBN 0-8335-1245-5.
New York: Alfred A. Knopf, 1990. 40 pages. ISBN 0-394-89861-3pbk.

New York: Golden Press Audio, 1992. ISBN 0-307-05883-2. Lexile 690. Grades K to 3.

There is no money to purchase a new coat for Anna in the difficult times after World War II, so her mother sells her few remaining valuables to purchase the materials and services of a seamstress to make a new one.

American Library Association Notable Children's Books.

Grades 3 to 6

Adler, David A. *One Yellow Daffodil: A Hanukkah Story.*
Refer to complete information under Grades Kindergarten to 2.

Bunting, Eve. *Gleam and Glow.*
Refer to complete information under Grades Kindergarten to 2.

De Trevino, Elizabeth. *Turi's Poppa.*
New York: Farrar, Straus & Giroux, 1968. 186 pages. ISBN 0-374-37887-8. (Out of print). Grades 3 to 6.

After World War II, eight-year-old Turi walks with his father from Budapest, Hungary, to Cremona, Italy, where his father hopes to get a job at a premier violin institute as its director.

Boston Globe-Horn Book Award.

Mead, Alice. *Girl of Kosovo.*
New York: Farrar, Straus & Giroux, 2001. 128 pages. ISBN 0-374-32620-7.
New York: Bantam Doubleday Dell Books for Young Readers, 2002. 128 pages. ISBN 0-440-41853-4. Grades 5 to 8.

An eleven-year-old Albanian girl experiences her family being devastated by war during the Serbian military attempt to expel them from their Kosovo village.

International Reading Association Notable Books for a Global Society.

Morpurgo, Michael. *The War of Jenkins Ear.*
New York: Philomel Books, 1995. 178 pages. ISBN 0-399-22735-0.
New York: Paperstar, 1997. 176 pages. ISBN 0-698-11550-3pbk. Lexile 750. Grades 6 to 9.

In 1952 at an English prep school, fighting breaks out between the boys in town and the students. Toby befriends a student who confides that he believes he is Jesus Christ in this story of friendship and betrayal. *American Library Association Best Books for Young Adults*.

Naidoo, Beverley. *The Other Side of Truth.*
New York: HarperCollins Children's Book Group, 2001. 272 pages. ISBN 0-06-029628-3. Lexile 710. Grades 6 to 8.

Sade Solaja is a twelve-year-old refugee who must flee her comfortable home in Lagos, Nigeria, in 1995 and care for her younger brother in the London streets.

American Library Association Notable Children's Books, Booklist Editors' Choice, The Bulletin of the Center for Children's Books Blue Ribbon Award, Carnegie Medal, Jane Addams Children's Book Award, National Council for the Social Studies Notable Children's Trade Books in the Field of Social Studies, National Council of Teachers of English Notable Children's Books in the English Language Arts, and *School Library Journal Best Book.*

Reiss, Johanna. *The Journey Back.*
First copyright 1976. Topeka, KS: Econo-Clad Books, 1987. 212 pages. ISBN 0-8335-0972-1.
New York: HarperTrophy, 1988. 224 pages. ISBN 0-06-447042-3pbk.
Prince Frederick, MD: Recorded Books unabridged audio, 2001. ISBN 0-7887-9960-6. Lexile 520. Grades 5 to 8.

After spending three years hiding from the Nazis, a thirteen-year-old Jewish girl is reunited with her family in Holland and struggles to regain a semblance of family life in 1945 after World War II. The sequel to *The Upstairs Room*.

National Jewish Book Award, Newbery Honor Book, National Council for the Social Studies Notable Children's Trade Books in the Field of Social Studies, and *New York Public Library Books for the Teen Age*.

Zeifert, Harriet. *A New Coat for Anna.*
Refer to complete information under Grades Kindergarten to 2.

Zephaniah, Benjamin. *Refugee Boy.*
New York: Bloomsbury Children's Books, 2002. 291 pages. ISBN 1-58234-763-8. Grades 5 to 8.

A fourteen-year-old refugee boy is forced to adjust to life in London as a foster child while his Eritrean mother and Ethiopian father fight for peace in Africa.

National Council for the Social Studies Notable Social Studies Trade Books for Young People.

Grades 7 and 8

Duder, Tessa. *Alex in Rome.*
New York: Houghton Mifflin Co., 1992. 166 pages. ISBN 0-395-62879-2. Grades 7 to Young Adult.

Fifteen-year-old Alex finds romance in Rome, Italy, while competing in the 1960 Olympics for the New Zealand Olympic swim team. The sequel to *In Lane Three, Alex Archer.*

AIM Children's Book Award and *Esther Glen Award.*

Duder, Tessa. *In Lane Three, Alex Archer.*
New York: Houghton Mifflin Co., 1989. 176 pages. ISBN 0-395-50927-0. Lexile 910. Grades 7 to Young Adult.

Fifteen-year-old Alex trains for six years and has to overcome personal trauma and hardship as she competes for a place on the 1960 Olympic swim team to represent New Zealand in Rome, Italy.

AIM Children's Book Award and *Esther Glen Award.*

Magorian, Michelle. *Back Home.*
First copyright 1984. New York: HarperCollins Children's Book Group, 1992. 375 pages. ISBN 0-06-440411-0pbk. Grades 7 to 10.

After being evacuated to America for five years during World War II, a young girl returns home to an English boarding school and a difficult relationship with her parents.

American Library Association Best Books for Young Adults and *New York Public Library Children's Books.*

Mead, Alice. *Adem's Cross.*
New York: Farrar, Straus & Giroux, 1996. 144 pages. ISBN 0-374-30057-7.
New York: Laurel Leaf Library, 1998. 132 pages. ISBN 0-440-22735-6pbk. Lexile 660. Grades 7 to Young Adult.

Adem is a fourteen-year-old Albanian boy trying to survive the brutality of Serbian controlled Kosovo in 1993. His sister is gunned down while reading a protest poem, his father is targeted and beaten, and Adem suffers as well.

American Library Association Best Books for Young Adults.

Mead, Alice. *Girl of Kosovo.*
Refer to complete information under Grades 3 to 6.

Morpurgo, Michael. *The War of Jenkins Ear.*
Refer to complete information under Grades 3 to 6.

Naidoo, Beverley. *The Other Side of Truth.*
Refer to complete information under Grades 3 to 6.

Reiss, Johanna. *The Journey Back.*
Refer to complete information under Grades 3 to 6.

Zephaniah, Benjamin. *Refugee Boy.*
Refer to complete information under Grades 3 to 6.

Chapter 18

Africa

Grades Kindergarten to 2

Grifalconi, Ann. *The Village That Vanished.*
Kadir Nelson, illustrator. New York: Dial Books for Young Readers, 2002. 40 pages. ISBN 0-8037-2623-6. Grades 2 to 5.

A young Yao girl and her mother devise a way to help their fellow African villagers escape approaching slave traders.

Jane Addams Children's Book Award Honor Book and *National Council for the Social Studies Notable Social Studies Trade Books for Young People.*

Medearis, Angela Shelf. *Seven Spools of Thread.*
Daniel Minter, illustrator. Morton Grove, IL: Albert Whitman & Company, 2000. 40 pages. ISBN 0-8075-7315-9. Lexile 450. Grades K to 3.

Seven African Ashanti brothers learn to cooperate when they are given the task of making gold from seven spools of thread in this tale instructive of Kwanzaa principles.

Storytelling World Award.

Sisulu, Elinor Batezat. *The Day Gogo Went to Vote: South Africa, April 1994.*
Boston: Little, Brown & Company, 1996. 32 pages. ISBN 0-316-70267-6 and 0-316-70271-4pbk. Lexile 780. Grades K to 3.

Six-year-old Thembi accompanies her grandmother to vote in the first democratic election in which black South Africans are allowed to participate.

International Reading Association Notable Books for a Global Society.

Wisniewski, David. *Sundiata: Lion King of Mali.*
New York: Clarion Books, 1992. 32 pages. ISBN 0-395-61302-7 and 0-395-76481-5pbk. Lexile AD820. Grades 2 to 4

In 13th century Mali, Sundiata, son of the king's second wife, overcomes physical handicap and social disgrace to return and rule Mali when he is eighteen years old.

American Library Association Notable Children's Books.

Grades 3 to 6

Burns, Khephra. *Mansa Musa.*
Dian and Leo Dillon, illustrators. San Diego, CA: Gulliver Books, 2001. 56 pages. ISBN 0-15-200375-4. Grades 4 to 6.

Fourteen-year-old Kankan is kidnapped by slave traders, but he eventually returns to his homeland to become Mansa Musa, king of 14th century Mali.

National Council for the Social Studies Notable Children's Trade Books in the Field of Social Studies.

Carter, Peter. *The Sentinels.*
New York: Oxford University Press, 1980. 199 pages. ISBN 0-19-271438-4. (Out of print). Grades 4 to 7.

In 1840, a slave and a shipwrecked man from an anti-slavery patrol ship help each other survive on an African coast until they are rescued.

Guardian Fiction Prize.

Farmer, Nancy. *A Girl Named Disaster.*
New York: Orchard Books, 1996. 309 pages. ISBN 0-531-09539-8.
New York: Puffin Books, 1998. 309 pages. ISBN 0-14-038635-1pbk.
Prince Frederick, MD: Recorded Books unabridged audio, 1997. ISBN 0-7887-1342-6. Lexile 730. Grades 6 to 9.

Nhamo, an eleven-year-old Shona girl, flees an arranged marriage in 1981 South Africa by taking the village boat in an attempt to find her father's family in Zimbabwe. The boat goes astray, and Nhamo must sur vive on an island before she finally reaches her destiny.

American Library Association Best Books for Young Adults, American Library Association Notable Children's Books, Newbery Honor Book, and *School Library Journal Best Book.*

Grifalconi, Ann. *The Village That Vanished.*
Refer to complete information under Grades Kindergarten to 2.

Hansen, Joyce. *The Captive.*
New York: Scholastic, 1994. 195 pages. ISBN 0-590-41625-1.
New York: Scholastic, 1995. 195 pages. ISBN 0-590-41624-3pbk. Lexile 810. Grades 5 to Young Adult.

In a story based on an actual slave narrative, Kofi, the prince of a West African village, is betrayed, kidnapped, and sold into slavery in Massachusetts. While working for a New England family of Puritans, he studies the English language and a shipbuilder gives him the chance to return home.

Coretta Scott King Award Honor Book and *National Council for the Social Studies Notable Children's Trade Books in the Field of Social Studies.*

Kurtz, Jane. *The Storyteller's Beads.*
Michael Bryant, illustrator. San Diego, CA: Gulliver Books, 1998. ISBN 0-15-20174-2. Lexile 750. Grades 5 to 8.

A young Christian orphan and a blind Jewish girl learn to rely on each other while fleeing Ethiopian persecution in the 1980s.

International Reading Association Notable Books for a Global Society.

Lester, Julius. *Pharaoh's Daughter: A Novel of Ancient Egypt.*
San Diego, CA: Silver Whistle, 2000. 192 pages. ISBN 0-15-201826-3.
New York: HarperTrophy, 2002. 192 pages. ISBN 0-06-440469-4. Lexile 720. Grades 4 to 6.

The Biblical story of Moses as seen through the eyes of a brother and sister.

International Reading Association Children's Choices.

Levitin, Sonia. *Dream Freedom.*
San Diego, CA: Silver Whistle, 2000. 288 pages. ISBN 0-15-202404-2.
Lexile 670. Grades 5 to 8.

Based on a true story of contemporary enslavement in Sudan where thousands of members of the Dinka and Nuba tribes are captured and forced into hard labor. A group of students in Denver, Colorado raises money to free slaves and educate others of their plight.

International Reading Association Notable Books for a Global Society and *National Council for the Social Studies Notable Children's Trade Books in the Field of Social Studies.*

McGraw, Eloise. *The Golden Goblet.*
First copyright 1961. Magnolia, MA: Peter Smith Publishers, 1988. 248 pages. ISBN 0-8446-6342-5. Lexile 930. Grades 5 to 9.

In this ancient Egyptian mystery, a young boy named Ranofer thwarts his evil half-brother's attempt to steal a golden goblet and assures himself a place as a goldsmith's apprentice because of his courage.

Newbery Honor Book.

Medearis, Angela Shelf. *Seven Spools of Thread.*
Refer to complete information under Grades Kindergarten to 2.

Naidoo, Beverley. *The Other Side of Truth.*
New York: HarperCollins Children's Book Group, 2001. 272 pages. ISBN 0-06-029628-3. Lexile 710. Grades 6 to 8.

Sade Solaja is a twelve-year-old refugee who must flee her comfortable home in Lagos, Nigeria, in 1995 and care for her younger brother in the London streets.

American Library Association Notable Children's Books, Booklist Editors' Choice, The Bulletin of the Center for Children's Books Blue Ribbon Award, Carnegie Medal, Jane Addams Children's Book Award, National Council for the Social Studies Notable Children's Trade Books in the Field of Social Studies, National Council of Teachers of English Notable Children's Books in the English Language Arts, and *School Library Journal Best Book.*

Naidoo, Beverley. *Out of Bounds: Seven Stories of Conflict and Hope.*
New York: HarperCollins Children's Book Group, 2003. 192 pages. ISBN 0-06-050799-3. Grades 5 to 8.

The effects of fifty-two years of South African apartheid are revealed through this anthology of short stories regarding children of diverse ethnic backgrounds.

Parent's Choice Silver Award.

Reboul, Antoine. *Thou Shalt Not Kill.*
Stephanie Craig, translator. Chatham, New York: S. G. Phillips, 1969. 157 pages. ISBN 0-87599-1610-0. Grades 6 to Young Adult.

Lost in the Sinai Desert after a battle during the Israel-Arab War of 1967, a fourteen-year-old Egyptian boy and an Israeli girl find that they must trust each other in order to survive.

Grand Prize of the Salon de L'Enfance.

Schur, Maxine. *When I Left My Village.*
Brian Pinkney, illustrator. New York: Dial Books for Young Readers, 1996. 62 pages. ISBN 0-8037-1561-7. Grades 3 to 6.

A Jewish family endures a difficult and treacherous journey from Ethiopia to Israel in an attempt to gain freedom.

International Reading Association Notable Books for a Global Society.

Sisulu, Elinor Batezat. *The Day Gogo Went to Vote: South Africa, April 1994.*
Refer to complete information under Grades Kindergarten to 2.

Wisniewski, David. *Sundiata: Lion King of Mali.*
Refer to complete information under Grades Kindergarten to 2.

Zephaniah, Benjamin. *Refugee Boy.*
New York: Bloomsbury Children's Books, 2002. 291 pages. ISBN 1-58234-763-8. Grades 5 to 8.

A fourteen-year-old refugee boy is forced to adjust to life in London as a foster child while his Eritrean mother and Ethiopian father fight for peace in Africa.

National Council for the Social Studies Notable Social Studies Trade Books for Young People.

Grades 7 and 8

Berry, James. *Ajeemah and His Son.*
Topeka, KS: Econo-Clad Books, 1999. 83 pages. ISBN 0-7857-2319-6. New York: HarperTrophy, 1994. 96 pages. ISBN 0-06-44023-0pbk. Lexile 760. Grades 7 to Young Adult.

Eighteen-year-old Atu and his father, Ajeemah, are walking to see his intended bride in Africa when they are captured and sold as slaves in 1807 Jamaica. Each spends the rest of his life trying to reunite with the other and fighting for freedom. Atu succeeds, but his father does not.

American Library Association Best Books for Young Adults, American Library Association Notable Children's Books, Booklist Editors' Choice, Boston Globe-Horn Book Award, The Bulletin of the Center for Children's Books Blue Ribbon Award, Horn Book Fanfare Honor List, National Council for the Social Studies Notable Children's Trade Books in the Field of Social Studies, and *New York Public Library Books for the Teen Age*.

Carter, Peter. *The Sentinels.*
Refer to complete information under Grades 3 to 6.

Farmer, Nancy. *A Girl Named Disaster.*
Refer to complete information under Grades 3 to 6.

Hansen, Joyce. *The Captive.*
Refer to complete information under Grades 3 to 6.

Kurtz, Jane. *The Storyteller's Beads.*
Refer to complete information under Grades 3 to 6.

Levitin, Sonia. *Dream Freedom.*
Refer to complete information under Grades 3 to 6.

McGraw, Eloise. *The Golden Goblet.*
Refer to complete information under Grades 3 to 6.

Naidoo, Beverley. *The Other Side of Truth.*
Refer to complete information under Grades 3 to 6.

Naidoo, Beverley. *Out of Bounds: Seven Stories of Conflict and Hope.*
Refer to complete information under Grades 3 to 6.

Quintana, Anton. *The Baboon King.*
John Nieuwenhuizen, translator. New York: Walker & Company, 1999. 192 pages. ISBN 0-8027-8711-8.
New York: Laurel Leaf Library, 2001. 183 pages. ISBN 0-440-22907-3pbk. Lexile 850. Grades 8 to Young Adult.

In this contemporary African novel, Morengaru is cast out by his tribe after he accidentally kills a man. Attempting to survive in the wilderness, he comes across a troop of baboons and is forced to defend himself against their king. He kills the king and, although maimed, Morengaru is accepted as the new baboon king.

Mildred L. Batchelder Award and *Parent's Choice Gold Award.*

Reboul, Antoine. *Thou Shalt Not Kill.*
Refer to complete information under Grades 3 to 6.

Zephaniah, Benjamin. *Refugee Boy.*
Refer to complete information under Grades 3 to 6.

Chapter 19

Armenia, Turkey, Israel, and the Middle East

Grades Kindergarten to 2

Heide, Florence Parry and Judith Heide Gilliland. *House of Wisdom.*
Mary Grandpre, illustrator. New York: DK Publishing, 1999. 48 pages.
ISBN 0-7894-2562-9. Lexile AD 700. Grades K to 4.

Young Ishaq is shown the caliph's library, the "house of wisdom,"
by his father who is a scribe in 9th century Baghdad. This beautifully
illustrated book shows the ancient architectural wonders of old Baghdad.
Middle East Book Award.

Zeman, Ludmila. *The Last Quest of Gilgamesh.*
Plattsburgh, New York: Tundra Books of Northern New York, 1995. 22
pages. ISBN 0-88776-328-6 and 0-88776-380-4pbk. Grades K to 6.

An intricately illustrated retelling of the Epic of Gilgamesh that was
first carved onto clay tablets in Mesopotamia five thousand years ago.
Governor General's Awards for Children's Literature.

Grades 3 to 6

Barrett, Tracy. *Anna of Byzantium.*
New York: Delacorte, 1999. 224 pages. ISBN 0-385-32626-2.
New York: Laurel Leaf Library, 2002. 224 pages. ISBN 0-440-41536-
5pbk. Lexile 910. Grades 6 to 10.

Told as a flashback, this book chronicles the life of Anna Commena,
who is raised as a princess in the 11th century Byzantium Empire.
Booklist Editors' Choice.

Chaikin, Miriam. *Alexandra's Scroll: The Story of the First Hanukkah.*
New York: Henry Holt & Co., 2002. 115 pages. ISBN 0-8050-6384-6.
Grades 4 to 7.

A young Jewish girl keeps a diary that describes the events of the
Maccabee-led Jewish rebellion that is remembered with the celebration
of Hanukkah.

Association of Jewish Libraries Award Notable Book.

Clinton, Cathryn. *A Stone in My Hand.*
Cambridge, MA: Candlewick Press, 2002. 191 pages. ISBN 0-7636-
1388-6. Grades 5 to 8.

An eleven-year-old girl living in a Palestinian Gaza community experiences violence and terrorism between Jews and Palestinians during
the 1988 year of the Infitada.

Booklist Editors' Choice, Children's Literature Choices, and *International Reading Association Notable Books for a Global Society.*

Dalokay, Vedat. *Sister Shako and Kolo the Goat: Memories of My
Childhood in Turkey.*
Guner Ener, translator. New York: Lothrop, Lee & Shepard Books,
1994. 96 pages. ISBN 0-688-13271-5. Lexile 950. Grades 5 to 7.

A nostalgic memoir of growing up in eastern Turkey and a ten-year-
old boy's transforming encounter with a remarkable woman. Left alone
with her goats after her husband and sons are killed in a vendetta, Sister
Shako survives by living in her father-in-law's old stable.

Mildred L. Batchelder Award Honor Book.

Ellis, Deborah. *The Breadwinner.*
Toronto, Canada: Groundwood Books, 2001. 170 pages. ISBN 0-88899-
419-2 and 0-88899-416-8pbk.
Old Greenwich, CT: Listening Library Unabridged Audio, 2002. ISBN
0-8072-0973-2. Grades 4 to 7.

An eleven-year-old Afghanistan girl cuts her hair and disguises herself as a boy in order to earn money to support her desperate family after
her father is arrested by the Taliban.

Middle East Book Award.

Ellis, Deborah. *Parvana's Journey.*
Toronto, Canada: Groundwood Books, 2002. 199 pages. ISBN 0-88899-
514-8 and 0-88899-519-9pbk. Grades 5 to 8.

In this sequel to *The Breadwinner,* twelve-year-old Parvana masquerades as a boy after war breaks out and her father dies, and joins with

other displaced children to find the rest of her family.

American Library Association Best Books for Young Adults, Canadian Library Association Book of the Year for Children Award Honor Book, International Reading Association Notable Books for a Global Society, and *Jane Addams Children's Book Award.*

Fletcher, Susan. *Shadow Spinner.*
New York: Simon & Schuster, 1998. 219 pages. ISBN 0-689-81852-1.
Prince Frederick, MD: Recorded Books unabridged audio, 1998. ISBN 0-7887-2977-2 and 0-7887-4649-9cd. Lexile 710. Grades 5 to 8.

Based on the classic *Arabian Nights,* a thirteen-year-old crippled girl assists Shahrazad in gathering stories to help save the queen's life.

International Reading Association Notable Books for a Global Society and *Storytelling World Award Honor Book.*

Heide, Florence Parry and Judith Heide Gilliland. *House of Wisdom.*
Refer to complete information under Grades Kindergarten to 2.

Laird, Elizabeth. *Kiss the Dust.*
Topeka, KS: Econo-Clad Books, 1999. 278 pages. ISBN 0-613-02304-8.
New York: Puffin Books, 1994. 288 pages. ISBN 0-14-036855-8pbk.
Lexile 850. Grades 5 to Young Adult.

Set in the mid-1980s during the Iran-Iraq war, a Kurdish refugee family experiences trauma and hardship as they flee their bombed home in northern Iraq. They escape to the mountains, move to an insect-infested refugee camp in Iran, and finally negotiate a passage to London.

American Library Association Best Books for Young Adults.

Nye, Naomi Shihab. *Habibi.*
Raul Colon, illustrator. New York: Simon & Schuster, 1997. 144 pages.
ISBN 0-689-80149-1.
Prince Frederick, MD: Recorded Books unabridged audio, 1999. ISBN 0-7887-3532-2. Lexile 850. Grades 5 to 9.

Fourteen-year-old Liyana undergoes a difficult adjustment after her family moves to Jerusalem from St. Louis, Missouri, and she is the only "outsider" at an Armenian school.

International Reading Association Notable Books for a Global Society, Jane Addams Children's Book Award, and *Middle East Book Award.*

Orlev, Uri. *The Lady with the Hat.*
Hillel Halkin, translator. New York: Houghton Mifflin Co., 1995. 183 pages. ISBN 0-395-69957-6.

New York: Puffin Books, 1997. 192 pages. ISBN 0-14-038571-1pbk. Lexile 840. Grades 6 to Young Adult.

Seventeen-year-old Yulek survives the Holocaust and in 1947 tries to return to his Polish home, only to confront more anti-Semitism. He flees to Palestine while his aunt, who is married to a Christian, tries to find him. He befriends a Jewish girl who hid from the Nazis in a convent and eventually becomes a nun.

American Library Association Best Books for Young Adults, American Library Association Notable Children's Books, and *Mildred L. Batchelder Award.*

Reboul, Antoine. *Thou Shalt Not Kill.*
Stephanie Craig, translator. Chatham, New York: S. G. Phillips, 1969. 157 pages. ISBN 0-87599-1610-0. Grades 6 to Young Adult.

Lost in the Sinai Desert after a battle during the Israel-Arab War of 1967, a fourteen-year-old Egyptian boy and an Israeli girl find that they must trust each other in order to survive.

Grand Prize of the Salon de L'Enfance.

Schur, Maxine. *When I Left My Village.*
Brian Pinkney, illustrator. New York: Dial Books for Young Readers, 1996. 62 pages. ISBN 0-8037-1561-7. Grades 3 to 6.

A Jewish family endures a difficult and treacherous journey from Ethiopia to Israel in an attempt to gain freedom.

International Reading Association Notable Books for a Global Society.

Zeman, Ludmila. *The Last Quest of Gilgamesh.*
Refer to complete information under Grades Kindergarten to 2.

Grades 7 and 8

Bagdasarian, Adam. *Forgotten Fire.*
New York: DK Publishing, 2000. 288 pages. ISBN 0-7894-2627-7. New York: Laurel Leaf Library, 2002. 288 pages. ISBN 0-440-22917-0pbk. Lexile 1050. Grades 8 to Adult.

Twelve-year-old Vahan is forced to flee for his life after his father and older brothers are shot to death. The novel chronicles his survival through three years of unspeakable horror until he is able to escape to the safe haven of Constantinople. Based on the experiences of the author's great-uncle during the 1915 Armenian genocide at the hands of the Turkish government.

Booklist Editors' Choice, International Reading Association Notable Books for a Global Society, and *National Book Award for Young People's Literature.*

Barrett, Tracy. *Anna of Byzantium.*
Refer to complete information under Grades 3 to 6.

Carmi, Daniella. *Samir and Yonatan.*
Yael Lotan, translator. New York: Scholastic, 2000. 183 pages. ISBN 0-439-13504-4 and 0-439-13523-0pbk. Lexile 810. Grades 7 to Young Adult.

When a young Palestinian boy goes to an Israeli hospital, he befriends an Israeli boy. Together they imagine a trip away from the occupied zones and the suffering of their families.

International Board on Books for Young People Honor Book, International Reading Association Notable Books for a Global Society, Middle East Book Award, and *Mildred L. Batchelder Award.*

Chaikin, Miriam. *Alexandra's Scroll: The Story of the First Hanukkah.*
Refer to complete information under Grades 3 to 6.

Clinton, Cathryn. *A Stone in My Hand.*
Refer to complete information under Grades 3 to 6.

Dalokay, Vedat. *Sister Shako and Kolo the Goat: Memories of My Childhood in Turkey.*
Refer to complete information under Grades 3 to 6.

Ellis, Deborah. *The Breadwinner.*
Refer to complete information under Grades 3 to 6.

Ellis, Deborah. *Parvana's Journey.*
Refer to complete information under Grades 3 to 6.

Fletcher, Susan. *Shadow Spinner.*
Refer to complete information under Grades 3 to 6.

Haugaard, Erik. *The Rider and His Horse.*
Leo Dillon and Diane Dillon, illustrators. New York: Houghton Mifflin Co., 1968. 243 pages. ISBN 0-395-06801-0. (Out of print). Grades 7 to 10.

A young Jewish man battles at Masada against the Romans and lives to create a true historical record of events.
Phoenix Award.

Laird, Elizabeth. *Kiss the Dust.*
Refer to complete information under Grades 3 to 6.

Nye, Naomi Shihab. *Habibi.*
Refer to complete information under Grades 3 to 6.

Orlev, Uri. *The Lady with the Hat.*
Refer to complete information under Grades 3 to 6.

Reboul, Antoine. *Thou Shalt Not Kill.*
Refer to complete information under Grades 3 to 6.

Speare, Elizabeth George. *The Bronze Bow.*
First copyright 1961. Topeka, KS: Econo-Clad Books, 1999. 256 pages. ISBN 0-8085-3900-0.
New York: Houghton Mifflin Co., 1997. 254 pages. ISBN 0-395-13719-5pbk.
Prince Frederick, MD: Recorded Books unabridged audio, 2001. ISBN 0-7887-5363-9. Lexile 760. Grades 7 to Young Adult.
Eighteen-year-old Daniel resents Palestinian Romans after they crucify his father and uncle. He is sold to a blacksmith who leaves his work to follow Jesus of Galilee. Daniel is slowly won over by the teachings of the gentle man.
International Board on Books for Young People and Newbery Medal.

Wilentz, Amy. *Martyr's Crossing.*
New York: Simon & Schuster. 2001. 320 pages. ISBN 0-684-85436-8.
New York: Ballantine Books, 2002. 320 pages. ISBN 0-345-44983-5pbk.
Grades 8 to Young Adult.
The Israeli-Palestinian conflict is at the center of this novel that focuses on individual people on both sides, including an Israeli border guard and a young Palestinian mother whose child needs medical help.
Booklist Editors' Choice.

Chapter 20

China, Korea, India, Pakistan, and Tibet

Grades Kindergarten to 2

Balgassi, Haemi. *Peacebound Trains.*
Chris K. Soentpiet, illustrator. New York: Clarion Books, 1996. 48 pages. ISBN 0-395-72093-1 and 0-618-04030-7pbk. Lexile AD620. Grades 1 to 4.

While watching for trains that will eventually return young Sumi's mother from army service, Sumi's grandmother tells her a story that reveals her family's plight to escape the communist invasion of Seoul, Korea in 1950.

International Reading Association Notable Books for a Global Society.

Bridges, Shirin Yim. *Ruby's Wish.*
Sophie Blackall, illustrator. San Francisco, CA: Chronicle Books, 2002. 36 pages. ISBN 0-8118-3490-5. Grades K to 3.

Over one hundred children live in this traditional Chinese household where a girl breaks tradition and seeks higher education, enabled by the generosity of her grandfather.

Bay Area Book Reviewers Association Award.

Demi. *The Donkey and the Rock.*
New York: Henry Holt & Co., 1999. 32 pages. ISBN 0-8050-5959-8. Lexile AD750. Grades K to 3.

A Tibetan King ruling a town full of foolish people puts a donkey and a rock on trial to settle a dispute between two honest men in 550 B.C.

   Aesop Accolade.

Park, Frances and Ginger Park. *My Freedom Trip: A Child's Escape from North Korea.*
Honesdale, PA: Boyd Mills Press, 1998. 32 pages. ISBN 1-56397-468-1.
Lexile 510. Grades 1 to 5.

   The story of a child's escape in the middle of the night from North Korea to South Korea just prior to the outbreak of the Korean War.

   International Reading Association Notable Books for a Global Society.

Grades 3 to 6

Balgassi, Haemi. *Peacebound Trains.*
Refer to complete information under Grades Kindergarten to 2.

Bridges, Shirin Yim. *Ruby's Wish.*
Refer to complete information under Grades Kindergarten to 2.

Choi, Sook Nyul. *Echoes of the White Giraffe.*
New York: Houghton Mifflin Co., 1993. 137 pages. ISBN 0-395-64721-5.
New York: Bantam Books, 1995. 137 pages. ISBN 0-440-40970-5pbk.
Lexile 870. Grades 6 to 10.

   In this sequel to the autobiographical *Year of Impossible Goodbyes*, Sookan is now fifteen years old in 1952 and trying to survive as a refugee in the Korean city of Pusan on a mountain where a poet awakens everyone by yelling "good morning" from one of its peaks. She begins a forbidden romance and waits for word on her father and brothers who are missing in the war. She finally decides to pursue an education in the United States.

   American Library Association Notable Children's Books.

Choi, Sook Nyul. *Year of Impossible Goodbyes.*
New York: Houghton Mifflin Co., 1991. 171 pages.
ISBN 0-395-57419-6.
New York: Yearling, 1993. 169 pages. ISBN 0-440-40759-1pbk.
Prince Frederick, MD: Recorded Books unabridged audio, 1998. ISBN 0-7887-2224-7. Lexile 840. Grades 5 to 9.

When World War II ends in 1945, the Japanese leave North Korea and the Russians begin to invade. Ten-year-old Sookan, her mother, and a brother are separated from her father and three older brothers as they try to escape across the thirty-eighth parallel.

The Bulletin of the Center for Children's Books Blue Ribbon Award and *School Library Journal Best Book.*

Dejong, Meindert. *The House of Sixty Fathers.*
Maurice Sendak, illustrator. First copyright 1956. New York: Harper-Collins Children's Book Group, 1990. 189 pages. ISBN 0-06-021481-3 and 0-06-440200-2pbk.
New York: American School Publishers unabridged audio, 1987. ISBN 0-394-7000-5. Lexile 820. Grades 5 to 8.

After escaping from the Japanese with his family, young Tien Pao starts floating downriver in his boat near where his parents are working at an American airfield. He ends up in Japanese-held territory in China and must walk back to the airfield. He assists an American pilot who crashed, and other Americans help him.

American Library Association Notable Children's Books, The Child Study Committee Children's Book Award, International Board on Books for Young People, and *Newbery Honor Book.*

Demi. *The Donkey and the Rock.*
Refer to complete information under Grades Kindergarten to 2.

McCaughrean, Geraldine. *The Kite Rider.*
New York: HarperCollins Children's Book Group, 2002. 288 pages. ISBN 0-06-623874-9 and 0-06-441091-9pbk. Lexile 900. Grades 5 to 9.

In order to save his widowed mother from a horrible re-marriage in 13th century China, a twelve-year-old boy becomes a circus kite rider and meets the great Mongol ruler Kublai Khan.

American Library Association Best Books for Young Adults, American Library Association Notable Children's Books, Children's Literature Choices, International Reading Association Notable Books for a Global Society, National Council for the Social Studies Notable Social Studies Trade Books for Young People, and *School Library Journal Best Book.*

Neuberger, Anne E. *The Girl-Son.*
Minneapolis, MN: The Lerner Publishing Group, 1994. 131 pages. ISBN 0-87614-846-1 and 1-57505-077-3pbk. Lexile 740. Grades 4 to 7.

Based on the true story of Induk Pahk who was born in North Korea in 1896 and lived happily until she was six years old when her father died. Because women were not allowed to own property, the house and farm were given to a male cousin, but Induk's mother refused to live with her husband's family. Determined that her daughter would get a good education, Induk's mother dressed her as a boy and sent her to school until a girl's school opened. She now is a teacher, lecturer, and political activist.

National Council for the Social Studies Notable Children's Trade Books in the Field of Social Studies and *Society of School Librarians International Book Award Outstanding Book.*

Park, Frances and Ginger Park. *My Freedom Trip: A Child's Escape from North Korea.*

Refer to complete information under Grades Kindergarten to 2.

Park, Linda Sue. *A Single Shard.*

New York: Clarion Books, 2001. 152 pages. ISBN 0-395-97827-0. Old Greenwich, CT: Listening Library abridged audio, 2002. ISBN 0-8072-0701-2. Lexile 920. Grades 5 to 8.

Set in 12th century Korea, poor and orphaned twelve-year-old Tree-ear works for a master potter to pay off a debt after dropping one of his pieces. Tree-ear's courage, loyalty, and determination bring the potter acceptance and success.

American Library Association Best Books for Young Adults, American Library Association Notable Children's Books, Booklist Editors' Choice, Booklist Top Ten Historical Fiction for Youth, Children's Literature Choices, International Reading Association Notable Books for a Global Society, Newbery Medal, and *School Library Journal Best Book.*

Park, Linda Sue. *When My Name Was Keoko: A Novel of Korea in World War II.*

New York: Clarion Books, 2002. 208 pages. ISBN 0-618-13335-6. Lexile 610. Grades 5 to 9.

A brother and sister struggle to maintain their identity in Japanese-occupied Korea from 1940 to 1945.

American Library Association Best Books for Young Adults, American Library Association Notable Children's Books, Children's Literature Choices, International Reading Association Notable Books for a Global Society, Jane Addams Children's Book Award Honor Book, National Council for the Social Studies Notable Social Studies Trade Books for Young People, Publishers Weekly Best Children's Books, and *School Library Journal Best Book.*

Sis, Peter. *Tibet: Through the Red Box.*
New York: Farrar, Straus & Giroux, 1998. 64 pages. ISBN 0-374-37552-6. Lexile AD870. Grades 4 to 7.

Based on the true story of the author's father, this is a diary recollection of a journey to Tibet in the 1950s when he is separated from his film crew, caught in a blizzard, nursed back to health by the gentle Yetis, and sheltered by Monks. He eventually meets the Dalai Lama.

American Library Association Notable Children's Books, Caldecott Honor Book, and *Riverbank Review Children's Books of Distinction Award.*

Staples, Suzanne. *Shabanu Daughter of the Wind.*
Topeka, KS: Econo-Clad Books, 1999. 240 pages. ISBN 0-8335-5154-X.
New York: Random House, 1991. 240 pages. ISBN 0-679-81030-7pbk.
Prince Frederick, MD: Recorded Books unabridged audio, 1994. ISBN 0-7887-0189-4. Lexile 970. Grades 5 to Young Adult.

Set in the Cholistan desert area of modern Pakistan, eleven-year-old Shabanu attempts to run away from her family of nomadic camel herders rather than marry a man chosen for her in order to settle a feud.

American Library Association Best Books for Young Adults, American Library Association Notable Children's Books, Horn Book Fanfare Honor List, International Reading Association Teachers' Choices, National Council for the Social Studies Notable Children's Trade Books in the Field of Social Studies, and *Newbery Honor Book.*

Whelan, Gloria. *Homeless Bird.*
New York: HarperCollins Children's Book Group, 2000. 240 pages. ISBN 0-06-028454-4 and 0-06-440200-2pbk.
New York: Bantam Books unabridged audio, 2001. ISBN 0-8072-6181-5. Lexile 800. Grades 4 to 8.

After thirteen-year-old Koly is forced to marry, she is promptly widowed and cast out in an Indian society that rejects widowed girls. She uses her gift for embroidery to become self-sufficient and ultimately finds love.

Booklist Editors' Choice, International Reading Association Notable Books for a Global Society, and *National Book Award for Young People's Literature.*

Grades 7 and 8

Choi, Sook Nyul. *Echoes of the White Giraffe.*
Refer to complete information under Grades 3 to 6.

Choi, Sook Nyul. *Year of Impossible Goodbyes.*
Refer to complete information under Grades 3 to 6.

Dejong, Meindert. *The House of Sixty Fathers.*
Refer to complete information under Grades 3 to 6.

Dickinson, Peter. *Tulku.*
First copyright 1979. Magnolia, MA: Peter Smith Publishers, 1995. 288 pages. ISBN 0-8446-6830-3. (Out of print). Grades 7 to 10.
    Theo escapes the destruction of his father's mission and the murder of his father during the Boxer Rebellion in 1900 China. He is adopted by Mrs. Jones, a British botanist, who flees with him to Tibet where he experiences Buddhist teachings before his departure to England.
    Carnegie Medal, International Board on Books for Young People, and *Whitbread Book Award.*

McCaughrean, Geraldine. *The Kite Rider.*
Refer to complete information under Grades 3 to 6.

Neuberger, Anne E. *The Girl-Son.*
Refer to complete information under Grades 3 to 6.

Park, Linda Sue. *A Single Shard.*
Refer to complete information under Grades 3 to 6.

Park, Linda Sue. *When My Name Was Keoko: A Novel of Korea in World War II.*
Refer to complete information under Grades 3 to 6.

Sis, Peter. *Tibet: Through the Red Box.*
Refer to complete information under Grades 3 to 6.

Staples, Suzanne. *Shabanu Daughter of the Wind.*
Refer to complete information under Grades 3 to 6.

Tan, Amy. *Joy Luck Club.*
New York: Putnam, 1989. 288 pages. ISBN 0-399-13420-4.

New York: Random House, 1991. 288 pages. ISBN 0-679-72768-Xpbk.
Los Angeles, CA: Dove Audio, 1989. ISBN 1-55800-206-5.(VHS/DVD)
Lexile 930. Grades 8 to Adult.

In 1949, four Chinese women from different families that recently
immigrated to San Francisco begin to meet and share their stories. Forty
years and two generations later, they continue their gathering called the
Joy Luck Club.

American Library Association Best Books for Young Adults.

Vijayaraghavan, Vineeta. *Motherland.*
New York: Soho Press, 2001. 256 pages. ISBN 1-56947-217-3 and 1-
56947-283-1pbk. Lexile 980. Grades 7 to Young Adult.

A teenager born in India and raised in America is sent back to India
for a summer. She learns the cause of the estrangement with her mother
while reacquainting herself with her culture.

Alex Award and *American Library Association Best Books for Young
Adults.*

Whelan, Gloria. *Homeless Bird.*
Refer to complete information under Grades 3 to 6.

Chapter 21

Vietnam and Thailand

Grades Kindergarten to 2

Breckler, Rosemary. *Sweet Dried Apples: A Vietnamese Wartime Childhood.*
Deborah Kogan Ray, illustrator. New York: Houghton Mifflin, 1996. 28 pages. ISBN 0-395-73570-X. Grades 1 to 4.

A young child reveals how her village is destroyed by fire and her herbalist grandfather dies during the Vietnamese conflict.

International Reading Association Notable Books for a Global Society.

Shea, Pegi Deitz. *The Whispering Cloth: A Refugee's Story.*
Anita Riggio, illustrator; You Yang, stitcher. Topeka, KS: Econo-Clad Books, 1999. 32 pages. ISBN 0-613-01253-4.
Honesdale, PA: Boyd Mills Press, 1996. 32 pages. ISBN 1-56397-623-4pbk. Lexile AD780. Grades K to 4.

Set in the mid 1970s, a young Hmong girl survives in a Thai refugee camp while learning how to stitch a pa'ndau story cloth depicting the murder of her parents and her escape in a basket on her grandmother's back.

International Reading Association Notable Books for a Global Society, International Reading Association Teachers' Choices, National Council for the Social Studies Notable Children's Trade Books in the Field of Social Studies, and *National Council of Teachers of English Notable Trade Books in the Language Arts.*

Grades 3 to 6

Breckler, Rosemary. *Sweet Dried Apples: A Vietnamese Wartime Childhood.*
Refer to complete information under Grades Kindergarten to 2.

Myers, Walter Dean. *Patrol: An American Soldier in Vietnam.*
Ann Grifalconi, illustrator. New York: HarperCollins Children's Book Group, 2002. 40 pages. ISBN 0-06-028363-7. Lexile 280. Grades 3 to 8.
The emotions of a frightened young American soldier fighting in the Vietnam War are demonstrated in this picture book for older readers.
The Bulletin for the Center for Children's Books Blue Ribbon Award, Children's Literature Choices, Jane Addams Children's Book Award, and *National Council for the Social Studies Notable Social Studies Trade Books for Young People.*

Shea, Pegi Deitz. *The Whispering Cloth: A Refugee's Story.*
Refer to complete information under Grades Kindergarten to 2.

Grades 7 and 8

Garland, Sherry. *Song of the Buffalo Boy.*
Topeka, KS: Econo-Clad Books, 1999. 282 pages. ISBN 0-7857-3553-4. San Diego, CA: Harcourt Children's Books, 1994. 282 pages. ISBN 0-15-200098-4pbk. Lexile 900. Grades 7 to Young Adult.
Seventeen-year-old Loi is the offspring of an American soldier and a Vietnamese woman who was forced to prostitute herself during the war. Shunned and mistreated because of her mixed heritage, Loi runs away to Ho Chi Minh City with a local boy she loves in order to escape an arranged marriage to an older man. She hopes to eventually find her way to America.
American Library Association Best Books for Young Adults, National Council for the Social Studies Notable Children's Trade Books in the Field of Social Studies, and *New York Public Library Books for the Teen Age.*

Jones, Adrienne. *Long Time Passing.*
New York: HarperCollins Children's Book Group, 1990. 245 pages. ISBN 0-06-023056-8. (Out of print). Grades 7 to Young Adult.
Jonas makes the difficult decision to enroll in the army in 1969 in an

attempt to find his father who is missing in action in Vietnam.
New York Public Library Books for the Teen Age.

Myers, Walter Dean. *Fallen Angels.*
Topeka, KS: Econo-Clad Books, 1999. 309 pages. ISBN 0-8335-3180-8.
New York: Scholastic, 1991. 309 pages. ISBN 0-590-40943-3pbk. Lexile 650. Grades 7 to Young Adult.
A powerful story about a seventeen-year-old African American boy, Richie Perry, who graduates from high school in 1967 and is sent on a tour of duty in the bloody battlefields of Vietnam.
American Library Association Best Books for Young Adults, American Library Association Quick Picks for Reluctant Young Adult Readers, Booklist Editors' Choice, Coretta Scott King Award, Horn Book Fanfare Honor List, and *School Library Journal Best Book.*

Myers, Walter Dean. *Patrol: An American Soldier in Vietnam.*
Refer to complete information under Grades 3 to 6.

O'Brien, Tim. *The Things They Carried.*
New York: Houghton Mifflin Co., 1990. 273 pages. ISBN 0-395-51598-X.
New York: Broadway Books, 1999. 246 pages. ISBN 0-7679-0289-0pbk. Lexile 880. Grades 8 to Young Adult.
A collection of short stories reflecting the author's experiences in Vietnam.
American Library Association 100 Best Books for Teens and *Pulitzer Prize Finalist.*

White, Ellen. *The Road Home.*
New York: Scholastic, 1995. 469 pages. ISBN 0-590-46737-9. (Out of print). Lexile 850. Grades 8 to Young Adult.
Twenty-two-year-old Rebecca Phillips is a nurse who has seen bloodshed, horror, and suffering in Vietnam. When her helicopter crashes in the jungle, she faces a brutal showdown for survival that changes her and makes it difficult to cope once she returns to Boston, so she travels to Colorado to locate a fellow survivor.
American Library Association Best Books for Young Adults.

Chapter 22

Japan

Grades Kindergarten to 2

James, J. Alison. *The Drums of Noto Hanto.*
Tsukushi, illustrator. New York: DK Publishing, 1999. 40 pages. ISBN 0-7894-2574-2. Grades K to 4.

Japanese villagers save themselves by beating drums and wearing fearsome masks to scare away a boatload of samurais sent by a greedy warlord in 1576. A festival is held each year on the seacoast of Japan to commemorate this event.

National Council for the Social Studies Notable Children's Trade Books in the Field of Social Studies.

Say, Allen. *Grandfather's Journey.*
New York: Houghton Mifflin Co., 1993. 32 pages. ISBN 0-395-57035-2. Lexile AD650. Grades K to 3.

A Japanese American man recounts his grandfather's journey to America, which he also undertakes in the early 20th century, and the feelings of being torn by his love for two different countries.

Booklist Editors' Choice, Boston Globe-Horn Book Award, The Bulletin of the Center for Children's Books Blue Ribbon Award, Caldecott Medal, and *School Library Journal Best Book.*

Say, Allen. *Tea With Milk.*
New York: Houghton Mifflin Co., 1999. 32 pages. ISBN 0-395-90495-1. Lexile AD450. Grades K to 3.

A young Japanese American girl is caught between two cultures in San Francisco. Her family moves back to Japan, which creates new problems for her.

American Library Association Notable Children's Books and *International Reading Association Notable Books for a Global Society.*

Grades 3 to 6

Haugaard, Erik. *The Boy and the Samurai.*
New York: Houghton Mifflin Co., 1991. 221 pages. ISBN 0-395-56398-4 and 0-618-07039-7pbk.
Prince Frederick, MD: Recorded Books unabridged audio, 1993. ISBN 1-55690-780-X. Lexile 700. Grades 5 to 9.

An orphan living on the streets in civil war-torn 16th century Japan helps a samurai rescue his wife from imprisonment by a warlord so they can all flee to a more peaceful life.
Parent's Choice Award.

Haugaard, Erik. *The Revenge of the Forty-Seven Samurai.*
New York: Houghton Mifflin Co., 1995. 226 pages. ISBN 0-395-70809-5. Grades 6 to Young Adult.

In 1700 feudal Japan, a servant boy named Jiro is chosen to spy for his samurai master in a plot with forty-seven other samurai who are attempting to avenge their master's unjust death. Based on a true story that is commemorated in modern Japan.
American Library Association Best Books for Young Adults and *American Library Association Notable Children's Books.*

James, J. Alison. *The Drums of Noto Hanto.*
Refer to complete information under Grades Kindergarten to 2.

Maruki, Toshi. *Hiroshima, No Pika.*
New York: Morrow, 1982. 48 pages. ISBN 0-688-01297-3. (Out of print). Lexile AD620. Grades 4 to 7.

The heartbreaking story as told by a mother of what happened to her family when the atomic bomb was dropped on Hiroshima in 1945.
American Library Association Notable Children's Books, Jane Addams Children's Book Award, and *Mildred L. Batchelder Award.*

Paterson, Katherine. *The Master Puppeteer.*
Haru Wells, illustrator. First copyright 1975. Topeka, KS: Econo-Clad Books, 1999. 179 pages. ISBN 0-8085-4372-5.
New York: HarperCollins Children's Book Group, 1989. 179 pages.

ISBN 0-06-440281-9pbk. Lexile 860. Grades 5 to 9.

A thirteen-year-old boy describes the famine and discontent of 18th century Osaka, Japan, and the world of puppeteers in which he is forced to live.

American Library Association Notable Children's Books of 1976 to 1980, National Book Award for Young People's Literature, and *School Library Journal Best Book.*

Paterson, Katherine. *Of Nightingales That Weep.*
Haru Wells, illustrator. First copyright 1974. Topeka, KS: Econo-Clad Books, 1999. 170 pages. ISBN 0-8335-4540-X.
New York: HarperCollins Children's Book Group, 1989. 172 pages. ISBN 0-06-440282-7pbk. Lexile 950. Grades 5 to 9.

Takiko accepts a position at the imperial Japanese court after her samurai father dies and her mother remarries an ugly potter. After falling in love with an enemy soldier and suffering an accident, Takiko discovers the inner beauty of her mother's husband.

American Library Association Notable Children's Books of 1976 to 1980 and *Phoenix Award.*

Say, Allen. *Grandfather's Journey.*
Refer to complete information under Grades Kindergarten to 2.

Say, Allen. *Tea With Milk..*
Refer to complete information under Grades Kindergarten to 2.

Watkins, Yoko Kawashima. *My Brother, My Sister and I.*
Topeka, KS: Econo-Clad Books, 1999. 233 pages. ISBN 0-7857-9137-X.
New York: Aladdin Paperbacks, 1996. 233 pages. ISBN 0-689-80656-6pbk. Lexile 750. Grades 6 to Young Adult.

In this sequel to the fictionalized biography *So Far from the Bamboo Grove,* thirteen-year-old Yoko and her brother and sister try to survive poverty in Japan, while Yoko is forced to conceal the death of their mother from the school she hates to attend and her brother is accused of crimes he did not commit. After her sister is injured in a fire, Yoko and her brother assist her in the hospital while she recovers. Their father finally returns from a Siberian prison, much aged from the experience.

American Library Association Best Books for Young Adults, New York Times Notable Books of the Year, Parenting Magazine Best Book, and *Publishers Weekly Best Books of the Year.*

Watkins, Yoko Kawashima and Jean Fritz. *So Far from the Bamboo Grove.*
Topeka, KS: Econo-Clad Books, 1999. 183 pages. ISBN 0-8335-2663-4.
New York: Beech Tree, 1994. 183 pages. ISBN 0-688-13115-8pbk. Lexile 730. Grades 5 to 9.

Yoko is an eleven-year-old Japanese girl living with her family in Korea. When World War II comes to an end, her family is forced to flee back to Japan, where they feel unwelcome.
American Library Association Notable Children's Books.

Yep, Laurence. *Hiroshima: A Novella.*
New York: Scholastic, 1995. 56 pages. ISBN 0-590-29832-2 and 0-590-20833-0pbk.
Prince Frederick, MD: Recorded Books unabridged audio, 1997. ISBN 0-7887-1111-3. Lexile 660. Grades 5 to 7.

Chronicles the bombing of Hiroshima in 1945 and its citizens' struggles to survive despite death and devastation as seen through the eyes of a twelve-year-old Japanese girl.
Booklist Editors' Choice and *National Council for the Social Studies Notable Children's Trade Books in the Field of Social Studies.*

Grades 7 and 8

Haugaard, Erik. *The Boy and the Samurai.*
Refer to complete information under Grades 3 to 6.

Haugaard, Erik. *The Revenge of the Forty-Seven Samurai.*
Refer to complete information under Grades 3 to 6.

Haugaard, Erik. *The Samurai's Tale.*
Topeka, KS: Econo-Clad Books, 1999. 234 pages. ISBN 0-613-02772-8.
New York: Houghton Mifflin Co., 1990. 234 pages. ISBN 0-395-54970-1pbk. Lexile 960. Grades 7 to 10.

An orphan named Taro is taken in by a general who is serving the great warlord Taketa Shingen, and he grows up to be a samurai in 16th century Japan.
American Library Association Notable Children's Books.

Hoobler, Dorothy and Thomas Hoobler. *The Demon in the Teahouse.*
New York: Philomel Books, 2001. 208 pages. ISBN 0-399-23499-3.
Lexile 660. Grades 7 to 9.

This mystery set in 18th century Japan tries to find out who is setting fires and killing geishas. A famous samurai judge asked to solve the case strategically places his fourteen-year-old son in a position to discover clues.
Children's Literature Choices.

Maruki, Toshi. *Hiroshima, No Pika.*
Refer to complete information under Grades 3 to 6.

Paterson, Katherine. *The Master Puppeteer.*
Refer to complete information under Grades 3 to 6.

Paterson, Katherine. *Of Nightingales That Weep.*
Refer to complete information under Grades 3 to 6.

Watkins, Yoko Kawashima. *My Brother, My Sister and I.*
Refer to complete information under Grades 3 to 6.

Watkins, Yoko Kawashima and Jean Fritz. *So Far from the Bamboo Grove.*
Refer to complete information under Grades 3 to 6.

Yep, Laurence. *Hiroshima: A Novella.*
Refer to complete information under Grades 3 to 6.

Chapter 23

Australia, New Zealand, and the Pacific Islands

Grades Kindergarten to 2

No award winning books were found.

Grades 3 to 6

Gee, Maurice. *The Fat Man.*
New York: Simon & Schuster, 1997. 192 pages. ISBN 0-689-81182-9
and 0-689-82459-9pbk.
Topeka, KS: Econo-Clad Books, 1999. 192 pages. ISBN 0-613-17795-9.
Lexile 620. Grades 6 to 9.

A psychological thriller set in Depression-era New Zealand about a
fat man who returns to his home town to take revenge on those who tormented him while he was growing up. Twelve-year-old Colin becomes
caught in his schemes.
School Library Journal Best Book.

Griese, Arnold A. *The Wind Is Not a River.*
Glo Coalson, illustrator. First copyright 1978. Topeka, KS: Econo-Clad
Books, 1999. 113 pages. ISBN 0-7857-9740-8. Lexile 780. Grades 3 to
6.

Sasan and Sidak are Aleutian siblings living on the island of Attu in
1942. When they see Japanese soldiers invading their island, they escape
to the hills and must forage for food. While there, they decide to help a

wounded soldier.

National Council for the Social Studies Notable Children's Trade Books in the Field of Social Studies.

Mazer, Harry. *A Boy at War: A Novel of Pearl Harbor.*
New York: Simon & Schuster, 2001. 104 pages. ISBN 0-689-84161-2. Lexile 530. Grades 6 to 9.

After being mistaken for a Navy man, fourteen-year-old Adam is thrown into the sea to help save lives during the bombing of Pearl Harbor in 1941.

Children's Literature Choices.

Salisbury, Graham. *Under the Blood-Red Sun.*
New York: Delacorte, 1994. 246 pages. ISBN 0-385-32099-X.
New York: Yearling, 1995. 246 pages. ISBN 0-440-41139-4pbk.
Prince Frederick, MD: Recorded Books unabridged audio, 1995. ISBN 0-7887-0427-3 and 1-4025-2348-3cd. Lexile 640. Grades 5 to 8.

Growing up in Oahu, Tomikazu's world is destroyed when the Japanese attack Pearl Harbor. Tomi's Japan-born father and grandfather are arrested, and Tomi must help his mother and sister to survive.

American Library Association Best Books for Young Adults and *Scott O'Dell Award for Historical Fiction.*

Sperry, Armstrong. *Call It Courage.*
First copyright 1940. New York: Simon & Schuster, 1983. 96 pages. ISBN 0-02-786030-2.
Reading, MA: Scott Foresman, 1990. 95 pages. ISBN 0-689-71391-6pbk.
New York: Bantam Books unabridged audio, 1997. ISBN 0-553-47887-7.
Prince Frederick, MD: Recorded Books unabridged audio, 2000. ISBN 0-7887-4648-0cd.
Old Greenwich, CT: Listening Library abridged audio, 2002. ISBN 0-8072-0869-8. (VHS). Lexile 830. Grades 5 to 7.

Twelve-year-old Matufu must accept his mother's death and face his fears of the sea which took her life. In the process, he overcomes the shame he has brought to his father, the chief of his Polynesian island, in a culture which values courage.

American Library Association Notable Children's Books and *Newbery Medal.*

Grades 7 and 8

Duder, Tessa. *Alex in Rome.*
New York: Houghton Mifflin Co., 1992. 166 pages. ISBN 0-395-62879-2. Grades 7 to Young Adult.

Fifteen-year-old Alex finds romance in Rome, Italy, while competing in the 1960 Olympics for the New Zealand Olympic swim team. The sequel to *In Lane Three, Alex Archer.*

AIM Children's Book Award and *Esther Glen Award*

Duder, Tessa. *In Lane Three, Alex Archer.*
New York: Houghton Mifflin Co., 1989. 176 pages. ISBN 0-395-50927-0. Lexile 910. Grades 7 to Young Adult.

Fifteen-year-old Alex trains for six years and has to overcome personal trauma and hardship as she competes for a place on the 1960 Olympic swim team to represent New Zealand in Rome, Italy.

AIM Children's Book Award and *Esther Glen Award.*

Gee, Maurice. *The Fat Man.*
Refer to complete information under Grades 3 to 6.

Hartnett, Sonya. *Thursday's Child.*
Cambridge, MA: Candlewick Press, 2002. 261 pages. ISBN 0-7636-1620-6. Grades 7 to 10.

A seven-year-old girl relates the misfortunes her family and six other siblings suffer while trying to survive in an abandoned prospector's shack during the Australian Depression.

Children's Literature Choices and *Guardian Fiction Prize.*

Mazer, Harry. *A Boy at War: A Novel of Pearl Harbor.*
Refer to complete information under Grades 3 to 6.

Salisbury, Graham. *Under the Blood-Red Sun.*
Refer to complete information under Grades 3 to 6.

Sperry, Armstrong. *Call It Courage.*
Refer to complete information under Grades 3 to 6.

Taylor, Theodore. *The Bomb.*
San Diego, CA: Harcourt Children's Books, 1995. 197 pages. ISBN 0-15-200867-5.
New York: Avon Books, 1997. 176 pages. ISBN 0-380-72723-4pbk.

Prince Frederick, MD: Recorded Books unabridged audio, 1996. ISBN 0-7887-0537-7. Lexile 830. Grades 7 to Young Adult.

In 1946, one year after the bombing of Nagasaki and Hiroshima, the U.S. Government needs to do further testing of atomic bombs and selects Bikini Atoll as its test site. The government tells the natives that they will be displaced for only two years after the blast, but sixteen-year-old Sorry Rinamu does not believe them. He does everything he can to stop the dropping of the bomb on his home. Almost fifty years after the test, Bikini Atoll still poisons anyone who tries to live on it.

American Library Association Best Books for Young Adults, International Reading Association Notable Books for a Global Society, National Council for the Social Studies Notable Children's Trade Books in the Field of Social Studies, New York Public Library Books for the Teen Age, and *Scott O'Dell Award for Historical Fiction.*

Chapter 24

Canada

Grades Kindergarten to 2

Debon, Nicolas. *A Brave Soldier.*
Toronto, CA: Groundwood Books, 2002. 32 pages. ISBN 0-88899-481-8. Grades 2 to 4.
A picture book with a Canadian theme portrays the brutality of World War I.
National Council for the Social Studies Notable Social Studies Trade Books for Young People.

Martin, Jacqueline Briggs. *The Lamp, the Ice, and the Boat Called Fish.*
Beth Krommes, illustrator. New York: Houghton Mifflin Co., 2001. 48 pages. ISBN 0-618-00341-X. Lexile 810. Grades 2 to 4.
In 1913, a Canadian research boat becomes trapped in ice during an Arctic expedition, and the men learn to survive by using Inupiat cultural traditions.
American Library Association Notable Children's Books, Golden Kite Award, and *National Council for the Social Studies Notable Children's Trade Books in the Field of Social Studies.*

Grades 3 to 6

Boraks-Nemetz, Lillian. *The Old Brown Suitcase: A Teenager's Story of War and Peace.*
Port Angeles, WA: Ben-Simon, 1994. 148 pages. ISBN 0-914539-10-8.
Grades 6 to 10.
    The story of fourteen-year-old Slava who comes to Canada from a Warsaw, Poland ghetto. She struggles with memories of the Holocaust and the adjustments her Jewish family must make in order to prosper in their new home.
    Sheila A. Egoff Prize.

Cooney, Caroline. *The Ransom of Mercy Carter.*
New York: Delacorte, 2001. 249 pages. ISBN 0-385-32615-7.
New York: Laurel Leaf Library, 2002. 256 pages. ISBN 0-440-22775-5.
Lexile 730. Grades 6 to 8.
    Kahnawake Mohawk Indians raid a Deerfield, Massachusetts village and kidnap 100 settlers, forcing them on a difficult winter trek to Canada. Eleven-year-old Mercy learns to appreciate the Kahnawake way of life while waiting to be ransomed.
    International Reading Association Notable Books for a Global Society.

Debon, Nicolas. *A Brave Soldier.*
Refer to complete information under Grades Kindergarten to 2.

Demers, Barbara. *Willa's New World.*
Regina, Saskatchewan Canada: Coteau Books, 1999. 303 pages. ISBN 1-55050-150-Xpbk. Lexile 1030. Grades 5 to 8.
    At the turn of the 19th century, a fifteen-year-old orphan is roughly cast aside by a relative and transported from Canada to a trading post on Hudson's Bay where she befriends a Native American girl named Amelia. She learns strength and independence through her hardships.
    American Library Association Top Ten Historical Fiction for Youth.

Doyle, Brian. *Mary Ann Alice.*
Toronto, Canada: Ground Books, 2002. 172 pages. ISBN 0-88899-453-2 and 0-88899-551-2pbk. Grades 4 to 7.
    A young girl passionate about geology watches the effect the 1926 building of a damn on the Gatineau River has on her Canadian town.
    Riverbank Review Children's Books of Distinction.

Ellis, Sarah. *Next-Door Neighbors.*
New York: Macmillan Publishing Co., 1990. 154 pages. ISBN 0-689-50495-0. Lexile 680. Grades 4 to 7.

Twelve-year-old Peggy is a minister's daughter. When her father moves the family to Vancouver in 1957, Peggy befriends a young Russian immigrant and the Chinese gardner who works next door.
School Library Journal Best Book.

Horne, Constance. *The Tenth Pupil.*
Vancouver, Canada: Ronsdale Press, 2001. 162 pages. ISBN 0-921870-86-8. Grades 4 to 7.

Set in pre-World War II Vancouver Island, Canada, eleven-year-old Trudy encounters racism when a Japanese boy becomes a student at her one-room schoolhouse.
Canadian Library Association Notable Book.

Hudson, Jan. *Dawn Rider.*
New York: Putnam, 1990. 175 pages. ISBN 0-399-22178-6.
New York: Puffin Books, 2000. 176 pages. ISBN 0-698-11859-6pbk. Lexile 760. Grades 6 to Young Adult.

Sixteen-year-old Kit Fox, a Blackfoot Indian in 1750 Canada, is not allowed to train a horse her tribe stole from the enemy, but she secretly learns to ride it. When the enemy invades, Kit Fox races the horse to a nearby tribe for guns.
Writer's Guild of Alberta Awards for Excellence.

Hudson, Jan. *Sweetgrass.*
New York: Philomel Books, 1989. 160 pages. ISBN 0-399-21721-5.
New York: Paperstar, 1999. 168 pages. ISBN 0-698-11763-8pbk. Lexile 640. Grades 6 to 9.

Fifteen-year-old Sweetgrass is the oldest unmarried girl in her Blackfoot tribe in the 1800s, but her father feels she is too immature to marry the boy she loves. Then a smallpox epidemic strikes her family, and Sweetgrass works hard to save them, thus proving her maturity.
American Library Association Notable Children's Books, Canada Council Children's Literature Prize, Canadian Library Association Book of the Year for Children Award, Governor General's Award for Children's Literature, International Board on Books for Young People, and *School Library Journal Best Book.*

Lunn, Janet. *Shadow in Hawthorn Bay.*
New York: Scribner, 1987. 192 pages. ISBN 0-684-18843-0. (Out of print). Grades 5 to 9.

In 1800 Scotland, Mairi "hears" her cousin's voice from Canada telling her to immigrate there. When she arrives, she learns that he recently drowned. Despite this tragedy, she marries and begins a new life.

Canada Council Children's Literature Prize, Canadian Library Association Book of the Year for Children Award, and *International Board on Books for Young People.*

Martin, Jacqueline Briggs. *The Lamp, the Ice, and the Boat Called Fish.*
Refer to complete information under Grades Kindergarten to 2.

Matas, Carol. *Sparks Fly Upward.*
New York: Clarion Books, 2002. 181 pages. ISBN 0-618-5964-9. Grades 4 to 7.

A twelve-year-old Canadian girl experiences anti-Semitism when she is forced to live with a Christian foster family at the turn of the 20th century.

Association of Jewish Libraries Award Notable Book and *National Council for the Social Studies Notable Social Studies Trade Books for Young People.*

Sterling, Shirley. *My Name is Seepeetza.*
Toronto, Canada: Groundwood Books, 1997. 128 pages. ISBN 0-88899-290-4 and 0-88899-165-7pbk. Lexile 720. Grades 5 to 8.

A young Native American girl is forced by the Canadian government to reside in a boarding school taught by nuns where she has to change her name to Martha and is not allowed to participate in her culture. Her experiences are related via a diary when she is in sixth grade.

Sheila A. Egoff Prize.

Yee, Paul. *Dead Man's Gold and Other Stories.*
Harvey Chan, illustrator. Toronto, Canada: Groundwood Books, 2002. 112 pages. ISBN 0-88899-475-3. Grades 6 to 9.

Ten ghost stories that reveal the history of hard labor and prejudice experienced by Chinese immigrants during the mid-19th and early 20th centuries in Canada.

International Reading Association Notable Books for a Global Society.

Grades 7 and 8

Boraks-Nemetz, Lillian. *The Old Brown Suitcase: A Teenager's Story of War and Peace.*
Refer to complete information under Grades 3 to 6.

Cooney, Caroline. *The Ransom of Mercy Carter.*
Refer to complete information under Grades 3 to 6.

Demers, Barbara. *Willa's New World.*
Refer to complete information under Grades 3 to 6.

Doyle, Brian. *Mary Ann Alice.*
Refer to complete information under Grades 3 to 6.

Ellis, Sarah. *Next-Door Neighbors.*
Refer to complete information under Grades 3 to 6.

Horne, Constance. *The Tenth Pupil.*
Refer to complete information under Grades 3 to 6.

Hudson, Jan. *Dawn Rider.*
Refer to complete information under Grades 3 to 6.

Hudson, Jan. *Sweetgrass.*
Refer to complete information under Grades 3 to 6.

Lunn, Janet. *Shadow in Hawthorn Bay.*
Refer to complete information under Grades 3 to 6.

Matas, Carol. *Sparks Fly Upward.*
Refer to complete information under Grades 3 to 6.

McKay, Sharon. *Charlie Wilcox.*
Toronto, Canada: Stoddart Kids, 2000. 221 pages. ISBN 0-7737-6093-8. Grades 7 to 10.
Fourteen-year-old Charlie accidentally boards a boat in Canada that is bound for England with soldiers to fight in World War I. While there, he fights in the war and cares for the wounded.
Geoffrey Bilson Award for Historical Fiction for Young People.

Morrissey, Donna. *Kit's Law.*
New York: Mariner Books, 2001. 384 pages. ISBN 0-618-10927-7pbk.
Fredericton, New Brunswick, Canada: Goose Lane Editions abridged
audio, 2001. ISBN 0-86492-283-3. Grades 7 to Young Adult.

After her grandmother dies, fourteen-year-old Kit is forced to take
care of her mentally impaired mother while living in a ramshackle cot-
tage on the outer banks of Newfoundland.
Alex Award.

Rylant, Cynthia. *I Had Seen Castles.*
San Diego, CA: Harcourt Children's Books, 1993. 97 pages. ISBN 0-15-
238003-5 and 0-15-200374-6pbk. Lexile 950. Grades 7 to Young Adult.

Now an old retired professor in Canada, John is haunted by memories of enlisting to fight in World War II despite the urging of his girlfriend to become a conscientious objector, a decision which forced him
to face the horrors of war, lose his girlfriend, and change his life forever.
New York Public Library Books for the Teen Age.

Sterling, Shirley. *My Name is Seepeetza.*
Refer to complete information under Grades 3 to 6.

Yee, Paul. *Dead Man's Gold and Other Stories.*
Refer to complete information under Grades 3 to 6.

Chapter 25

Mexico, Central and South America, and the Caribbean

Grades Kindergarten to 2

No award winning books were found.

Grades 3 to 6

Alvarez, Julia. *Before We Were Free.*
New York: The Knopf Publishing Group, 2002. 166 pages. ISBN 0-375-81544-9. Lexile 890. Grades 6 to 10.

Diary format reveals the suffering twelve-year-old Anita's family experience while being terrorized by the Trujillo dictatorship of the Dominican Republic. Her relatives are forced into hiding, resulting in eventual immigration to the United States.

American Library Association Best Books for Young Adults, American Library Association Notable Children's Books, Americas Award for Children's and Young Adult Literature, and *National Council for the Social Studies Notable Social Studies Trade Books for Young People.*

Amado, Elisa and Antonio Skarmeta. *The Composition.*
Toronto, Canada: Groundwood Books, 2000. 32 pages. ISBN 0-88899-390-0. Lexile 420. Grades 3 to 6.

Young children are pressured to betray their parents in this Latin American story of political dictatorship.

Americas Award for Children's and Young Adult Literature and *Jane Addams Children's Book Award Honor Book.*

Clark, Ann Nolan. *Secret of the Andes.*
Jean Charlot, illustrator. Topeka, KS: Econo-Clad Books, 1999. 120 pages. ISBN 0-7857-7245-6.
New York: Viking, 1976. 120 pages. ISBN 0-14-030926-8pbk. Lexile 710. Grades 3 to 6.

A young Incan boy lives in the mountains of Peru and tends llamas while searching for the meaning of family.
Newbery Medal.

Dorris, Michael. *Morning Girl.*
Topeka, KS: Econo-Clad Books, 1999. 74 pages. ISBN 0-7857-3845-2.
New York: Hyperion, 1999. 74 pages. ISBN 0-7868-1358-Xpbk. Lexile 980. Grades 3 to 7.

In 1492, life is different for Taino Indian siblings Morning Girl and Star Boy after Columbus arrives and imposes cultural changes on their Bahama island.
Scott O'Dell Award for Historical Fiction.

Garland, Sherry. *In the Shadow of the Alamo.*
San Diego, CA: Gulliver Books, 2001. 282 pages. ISBN 0-15-201744-5. Grades 6 to 8.

Fifteen-year-old Lorenzo is forced to march and fight at the Alamo after the Mexican army captures his village.
National Council for the Social Studies Notable Children's Trade Books in the Field of Social Studies.

Garland, Sherry. *Voices of the Alamo.*
Ronald Himler, illustrator. New York: Scholastic Trade, 2000. 40 pages. ISBN 0-590-98833-6. Lexile 970. Grades 4 to 8.

A picture book for older readers, it describes events leading up to the thirteen-day siege of the Alamo as told by sixteen different people.
National Council for the Social Studies Notable Children's Trade Books in the Field of Social Studies.

Hausman, Gerald and Uton Hinds. *The Jacob Ladder.*
New York: Orchard Books, 2001. 128 pages. ISBN 0-531-30331-4. Lexile 690. Grades 5 to 7.

A twelve-year-old Jamaican boy helps to hold his family together in the 1960s after his father leaves them in poverty and moves in with the woman next door.
National Council for the Social Studies Notable Children's Trade Books in the Field of Social Studies.

Ibbotson, Eva. *Journey to the River Sea.*
Kevin Hawkes, illustrator. New York: Penguin Putnam, 2002. 336 pages.
ISBN 0-525-46739-4.
Prince Frederick, MD: Recorded Books unabridged audio, 2002. ISBN
1-4025-2736-5. Lexile 860. Grades 5 to 7.

In 1910, an orphaned girl and her governess are sent to live with un-
familiar relatives on a rubber plantation in Brazil, where they persevere
to realize their dream of exploring the Amazon.

American Library Association Notable Children's Books, Booklist
Top Ten Historical Fiction for Youth, School Library Journal Best Book,
and *Smithsonian Magazine Notable Books for Children.*

Ryan, Pam Munoz. *Esperanza Rising.*
New York: Scholastic Trade, 2000. 262 pages. ISBN 0-439-12041-1 and
0-439-12042-Xpbk.
New York: Bantam Books unabridged audio, 2001. ISBN 0-8072-6207-
2. Lexile 750. Grades 5 to 8.

Privileged fourteen-year-old Esperanza is forced to move from Mexico to the United States to work in an agricultural labor camp after her
father dies and her mother falls ill. Her transition is made even more difficult when she witnesses the injustices economic difficulties impose
upon others during the Depression.

American Library Association Notable Children's Books, Interna-
tional Reading Association Notable Books for a Global Society, Jane
Addams Children's Book Award, National Council for the Social Studies
Notable Children's Trade Books in the Field of Social Studies, and *Pura*
Belpre Award.

Taylor, Theodore. *The Cay.*
First copyright 1969. New York: Random House, 1987. 138 pages. ISBN
0-385-07906-0.
New York: Avon Books, 1995. 144 pages. ISBN 0-380-00142-Xpbk.
New York: Bantam Books abridged audio, 1992. ISBN 0-553-47038-3.
Lexile 860. Grades 6 to 9.

When the freighter on which they are traveling is torpedoed by a
German submarine in 1942 during World War II, an adolescent white
boy, blinded by a head injury he sustained during the ship's explosion,
and an old black man are stranded on a tiny Caribbean island. The boy
acquires an appreciation for the vision, courage, and love of his old companion.

American Library Association Notable Children's Book, Child Study
Children's Book Committee Children's Book of the Year, Children's Lit-

erature Council of Southern California Book Award, Commonwealth Club of California Book Award, Cooperative Children's Book Center Children's Book of the Year, Jane Addams Children's Book Award, and *Lewis Carroll Shelf Award.*

Temple, Frances. *Tonight by Sea.*
New York: Orchard Books, 1995. 152 pages. ISBN 0-531-06899-4.
New York: HarperCollins Children's Book Group, 1997. 160 pages. ISBN 0-06-440670-9pbk. Lexile 750. Grades 5 to 8.

A teenager assists her uncle in building a boat to escape the oppressive and violent Haitian military regime.

International Reading Association Notable Books for a Global Society.

Veciana-Suarez, Ana. *Flight to Freedom. ("First Person Fiction Series").*
New York: Orchard Books, 2002. 208 pages. ISBN 0-439-38199-1. Grades 6 to 9.

Thirteen-year-old Yara keeps a diary where she describes her transition through immigration from 1967 Havana, Cuba to her new life in Miami, Florida.

National Council for the Social Studies Notable Social Studies Trade Books for Young People.

Grades 7 and 8

Abelove, Joan. *Go and Come Back.*
New York: DK Publishing, 1998. 176 pages. ISBN 0-7894-2476-2.
New York: Puffin Books, 2000. 192 pages. ISBN 0-14-130694-7pbk. Lexile 620. Grades 8 to Young Adult.

A fictional visit from anthropologists studying a Peruvian tribe in the Amazon jungle as seen through the eyes of a Peruvian teenager. Insightful study of a primitive culture.

American Bookseller Pick of the Lists, American Library Association Best Books for Young Adults, American Library Association Notable Children's Books, Booklist Editors' Choice, The Bulletin of the Center for Children's Books Blue Ribbon Award, Horn Book Fanfare Honor List, Publishers Weekly Best Books of the Year, and *School Library Journal Best Book.*

Alvarez, Julia. *Before We Were Free.*
Refer to complete information under Grades 3 to 6.

Berry, James. *Ajeemah and His Son.*
Topeka, KS: Econo-Clad Books, 1999. 83 pages. ISBN 0-7857-2319-6.
New York: HarperTrophy, 1994. 96 pages. ISBN 0-06-44023-0pbk. Lexile 760. Grades 7 to Young Adult.

Eighteen-year-old Atu and his father, Ajeemah, are walking to see his intended bride in Africa when they are captured and sold as slaves in 1807 Jamaica. Each spends the rest of his life trying to reunite with the other and fighting for freedom. Atu succeeds, but his father does not.

American Library Association Best Books for Young Adults, American Library Association Notable Children's Books, Booklist Editors' Choice, Boston Globe-Horn Book Award, The Bulletin of the Center for Children's Books Blue Ribbon Award, Horn Book Fanfare Honor List, National Council for the Social Studies Notable Children's Trade Books in the Field of Social Studies, and *New York Public Library Books for the Teen Age.*

Dorris, Michael. *Morning Girl.*
Refer to complete information under Grades 3 to 6.

Garland, Sherry. *In the Shadow of the Alamo.*
Refer to complete information under Grades 3 to 6.

Garland, Sherry. *Voices of the Alamo.*
Refer to complete information under Grades 3 to 6.

Hausman, Gerald and Uton Hinds. *The Jacob Ladder.*
Refer to complete information under Grades 3 to 6.

Ibbotson, Eva. *Journey to the River Sea.*
Refer to complete information under Grades 3 to 6.

Ryan, Pam Munoz. *Esperanza Rising.*
Refer to complete information under Grades 3 to 6.

Taylor, Theodore. *The Cay.*
Refer to complete information under Grades 3 to 6.

Temple, Frances. *Tonight by Sea.*
Refer to complete information under Grades 3 to 6.

Veciana-Suarez, Ana. *Flight to Freedom. ("First Person Fiction Series").*

Refer to complete information under Grades 3 to 6.

III

MYTHS AND FOLKTALES

Chapter 26

American

African American

Farmer, Nancy. *Casey Jones's Fireman: The Story of Sim Webb.*
James Bernardin, illustrator. New York: Phyllis Fogelman Books, 1999.
40 pages. ISBN 0-8037-1929-9. Lexile 390. Grades K to 3.

Sim Webb is an African American fireman who worked with the
legendary Casey Jones during the disaster of the "Cannonball Express"
in the late 19th century.

Booklist Editors' Choice.

Hamilton, Virginia. *A Ring of Tricksters: Animal Tales from America,*
the West Indies, and Africa.
Barry Moser, illustrator. New York: Blue Sky Press, 1998. 112 pages.
ISBN 0-590-47374-3. Lexile 550. Grades 3 to 6.

Eleven animal trickster tales follow the migration of African culture
from Africa to the West Indies and America.

International Reading Association Notable Books for a Global Soci-
ety.

Hamilton, Virginia. *Her Stories: African American Folktales, Fairy*
Tales, and True Tales.
Leo and Diane Dillon, illustrators. New York: Scholastic, 1995. 128
pages. ISBN 0-590-47370-0. Lexile 880. Grades 3 to 6.

Twenty-five tales from the female African American tradition.

Coretta Scott King Award, International Reading Association Not-
able Books for a Global Society, and *Storytelling World Award Honor*
Book.

Hamilton, Virginia. *The People Could Fly: American Black Folktales.*
Leo and Diane Dillon, illustrators. New York: Random House, 2000. 192
pages. ISBN 0-375-80471-4.
New York: Alfred A. Knopf, 1993. 178 pages. ISBN 0-679-84336-1pbk.
Lexile 680. Grades K to 3.
      Twenty-four African American folktales about animals, the super-
natural, and the desire for freedom from slavery.
      Coretta Scott King Award.

Hamilton, Virginia. *When Birds Could Talk & Bats Could Sing: The
Adventures of Bruh Sparrow, Sis Wren and Their Friends.*
Barry Moser, illustrator. New York: Scholastic, 1996. 72 pages. ISBN 0-
590-47372-7. Lexile 620. Grades 3 to 6.
      Eight folktales first collected from African American slaves on
Southern plantations.
      Anne Izard Storytellers' Choice Award.

Hurston, Zora Neale. *Every Tongue Got to Confess: Negro Folktales
from the Gulf States.*
New York: HarperCollins Children's Book Group, 2001. 320 pages.
ISBN 0-06-018893-6 and 0-06-093454-9pbk.
New York: HarperAudio unabridged audio, 2001. ISBN 0-694-52645-2.
      This extensive collection of five hundred folktales from the African
American tradition was compiled by the anthropologist-author as a result
of her travels through the American South during the 1920s. This re-
source book is best used by teachers and adults.
      Storytelling World Award Honor Book.

Lester, Julius. *Further Tales of Uncle Remus: The Misadventures of
Brer Rabbit, Brer Fox, Brer Wolf, the Doodang, and Other Creatures.*
Jerry Pinkney, illustrator. New York: Penguin Putnam, 1990. 148 pages.
ISBN 0-8037-0610-3. Grades K to 6.
      Thirty-three humorous African American folktales feature the antics
of animals as they try to outsmart each other.
      Anne Izard Storytellers' Choice Award.

McGill, Alice. *In the Hollow of Your Hand: Slave Lullabies.*
Michael Cummings, illustrator. New York: Houghton Mifflin Co., 2000.
40 pages. ISBN 0-395-85755-4. Grades K to 7.
      Forty folk lullabies communicate the experience of family life under
slavery. Illustrated with full-page quilt collages. Includes a CD of the

songs.

Aesop Accolade.

Reneaux, J. J. *How Animals Saved the People: Animal Tales from the South.*
James Ransome, illustrator. New York: HarperCollins Children's Book Group, 2001. 64 pages. ISBN 0-688-16253-3 and 0-688-16254-1. Grades K to 3.

Eight folktales from the Southern United States that differ in their origin and dialect. Includes tales from African American, Appalachian, Cajun, Creole, and Native American traditions.

International Reading Association Children's Choices and *National Council for the Social Studies Notable Children's Trade Books in the Field of Social Studies.*

San Souci, Robert D. *Callie Ann and Mistah Bear.*
Don Daily, illustrator. New York: Dial Books for Young Readers, 2000. 32 pages. ISBN 0-8037-1766-0. Lexile AD580. Grades K to 3.

Young Callie Ann outwits the crafty Mistah Bear when he comes in disguise to court her mother in this Southern African American folktale.

National Council for the Social Studies Notable Children's Trade Books in the Field of Social Studies.

San Souci, Robert. *The Hired Hand: An African-American Folktale.*
Jerry Pinkney, illustrator. New York: Dial Books for Young Readers, 1997. 40 pages. ISBN 0-8037-1296-0 and 0-8037-1640-0pbk. Lexile AD670. Grades K to 3.

Additional help is hired at the sawmill because the owner's son is so lazy. Disaster results when the son tries to imitate the magic bestowed by the hired hand, and a lesson in morality is learned.

Aesop Prize and *National Council for the Social Studies Notable Children's Trade Books in the Field of Social Studies.*

San Souci, Robert D. *The Secret of the Stones: A Folktale.*
James Ransome, illustrator. New York: Phyllis Fogelman Books, 2000. 40 pages. ISBN 0-8037-1640-0. Lexile AD700. Grades K to 3.

Drawn from Zaire and the African American culture of the Arkansas Ozarks, this tale is about a childless couple that must break an enchanted spell to release two orphaned children who have been transformed into stones.

National Council for the Social Studies Notable Children's Trade Books in the Field of Social Studies.

San Souci, Robert D. and Jane Yolen. *Cut from the Same Cloth: American Women of Myth, Legend and Tall Tale.*
Brian Pinkney, illustrator. New York: Philomel Books, 1993. 140 pages. ISBN 0-399-21987-0.
New York: Penguin Putnam, 2000. 160 pages. ISBN 0-698-11811-1pbk. Lexile 1050. Grades 3 to 6.
　　This collection of tales from all areas of the country features fifteen of America's little-known heroines as told in the Native American, African American, Anglo American, Eskimo, and Hawaiian traditions.
　　Aesop Prize.

Stevens, Janet. *Tops & Bottoms.*
San Diego, CA: Harcourt Children's Books, 1995. 40 pages. ISBN 0-15-292851-0. Lexile 580. Grades K to 3.
　　In a story rooted in European folktales and Southern American slave stories, Bear and Hare are involved in a gardening partnership, with the rabbit eventually outwitting the lazy bear.
　　Caldecott Honor Book and *Storytelling World Award Honor Book.*

Native American

Bania, Michael. *Kumak's House: A Tale of the Far North.*
Portland, OR: Alaska Northwest Books, 2002. 32 pages. ISBN 0-88240-540-3. Grades K to 3.
　　A wise Inupiat elder helps a complaining Eskimo family to feel grateful for the home they have.
　　National Council for the Social Studies Notable Social Studies Trade Books for Young People.

Banyon, Kay Thorpe and Robert H. Bushyhead. *Yonder Mountain: A Cherokee Legend.*
Kristina Rodanas, illustrator. Tarrytown, NY: Marshall Cavendish Corporation, 2002. 32 pages. ISBN 0-7614-5113-7. Grades K to 3.
　　Cherokee Chief Sky sends three young men on a journey that will prove which one will be his successor.
　　National Council for the Social Studies Notable Social Studies Trade Books for Young People.

Bierhorst, John, editor. *The Dancing Fox: Arctic Folktales.*
Mary K. Okheena, illustrator. New York: Morrow, 1997. 192 pages. ISBN 0-688-14406-3. Grades 4 to 6.

Eighteen stories that are filled with universal human experiences introduce the Inuit cultures of Alaska, Canada, and Greenland.
National Council for the Social Studies Notable Children's Trade Books in the Field of Social Studies.

Bierhorst, John, editor. *The Deetkatoo: Native American Stories about Little People.*
Ron Hilbert Coy, illustrator. New York: William Morrow & Co., 1998. 160 pages. ISBN 0-688-14837-9. Grades 3 to 12.
Twenty-two Native American tales from fourteen different cultures remind us that even the smallest beings can be powerful.
Aesop Accolade.

Bruchac, Joseph. *Between Earth and Sky: Legends of Native American Sacred Places.*
San Diego, CA: Harcourt Children's Books, 1996. 32 pages. ISBN 0-15-200042-9 and 0-15-202062-4pbk. Lexile AD780. Grades 2 to 5.
A Native American man explains the importance of ten sacred places to his nephew by retelling ten native American legends.
International Reading Association Notable Books for a Global Society.

Bruchac, Joseph. *How Chipmunk Got His Stripes: A Tale of Bragging and Teasing.*
Jose Aruego and Ariane Dewey, illustrators. New York: Penguin Putnam, 2001. 32 pages. ISBN 0-8037-2404-7. Lexile AD260. Grades K to 3.
The teasing chipmunk obtains his stripes from the claw marks of a prideful bear after angering him in this Native American tale.
Children's Literature Choices and *National Council for the Social Studies Notable Children's Trade Books in the Field of Social Studies.*

Bruchac, Joseph. *Skeleton Man.*
New York: HarperCollins Children's Book Group, 2001. 128 pages. ISBN 0-06-029075-7. Lexile 730. Grades 5 to 9.
Molly relies on a Mohawk legend to figure out the reason for the disappearance of her parents and the identity of the mysterious man who claims to be a relative.
American Library Association Notable Children's Books and *School Library Journal Best Book.*

Bruchac, Joseph and Gayle Ross. *The Story of the Milky Way: A Cherokee Tale.*
Virginia Stroud, illustrator. New York: Dial Books for Young Readers, 1995. 32 pages. ISBN 0-8037-1737-7. Lexile AD590. Grades K to 3.

A spirit dog, discovered stealing cornmeal, leaps into the sky. Each of the grains of cornmeal falling from his mouth becomes a star that helps to form the Milky Way.

Aesop Accolade.

Charles, Veronika Martenova. *Maiden of the Mist: A Legend of Niagara Falls.*
Toronto, Canada: Stoddart Kids, 2001. 32 pages. ISBN 0-7737-3297-7. Lexile 500. Grades 1 to 3.

The brave daughter of a chief sacrifices herself to the god of the Niagara River to relieve the sickness and suffering of her Native American tribe.

Storytelling World Award Honor Book.

Dabcovich, Lydia. *The Polar Bear Son: An Inuit Tale.*
New York: Clarion Books, 1997. 32 pages. ISBN 0-395-72766-9 and 0-395-97567-0pbk. Lexile AD470. Grades K to 3.

The gentle story of a woman and her adopted polar bear son who continues to provide for her even after he is forced to leave her village.

National Council for the Social Studies Notable Children's Trade Books in the Field of Social Studies

DePaola, Tomie. *The Legend of the Bluebonnet.*
New York: Penguin Putnam, 1986. 30 pages. ISBN 0-399-20937-9 and 0-698-11359-4pbk. Lexile 740. Grades K to 3.

A Comanche legend that tells how the state flower of Texas, the bluebonnet, originated.

American Bookseller Pick of the Lists, Booklist Editors' Choice, and *National Council for the Social Studies Notable Children's Trade Books in the Field of Social Studies.*

DePaola, Tomie. *The Legend of the Indian Paintbrush.*
New York: Penguin Putnam, 1996. 40 pages. ISBN 0-399-21534-4 and 0-698-11360-8pbk. Lexile AD840. Grades K to 3.

An old Texas legend about the first blooming of Wyoming's state flower, the Indian paintbrush.

American Bookseller Pick of the Lists and *National Council for the*

Social Studies Notable Children's Trade Books in the Field of Social Studies.

Digennaro, Jacqueline and Mary Helen Pelton. *Images of a People: Tlingit Myths and Legends.*
Jennifer Brady Morales, illustrator. Englewood, CO: Libraries Unlimited, 1992. 170 pages. ISBN 0-87287-918-6. Grades 4 to 12.
More than twenty stories from the Alaskan Tlingit tradition are accompanied by information on its culture, history, and art.
Anne Izard Storytellers' Choice Award.

Duncan, Barbara R., editor. *Living Stories of the Cherokee.*
Chapel Hill, NC: University of North Carolina Press, 1998. 272 pages. ISBN 0-8078-2411-9 and 0-8078-4719-4pbk.
This anthology of seventy-two traditional and contemporary tales from the Eastern Band of Cherokee Indians in North Carolina is meant to be used as a resource by older readers and adults.
Storytelling World Award Honor Book.

Field, Edward. *Magic Words.*
Stefano Vitale, illustrator. San Diego, CA: Gulliver Books, 1998. 32 pages. ISBN 0-15-201498-5. Lexile 880. Grades K to 5.
Based on Netsilek Inuit songs and legends gathered by Knud Ramussen during an expedition, this collection of poems describes myths about the creation of the universe.
National Council for the Social Studies Notable Children's Trade Books in the Field of Social Studies.

French, Fiona. *Lord of the Animals: A Miwok Indian Creation Myth.*
Brookfield, CT: Millbrook Press, 1997. 32 pages. ISBN 0-7613-0112-7. Grades K to 3.
The story of man's creation from the Miwok Indian tradition of coastal California.
National Council for the Social Studies Notable Children's Trade Books in the Field of Social Studies.

Goble, Paul. *The Girl Who Loved Wild Horses.*
New York: Atheneum Books for Young Readers, 2001. 29 pages. ISBN 0-689-84504-9 and 0-689-71696-6pbk. Lexile 670. Grades K to 3.
A Plains Indian girl befriends a wild stallion and, although she is fond of her people, she chooses to live among the horses.
Caldecott Medal.

Goble, Paul. *The Legend of the White Buffalo Woman.*
Washington, D.C.: National Geographic Society, 1998. 32 pages. ISBN
0-7922-7074-6 and 0-7922-6552-1pbk. Lexile 850. Grades 4 to 8.

   The sacred legend of the Lakota people about a great flood that kills
almost all life on earth, but the nation is reborn from the union of a
woman and an eagle. The arrival of the powerful White Buffalo Woman
gives the Lakota people the sacred calf pipe, a gift from the Great Spirit.
   Aesop Accolade.

Goble, Paul. *Love Flute.*
Topeka, KS: Econo-Clad Books, 1999. 32 pages. ISBN 0-613-05407-5.
New York: Aladdin Paperbacks, 1997. 32 pages. ISBN 0-689-81683-
9pbk. Lexile AD630. Grades 3 to 6.

   Elk Men give a shy young man a flute made by the birds and animals
to enable him to express his love for a beautiful girl in this Native American tale.
   Aesop Prize and *Anne Izard Storytellers' Choice Award.*

Goble, Paul. *Storm Maker's Tipi.*
New York: Atheneum Books for Young Readers, 2001. 40 pages. ISBN
0-689-84137-X. Lexile AD610. Grades K to 5.

   In this story from the Blackfoot tradition, Storm Maker saves the
lives of Sacred Otter and his son and teaches them the art of tipi spiritual
painting. Includes instructions on how to construct a tipi.
   *National Council for the Social Studies Notable Children's Trade
Books in the Field of Social Studies.*

Goldin, Barbara Diamond. *The Girl Who Lived with the Bears.*
Andrew Plewes, illustrator. San Diego, CA: Harcourt Children's Books,
1997. 40 pages. ISBN 0-15-200684-2. Lexile 670. Grades K to 5.

   After the daughter of a chief insults the bear people, she is forced to
live among them.
   *American Bookseller Pick of the Lists, National Council for the So-
cial Studies Notable Children's Trade Books in the Field of Social Studies,* and *Storytelling World Award Honor Book.*

Hinton, Leanne, translator. *Ishi's Tale of Lizard.*
Susan L. Roth, illustrator. Berkeley, CA: Heyday Books, 2000. 32 pages.
ISBN 1-890771-32-5pbk. Grades K to 3.

   The adventures of an arrow-making lizard as told to anthropologists
in 1911 by Ishi, the last remaining member of the California Yahi Indians after he emerged from the foothills of California where he had been

hiding for forty years.
Aesop Accolade.

Jacob, Murv. *The Great Ball Game of the Birds and Animals.*
Albuquerque, NM: University of New Mexico Press, 2002. 32 pages.
ISBN 0-8263-2913-6. Grades K to 3.
The birds make wings for a bat and squirrel to meet a stickball challenge against larger animals in this Cherokee tale.
Oklahoma Book Award.

Kusugak, Michael Arvaarluk. *Northern Lights: The Soccer Trails.*
Vladyana Krykorka, illustrator. Ontario, Canada: Annick Press, 1993. 24
pages. ISBN 1-55037-339-0 and 1-55037-338-2pbk.
Topeka, KS: Econo-Clad Books, 1999. 24 pages. ISBN 0-7857-2207-6.
Lexile AD590. Grades 3 to 6.
An Inuit tale, explaining the origin of the northern lights, about the
souls of the dead playing soccer using a walrus head for the ball. Told by
a young Inuit girl's grandmother to assist the girl with her grief after her
mother dies. Illustrated with paintings and photographs of Inuit beadwork.
Aesop Accolade, Canadian Library Association Notable Book, and
Ruth Schwartz Children's Book Award.

Lelooska, Chief and Christine Normandin. *Echoes of the Elders.*
Andrea Danese, editor. New York: DK Publishing, 1997. 40 pages.
ISBN 0-7894-2455-X. Lexile 760. Grades 3 to 6.
Five Northwest Coast Indian tales by the late Chief Lelooska of
Cherokee heritage. Includes paintings by the chief and a CD of him telling the stories.
Aesop Prize and *International Reading Association Notable Books
for a Global Society.*

Lelooska, Chief and Christine Normandin. *Spirit of the Cedar People.*
New York: DK Publishing, 1998. 40 pages. ISBN 0-7894-2571-8. Lexile
AD730. Grades K to 6.
This companion volume to *Echoes of the Elders* features five additional tales from the Northwest Coast Indian tradition. A CD featuring
the voice of Chief Lelooska accompanies this collection
American Library Association Notable Children's Books and *Anne
Izard Storytellers' Choice Award.*

Luenn, Nancy. *Miser on the Mountain: A Nisqually Legend of Mount Rainier.*
Pierr Morgan, illustrator. Seattle, WA: Sasquatch Books, 1997. 32 pages. ISBN 1-57061-082-7. (Out of print). Grades K to 4.

A Northwest Coast Indian legend regarding the quest of an old man on the summit of Mount Rainier.

Storytelling World Award Honor Book.

Lunge-Larsen, Lise and Margi Preus. *The Legend of the Lady Slipper.*
Andrea Arroyo, illustrator. New York: Houghton Mifflin Co., 1999. 32 pages. ISBN 0-395-90512-5. Grades K to 3.

A courageous young Ojibwa girl becomes stuck during a blizzard while on her way to a neighboring village to get herbs to heal those who are ill, and she discards her moccasins to free herself. When she returns to their location in the spring, she finds a patch of pink and white flowers in the shape of her shoes.

National Council for the Social Studies Notable Children's Trade Books in the Field of Social Studies.

Manitonquat. *The Children of the Morning Light: Wampanoag Tales As Told by Manitonquat.*
Mary Arquette, illustrator. New York: Macmillan Publishing Co., 1994. 80 pages. ISBN 0-02-765905-4. Grades 3 to 6.

Seven creation stories and four legends from the eastern Massachusetts Wampanoag tradition are shared by Native American storyteller, Manitonquat.

Anne Izard Storytellers' Choice Award.

McDermott, Gerald. *Arrow to the Sun: A Pueblo Indian Tale.*
New York: Viking, 1974. 42 pages. ISBN 0-670-13369-8 and 0-14-050211-4pbk. Lexile 480. Grades 3 to 6.

An adaptation of the Pueblo Indian myth about a boy's search for his father that explains how the spirit of the Sun was brought to the Earth.

Caldecott Medal.

McDermott, Gerald. *Raven: A Trickster Tale from the Pacific Northwest.*
San Diego, CA: Harcourt Children's Books, 1993. 32 pages. ISBN 0-15-265661-8 and 0-15-202449-2pbk. Lexile AD380. Grades K to 3.

Raven attempts to steal the sun from the Sky Chief in order to light the world.

Caldecott Honor Book.

Norman, Howard A. *The Girl Who Dreamed Only Geese: And Other Tales of the Far North.*
Diane and Leo Dillon, illustrators. San Diego, CA: Harcourt Children's Books, 1997. 164 pages. ISBN 0-15-230979-9. Lexile 600. Grades 3 to 6.

Ten Inuit tales from Siberia, Alaska, the Canadian Arctic, and Greenland.

Aesop Accolade and *Anne Izard Storytellers' Choice Award.*

Norman, Howard A. *Trickster and the Fainting Birds.*
Tom Pohrt, illustrator. San Diego, CA: Gulliver Books, 2000. 96 pages. ISBN 0-15-200888-8. Lexile 550. Grades K to 3.

Illustrated with forty-two paintings, these seven tales from the Algonquin Cree tradition feature the troublesome Trickster and his humorous antics.

Aesop Prize.

Pollock, Penny. *The Turkey Girl: A Zuni Cinderella.*
Ed Young, illustrator. Boston: Little, Brown & Company, 1996. 32 pages. ISBN 0-316-71314-7. Lexile 860. Grades K to 3.

A young girl who tends turkeys realizes her dream of going to the Dance of the Sacred Bird with the assistance of one of the turkeys who helps her make a magical dress. When the girl breaks her promise to return before sunrise, all the turkeys abandon her in this New Mexican Zuni Indian tale.

Aesop Accolade.

Reneaux, J. J. *How Animals Saved the People: Animal Tales from the South.*
James Ransome, illustrator. New York: HarperCollins Children's Book Group, 2001. 64 pages. ISBN 0-688-16253-3 and 0-688-16254-1. Grades K to 3.

Eight folktales from the Southern United States that differ in their origin and dialect. Includes tales from African American, Appalachian, Cajun, Creole, and Native American traditions.

International Reading Association Children's Choices and *National Council for the Social Studies Notable Children's Trade Books in the Field of Social Studies.*

Rodanas, Kristina. *Follow the Stars.*
Tarrytown, NY: Marshall Cavendish, 1998. 32 pages. ISBN 0-7614-5029-7. Lexile AD490. Grades K to 3.

Animals suffering from an everlasting winter search for the birds of summer and explain the origin of the North Star in this gentle retelling of an Ojibwa tale.

National Council for the Social Studies Notable Children's Trade Books in the Field of Social Studies.

Ross, Gayle. *How Rabbit Tricked Otter: And Other Cherokee Trickster Stories.*
Murv Jacob, illustrator. New York: HarperCollins Children's Book Group, 1994. 80 pages. ISBN 0-06-021285-3.
New York: Caedmon Audio, 1996. ISBN 1-55994-542-7. Lexile 870. Grades 3 to 6.

Fifteen tales from the Cherokee oral tradition featuring the trickster Rabbit.

Anne Izard Storytellers' Choice Award.

San Souci, Robert D. and Jane Yolen. *Cut from the Same Cloth: American Women of Myth, Legend and Tall Tale.*
Brian Pinkney, illustrator. New York: Philomel Books, 1993. 140 pages. ISBN 0-399-21987-0.
New York: Penguin Putnam, 2000. 160 pages. ISBN 0-698-11811-1pbk. Lexile 1050. Grades 3 to 6.

This collection of tales from all areas of the country features fifteen of America's little-known heroines as told in the Native American, African American, Anglo American, Eskimo, and Hawaiian traditions.

Aesop Prize.

Simms, Laura. *The Bone Man: A Native American Modoc Tale.*
Michael McCurdy, illustrator. New York: Disney Press, 1997. 32 pages. ISBN 0-7868-2074-8. Lexile 530. Grades K to 3.

A terrible giant and a small Modoc boy clash in this Native American tale that includes scratchboard illustrations.

American Library Association Notable Children's Books.

Talashoema, Herschel. *Coyote and Little Turtle: A Traditional Hopi Tale.*
Emory Sekaquaptewa, editor. Santa Fe, NM: Clear Light Books, 1993. 90 pages. ISBN 0-940666-84-7. (Out of print). Grades K to 3.

A story told in both Hopi and English with ninety Hopi drawings in color.

Aesop Accolade.

Turtle, Eagle Walking. *Full Moon Stories: Thirteen Native American Legends.*
New York: Disney Press, 1997. 48 pages. ISBN 0-7868-2175-2. Grades 3 to 6.

Thirteen stories that revolve around the thirteen full moons of the year as the organizing theme to convey Arapahoe Indian traditions.

Aesop Accolade.

Ude, Wayne. *Maybe I Will Do Something: Seven Coyote Tales.*
Abigail Rorer, illustrator. New York: Houghton Mifflin Co., 1993. 75 pages. ISBN 0-395-65233-2. Grades 5 to 10.

The coyote is the central figure in these seven tales that use Native American cultural traditions to explain the origin of the world.

Anne Izard Storytellers' Choice Award.

Van Laan, Nancy. *Shingebiss: An Ojibwe Legend.*
Betsy Bowen, illustrator. New York: Houghton Mifflin Co., 1997. 32 pages. ISBN 0-395-82745-0 and 0-618-21616-2. Grades K to 4.

Woodcuts illustrate this story of a merganser duck that challenges the fierce Winter Maker in his attempt to survive the winter.

National Council for the Social Studies Notable Children's Trade Books in the Field of Social Studies.

Webster, M. L. *On the Trail Made of Dawn: American Indian Creation Myths.*
North Haven, CT: Shoe String Press, 2001. 96 pages. ISBN 0-208-02497-2. Grades 4 to 6.

Thirteen Native American cultures are represented in this collection of creation tales.

Storytelling World Award Honor Book.

Yamane, Linda. *When the World Ended, How Hummingbird Got Fire, How People Were Made: Rumsien Ohlone Stories.*
Berkeley, CA: Oyate, 1995. 48 pages. ISBN 0-96251-751-8pbk. Grades 3 to 6.

Three California Ohlone stories retold and illustrated.

Aesop Accolade.

Southern

Artell, Mike. *Petite Rouge: A Cajun Red Riding Hood.*
Jim Harris, illustrator. New York: Dial Books for Young Readers, 2001.
32 pages. ISBN 0-8037-2514-0. Lexile 870. Grades K to 3.
   A classic folktale retold in the Southern Cajun tradition.
   National Council for the Social Studies Notable Children's Trade Books in the Field of Social Studies and *Storytelling World Award.*

Brooks, Stephen and Annette J. Bruce. *Sandspun.*
Sarasota, FL: Pineapple Press, 2001. 176 pages. ISBN 1-56164-242-8 and 1-56164-243-6pbk.
   This anthology of folktales by the best of Florida's storytellers is best used with older readers.
   Storytelling World Award Honor Book.

Davis, Donald D. *Jack Always Seeks His Fortune: Authentic Appalachian Jack Tales.*
New York: August House, 1992. 176 pages. ISBN 0-87483-281-0 and 0-87483-280-2pbk. Grades 3 to 7.
   A collection of thirteen tales about Jack from the Southern Appalachian Mountains.
   Anne Izard Storytellers' Choice Award.

Doucet, Sharon Arms. *Lapin Plays Possum: Trickster Tales from the Louisiana Bayou.*
New York: Farrar, Straus & Giroux, 2002. 64 pages. ISBN 0-374-34328-4. Grades K to 3.
   Three Cajun folktales where rabbit "Lapin" plays tricks to outwit hyena "Bouki".
   Children's Literature Choices.

Doucet, Sharon Arms. *Why Lapin's Ears Are Long: And Other Tales from the Louisiana Bayou.*
David Catrow, illustrator. New York: Orchard Books, 1997. 64 pages. ISBN 0-531-33041-9. (Out of print). Grades K to 4.
   Three Creole-Cajun folktales that originated in West Africa about the rabbit trickster, Lapin.
   Storytelling World Award Honor Book.

Johnson, Paul Brett. *Jack Outwits the Giants.*
New York: Margaret K. McElderry Books, 2002. 32 pages. ISBN 0-689-83902-2. Grades K to 3.

Clever Jack outwits a pair of hungry giants in this Appalachian folktale.

National Council for the Social Studies Notable Social Studies Trade Books for Young People and *Storytelling World Award Honor Book.*

Reneaux, J. J. *Cajun Folktales.*
New York: August House, 1992. 176 pages. ISBN 0-87483-283-7 and 0-87483-282-9pbk.
New York: August House audio, 1994. ISBN 0-87483-383-3. Grades 3 to 6.

Twenty-seven traditional Cajun tales are retold by a nationally acclaimed storyteller.

Anne Izard Storytellers' Choice Award.

Reneaux, J. J. *How Animals Saved the People: Animal Tales from the South.*
James Ransome, illustrator. New York: HarperCollins Children's Book Group, 2001. 64 pages. ISBN 0-688-16253-3 and 0-688-16254-1. Grades K to 3.

Eight folktales from the Southern United States that differ in their origin and dialect. Includes tales from African American, Appalachian, Cajun, Creole, and Native American traditions.

International Reading Association Children's Choices and *National Council for the Social Studies Notable Children's Trade Books in the Field of Social Studies.*

Reneaux, J. J. *Why Alligator Hates Dog: A Cajun Folktale.*
Donnie Green, illustrator. New York: August House, 1995. 32 pages. ISBN 0-87483-412-0 and 0-87483-621-2pbk. Grades K to 3.

A Cajun tale about a sassy dog that outwits an alligator.

Aesop Accolade.

Salley, Coleen. *Epossumondas.*
Janet Stevens, illustrator. San Diego, CA: Harcourt Children's Books, 2002. 40 pages. ISBN 0-15-216748-X. Grades K to 2.

A Louisiana possum takes his mother's instructions literally in this hilarious rendition of the Southern legend of Epaminondas.

Children's Literature Choices.

Thomassie, Tynia. *Feleciana Meets d'Loup Garou: A Cajun Tall Tale.*
Cat Bowman Smith, illustrator. Boston: Little, Brown & Company, 1998.
32 pages. ISBN 0-316-84133-1. (Out of print). Lexile 590. Grades K to
3.

A young girl and the legendary werewolf of the bayou who eats
naughty children chase each other around until the werewolf reveals to
her how he handles his bad days.

*National Council for the Social Studies Notable Children's Trade
Books in the Field of Social Studies.*

Wooldridge, Connie Nordhielm. *Wicked Jack.*
Will Hildebrand, illustrator. New York: Holiday House, 1995. 32 pages.
ISBN 0-8234-1101-X and 0-8234-1292-Xpbk. Grades K to 3.

An adaptation of the Southern folktale "Wicked John and the Devil."
A blacksmith defeats the devil and his young sons with a chair that won't
stop rocking, a sledgehammer that won't stop pounding, and a fire bush
that keeps on sticking.

Aesop Accolade.

Southwestern

Hayes, Joe. *Here Comes the Storyteller.*
Richard Baron, photographer. El Paso, TX: Cinco Puntos Press, 1996. 80
pages. ISBN 0-938317-25-3pbk. Grades 3 to 6.

Nine favorite Southwestern United States tales with photographs illustrating the gestures, poses, and facial expressions of the storyteller.

Youth Storytelling Pegasus Award.

Hayes, Joe. *Little Gold Star.*
Gloria Osuna Perez, illustrator. Lucia Angela Perez, illustrator. El Paso,
TX: Cinco Puntos Press, 2002. 30 pages. ISBN 0-938317-68-7. Grades K
to 3.

In this Hispanic variation of the Cinderella story from New Mexico,
Arcia and her wicked stepsisters encounter a hawk that leaves them
transformed.

Storytelling World Award Honor Book.

Hopkins, Jackie Mims. *The Horned Toad Prince.*
Michael Austin, illustrator. Atlanta, GA: Peachtree Publishers, 2000. 32
pages. ISBN 1-56145-195-9. Lexile 670. Grades K to 3.

A Southwestern cowgirl owes a horny toad three favors after he re-

trieves her hat in this retelling of "The Frog Prince."
Storytelling World Award Honor Book.

Mitchell, Marianne. *Joe Cinders.*
Bryan Langdo, illustrator. New York: Henry Holt and Company, 2002.
48 pages. ISBN 0-8050-6529-6. Grades K to 2.
 Joe wins the heart of a girl in this alternative version of a Southwestern male Cinderella story.
Storytelling World Award Honor Book.

Multiregional

Andersen, Hans Christian. *The Little Match Girl.*
Jerry Pinkney, illustrator. New York: Phyllis Fogelman Books, 1999. 32
pages. ISBN 0-8037-2314-8. Grades K to 3.
 A tragic classic set at the beginning of the 20th century about a poverty-stricken girl who sells matches on an American street corner.
National Council for the Social Studies Notable Children's Trade Books in the Field of Social Studies and *Parent's Choice Gold Award.*

Aylesworth, Jim. *The Tale of Tricky Fox: A New England Trickster Tale.*
New York: Scholastic, 2001. 32 pages. ISBN 0-439-09543-3. Lexile
AD610. Grades K to 3.
 Tricky Fox outwits many people before he encounters a teacher who, he discovers, is not as easy to fool as other humans.
Storytelling World Award Honor Book.

Baker, Holly C., Amy J. Kotkin and Steven J. Zeitlin. *A Celebration of American Family Folklore.*
Cambridge, MA: Yellow Moon Press, 1992. 304 pages. ISBN 0-938756-36-2pbk.
 The authors gathered these stories over a period of four consecutive summers at the Smithsonian Folklife Festival. This anthology is best used with older children.
Anne Izard Storytellers' Choice Award.

Birdseye, Tom. *Look Out, Jack! The Giant Is Back.*
Will Hillenbrand, illustrator. New York: Holiday House, 2001. 32 pages.
ISBN 0-8234-1450-7. Lexile AD560. Grades K to 3.
 Jack moves to America in this extension of the beanstalk tale

wherein the giant is dead, but his big brother is out for revenge.
Storytelling World Award.

DePaola, Tomie. *Christopher: The Holy Giant.*
New York: Holiday House, 1994. 32 pages. ISBN 0-8234-0862-0 and 0-8234-1169-9pbk. Lexile AD680. Grades K to 3.

An interpretation of the legend of St. Christopher, who was originally a giant named Reprobus. In his attempt to serve the world's most powerful king, St. Christopher finds Christ in the form of a young child when he assists travelers across a turbulent river.
Aesop Accolade.

DeSpain, Pleasant. *Sweet Land of Story: Thirty-Six American Tales to Tell.*
Donald Bell, illustrator. New York: August House, 2000. 192 pages. ISBN 0-87483-569-0 and 0-87483-600-Xpbk. Grades 4 to 6.

A wide variety of short tales organized by regions of the United States. Introductory remarks give insight into the people and cultures of the selected regions.
National Council for the Social Studies Notable Children's Trade Books in the Field of Social Studies.

Fleming, Candace. *The Hatmaker's Sign: A Story.*
Robert Andrew Parker, illustrator. New York: Orchard Books, 1998. 32 pages. ISBN 0-531-30075-7 and 0-531-07174-Xpbk. Lexile 410. Grades K to 5.

This tale is based on a parable Benjamin Franklin told Thomas Jefferson while Congress was demanding that Jefferson rewrite sections of the Declaration of Independence. Upon consultation with others, a Boston hatmaker eliminates words from his store sign until it is finally blank.
Aesop Accolade and *Storytelling World Award Honor Book.*

Goodall, Jane. *The Eagle & the Wren: A Fable.*
Alexander Reichstein, illustrator. New York: North-South Books, 2000. 40 pages. ISBN 0-7358-1381-7. Lexile AD420. Grades K to 3.

The lark, dove, vulture, and eagle all claim to fly the highest. They have a contest, with a surprise outcome that illustrates how we depend upon each other.
National Council for the Social Studies Notable Children's Trade Books in the Field of Social Studies and *Storytelling World Award Honor Book.*

Guthrie, Woody. *This Land Is Your Land.*
Kathy Jacobsen, illustrator. Pete Seeger, contributor. Boston: Little,
Brown & Company, 1998. 32 pages. ISBN 0-316-39215-4. Lexile NP.
Grades K to 3.

A picture-book tribute to a popular American song.
American Library Association Notable Children's Books.

Hicks, Ray and Lynn Salsi. *The Jack Tales.*
Owen Smith, illustrator. New York: Callaway Editions, 2000. 40 pages.
ISBN 0-935112-58-8. Grades 3 to 5.

Three tales about Jack ("Jack and the Northwest Wind," "Jack and
the Bean Tree," and "Jack and the Robbers") are retold and humorously
illustrated. Includes a CD.
Booklist Top Ten Folklore Books for Youth.

Isaacs, Anne. *Swamp Angel.*
Paul Zelinsky, illustrator. New York: Dutton Children's Books, 1994. 40
pages. ISBN 0-525-45271-0.
New York: Puffin Books, 2000. 48 pages. ISBN 0-14-055908-6pbk.
Lexile AD1020. Grades K to 3.

An American tall tale about the competition between a Tennessee
woodswoman and a very hungry bear that changes the North American
landscape.
*American Library Association Notable Children's Books, Booklist
Editors' Choice, Boston Globe-Horn Book Award Honor Book, Calde-
cott Honor Book, New York Times Best Illustrated Book of the Year,
Publishers Weekly Best Books of the Year*, and *School Library Journal
Best Book.*

Lester, Julius. *John Henry.*
Jerry Pinkney, illustrator. New York: Dial Books for Young Readers,
1994. 40 pages. ISBN 0-8037-1606-0.
New York: Puffin Books, 1999. 40 pages. ISBN 0-14-056622-8pbk.
Lexile AD720. Grades K to 3.

An original American tall tale of how John Henry raced against and
beat a steam drill.
*Aesop Prize, American Library Association Notable Children's
Books, Boston Globe-Horn Book Award, The Bulletin of the Center for
Children's Books Children's Book Award, Caldecott Honor Book, Horn
Book Fanfare Honor List, National Council for the Social Studies Nota-
ble Children's Trade Books in the Field of Social Studies, Society of Il-
lustrators Gold Medal*, and *Storytelling World Award Honor Book.*

Lewis, J. Patrick. *The Shoe Tree of Chagrin.*
Chris Sheban, illustrator. Mankato, MN: Creative Editions, 2001. 32
pages. ISBN 1-56846-173-9. Grades 1 to 4.

In this original Ohio tall tale, an elderly cobbler who makes shoes for
the entire Ohio Valley is prevented from returning promptly to the area
by her age and inclement weather. The shoes she made are found hung
from a tree at the edge of town, thus demonstrating the woman's integ-
rity and hard work.

Golden Kite Award.

Lobel, Arnold. *Fables.*
New York: HarperCollins Children's Book Group, 1980. 40 pages. ISBN
0-06-023973-5 and 0-06-443046-4pbk. Lexile 540. Grades K to 3.

Twenty short original American fables about an array of animal
characters.

American Library Association Notable Children's Books and *Caldecott Medal.*

Murphy, Shirley Rousseau. *Wind Child.*
Diane and Leo Dillon, illustrators. New York: HarperCollins Children's
Book Group, 1999. 40 pages. ISBN 0-06-024903-X. (Out of print).
Grades K to 3.

Born of a human mother and the East Wind, a young girl becomes a
weaver in an attempt to find a husband and ease her loneliness.

Parent's Choice Award.

Philip, Neil. *Stockings of Buttermilk: American Folktales.*
Jacqueline Mair, illustrator. New York: Houghton Mifflin Co., 1999. 128
pages. ISBN 0-395-84980-2. Lexile 870. Grades 3 to 6.

These eighteen American folktales from eleven states are based on
traditional tales from the British Isles, France, Germany, and Spain. Illustrations are in the style of American folk art.

Aesop Accolade.

San Souci, Robert D. and Jane Yolen. *Cut from the Same Cloth:
American Women of Myth, Legend and Tall Tale.*
Brian Pinkney, illustrator. New York: Philomel Books, 1993. 140 pages.
ISBN 0-399-21987-0.
New York: Penguin Putnam, 2000. 160 pages. ISBN 0-698-11811-1pbk.
Lexile 1050. Grades 3 to 6.

This collection of tales from all areas of the country features fifteen
of America's little-known heroines as told in the Native American, Afri-

can American, Anglo American, Eskimo, and Hawaiian traditions.
Aesop Prize.

Schanzer, Rosalyn. *Davy Crockett Saves the World.*
New York: HarperCollins Children's Book Group, 2001. 32 pages. ISBN 0-688-16991-0. Lexile 890. Grades 5 to 8.
Brave Davy Crockett faces down Halley's comet in this original tall tale. The text is accompanied by oversized illustrations that match the story's humor.
Booklist Editors' Choice.

Seeger, Pete and Paul Dubois Jacobs. *Pete Seeger's Storytelling Book.*
San Diego, CA: Harcourt Children's Books, 2000. 288 pages. ISBN 0-15-100370-X and 0-15-601311-8pbk. Grades 3 to 7.
More than twenty-five of this famous storyteller's favorite tales are recounted in this collection from the oral tradition of the United States.
Youth Storytelling Pegasus Award.

Walker, Paul Robert. *Big Men, Big Country: A Collection of American Tall Tales.*
James Bernardin, illustrator. San Diego, CA: Harcourt Children's Books, 1993. 79 pages. ISBN 0-15-207136-9 and 0-15-202625-8pbk. Grades 3 to 6.
Nine tall tales about the escapades of such heroes as Davy Crockett, Paul Bunyan, John Henry, Pecos Bill, and other mythical as well as historical figures. A note at the end of each tale gives information about its origin and the life of the man it is based upon.
Aesop Accolade.

Wardlaw, Lee. *Punia and the King of Sharks: A Hawaiian Folktale.*
Felipe Davalos, illustrator. New York: Dial Books for Young Readers, 1997. 32 pages. ISBN 0-8037-1682-6. Lexile AD700. Grades K to 3.
A young Polynesian boy tricks the King of Sharks out of lobsters to feed his mother and village.
National Council for the Social Studies Notable Children's Trade Books in the Field of Social Studies.

Willey, Margaret. *Clever Beatrice: An Upper Peninsula Conte.*
Heather Solomon, illustrator. New York: Atheneum Books for Young Readers, 2001. 40 pages. ISBN 0-689-83254-0. Lexile 470. Grades K to 3.
In this brains versus brawn tall tale of the upper peninsula of Michi-

gan, a young girl tricks a giant out of his gold coins to assist her impoverished mother.

American Library Association Notable Children's Books, The Bulletin of the Center for Children's Books Blue Ribbon Award, Charlotte Zolotow Award, and *Children's Literature Choices.*

Chapter 27

International

African

Aardema, Verna. *Why Mosquitoes Buzz in Peoples Ears: A West African Tale.*
Leo D. Dillon, illustrator. New York: Dial Books for Young Readers, 1984. 30 pages. ISBN 0-8037-6089-2.
New York: Penguin Putnam, 1978. 30 pages. ISBN 0-14-054905-6pbk. Lexile 770. Grades K to 3.
A mosquito tells a story about a jungle disaster that reveals the secret of its buzz.
American Library Association Notable Children's Books and *Caldecott Medal.*

Andersen, Hans Christian. *The Nightingale.*
Jerry Pinkney, illustrator. New York: Phyllis Fogelman Books, 2002. 40 pages. ISBN 0-8037-2464-0. Grades K to 3.
The nightingale returns from banishment to revive a dying King with its beautiful song in this classic tale set in Morocco instead of China.
National Council for the Social Studies Notable Social Studies Trade Books for Young People.

Bryan, Ashley. *Lion and the Ostrich Chicks: And Other African Folktales.*
New York: Aladdin Paperbacks, 1996. 96 pages. ISBN 0-689-80713-9pbk. Grades K to 3.
Four stories representing various cultures of Africa.
Coretta Scott King Award Honor Book.

Bryan, Ashley. *The Ox of the Wonderful Horns: And Other African Folktales.*
New York: Atheneum Books for Young Readers, 1993. 42 pages. ISBN 0-689-31799-9. Grades K to 4.

Five traditional tales from Africa feature animals and the story of a chief's son who is tormented by his father's many wives.

Anne Izard Storytellers' Choice Award.

Dayrell, Elphinstone. *Why the Sun and the Moon Live in the Sky: An African Folktale.*
Blair Lent, illustrator. New York: Houghton Mifflin Co., 1968. 32 pages. ISBN 0-395-29609-9 and 0-395-53963-3pbk. Lexile 570. Grades K to 3.

An African folktale that explains how the sun and the moon, original inhabitants of the earth, came to live in the sky.

American Library Association Notable Children's Books and *Horn Book Fanfare Honor List.*

Diakite, Baba Wague. *The Hatseller and the Monkeys: A West African Folktale.*
New York: Scholastic, 1999. 32 pages. ISBN 0-590-96069-5. Lexile AD650. Grades K to 3.

A hatseller falls asleep under a mango tree, and a group of mischievous monkeys swipe his wares. He is able to figure out how to retrieve his hats only after he eats the mangoes.

Aesop Accolade and *International Reading Association Notable Books for a Global Society.*

Diakite, Baba Wague. *The Hunterman and the Crocodile: A West African Folktale.*
New York: Scholastic, 1997. 32 pages. ISBN 0-590-89828-0. Lexile AD800. Grades K to 3.

Illustrated with ceramic tile paintings, this humorous folktale is about a hunter and a crocodile that take turns being captive and captor as they learn the important lesson of living in harmony with nature.

American Library Association Notable Children's Books and *National Council for the Social Studies Notable Children's Trade Books in the Field of Social Studies.*

Echewa, T. Obinkaram. *The Magic Tree: A Folktale from Nigeria.*
New York: Morrow, 1999. 32 pages. ISBN 0-688-16232-0. Lexile AD680. Grades K to 3.

A mistreated orphaned boy finds a magic tree and becomes powerful in his African village.

Booklist Editors' Choice and *International Reading Association Notable Books for a Global Society.*

Gershator, Phillis. *Only One Cowry: A Dahomean Tale.*
David Soman, illustrator. New York: Orchard Books, 2000. 32 pages. ISBN 0-531-33288-8. Grades K to 3.

A clever young man and the beautiful daughter of a chief trick a stingy king into supplying lavish gifts in this African folktale.

National Council for the Social Studies Notable Children's Trade Books in the Field of Social Studies.

Gershator, Phillis. *Zzzng! Zzzng! Zzzng!: A Yoruba Tale.*
Greg Henry and Theresa Smith, illustrators. New York: Scholastic, 1997. 32 pages. ISBN 0-531-09523-1. Grades K to 3.

Angry Mosquito learns to buzz and bite after suffering rejection from Ear, Arm, and Leg.

Anne Izard Storytellers' Choice Award.

Hamilton, Virginia. *A Ring of Tricksters: Animal Tales from America, the West Indies, and Africa.*
Barry Moser, illustrator. New York: Blue Sky Press, 1998. 112 pages. ISBN 0-590-47374-3. Lexile 540. Grades 3 to 6.

Eleven animal trickster tales follow the migration of African culture from Africa to the West Indies and America.

International Reading Association Notable Books for a Global Society.

Hyman, Katrin. *Sense Pass King: A Story from Cameroon.*
Trina Schart Hyman, illustrator. New York: Holiday House, 2002. 32 pages. ISBN 0-8234-1557-5. Grades K to 3.

A gifted girl earns the nickname Sense Pass King by outwitting a royal ruler in this traditional African folktale.

National Council for the Social Studies Notable Social Studies Trade Books for Young People.

Kituku, Vincent Muli. *East African Folktales: The Voice of Mukamba.*
New York: August House, 1997. 93 pages. ISBN 0-87483-489-9pbk. Grades 6 to 12.

A bilingual collection of eighteen folktales in English and Kenyan

Kikamba. Each tale is followed by a brief explanation of African customs.

Youth Storytelling Pegasus Award.

Knutson, Barbara. *How the Guinea Fowl Got Her Spots: A Swahili Tale of Friendship.*
Minneapolis, MN: The Lerner Publishing Group, 1991. 32 pages. ISBN 0-87614-416-4 and 0-87614-537-7pbk. Lexile AD730. Grades K to 3.

The guinea fowl protects her friend, the cow, from being eaten by the lion and in return gets sprinkled with milk for protective coloring in this African folktale.

Anne Izard Storytellers' Choice Award.

LaTeef, Nelda. *The Hunter and the Ebony Tree.*
North Kingston, RI: Moon Mountain, 2002. 32 pages. ISBN 0-9677929-9-1. Grades K to 3.

A wise hunter enlists the help of his forest friends to assist him in outwitting the father of the beautiful girl he wants to marry in this African folktale.

Storytelling World Award Honor Book.

Lexau, Joan M. *Crocodile and Hen: A Bakongo Folktale.*
Doug Cushman, illustrator. New York: HarperCollins Children's Book Group, 2001. 48 pages. ISBN 0-06-028486-2 and 0-06-028487-0. Lexile 120. Grades K to 3.

Based on a folktale from the Republic of Congo, a hen outwits a crocodile that is determined to eat her by calling him her brother.

National Council for the Social Studies Notable Children's Trade Books in the Field of Social Studies.

Lippert, Margaret H. and Won-Ldy Paye. *Head, Body, Legs: A Story from Liberia.*
Julie Paschkis, illustrator. New York: Henry Holt & Co., 2002. 32 pages. ISBN 0-8050-6570-9. Grades Pre-K to 2.

This humorous African folktale reveals that head, body, arms, and legs can accomplish more when they cooperate with each other.

Aesop Accolade, American Library Association Notable Children's Book, The Bulletin for the Center for Children's Books Blue Ribbon Award, and *Children's Literature Choices.*

MacDonald, Margaret Read. *Mabela the Clever.*
Tim Coffey, illustrator. Morton Grove, IL: Albert Whitman & Co., 2001.
32 pages. ISBN 0-8075-4902-9. Lexile AD380. Grades K to 3.

A village's mice are tricked by a clever cat into believing that they belong to a secret society, only to be rescued by the littlest mouse of them all in this African folktale.

Aesop Accolade, Charlotte Zolotow Award Highly Commended Book, Children's Literature Choices, and *Storytelling World Award.*

Mandela, Nelson, editor. *Nelson Mandela's Favorite African Folktales.*
New York: W.W. Norton, 2002. 144 pages. ISBN 0-393-05212-5. Grades 1 to 5.

Thirty-two African legends by numerous authors and illustrators are presented in this anthology.

Storytelling World Award Honor Book.

McDermott, Gerald. *Zomo the Rabbit: A Trickster Tale from West Africa.*
San Diego, CA: Harcourt Children's Books, 1992. 30 pages. ISBN 0-15-299967-1 and 0-15-201010-6pbk. Lexile 370. Grades K to 3.

Zomo the rabbit acquires his speed while trying to obtain wisdom from Sky God, who challenges him with three impossible tasks.

Anne Izard Storytellers' Choice Award.

Medearis, Angela Shelf. *Seven Spools of Thread.*
Daniel Minter, illustrator. Morton Grove, IL: Albert Whitman & Company, 2000. 40 pages. ISBN 0-8075-7315-9. Lexile 430. Grades K to 3.

Seven African Ashanti brothers learn to cooperate when they are given the task of making gold from seven spools of thread in this tale instructive of Kwanzaa principles.

Storytelling World Award.

Mollel, Tololwa M. *The Orphan Boy.*
Paul Morin, illustrator. New York: Houghton Mifflin Co., 1991. 32 pages. ISBN 0-89919-985-2 and 0-395-72079-6pbk. Lexile AD560. Grades K to 3.

This traditional folktale from Africa explains why the star Kileken (Venus) appears in the sky at both morning and night.

American Bookseller Pick of the Lists, American Library Association Notable Children's Books, National Council for the Social Studies Notable Children's Trade Books in the Field of Social Studies, Parent's

Choice Storybook Honor Award, and *Storytelling World Award Honor Book.*

Offodile, Buchi. *The Orphan Girl and Other Stories: West African Folk Tales.*
Northampton, MA: Interlink Publishing Group, 2001. 272 pages. ISBN 1-56656-375-5. Grades 6 to 8.

An anthology of folktales representing the diversity of cultures in West Africa with basic geographical information.

Storytelling World Award Honor Book.

Olaleye, Isaac. *In the Rainfield: Who is the Greatest?*
Ann Grifalconi, illustrator. New York: Scholastic, 2000. 32 pages. ISBN 0-590-48363-3. Lexile AD380. Grades K to 3.

A Nigerian folktale where Fire, Wind, and Rain compete to see who is the greatest.

National Council for the Social Studies Notable Children's Trade Books in the Field of Social Studies and *Parent's Choice Silver Award.*

Paye, Won-Ldy and Margaret Lippert. *Why Leopard Has Spots: Dan Stories from Liberia.*
Ashley Bryan, illustrator. New York: Raintree Steck-Vaughn Publishers, 1998. ISBN 0-8172-5156-1 and 0-8172-7980-6pbk.
Golden, CO: Fulcrum Publishing, 1999. 64 pages. ISBN 1-55591-991-Xpbk. Lexile 580. Grades 3 to 6.

Six humorous West African tales from Liberia.

Aesop Accolade, Anne Izard Storytellers' Choice Award, and *Storytelling World Award Honor Book.*

Shepard, Aaron. *Master Man: A Tall Tale of Nigeria.*
David Wisniewski, illustrator. New York: HarperCollins Children's Book Group, 2000. 32 pages. ISBN 0-688-13783-0. Lexile 340. Grades K to 3.

A foolish man brags about his strength in this tale that explains the origin of thunder in the sky.

Children's Literature Choices.

Steptoe, John. *Mufaro's Beautiful Daughters: An African Tale.*
New York: Lothrop, Lee & Shepard Books, 1987. 32 pages. ISBN 0-688-04045-4 and 0-688-12935-8pbk. Lexile AD 720. Grades K to 3.

An African Cinderella tale of the two daughters of Mufaro who go before a king who is seeking a wife. One of the daughters is mean and

spiteful, while the other is beautiful and kind.
Coretta Scott King Award.

Wisniewski, David. *Sundiata: Lion King of Mali.*
New York: Clarion Books, 1992. 32 pages. ISBN 0-395-61302-7 and 0-395-76481-5pbk. Lexile AD820. Grades 2 to 4.

In 13th century Mali, Sundiata, son of the king's second wife, overcomes physical handicap and social disgrace to return and rule Mali when he is eighteen years old.
American Library Association Notable Children's Books.

Armenian

San Souci, Robert D. *A Weave of Words: An Armenian Tale.*
Raul Colon, illustrator. New York: Orchard Books, 1998. 32 pages. ISBN 0-531-30053-6. Lexile 720. Grades 2 to 5.

A lazy prince who learns to read, write, and weave in order to win his love's hand in marriage finds later that his new skills will save him.
Storytelling World Award Honor Book.

Australian

Morin, Paul. *Animal Dreaming: An Aboriginal Dreamtime Story.*
San Diego, CA: Silver Whistle, 1998. 32 pages. ISBN 0-15-20004-2. Grades K to 5.

Animals from long ago create a world in which they live harmoniously in this Australian Aboriginal tale told to a young boy by his elders.
International Reading Association Notable Books for a Global Society and *National Council for the Social Studies Notable Children's Trade Books in the Field of Social Studies.*

Rhodes, Timothy. *The Singing Snake.*
Stefan Czernecki, illustrator. New York: Hyperion, 1993. 40 pages. ISBN 0-920534-97-X. (Out of print). Grades K to 3.

An Australian folktale about a snake that wins a singing contest.
Storytelling World Award Honor Book.

Roth, Susan L. *The Biggest Frog in Australia.*
Topeka, KS: Econo-Clad Books, 2000. 32 pages. ISBN 0-613-28423-2.

New York: Aladdin Paperbacks, 2000. 32 pages. ISBN 0-689-83314-8pbk. Lexile 670. Grades K to 3.

An immense frog drinks up all the water on the continent, and all the other animals try to make him laugh so the water will come spilling out.

Aesop Accolade.

British

Barber, Antonia. *The Mousehole Cat.*
Nicola Bayley, illustrator. Topeka, KS: Econo-Clad Books, 1996. 40 pages. ISBN 0-613-26291-3.
New York: Simon & Schuster, 1996. 40 pages. ISBN 0-689-80837-2pbk. Lexile AD1030. Grades K to 3.

Based on a Cornish legend, an old fisherman and his cat battle a fierce storm and save Mousehole, their little British fishing village.

Anne Izard Storytellers' Choice Award.

Cullen, Lynn. *Godiva.*
Kathryn Hewitt, illustrator. New York: Golden Books, 2001. 32 pages. ISBN 0-307-41175-3. Grades 1 to 3.

Kind and compassionate Godiva accepts her wealthy husband's challenge to ride through the streets naked in order to get him to lower taxes for the townspeople of the British village of Coventry.

Storytelling World Award Honor Book.

MacDonald, Margaret Read. *The Old Woman Who Lived in a Vinegar Bottle: A British Fairy Tale.*
Nancy Dunaway Fowlkes, illustrator. New York: August House, 1995. 32 pages. ISBN 0-87483-415-5. Grades K to 3.

A kind fairy grants the wishes of an old woman to move out of a vinegar bottle and into ever grander accommodations. The fairy finally realizes that the old woman will never be content and returns her to the vinegar bottle.

Storytelling World Award Honor Book.

Morpurgo, Michael. *Arthur, High King of Britain.*
Michael Foreman, illustrator. San Diego, CA: Harcourt Children's Books, 1995. 144 pages. ISBN 0-15-200080-1. Lexile 760. Grades 4 to 7.

King Arthur tells his legends to a twelve-year-old boy who lies in a

cave recovering from a near-drowning.
Storytelling World Award Honor Book.

Philip, Neil. *Celtic Fairy Tales.*
Isabelle Brent, illustrator. New York: Viking, 1999. 144 pages. ISBN 0-670-88387-5. Grades 3 to 6.

Twenty tales illustrated with ornate patterns of the Celts from the traditions of Brittany, Cornwall, Ireland, Scotland, and Wales.
National Council for the Social Studies Notable Children's Trade Books in the Field of Social Studies.

Cambodian

Ho, Mifong. *Brother Rabbit.*
Jean Tseng, illustrator. Saphan Ras, translator. New York: HarperCollins Children's Book Group, 1997. 32 pages. ISBN 0-688-12553-0. Grades K to 3.

A Cambodian folktale where a rabbit outwits a crocodile, two elephants, and a woman.
Storytelling World Award Honor Book.

Canadian

Bierhorst, John, editor. *The Dancing Fox: Arctic Folktales.*
Mary K. Okheena, illustrator. New York: Morrow, 1997. 192 pages. ISBN 0-688-14406-3. Grades 4 to 6.

Eighteen stories that are filled with universal human experiences introduce the Inuit cultures of Alaska, Canada, and Greenland.
National Council for the Social Studies Notable Children's Trade Books in the Field of Social Studies.

Dabcovich, Lydia. *The Polar Bear Son: An Inuit Tale.*
New York: Clarion Books, 1997. 32 pages. ISBN 0-395-72766-9 and 0-395-97567-0pbk. Lexile AD470. Grades K to 3.

The gentle story of a woman and her adopted polar bear son who continues to provide for her even after he is forced to leave her village.
National Council for the Social Studies Notable Children's Trade Books in the Field of Social Studies.

Field, Edward. *Magic Words.*
Stefano Vitale, illustrator. San Diego, CA: Gulliver Books, 1998. 32 pages. ISBN 0-15-201498-5. Lexile 880. Grades K to 5.

Based on Netsilek Inuit songs and legends gathered by Knud Ramussen during an expedition, this collection of poems describes myths about the creation of the universe.

National Council for the Social Studies Notable Children's Trade Books in the Field of Social Studies.

Kusugak, Michael Arvaarluk. *Northern Lights: The Soccer Trails.*
Vladyana Krykorka, illustrator. Ontario, Canada: Annick Press, 1993. 24 pages. ISBN 1-55037-339-0 and 1-55037-338-2pbk.
Topeka, KS: Econo-Clad Books, 1999. 24 pages. ISBN 0-7857-2207-6. Lexile AD590. Grades 3 to 6.

An Inuit tale, explaining the origin of the northern lights, about the souls of the dead playing soccer using a walrus head for the ball. Told by a young Inuit girl's grandmother to assist the girl with her grief after her mother dies. Illustrated with paintings and photographs of Inuit beadwork.

Aesop Accolade, Canadian Library Association Notable Book, and *Ruth Schwartz Children's Book Award.*

Lelooska, Chief and Christine Normandin. *Echoes of the Elders.*
Andrea Danese, editor. New York: DK Publishing, 1997. 40 pages. ISBN 0-7894-2455-X. Lexile 760. Grades 3 to 6.

Five Northwest Coast Indian tales by the late Chief Lelooska of Cherokee heritage. Includes paintings by the chief, and a CD of him telling the stories.

Aesop Prize.

Lelooska, Chief and Christine Normandin. *Spirit of the Cedar People.*
New York: DK Publishing, 1998. 40 pages. ISBN 0-7894-2571-8. Lexile AD730. Grades K to 6.

This companion volume to *Echoes of the Elders* features five additional tales from the Northwest Coast Indian tradition. A CD featuring the voice of Chief Lelooska accompanies this collection.

American Library Association Notable Children's Books and *Anne Izard Storytellers' Choice Award.*

Norman, Howard A. *The Girl Who Dreamed Only Geese: And Other Tales of the Far North.*
Diane and Leo Dillon, illustrators. San Diego, CA: Harcourt Children's

Books, 1997. 164 pages. ISBN 0-15-230979-9. Lexile 600. Grades 3 to
6.

Ten Inuit tales from Siberia, Alaska, the Canadian Arctic, and
Greenland.

Aesop Accolade and *Anne Izard Storytellers' Choice Award.*

Central American and Caribbean

Berry, James R. *First Palm Trees: An Anancy Spiderman Story.*
Greg Couch, illustrator. New York: Simon & Schuster, 1997. 40 pages.
ISBN 0-689-81060-1. Grades K to 3.

Greedy Anancy is forced to share the king's reward with the spirits
of sun, water, earth, and air after he convinces them to create the earth's
first palm trees in this West Indian tale.

*National Council for the Social Studies Notable Children's Trade
Books in the Field of Social Studies.*

DeSpain, Pleasant. *The Emerald Lizard: Fifteen Latin American Tales
to Tell in English and Spanish.*
Don Bell, illustrator. Mario Lamo-Jimenez, translator. New York: August House, 1999. 192 pages. ISBN 0-87483-551-8 and 0-87483-552-
6pbk. Grades 3 to 7.

Fifteen traditional Latin American folktales, legends, and myths collected from fifteen different countries are retold in both English and
Spanish.

*National Council for the Social Studies Notable Children's Trade
Books in the Field of Social Studies.*

Gonzalez, Lucia M. *The Bossy Gallito.*
Lulu Delacre, illustrator. New York: Scholastic, 1999. 32 pages. ISBN 0-
439-06757-Xpbk. Lexile 670. Grades K to 3.

A folktale from Cuba featuring a rooster on his way to a wedding
that is told both in English and Spanish.

Aesop Accolade.

Hamilton, Virginia. *The Girl Who Spun Gold.*
Diane and Leo Dillon, illustrators. New York: Blue Sky Press, 2000. 40
pages. ISBN 0-590-47378-6. Lexile AD360. Grades K to 2.

A West Indian version of the Rumplestiltskin story with a surprising and happy ending.

Booklist Editors' Choice and *Booklist Top Ten Folklore Books for Youth.*

Hausman, Gerald. *Doctor Bird: Three Lookin' Up Tales from Jamaica.*
Ashley Wolff, illustrator. New York: Philomel Books, 1998. 40 pages. ISBN 0-399-22744-X. Lexile 800. Grades K to 3.

Three West Indian folktales featuring Dr. Bird, a clever humming-bird and the national bird of Jamaica.

National Council for the Social Studies Notable Children's Trade Books in the Field of Social Studies.

Hausman, Gerald. *Duppy Talk: West Indian Tales of Mystery and Magic.*
New York: Simon & Schuster, 1994. 102 pages. ISBN 0-671-89000-X. Grades 3 to 6.

Six Jamaican folktales based on African tribal storytelling. Each tale opens with a Jamaican proverb, and the final chapter discusses each saying's origin and meaning.

Aesop Accolade.

Keens-Douglas, Richardo. *La Diablesse and the Baby.*
Marie Lafrance, illustrator. Ontario, Canada: Annick Press, 1994. 24 pages. ISBN 1-55037-993-3 and 1-55037-992-5pbk. Lexile 810. Grades K to 3.

Granny outwits the legendary creature that roams the Caribbean to steal babies.

Storytelling World Award Honor Book.

Loya, Olga. *Momentos Magicos: Magic Moments.*
Carmen Lizardi-Rivera, translator. New York: August House, 1997. 160 pages. ISBN 0-87483-497-Xpbk. Grades 3 to 6.

Fifteen different Latin American folktales from the Caribbean, Central America, Mexico, and South America are presented bilingually and arranged into the four sections of scary stories, Trickster tales, strong women, and myths.

Aesop Accolade and *Storytelling World Award Honor Book.*

Montes, Marisa. *Juan Bobo Goes to Work: A Puerto Rican Folktale.*
Joe Cepeda, illustrator. New York: HarperCollins Children's Book Group, 2000. 32 pages. ISBN 0-688-16233-9. Grades K to 3.

Juan Bobo continuously loses his money and food on the way home from his jobs until he makes an ill rich girl laugh. Her father then pays him with a ham every Sunday.

American Library Association Notable Children's Books and *Pura Belpre Award.*

Perrault, Charles Centril, Robert D. San Souci, and Daniel R. San Souci. *Cendrillon: A Caribbean Cinderella.*
Brian Pinkney, illustrator. New York: Simon & Schuster, 1998. 40 pages. ISBN 0-689-80668-X. Lexile AD550. Grades K to 3.

A Creole version of the famous Cinderella story set on the island of Martinique.

American Library Association Notable Children's Books.

San Souci, Robert D. *The Faithful Friend.*
Brian Pinkney, illustrator. New York: Simon & Schuster, 1995. 40 pages. ISBN 0-02-786131-7.
New York: Aladdin Paperbacks, 1999. 40 pages. ISBN 0-689-82458-0pbk. Lexile 850. Grades K to 3.

A tale of romance, danger, and intrigue set on the island of Martinique and based on local lore. Two best friends, one black and one white, assist each other while pursuing true love.

Caldecott Honor Book and *Coretta Scott King Award Honor Book.*

San Souci, Robert D. *The Twins and the Bird of Darkness: A Hero Tale from the Caribbean.*
Terry Widener, illustrator. New York: Simon & Schuster, 2002. 40 pages. ISBN 0-689-83343-1. Grades K to 3.

Kind and cowardly twin brothers fight the bird of darkness in order to save Princess Marie in this Caribbean folktale.

National Council for the Social Studies Notable Social Studies Trade Books for Young People.

Chinese

Berger, Barbara Helen. *All the Way to Lhasa: A Tale from Tibet.*
New York: Philomel Books, 2002. 32 pages. ISBN 0-399-23387-3. Grades K to 3.

A Tibetan parable reveals how the slow and steady persistence of a young boy and his yak result in the ultimate reward of reaching the holy city of Lhasa first.

National Council for the Social Studies Notable Social Studies Trade

Books for Young People and *Parent's Choice Award Recommended Book.*

Bouchard, David. *Buddha in the Garden. ("Chinese Legends Series").*
Zhong-Yan Huang, illustrator. Vancouver, Canada: Raincoast Books, 2001. 32 pages. ISBN 1-55192-452-8. Grades 2 to 5.

With the assistance of a blind monk, a young orphan boy achieves enlightenment while tending a garden in a Buddhist monastery.

Canadian Library Association Notable Book.

Bouchard, David. *The Great Race.*
Zhong-Yang Huang, illustrator. Brookfield, CT: Millbrook Press, 1997. 32 pages. ISBN 0-7613-0305-7. Lexile AD680. Grades 3 to 6.

The origins of the zodiac are revealed by a grandmother to her young granddaughter in this tale that explains its significance in Chinese tradition.

National Council for the Social Studies Notable Children's Trade Books in the Field of Social Studies.

Casanova, Mary. *The Hunter: A Chinese Folktale.*
Ed Young, illustrator. New York: Atheneum Books for Young Readers, 2000. 32 pages. ISBN 0-689-82906-X. Lexile AD590. Grades K to 3.

A gifted Chinese scroll painter portrays the folktale of a young hunter, Hai Li Bu, and the pact he makes with the Dragon King of the Sea during a time of drought and famine.

Aesop Accolade, Booklist Editors' Choice, Booklist Top Ten Folklore Books for Youth, and *Parent's Choice Gold Award.*

Chen, Kerstin. *Lord of the Cranes: A Chinese Tale.*
J. Alison James, translator and Jian Jiang Chen, illustrator. New York: North-South Books, 2000. 36 pages. ISBN 0-7358-1192-X. Grades K to 3.

While testing people's kindness, the disguised Lord of the Cranes finds only one man who will offer him food. He rewards this man with three dancing cranes, thereby ensuring his prosperity.

National Council for the Social Studies Notable Children's Trade Books in the Field of Social Studies.

Creeden, Sharon. *Fair Is Fair: World Folktales of Justice.*
New York: August House, 1997. 190 pages. ISBN 0-87483-400-7 and 0-87483-4775-5pbk. Grades 4 to Adult.

A professional lawyer presents thirty international folktales from

China, Germany, Greece, Ireland, and Morocco that illustrate fairness under the law.

Aesop Prize and *Storytelling World Award Honor Book.*

Czernecki, Stefan. *The Cricket's Cage: A Chinese Folktale.*
New York: Disney Press, 1997. 32 pages. ISBN 0-7868-2234-1. Grades K to 3.

Kuai Xiang will lose his life if he cannot design a tower that pleases the emperor. He promises to build a better cage for the emperor's cricket before he is executed. After he draws a design for an ideal cage, the cricket shows Kuai a design for the emperor's tower.

Aesop Accolade, National Council for the Social Studies Notable Children's Trade Books in the Field of Social Studies, and *Storytelling World Award Honor Book.*

Davol, Margarite W. *The Paper Dragon.*
Robert Sabuda, illustrator. New York: Atheneum Books for Young Readers, 1998. 60 pages. ISBN 0-689-31992-4. Lexile 850. Grades 1 to 4.

A humble Chinese scroll painter agrees to confront a fire-breathing dragon before it destroys his village.

International Reading Association Notable Books for a Global Society.

Demi. *The Donkey and the Rock.*
New York: Henry Holt & Co., 1999. 32 pages. ISBN 0-8050-5959-8. Lexile AD750. Grades K to 3.

A Tibetan King ruling a town full of foolish people puts a donkey and a rock on trial to settle a dispute between two honest men in 550 B.C.

Aesop Accolade.

Demi. *The Empty Pot.*
New York: Henry Holt & Co., 1990. 32 pages. ISBN 0-8050-1217-6 and 0-8050-4900-2pbk. Lexile 630. Grades K to 3.

A courageous and honest young boy is chosen to be the next Chinese emperor after he passes a test given by the old emperor.

Anne Izard Storytellers' Choice Award.

Kimmel, Eric A. *Ten Suns: A Chinese Legend.*
Yongsheng Xuan, illustrator. New York: Holiday House, 1998. 32 pages. ISBN 0-8234-1317-9. Lexile AD530. Grades K to 3.

When the ten "suns" (sons) of a sky emperor endanger the world by walking across the sky together, their father sacrifices nine of them to save the earth.

National Council for the Social Studies Notable Children's Trade Books in the Field of Social Studies.

Louie, Ai-Ling. *Yeh Shen: A Cinderella Story from China.*
Ed Young, illustrator. New York: Putnam, 1982. 31 pages. ISBN 0-399-20900-X.
New York: Paperstar, 1996. 32 pages. ISBN 0-698-11388-8pbk. Lexile AD840. Grades K to 3.

A Cinderella story in which a young girl overcomes a wicked stepmother and stepsister to become the bride of a prince. The story is based on ancient Chinese manuscripts that were written one thousand years before the earliest European version.

American Library Association Notable Children's Books, Boston Globe-Horn Book Award Honor Book, International Reading Association Children's Choices, International Reading Association Teachers' Choices, and *School Library Journal Best Book of the Year.*

McCully, Emily Arnold. *Beautiful Warrior: The Legend of Nun's Kung Fu.*
New York: Scholastic, 1998. 40 pages. ISBN 0-590-37487-7. Lexile AD630. Grades K to 3.

A kung fu story about two legendary women in 17th century China. The first is a child prodigy whose father teaches her the five pillars of learning and the martial arts. She becomes a nun known as Wu Mei, "Beautiful Warrior," who then saves a young girl and teaches her the art that changes the girl's life.

American Library Association Notable Children's Books.

Morimoto, Junko. *The Two Bullies.*
Isao Morimoto, translator. New York: Crown, 1999. 32 pages. ISBN 0-517-80061-6. (Out of print). Lexile AD370. Grades K to 3.

Two bullies, one from Japan and the other from China, are considered strongmen in their respective countries. They inadvertently intimidate each other before ever meeting, so they never meet to fight as a result.

American Library Association Notable Children's Books and *Australia's Children's Book of the Year Award.*

Porte, Barbara Ann. *Hearsay: Strange Tales from the Middle Kingdom.*
Rosemary Feit Covey, illustrator. New York: Greenwillow Books, 1998.
144 pages. ISBN 0-688-15381-X. Grades 4 to 7.

Fifteen ancient and original tales with a time frame that spans centuries are drawn from Chinese folklore and culture.
Anne Izard Storytellers' Choice Award.

Provensen, Alice. *The Master Swordsman & The Magic Doorway: Two Legends from Ancient China.*
New York: Simon & Schuster, 2001. 40 pages. ISBN 0-689-83232-X.
Lexile 450. Grades K to 3.

The first tale portrays an ancient master who teaches a young boy to become a master swordsman, who then uses his sword to become a master chef. The second is about a painter who outwits an emperor.
National Council for the Social Studies Notable Children's Trade Books in the Field of Social Studies.

Sanfield, Steve. *Just Rewards: Or Who Is That Man in the Moon & What's He Doing Up There Anyway?*
New York: Orchard Books, 1996. 32 pages. ISBN 0-531-08885-5.
Grades K to 3.

Two men treat the same sparrow differently in this Chinese folktale, and each end up with what he deserves.
Storytelling World Award Honor Book.

San Souci, Robert D. *Fa Mulan: The Story of a Woman Warrior.*
Jean Tseng and Mou-Sien Tseng, illustrators. New York: Hyperion, 1998. 32 pages. ISBN 0-7868-0346-0 and 0-7868-1421-7pbk. Lexile 780. Grades K to 3.

A brave Chinese girl masquerades as a boy in order to take her aged father's place in the Khan's army to fight against the Tartars.
Storytelling World Award Honor Book and *International Reading Association Notable Books for a Global Society.*

Schroeder, Alan. *The Stone Lion.*
Todd L. W. Doney, illustrator. New York: Scribner, 1994. 32 pages.
ISBN 0-684-19578-X. Grades K to 3.

After Drashi and his widowed mother are thrown out of their Tibetan home by his greedy brother, Drashi's honesty and respect is rewarded with a bucket of gold by the fierce stone Guardian of the Mountain.
Storytelling World Award Honor Book.

Simonds, Nina and Leslie Swartz. *Moonbeams, Dumplings & Dragon Boats: A Treasury of Chinese Tales, Activities & Recipes.*
Meilo So, illustrator. San Diego, CA: Gulliver Books, 2002. 80 pages. ISBN 0-15-201983-9. Grades 3 to 7.

The five Chinese festivals of the Chinese New Year, the Lantern Festival, Zing Ming, the Dragon Boat Festival, and the Moon Festival are represented in this collection of folktales and activities.

Children's Literature Choices and *Smithsonian Magazine Notable Books for Children.*

Tseng, Grace. *White Tiger, Blue Serpent.*
Jean and Mou-Sien Tseng, illustrators. New York: Lothrop, Lee & Shepard Books, 1999. ISBN 0-688-12515-8 and 0-688-12516-8. Lexile AD860. Grades K to 3.

A young Chinese boy faces many dangers as he tries to retrieve a beautiful brocade woven by his mother and stolen by a greedy goddess.

National Council for the Social Studies Notable Children's Trade Books in the Field of Social Studies.

Ye, Ting-Xing. *Weighing the Elephant.*
Suzane Langlois, illustrator. Ontario, Canada: Annick Press, 1998. 32 pages. ISBN 1-55037-527-X and 1-55037-526-1pbk. Lexile AD920. Grades K to 3.

A young boy helps save a baby elephant from banishment in this math-related Chinese folktale.

Storytelling World Award Honor Book.

Yep, Laurence. *The Dragon Prince: A Chinese Beauty and the Beast Tale.*
Kam Mak, illustrator. New York: HarperCollins Children's Book Group, 1997. 32 pages. ISBN 0-06-024381-3 and 0-06-443518-0pbk. Lexile 820. Grades K to 6.

A threatened farmer is forced to promise his seven daughters in marriage to a terrifying dragon. Six run away, but the seventh marries the dragon and transforms him into a handsome prince.

American Bookseller Pick of the Lists and *National Council for the Social Studies Notable Children's Trade Books in the Field of Social Studies.*

Yep, Laurence. *Tiger Woman.*
Robert Roth, illustrator. Mahwah, NJ: Troll Communications, 1995. 32 pages. ISBN 0-8167-3464-X. Grades K to 3.

A selfish old woman is transformed into a series of animals until she repents of her ways after an encounter with a needy beggar in this retelling of a Shantung folk tale.

Storytelling World Award Honor Book.

Young, Ed. *Monkey King.*
New York: HarperCollins Children's Book Group, 2001. 40 pages. ISBN 0-06-027919-2 and 0-06-027950-8. Lexile AD710. Grades K to 3.

The trickster Monkey King uses his magic for mischief until Buddha traps him and releases him five hundred years later so the Monkey King can continue on his path to enlightenment in this Chinese folktale from the T'ang Dynasty.

National Council for the Social Studies Notable Children's Trade Books in the Field of Social Studies.

Czech

Martin, Rafe. *The Twelve Months.*
Toronto, Canada: Stoddart Kids, 2001. 32 pages. ISBN 0-7737-3249-7. Grades 1 to 4.

In this Cinderella tale from the former Czechoslovakia, a young girl is sent into the harsh winter by her cruel aunt and cousin to achieve impossible tasks. Her success is assisted by the twelve months of the year who appear in the form of twelve men.

Storytelling World Award Honor Book.

Danish

Andersen, Hans Christian. *The Steadfast Tin Soldier.*
Fred Marcellino, illustrator; Tor Seidler, photographer. New York: HarperCollins Children's Book Group, 1992. 32 pages. ISBN 0-06-205000-1 and 0-06-205900-9pbk. Lexile AD590. Grades K to 3.

First published during the Christmas holidays in 1838, this tale is about the perilous adventure of a toy soldier whose love for a paper dancing girl culminates in tragedy for both of them.

Booklist Editors' Choice and *New York Times Ten Best Picture Books of the Year.*

Andersen, Hans Christian. *The Ugly Ducking.*
Jerry Pinkney, illustrator. New York: Morrow Junior, 1999. 40 pages.
ISBN 0-688-15932-X. Lexile AD650. Grades K to 3.
The classic tale of how an ugly ducking develops into a beautiful swan.
American Library Association Notable Children's Books and Caldecott Honor Book.

Deedy, Carmen Agra. *The Yellow Star: The Legend of King Christian X of Denmark.*
Henri Sorenson, illustrator. Atlanta, GA: Peachtree Publishers, 2000. 32 pages. ISBN 1-56145-208-4. Lexile AD550. Grades 2 to 6.
The story of the heroic King of Denmark who wore a Jewish Star of David and defied the Nazis during the occupation of his country during World War II. More than 7,000 Jews were smuggled to safety under his leadership.
Christopher Award, International Reading Association Notable Books for a Global Society, International Reading Association Teachers' Choices, Jane Addams Children's Book Award, National Council for the Social Studies Notable Children's Trade Books in the Field of Social Studies, Parent's Choice Gold Award, and *Storytelling World Award Honor Book.*

MacDonald, Margaret Read. *Fat Cat: A Danish Folktale.*
Julie Paschkis, illustrator. New York: August House, 2001. 32 pages. ISBN 0-87483-616-6. Grades K to 3.
A greedy cat with a voracious appetite swallows many people and animals until he swallows a mouse that cuts him open and allows the others to escape.
Parent's Choice Award Recommended Book.

Finnish

McNeil, M. E. A. *The Magic Storysinger: A Tale from the Finnish Epic Kalevala.*
Owings Mills, MD: Stemmer House Publishers, 1993. 112 pages. ISBN 0-88045-128-9. Grades 1 to 6.
The adventures of Vaino, a storysinger who sings magical tales of spells, enchantments, and strong female characters.
Aesop Accolade.

Shepard, Aaron. *The Maiden of Northland: A Hero Tale of Finland.*
Carol Schwartz, illustrator. New York: Simon & Schuster, 1996. 40
pages. ISBN 0-689-80485-7. Grades 3 to 6.

Aila is the beautiful daughter of the ancient witch Louhi and the ob-
ject of a rivalry between two suitors in this free-verse retelling of the
great Finnish epic, the Kalevala.

Aesop Accolade.

French

Brown, Marcia. *Stone Soup.*
New York: Simon & Schuster, 1987. 48 pages. ISBN 0-684-92296-7 and
0-689-71103-4pbk. Lexile 480. Grades K to 3.

The story of three soldiers who manage to cook up a tasty soup by
outwitting a village full of wary French peasants.

American Library Association Notable Children's Books and *Caldecott Honor Book.*

Coxe, Molly. *Bunny and the Beast.*
Pamela Silin-Palmer, illustrator. New York: Random House, 2001. 32
pages. ISBN 0-375-80468-4. Grades K to 3.

A selfless bunny releases a bull terrier from a spell and transforms
him into a handsome bunny-prince in this retelling of a popular French
tale.

Storytelling World Award Honor Book.

DeFelice, Cynthia and Mary Demarsh. *Three Perfect Peaches: A
French Folktale.*
Irene Trivas, illustrator. New York: Orchard Books, 1995. 32 pages.
ISBN 0-531-06872-2. Lexile 820. Grades K to 3.

The youngest of three brothers delivers three perfect peaches to cure
the princess' illness and wins her hand in marriage.

Anne Izard Storytellers' Choice Award.

Lobel, Anita and Charlotte S. Huck. *Toads and Diamonds.*
New York: Morrow, 1996. 32 pages. ISBN 0-688-13680-X. Lexile
AD820. Grades K to 3.

A young girl's kindness is rewarded with gifts of flowers and jewels
while her stepsister's selfishness results in toads and snakes spewing
from her mouth in this retelling of a French folktale.

Storytelling World Award Honor Book.

Marcellino, Fred. *I, Crocodile.*
New York: HarperCollins Children's Book Group, 1999. 32 pages. ISBN 0-06-205168-7. Lexile AD300. Grades K to 3.

At Napoleon's request, an Egyptian crocodile is kidnapped and taken to Paris to be displayed in a public fountain.

American Library Association Notable Children's Book and New York Times Best Illustrated Book of the Year.

Perrault, Charles. *The Complete Fairy Tales of Charles Perrault.*
Sally Holmes, illustrator. Neil Philip and Nicoletta Simborowski, translators. New York: Clarion Books, 1993. 156 pages. ISBN 0-395-57002-6. Grades 4 to 6.

Eleven classic stories translated true to Perrault's original tellings include information about the origin and history of each tale.

Anne Izard Storytellers' Choice Award.

Perrault, Charles. *Puss in Boots.*
Fred Marcellino, illustrator; Malcolm Arthur, translator. New York: Farrar, Straus & Giroux, 1990. 32 pages. ISBN 0-374-36160-6. Lexile AD790. Grades K to 3.

A retelling of the story about a cat that made his master's fortune by trickery and cleverness.

American Library Association Notable Children's Books, Booklist Editors' Choice, Caldecott Honor Book, and *Publishers Weekly Best Books of the Year.*

Philip, Neil. *Celtic Fairy Tales.*
Isabelle Brent, illustrator. New York: Viking, 1999. 144 pages. ISBN 0-670-88387-5. Grades 3 to 6.

Twenty tales illustrated with ornate patterns of the Celts from the traditions of Brittany, Cornwall, Ireland, Scotland, and Wales.

National Council for the Social Studies Notable Children's Trade Books in the Field of Social Studies.

German

Babbitt, Natalie. *Ouch!*
Fred Marcellino, illustrator. Jacob and Wilhelm Grimm, original authors. New York: HarperCollins Children's Book Group, 1998. 32 pages. ISBN 0-06-205066-4. Lexile AD510. Grades K to 3.

This tale from the Grimm brothers was originally titled "The Giant with the Three Golden Hairs" and is about young Marco who started out as nobody special and ended up a king.

American Library Association Notable Children's Books and *Parent's Choice Award.*

Creeden, Sharon. *Fair Is Fair: World Folktales of Justice.*
New York: August House, 1997. 190 pages. ISBN 0-87483-400-7 and 0-87483-4775-5pbk. Grades 4 to Adult.

A professional lawyer presents thirty international folktales from China, Germany, Greece, Ireland, and Morocco that illustrate fairness under the law.

Aesop Prize and *Storytelling World Award Honor Book.*

Grimm, Jacob and Wilhelm. *Rapunzel.*
Paul Zelinsky, illustrator. New York: Dutton Children's Books, 1997. 48 pages. ISBN 0-525-4607-4. Lexile AD700. Grades K to 3.

This story originated in Italy and France and was adapted by the Grimm brothers of Germany. The illustrator has used the Renaissance style to embellish this fairy tale of a beautiful girl with long golden hair who is imprisoned in a lonely tower by a witch.

Caldecott Medal.

Grimm, Jacob and Wilhelm. *Rumpelstiltskin.*
Paul Zelinsky, illustrator. New York: Dutton Children's Books, 1986. 37 pages. ISBN 0-525-44265-0.
New York: Penguin Putnam, 1996. 37 pages. ISBN 0-14-055864-0pbk. Lexile 740. Grades K to 3.

A strange little man helps the miller's daughter spin straw into gold for the king on the condition that she give him her first born.

American Library Association Notable Children's Books and *Caldecott Honor Book.*

Kimmel, Eric A. *Iron John: Adapted from the Brothers Grimm.*
Trina Schart Hyman, illustrator. New York: Holiday House, 1994. 32 pages. ISBN 0-8234-1073-0 and 0-8234-1248-2pbk. Lexile AD510. Grades K to 3.

A young prince who is assisted by a spell-bound king falls in love with a servant girl and returns to the forest to rescue the king.

Storytelling World Award Honor Book.

Lesser, Rika. *Hansel and Gretel.*
Paul Zelinsky, illustrator. New York: Dutton Children's Books, 1999. 40 pages. ISBN 0-525-46152-3.
New York: Paperstar, 1996. 40 pages. ISBN 0-698-11407-8pbk. Lexile AD680. Grades K to 3.

Reminiscent of the earliest Grimm tale published in 1812, this beautifully illustrated book tells the story of the lost children of a poor woodcutter who discover a house made of bread, cakes, and candy that is occupied by a wicked witch who likes to eat children for dinner.

Caldecott Honor Book.

Stanley, Diane. *Rumpelstiltskin's Daughter.*
New York: Morrow, 1997. 32 pages. ISBN 0-688-14327-X.
New York: HarperTrophy, 2002. 32 pages. ISBN 0-06-441095-1pbk. Lexile AD570. Grades K to 3.

The miller's daughter is imprisoned by a greedy king who orders her to spin straw into gold. Rumpelstiltskin saves her, and she elopes with him. Years later, their daughter is captured by the same greedy king, but she outwits him and brings food and power to the starving people of the kingdom.

American Library Association Notable Children's Books, Land of Enchantment Children's Book Award, and *Storytelling World Award Honor Book.*

Greek

Bader, Barbara. *Aesop & Company: With Scenes from His Legendary Life.*
Arthur Geisert, illustrator. New York: Houghton Mifflin Co., 1999. 64 pages. ISBN 0-395-97496-8pbk. Grades 1 to 6.

Nineteen Aesop fables, complete with concluding morals, are illustrated with black and white etchings. An epilogue about Aesop and the myth surrounding his life is included and adds depth to the scholarly introduction.

Aesop Prize.

Balit, Christina, Plato Timaeus and Plato Critias. *Atlantis: The Legend of a Lost City.*
New York: Henry Holt & Co., 2000. 32 pages. ISBN 0-8050-6334-X. Lexile 750. Grades K to 5.

A picture book retelling of the story of Atlantis wherein Poseidon marries the beautiful Cleito. Their descendants incur the wrath of the gods, and a terrible curse is carried out that sinks the island forever to the bottom of the sea.

Booklist Top Ten Folklore Books for Youth.

Creeden, Sharon. *Fair Is Fair: World Folktales of Justice.*
New York: August House, 1997. 190 pages. ISBN 0-87483-400-7 and 0-87483-4775-5pbk. Grades 4 to Adult.

A professional lawyer presents thirty international folktales from China, Germany, Greece, Ireland, and Morocco that illustrate fairness under the law.

Aesop Prize and *Storytelling World Award Honor Book.*

D'Aulaire, Edgar Parin and Ingri D'Aulaire. *D'Aulaire's Book of Greek Myths.*
New York: Doubleday Broadway Publishing Group, 1962. 192 pages ISBN 0-385-01583-6 and 0-440-40694-3pbk.
New York: Airplay audio, 1996. ISBN 1-885608-14-4 and 1-885608-15-2cd. Lexile 1070. Grades 4 to 7.

A best-loved children's book about the gods, goddesses, kings, and heroes of ancient Greek mythology.

Horn Book Children's Classics.

Demi. *King Midas: The Golden Touch.*
Margaret K. McElderry Books, 2002. 48 pages. ISBN 0-689-3297-4. Grades K to 3.

A retelling of the popular folktale in which a king comes to regret his wish that everything he touches will turn to gold.

Children's Literature Choices.

Kindl, Patrice. *Lost in the Labyrinth.*
New York: Houghton Mifflin Company, 2002. 194 pages. ISBN 0-618-16684-X. Grades 5 to 9.

The ancient Greek legend of Theseus and the Minotaur is told through the eyes of the kind fourteen-year-old, Xenodice, the younger sister of ruthless Ariadne.

National Council for the Social Studies Notable Social Studies Trade Books for Young People.

Manna, Anthony L. and Christodoula Mitakidou. *Mr. Semolina-Semolinus: A Greek Folktale.*
Giselle Potter, illustrator. New York: Atheneum Books for Young Read-

ers, 1997. ISBN 0-689-81093-8. Grades K to 3.

A feisty princess creates a man out of sugar, almonds, and semolina wheat when she cannot find a perfect one to marry. After he is kidnapped by an evil queen, the princess must brave a perilous journey to get her stolen man back.

American Library Association Notable Children's Books.

Osborne, Mary Pope. *The Land of the Dead. ("Tales from the Odyssey, 2").*
New York: Hyperion, 2002. 105 pages. ISBN 0-7868-0771-7 and 0-7868-0929-9pbk. Grades 4 to 8.

This second book based on the ancient tales by Homer retells the continuous trials that occur to Odysseus and his men after they defeat the one-eyed giant and continue towards home.

Publishers Weekly Best Children's Books.

Osborne, Mary Pope. *The One-Eyed Giant. ("Tales from the Odyssey, 1").*
New York: Hyperion, 2002. 105 pages. ISBN 0-7868-07709 and 0-7868-0928-0pbk. Lexile 700. Grades 4 to 8.

First in a series of books based on the ancient tales of Homer. Odysseus fights in the Trojan War and encounters many dangerous, mythological creatures on his perilous journey home.

Publishers Weekly Best Children's Books.

Pinkney, Jerry. *Aesop's Fables.*
New York: SeaStar Books, 2000. 96 pages. ISBN 1-58717-000-0. Lexile 760. Grades 3 to 7.

More than sixty of Aesop's timeless fables have been humorously retold and beautifully illustrated.

Booklist Editors' Choice and *Booklist Top Ten Folklore Books for Youth.*

Richards, Jean. *The First Olympic Games: A Gruesome Greek Myth with a Happy Ending.*
Kat Thacker, illustrator. Brookfield, CT: Millbrook Press, 2000. 40 pages. ISBN 0-7613-1311-7. Grades K to 4.

An ancient Greek myth in which the gods restored Pelops after he was chopped up for stew by his father. He goes on to win a princess and kingdom, as well as establish the first Olympic games.

National Council for the Social Studies Notable Children's Trade Books in the Field of Social Studies.

Spinner, Stephanie. *Quiver.*
New York: The Knopf Publishing Group, 2002. 176 pages. ISBN 0-375-81489-2. Lexile 730. Grades 6 to 10.

A retelling of the classic legend of Atalanta, the fleet-footed female warrior who could outrun any man in ancient Greece.

National Council for the Social Studies Notable Social Studies Trade Books for Young People.

Van Hensbergen, Gijs and Jean Pierre Vernant. *The Universe, the Gods, and Men: Ancient Greek Myths.*
Linda Asher, translator. New York: HarperCollins Children's Book Group, 2001. 224 pages. ISBN 0-06-019775-7.

Best read by older readers, this collection of Greek myths was compiled from the recordings of bedtime stories the classicist Vernant told his grandson twenty-five years ago.

Storytelling World Award Honor Book.

Ward, Helen. *The Hare and the Tortoise: A Fable from Aesop.*
Brookfield, CT: Millbrook Press, 1999. 40 pages. ISBN 0-7613-0988-8. Lexile AD430. Grades K to 3.

Recounts the race between the boastful hare and the slow but persevering tortoise. Enhanced with the use of peepholes that allow readers to keep both the hare and tortoise in view at all times.

American Library Association Notable Children's Books.

Yolen, Jane. *Pegasus: The Flying Horse.*
Li Ming, illustrator. New York: Dutton Children's Books, 1998. 40 pages. ISBN 0-525-65244-2. Lexile AD530. Grades 3 to 6.

In this retelling of the classic Greek myth, Bellerophon tames the winged horse Pegasus with the help of the goddess Athena. He slays the three-headed Chimaera, but his great pride leads to his downfall.

Storytelling World Award Honor Book.

Hungarian

Greene, Ellin. *The Little Golden Lamb.*
Rosanne Litzinger, illustrator. New York: Houghton Mifflin Co., 2000. 32 pages. ISBN 0-395-71526-1. Grades K to 3.

A shepherd boy wins the hand of an ailing princess with the assistance of his little golden lamb in this Hungarian version of "The Golden

Goose."
Storytelling World Award Honor Book.

Molnar, Irma. *One Time Dog Market at Buda and Other Hungarian Folktales.*
Georgeta-Elena Enesel, illustrator. North Haven, CT: Linnet Books, 2001. 129 pages. ISBN 0-208-02505-7. Grades 3 to Adult.
    This anthology presenting twenty-three Hungarian folktales that feature important historical figures is full of cleverness and wit.
    Aesop Prize.

Indian

Arenson, Roberta. *Manu and the Talking Fish.*
New York: Barefoot Books, 2000. 32 pages. ISBN 1-84148-032-0. Grades K to 3.
    This folktale from India about a flood that destroys and then renews the world predates the biblical story about Noah. A rich Indian prince saves a little fish, who then rewards the prince by telling him how he can save his world from the destruction of the flood.
    National Council for the Social Studies Notable Children's Trade Books in the Field of Social Studies.

Bannerman, Helen. *The Story of Little Babaji.*
Fred Marcellino, illustrator. New York: HarperCollins Children's Book Group, 1996. 72 pages. ISBN 0-06-205064-8 and 0-06-008093-0pbk. Lexile AD740. Grades K to 3.
    A remake of the 1899 classic "The Story of Little Black Sambo" renames its characters Babaji, Mamaji, and Papaji and evokes images of the rich culture of India while telling the story of a boy and his encounter with bully tigers.
    American Library Association Notable Children's Books, Booklist Editors' Choices, and *National Council for the Social Studies Notable Children's Trade Books in the Field of Social Studies.*

Brown, Marcia. *Once a Mouse: A Fable Cut in Wood.*
New York: Simon & Schuster, 1989. 32 pages. ISBN 0-689-71343-6 and 0-684-12662-1pbk. Lexile AD530. Grades K to 3.
    A hermit's pet mouse becomes increasingly vain as it changes into a cat, a dog, and a tiger.
    Caldecott Medal.

Demi. *One Grain of Rice: A Mathematical Folktale.*
New York: Scholastic, 1997. 40 pages. ISBN 0-590-93998-X. Lexile AD830. Grades K to 6.
A clever girl outsmarts a selfish Indian raja and saves her village from starvation.
International Reading Association Notable Books for a Global Society and *National Council for the Social Studies Notable Children's Trade Books in the Field of Social Studies.*

Martin, Rafe. *The Brave Little Parrot.*
Susan Gaber, illustrator. New York: Putnam, 1998. 32 pages. ISBN 0-399-22825-X. Lexile 550. Grades K to 3.
In this Indian jakata tale which chronicles the past lives of Buddha, a small parrot's bravery during a forest fire is rewarded by a change in the color of his feathers.
Storytelling World Award Honor Book.

McKibbon, Hugh William. *The Token Gift.*
Scott Cameron, illustrator. Ontario, Canada: Annick Press, 1996. 32 pages. ISBN 1-55037-499-0 and 1-55037-498-2pbk. Lexile AD610. Grades 3 to 5.
After a boy who developed a popular board game in ancient India becomes an old man, he is rewarded by the king who grants him his wish of a single grain of rice that is to be doubled for each square on the chessboard. This causes a moral dilemma that is solved by an intelligent and honorable act by the old man.
Storytelling World Award Honor Book.

Ness, Caroline. *The Ocean of Story: Fairy Tales from India.*
Neil Philip, editor. Jacqueline Mair, illustrator. New York: Lothrop, Lee & Shepard Books. 128 pages. ISBN 0-688-13584-6. Grades 3 to 6.
Eighteen tales drawn from India's oral folklore traditions.
Anne Izard Storytellers' Choice Award.

Shepard, Aaron. *The Gifts of Wali Dad: A Tale of India and Pakistan.*
Daniel San Souci, illustrator. New York: Atheneum Books for Young Readers, 1995. 32 pages. ISBN 0-684-19445-7. (Out of print). Grades K to 3.
After a simple grass cutter named Wali Dad gives a bracelet to the Queen of Khaistan, he becomes the recipient of a more lavish gift, which he then gives away to a king. As he gives the gifts away in exasperation,

the gifts he receives in return become richer and richer.
Storytelling World Award Honor Book.

Indonesian

Sierra, Judy. *The Gift of the Crocodile: A Cinderella Story.*
Reynold Ruffins, illustrator. New York: Simon & Schuster, 2000. 40
pages. ISBN 0-689-82188-3. Lexile 590. Grades K to 3.
    A river crocodile helps a mistreated stepchild who respects all animals in this beautiful book set on the Spice Islands.
Booklist Top Ten Folklore Books for Youth.

Irish

Bateman, Teresa. *The Ring of Truth: An Original Irish Tale.*
Omar Rayyan, illustrator. New York: Holiday House, 1997. 32 pages.
ISBN 0-8234-1255-5 and 0-8234-1518-Xpbk. Lexile AD860. Grades K
to 4.
    Irish peddlar Patrick O'Kelley boasts that he can tell a bigger lie than
the king of the leprechauns. They trick Patrick into wearing the emerald
ring of truth, thereby provoking the wrath of the townspeople, but he ultimately wins a local contest.
Anne Izard Storytellers' Choice Award and *Storytelling World Award.*

Creeden, Sharon. *Fair Is Fair: World Folktales of Justice.*
New York: August House, 1997. 190 pages. ISBN 0-87483-400-7 and 0-87483-4775-5pbk. Grades 4 to Adult.
    A professional lawyer presents thirty international folktales from
China, Germany, Greece, Ireland, and Morocco that illustrate fairness
under the law.
Aesop Prize and *Storytelling World Award Honor Book.*

Doyle, Malachy. *Tales from Old Ireland.*
Niamh Sharkey, illustrator. New York: Barefoot Books, 2000. 96 pages.
ISBN 1-902283-97-X.
New York: Barefoot Books audio, 2001. ISBN 1-84148-403-2cd. Grades
3 to Adult.
    Seven classic folktales are retold with an Irish lilt to the prose.

National Council for the Social Studies Notable Children's Trade Books in the Field of Social Studies and *Parent's Choice Gold Award.*

Hague, Michael. *Kate Culhane: A Ghost Story.*
New York: SeaStar Books, 2001. 40 pages. ISBN 1-58717-058-2. Grades 4 to 8.

An eerie Irish folktale where young Kate Culhane outwits a ghost and saves the lives of three boys after she inadvertently steps on a newly dug grave.
Storytelling World Award Honor Book.

McNeil, Heather. *Celtic Breeze: Stories of the Otherworld from Scotland, Ireland, and Wales.*
Nancy Chien-Eriksen, illustrator. Englewood, CO: Libraries Unlimited, 2001. 200 pages. ISBN 1–56308-778-2 and 1-56308-961-0pbk.

Sixteen tales of the faery folk from Celtic lands is designed to be read by older readers and adults.
Storytelling World Award Honor Book.

Philip, Neil. *Celtic Fairy Tales.*
Isabelle Brent, illustrator. New York: Viking, 1999. 144 pages. ISBN 0-670-88387-5. Grades 3 to 6.

Twenty tales illustrated with ornate patterns of the Celts from the traditions of Brittany, Cornwall, Ireland, Scotland, and Wales.
National Council for the Social Studies Notable Children's Trade Books in the Field of Social Studies.

Talbot, Hudson. *O'Sullivan Stew.*
New York: Putnam, 1999. 40 pages. ISBN 0-399-23162-5.
New York: Puffin Books, 2002. 48 pages. ISBN 0-698-11889-8pbk. Grades K to 3.

Clever Kate saves her family with her storytelling ability after a king captures them while they are trying to retrieve a witch's stolen horse.
National Council for the Social Studies Notable Children's Trade Books in the Field of Social Studies.

Israeli and Jewish

Goldin, Barbara Diamond. *Child's Book of Midrash.*
Northvale, NJ: Jason Aronson Publishers, 1994. 124 pages. ISBN 0-87668-837-7. (Out of print).

Stories of heroic individuals are drawn from the Talmud and Midrash in this book of Jewish tales for older children.

Anne Izard Storytellers' Choice Award.

Goldin, Barbara Diamond. *Journeys with Elijah: Eight Tales of the Prophet.*

Jerry Pinkney, illustrator. San Diego, CA: Gulliver Books, 1999. 96 pages. ISBN 0-15-200445-9. Lexile 780. Grades K to 3.

Eight international stories celebrating the legend of the Jewish prophet Elijah from the Talmud span seventeen different centuries from ancient times to modern Israel.

American Library Association Notable Children's Books and *National Council for the Social Studies Notable Children's Trade Books in the Field of Social Studies.*

Jaffe, Nina, John Segal and Steve Zeitlin. *While Standing on One Foot: Puzzle Stories and Wisdom Tales from the Jewish Tradition.*

New York: Henry Holt & Co., 1993. 89 pages. ISBN 0-8050-2594-4 and 0-8050-5073-6pbk. Grades 4 to 7.

Seventeen folktales written in two parts pose questions to be solved and then reveal the conflict resolutions.

Anne Izard Storytellers' Choice Award and *Storytelling World Award Honor Book.*

Kimmel, Eric A. *A Cloak for the Moon.*

Katya Krenina, illustrator. New York: Holiday House, 2001. 32 pages. ISBN 0-8234-1493-0. Lexile AD420. Grades K to 3.

Based on a folktale attributed to the 18th century Jewish spiritual leader Rabbi Nachman of Bratslav, a tailor vows to make a cloak for the moon after it speaks to him through a dream.

Sydney Taylor Book Award.

Kimmel, Eric A. *Days of Awe: Stories for Rosh Hashanah and Yom Kippur.*

Erika Weihs, illustrator. New York: Puffin Books, 1996. 48 pages. ISBN 0-14-050271-8pbk. (Out of print). Grades 3 to 6.

Three stories of Jewish folklore focusing on the pillars of the Jewish High Holidays and emphasizing charity, prayer, and repentance are set in the locales of a shtetl, Moorish Spain, and the Holy Land.

Aesop Prize.

Kimmel, Eric A. *The Spotted Pony: A Collection of Hanukkah Stories.*
Leonard Everett Fisher, illustrator. New York: Holiday House, 1992. 70
pages. ISBN 0-8234-0936-8. Grades K to 6.
A Jewish folktale is told for each of the eight Hannukkah nights.
Anne Izard Storytellers' Choice Award.

Kimmel, Eric A. and Baal Shem Tov. *Gershon's Monster: A Story for
the Jewish New Year.*
Jon J. Muth, illustrator. New York: Scholastic, 2000. 32 pages. ISBN 0-
439-10839-X. Lexile AD400. Grades K to 4.
Gershon is a selfish and sinful man who bags up his sins and casts
them into the sea every year. After his wish for children is granted by a
rabbi, his sins come back to haunt him. While his children are playing by
the sea, they are nearly engulfed by a large black wave of Gershon's sins
until he cries out to God in repentance.
*National Council for the Social Studies Notable Children's Trade
Books in the Field of Social Studies.*

Pearl, Sydelle. *Elijah's Tears: Stories for the Jewish Holidays.*
Rossitza Skortcheva Penney, illustrator. New York: Henry Holt & Co.,
1996. 64 pages. ISBN 0-8050-4627-5. Grades 2 to 4.
The prophet Elijah appears in five stories set during four Jewish
holidays.
Storytelling World Award Honor Book.

Pinkney, Jerry. *Noah's Ark.*
New York: SeaStar Books, 2002. 40 pages. ISBN 1-58717-201-1.
Grades K to 4.
Noah and his family build an ark to save God's creatures from the
great flood in this rendition of the biblical story.
*American Library Association Notable Children's Books, Associa-
tion of Jewish Libraries Award Honor Book, Caldecott Honor Book,* and
Children's Literature Choices.

Prose, Francine. *You Never Know: A Legend of the Lamed-Vavniks.*
Mark Podwal, illustrator. New York: Greenwillow Books, 1998. 24
pages. ISBN 0-688-15806-4. Grades K to 3.
A poor shoemaker who prays first to relieve a town of drought and
then of floods is recognized by the rabbi as a lamed-vavnik, a holy man
who lives a life of such goodness that he has God's ear.
Anne Izard Storytellers' Choice Award.

Rush, Barbara and Howard Schwartz. *A Coat for the Moon and Other Jewish Tales.*
Michael Iofin, illustrator. Philadelphia, PA: Jewish Publication Society, 1999. 96 pages. ISBN 0-8276-0596-X and 0-8276-0736-9pbk. Grades K to 3.
A collection of fifteen Jewish folktales from around the world.
Anne Izard Storytellers' Choice Award.

Rush, Barbara and Howard Schwartz. *Wonder Child and Other Jewish Fairy Tales.*
New York: HarperCollins Children's Book Group, 1996. 66 pages. ISBN 0-06-023517-9. Grades 3 to 6.
Eight Jewish fairy tales from around the world.
Anne Izard Storytellers' Choice Award.

Schmidt, Gary D. *Mara's Stories: Glimmers in the Darkness.*
New York: Henry Holt & Co., 2001. 112 pages. ISBN 0-8050-6794-9. Grades 5 to 8.
Mara tells twenty-two Jewish folktales to women and children in a concentration camp during the Holocaust in order to distract them from their suffering.
Storytelling World Award Honor Book.

Schwartz, Howard. *The Day the Rabbi Disappeared: Jewish Holiday Tales of Magic.*
Monique Passicot, illustrator. New York: Viking, 2000. 128 pages. ISBN 0-670-88733-1. Grades K to 3.
Twelve tales of Jewish mysticism and magic from around the world that move through the Jewish calendar to encompass twelve Jewish holidays.
Aesop Prize and *Booklist Top Ten Folklore Books for Youth.*

Schwartz, Howard. *Invisible Kingdoms: Jewish Tales of Angels, Spirits, and Demons.*
Stephen Fieser, illustrator. New York: Harper Collins Children's Book Group, 2002. 68 pages. ISBN 0-06-027855-2. Grades 3 to 6.
This anthology of nine mystical Jewish tales features supernatural creatures from countries around the world.
Association of Jewish Libraries Award Notable Book and *Smithsonian Magazine Notable Books for Children.*

Schwartz, Howard. *Next Year in Jerusalem: 3000 Years of Jewish Stories.*
Topeka, KS: Econo-Clad Books, 1999. 64 pages. ISBN 0-613-08435-7. (Out of print). Lexile 1030. Grades 3 to 6.

Eleven Jewish tales, all set in Jerusalem, are gathered from different parts of the world and illustrated with soft watercolors.

Aesop Prize and *Storytelling World Award Honor Book.*

Shollar, Leah P. *Thread of Kindness: A Tzedakah Story.*
Yehudis Cohen, editor. Shoshana Mekibel, illustrator. New York: Hachai Publishing, 2000. 32 pages. ISBN 1-929628-01-3. Grades K to 3.

A poor Jewish couple who have been granted the blessing of wealth begin a thread of kindness and charity that they weave throughout their community.

Storytelling World Award Honor Book.

Silverman, Erica. *Raisel's Riddle.*
Susan Gaber, illustrator. New York: Farrar, Straus & Giroux, 1999. 40 pages. ISBN 0-374-36168-1. Lexile AD270. Grades K to 3.

Raisel is an orphan who is raised by her Talmudic scholar grandfather. After he dies, she finds work in the home of a distinguished rabbi, but she is mistreated by his jealous cook. Raisel's kindness, intelligence, and cleverness lead to her marriage to the rabbi's son in this East European version of a Cinderella tale.

American Library Association Notable Children's Books and *International Reading Association Notable Books for a Global Society.*

Walsman, Neil. *The Two Brothers: A Legend of Jerusalem.*
New York: Simon & Schuster, 1997. 40 pages. ISBN 0-689-31936-3. Grades 1 to 4.

King Solomon builds a holy temple on the spot where he observes two brothers treating each other with deep love and kindness, which leads to the creation of the ancient city of Jerusalem.

Storytelling World Award Honor Book.

Waxman, Sydell. *The Rooster Prince.*
Glora Carmi, illustrator. New York: Pitspopany Press, 2000. 48 pages. ISBN 0-943706-45-9 and 0-943706-49-1pbk. Grades 2 to 5.

A poor village boy cures a prince of acting like a rooster in this parable told by the great Jewish sage Rabbi Nachman of Bratslav.

Storytelling World Award Honor Book.

Wiesel, Elie. *King Solomon and His Magic Ring.*
Monique Passicot, illustrator. New York: Greenwillow Books, 1999. 51 pages. ISBN 0-688-16959-7. Lexile AD750. Grades K to 3.
  Twenty stories about King Solomon of ancient Jerusalem.
  Aesop Prize.

Wisniewski, David. *Golem.*
New York: Clarion Books, 1996. 31 pages. ISBN 0-395-72618-2. Lexile 690. Grades 4 to 7.
  Golem is the Hebrew word for "shapeless man." According to Jewish legend, Golem was created from clay by a rabbi in order to protect his people from persecution in the ghettos of 16th century Prague.
  American Library Association Notable Children's Books, Booklist Editors' Choice, Caldecott Medal, International Reading Association Notable Books for a Global Society, and *New York Times Best Illustrated Book of the Year.*

Wolkstein, Diane. *Esther's Story.*
Topeka, KS: Econo-Clad Books, 1999. 40 pages. ISBN 0-613-07718-0. Lexile 780. Grades 3 to 6.
  From the biblical Book of Esther, a young Jewish orphan girl becomes Queen of Persia. She risks her social status and life to save her people from certain death.
  Aesop Accolade.

Italian

Bedard, Michael. *The Wolf of Gubbio.*
Murray Kimber, illustrator. Toronto, Canada: Stoddart Kids, 2001. 24 pages. ISBN 0-7737-3250-0. Grades 2 to 4.
  A legend about the saint who talks to a wolf and saves a village.
  National Council for the Social Studies Notable Children's Trade Books in the Field of Social Studies.

Calvino, Italo. *Italian Folktales.*
George Martin, translator. San Diego, CA: Harcourt Children's Books, 1990. 763 pages. ISBN 0-15-145770-0 and 0-15-64549-0pbk. Lexile 830. Grades 6 to Adult.
  Two hundred lively Italian folktales.
  New York Times Notable Books of the Year.

Japanese

Bodkin, Odds and Gennady Spirin. *The Crane Wife.*
Sumiko Yagawa, illustrator. San Diego, CA: Gulliver Books, 1998. 32 pages. ISBN 0-15-201407-1 and 0-15-216350-6pbk. Lexile AD320. Grades K to 3.

A retelling of the traditional Japanese tale of a poor sail maker whose kindness to an injured crane is rewarded by the gift of a beautiful wife, but he loses her through greed and mistrust.

Booklist Editors' Choice, National Council for the Social Studies Notable Children's Trade Books in the Field of Social Studies, and *Storytelling World Award Honor Book.*

Kajikawa, Kimiko. *Yoshi's Feast.*
Yumi Heo, illustrator. New York: DK Publishing, 2000. 32 pages. ISBN 0-7894-2607-2. Lexile AD540. Grades K to 3.

A Japanese folktale about the humorous feud between two neighbors, one a fan maker and the other an eel catcher.

Booklist Editors' Choice and *International Reading Association Notable Books for a Global Society.*

Kimmel, Eric A. *Three Samurai Cats.*
Mordicai Gerstein, illustrator. New York: Holiday House, 2003. 32 pages. ISBN 0-8234-1742-5. Grades K to 3.

A Zen master cat uses the art of passive resistance against an opponent rat in this philosophical folktale from Japan.

Parent's Choice Silver Award.

Martin, Rafe. *The Hungry Tigress: Buddhist Myths, Legends, and Jataka Tales.*
Cambridge, MA: Yellow Moon Press, 1999. 290 pages. ISBN 0-938756-52-4pbk. Grades 3 to 8.

The largest English collection of Buddhist tales features stories of Buddha's birth and enlightenment as well as traditional jataka tales of Buddha in animal form. This collection also includes some contemporary tales of courage and perseverance.

Anne Izard Storytellers' Choice Award.

Martin, Rafe, editor. *Mysterious Tales of Japan.*
Tatsuro Kiuchi, illustrator. New York: Putnam, 1996. 74 pages. ISBN 0-399-22677-X. Grades 3 to 6.

Ten Japanese folktales with roots in the Shinto and Buddhist views of life. Every tale begins with a haiku poem.

Aesop Accolade, Anne Izard Storytellers' Choice Award, and *International Reading Association Notable Books for a Global Society.*

Melmed, Laura Krauss. *Little Oh.*
Jim Lamarche, illustrator. New York: Lothrop, Lee & Shepard Books, 1997. 32 pages. ISBN 0-688-14208-7. Lexile AD720. Grades K to 3.

A mother tells her son about a little origami doll that comes to life for her creator, a lonely Japanese woman.

American Library Association Notable Children's Books, Georgia Children's Picture Storybook Award, and *National Council for the Social Studies Notable Children's Trade Books in the Field of Social Studies.*

Morimoto, Junko. *The Two Bullies.*
Isao Morimoto, translator. New York: Crown, 1999. 32 pages. ISBN 0-517-80061-6. (Out of print). Lexile AD370. Grades K to 3.

Two bullies, one from Japan and the other from China, are considered strongmen in their respective countries. They inadvertently intimidate each other before meeting, so they never meet to fight as a result.

American Library Association Notable Children's Books and *Australia's Children's Book of the Year Award.*

Myers, Tim. *Basho and the Fox.*
Oki S. Han, illustrator. Tarrytown, NY: Marshall Cavendish, 2000. 32 pages. ISBN 0-7614-5068-8. Lexile AD490. Grades K to 3.

An honored 17th century Japanese poet struggles to create a haiku that will satisfy a fox.

Storytelling World Award Honor Book.

Paterson, Katherine. *The Tale of the Mandarin Ducks.*
Diane and Leo Dillon, illustrators. New York: Penguin Putnam, 1990. 36 pages. ISBN 0-525-67283-4 and 0-14-055739-3pbk. Lexile AD930. Grades K to 3.

A servant girl releases a captive mandarin duck and is sentenced to death by a cruel Japanese emperor, but the duck and his mate return to rescue the girl and her beloved.

Anne Izard Storytellers' Choice Award.

San Souci, Robert D. *The Silver Charm: A Folktale from Japan.*
Yoriko Ito, illustrator. New York: Doubleday, 2002. 32 pages. ISBN 0-385-32159-7. Grades K to 3.

In this Ainu folktale set on the island of Hokkaido, a puppy and a fox

cub retrieve a precious amulet a kidnapped child offers to an ogre in order to save his own life.
Storytelling World Award Honor Book.

Sierra, Judy. *Tasty Baby Belly Buttons: A Japanese Folktale.*
Meilo So, illustrator. New York: Alfred A. Knopf, 1999. 40 pages. ISBN 0-679-89369-5.
New York: Bantam Dell Publishing Group, 2001. 32 pages. ISBN 0-440-41738-4pbk. Lexile AD810. Grades K to 3.

Urikohime, a little girl who was born from a melon and has no belly button, is taught sword fighting and cooking by her elderly parents. She uses these skills to defend the village from the monstrous onis who steal babies to eat their tasty belly buttons.
American Library Association Notable Children's Books.

Snyder, Dianne. *The Boy of the Three-Year Nap.*
Allen Say, illustrator. New York: Houghton Mifflin Co., 1988. 32 pages. ISBN 0-395-44090-4. Lexile AD610. Grades K to 3.

A poor Japanese mother changes events to alter the lazy habits of her son.
American Library Association Notable Children's Books, Booklist Editors' Choice, Boston Globe-Horn Book Award, Caldecott Honor Book, and *School Library Journal Best Book.*

Waite, Michael P. *Jojofu.*
Yoriko Ito, illustrator. New York: Lothrop, Lee & Shepard Books, 1996. 32 pages. ISBN 0-688-13660-5. Grades K to 3.

A faithful hunting dog protects his Japanese master during a hunting trip in this folktale that is more than one thousand years old.
Storytelling World Award Honor Book.

Wells, Ruth. *The Farmer and the Poor God: A Folktale from Japan.*
Yoshi, illustrator. New York: Simon & Schuster, 1996. 26 pages. ISBN 0-689-80214-5. Grades K to 3.

After the actions of the Poor God cause a reversal of a family's impoverished status, the Rich God who moves in is sent away.
Storytelling World Award Honor Book.

Korean

Farley, Carol J. *Mr. Pak Buys a Story.*
Benrei Huang, illustrator. Topeka, KS: Econo-Clad Books, 1999. 32 pages. ISBN 0-613-22019-6.
Morton Grove, IL: Albert Whitman & Co., 1999. 32 pages. ISBN 0-8075-5179-1. Lexile 190. Grades K to 3.

A Korean couple bored with country life gives money to a servant and sends him to town to buy a story. A thief tricks the servant, but the story wreaks revenge later when the thief returns.
Storytelling World Award Honor Book.

Han, Suzanne Crowder. *The Rabbit's Tail: A Story from Korea.*
Richard Wehrman, illustrator. New York: Henry Holt & Co., 1999. 32 pages. ISBN 0-8050-4580-5. Grades K to 3.

A Korean folktale that explains how rabbits lost their original long tails.
National Council for the Social Studies Notable Children's Trade Books in the Field of Social Studies.

Mexican

Ada, Alma Flor. *The Lizard and the Sun.*
Felipe Davalos, illustrator. Reading, MA: Scott Foresman, 1999. 48 pages. ISBN 0-440-41531-4. Lexile AD580. Grades K to 3.

A little lizard persists in bringing the light and warmth of the sun back to ancient Mexico after it disappears in this bilingual folktale.
National Council for the Social Studies Notable Children's Trade Books in the Field of Social Studies.

Ada, Alma Flor, Rosalma Zubizarreta and Roger Drury. *Mediopollito Half-Chicken: A Folktale in Spanish and English.*
Kim Howard, illustrator. New York: Bantam Books, 1997. 40 pages. ISBN 0-440-41360-5pbk. Lexile 680. Grades K to 3.

A bilingual folktale explains how a half-chicken with one leg, one eye, and one wing ascends to the top of a weather vane.
Aesop Accolade.

DePaola, Tomie. *Adelita: A Mexican Cinderella Story.*
New York: Puffin Books, 2002. 32 pages. ISBN 0-399-23866-2. Grades

K to 3.

When Adelita's father dies, Adelita is consigned to the kitchen by her cruel stepmother until she wins the heart of a wealthy, eligible bachelor who was once a childhood friend.

National Council for the Social Studies Notable Social Studies Trade Books for Young People.

DeSpain, Pleasant. *The Emerald Lizard: Fifteen Latin American Tales to Tell in English and Spanish.*
Don Bell, illustrator. Mario Lamo-Jimenez, translator. New York: August House, 1999. 192 pages. ISBN 0-87483-551-8 and 0-87483-552-6pbk. Grades 3 to 7.

Fifteen traditional Latin American folktales, legends, and myths collected from fifteen different countries are retold in both English and Spanish.

National Council for the Social Studies Notable Children's Trade Books in the Field of Social Studies.

Ehlert, Lois. *Cuckoo: A Mexican Folktale.*
Gloria De Aragon, translator. San Diego, CA: Harcourt Children's Books, 1997. 40 pages. ISBN 0-15-200274-X and 0-15-202428-Xpbk. Lexile AD290. Grades 3 to 8.

The cuckoo bird loses her beautiful singing voice while trying to rescue seeds from a burning field in this bilingual story that retells a traditional Mayan legend.

National Council for the Social Studies Notable Children's Trade Books in the Field of Social Studies.

Gerson, Mary-Joan. *Fiesta Femenina: Celebrating Women in Mexican Folktale.*
Maya Christina Gonzalez, illustrator. New York: Barefoot Books, 2001. 64 pages. ISBN 1-84148-365-6. Grades 3 to 7.

Eight Mexican folktales feature courageous women from a variety of cultural traditions.

Aesop Prize and *National Council for the Social Studies Notable Children's Trade Books in the Field of Social Studies.*

Loya, Olga. *Momentos Magicos: Magic Moments.*
Carmen Lizardi-Rivera, translator. New York: August House, 1997. 160 pages. ISBN 0-87483-497-Xpbk. Grades 3 to 6.

Fifteen different Latin American folktales from the Caribbean, Central America, Mexico, and South America are presented bilingually and arranged into the four sections of scary stories, Trickster tales, strong women, and myths.

Aesop Accolade and *Storytelling World Award Honor Book.*

McDermott, Gerald. *Musicians of the Sun.*
New York: Simon & Schuster, 1997. 40 pages. ISBN 0-689-80706-6 and 0-689-83907-3pbk. Lexile 420. Grades K to 3.

A rhythmic retelling of an Aztec myth where the Lord of Night sends Wind to release the musicians the Sun is holding and bring them down to earth, where they spread color and joy while making music.

Aesop Accolade.

Middle Eastern

Balouch, Kristen. *The King & Three Thieves: A Persian Tale.*
C. Hennessy, editor. New York: Penguin Putnam, 2000. 32 pages. ISBN 0-670-88059-0. Grades K to 3.

When a king disguises himself and slips out of his palace in an attempt to feed the hungry, he comes across three men who tell him of their plan to rob the royal treasury. After he captures them, the king assists the men in using their special skills to aid the kingdom.

National Council for the Social Studies Notable Children's Trade Books in the Field of Social Studies.

Ben-Ezer, Ehud. *Hosni the Dreamer: An Arabian Tale.*
Uri Shulevitz, illustrator. New York: Farrar, Straus & Giroux, 1997. 32 pages. ISBN 0-374-33340-8. Grades K to 3.

Although considered a fool by his fellow shepherds, a wise verse purchased during a trip to the city saves Hosni's life and secures his future.

National Council for the Social Studies Notable Children's Trade Books in the Field of Social Studies.

Creeden, Sharon. *Fair Is Fair: World Folktales of Justice.*
New York: August House, 1997. 190 pages. ISBN 0-87483-400-7 and 0-87483-4775-5pbk. Grades 4 to Adult.

A professional lawyer presents thirty international folktales from China, Germany, Greece, Ireland, and Morocco that illustrate fairness under the law.

Aesop Prize and *Storytelling World Award Honor Book.*

Kherdian, David. *The Rose's Smile: Farizad of the Arabian Nights.*
Stephano Vitale, illustrator. New York: Henry Holt & Co., 1997. 40 pages. ISBN 0-8050-3912-0. (Out of print). Grades 2 to 4.

The lengthy tale about a beautiful maiden's quest to fulfill her destiny and release her brother from an evil spell is condensed in this picture-book version.

Storytelling World Award Honor Book.

Shepard, Aaron. *The Gifts of Wali Dad: A Tale of India and Pakistan.*
Daniel San Souci, illustrator. New York: Atheneum Books for Young Readers, 1995. 32 pages. ISBN 0-684-19445-7. (Out of print). Grades K to 3.

After a simple grass cutter named Wali Dad gives a bracelet to the Queen of Khaistan, he becomes the recipient of a more lavish gift, which he then gives away to a king. As he gives the gifts away in exasperation, the gifts he receives in return become richer and richer.

Storytelling World Award Honor Book.

Smith, Nora A. and Kate D. Wiggins, editors. *The Arabian Nights: Their Best Known Tales.*
Maxfield Parrish, illustrator. New York: Simon & Schuster, 1993. 344 pages. ISBN 0-684-19589-5 and 0-684-13809-3pbk. Grades 3 to 6.

One of the many retellings of the tales of Scheherazade.

Horn Book Children's Classics.

Young, Ed. *What About Me?*
New York: Philomel Books, 2002. 40 pages. ISBN 0-399-23624-4. Grades K to 3.

Based on a Sufi tale, a young boy is guided by a Grand Master to discover the secret of knowledge acquisition.

National Council for the Social Studies Notable Social Studies Trade Books for Young People.

Zeman, Ludmila. *Sinbad in the Land of the Giants.*
Toronto, Canada: Tundra Books, 2001. 30 pages. ISBN 0-88776-461-4. Grades 2 to 6.

A story originating from the tales of "A Thousand and One Nights," Sinbad and his crew are driven off course by fierce winds and face many hardships in the Land of Giants.

Canadian Library Association Notable Book.

Norwegian

D'Aulaire, Edgar Parin and Ingri D'Aulaire. *D'Aulaire's Norse Gods and Giants.*
Magnolia, MA: Peter Smith Publishers, 1993. 168 pages. ISBN 0-8664-6692-0.
New York: Doubleday Broadway Publishing Group, 1986. 168 pages. ISBN 0-385-23692-1pbk. Grades 2 to 6.

Oversized illustrations accompany the retelling of Norse myths that feature stories of Loki, Odin, and Thor.

Horn Book Children's Classics.

Huck, Charlotte. *The Black Bull of Norroway: A Scottish Tale.*
Anita Lobel, illustrator. New York: Greenwillow Books, 2001. 40 pages. ISBN 0-688-16901-5. Lexile AD700. Grades 2 to 4.

This Scottish folktale tells of three Norwegian sisters who hope for good marriages. The first two receive wealth, while the bravery and kindness of the third releases the Duke of Norway from an evil spell.

American Library Association Notable Children's Books, National Council for the Social Studies Notable Children's Trade Books in the Field of Social Studies, National Council of Teachers of English Notable Children's Books in the English Language Arts, and *Parent's Choice Silver Award.*

Lunge-Larsen, Lise. *The Race of the Birkebeiners.*
Mary Azarian, illustrator. New York: Houghton Mifflin Co., 2001. 32 pages. ISBN 0-618-10313-9. Lexile AD660. Grades K to 3.

The Birkebeiners are peasants trained to be fierce warriors under the guidance of the king of Norway. After his death, they risk their lives to save the queen and her infant son from a murderous rival tribe. Modern-day Norwegian Birkebeiner ski events are based on this legend.

Aesop Accolade, American Library Association Notable Children's Books, Children's Literature Choices, Parent's Choice Silver Award, and *Storytelling World Award Honor Book.*

Lunge-Larsen, Lise and Peter Christi Asbjrnsen. *The Troll With No Heart in His Body: And Other Tales of Trolls from Norway.*
Betsy Bowen, illustrator. New York: Houghton Mifflin Co., 1999. 96 pages. ISBN 0-395-91371-3. Lexile 830. Grades 3 to 7.

These nine stories about trolls are illustrated with polychrome woodcuts reminiscent of Norwegian folk art.

American Library Association Notable Children's Books, Anne Izard

Storytellers' Choice Award, and *National Council for the Social Studies Notable Children's Trade Books in the Field of Social Studies*.

Sanderson, Ruth. *The Crystal Mountain.*
Boston: Little, Brown & Company, 1999. 32 pages. ISBN 0-316-77092-2. Lexile 700. Grades K to 4.
This story set in 15th century Europe combines the Chinese legend of the magic brocade with a Norwegian folktale and is about a young man who rescues a beautiful tapestry and the Red Fairy from Crystal Mountain.
National Council for the Social Studies Notable Children's Trade Books in the Field of Social Studies.

Russian

Arnold, Katya. *Baba Yaga: A Russian Folktale.*
Topeka, KS: Econo-Clad Books, 1999. 32 pages. ISBN 0-613-09444-1.
New York: North-South Books, 1996. 32 pages. ISBN 1-55858-593-1pbk. Lexile AD510. Grades K to 3.
A Russian witch who has captured Young Tishka orders her daughter to cook him, but clever Tishka escapes and tricks the witch into eating her own daughter. Illustrated with Russian "lubok," a type of woodcut folk art.
Aesop Accolade.

Lewis, J. Patrick. *At the Wish of the Fish: A Russian Folktale.*
Katya Krenina, illustrator. New York: Atheneum Books for Young Readers, 1999. 32 pages. ISBN 0-689-81336-8. Grades K to 3.
A captured enchanted fish grants a simple man all his wishes in exchange for its freedom.
National Council for the Social Studies Notable Children's Trade Books in the Field of Social Studies.

Martin, Rafe. *The Language of Birds.*
Susan Gaber, illustrator. New York: Penguin Putnam, 2000. 32 pages. ISBN 0-399-22925-6. Lexile AD410. Grades K to 3.
Two boys who have been given ten gold coins by their father choose to spend their fortunes in different ways. One boy squanders it on himself, while the other saves the life of a baby bird and wins a princess in

marriage as a reward.

Booklist Top Ten Folklore Books for Youth and *Storytelling World Award Honor Book.*

McCaughrean, Geraldine. *Grandma Chickenlegs.*
Moira Kemp, illustrator. Minneapolis, MN: Carolrhoda Books, 1999. 32 pages. ISBN 1-57505-415-9. Grades K to 3.

A young girl outwits a wicked stepmother in this retelling of the classic Russian folktale about the witch Baba Yaga.

Storytelling World Award Honor Book.

Norman, Howard A. *The Girl Who Dreamed Only Geese: And Other Tales of the Far North.*
Diane and Leo Dillon, illustrators. San Diego, CA: Harcourt Children's Books, 1997. 164 pages. ISBN 0-15-230979-9. Lexile 600. Grades 3 to 6.

Ten Inuit tales from Siberia, Alaska, the Canadian Arctic, and Greenland.

Aesop Accolade and *Anne Izard Storytellers' Choice Award.*

Ogburn, Jacqueline K. *The Magic Nesting Doll.*
Toby Sherry, editor. Laurel Long, illustrator. New York: Dial Books for Young Readers, 2000. 32 pages. ISBN 0-8037-2414-4. Lexile 550. Grades K to 3.

After her grandmother's death, Katya travels with a Russian nesting doll that reveals a different magical animal each time it is opened. The magic helps defeat an evil wizard and release a frozen prince from the wizard's spell.

Storytelling World Award Honor Book.

San Souci, Robert D. *Peter and the Blue Witch Baby.*
Alexi Natchev, illustrator. New York: Doubleday Broadway Publishing Group, 2000. 32 pages. ISBN 0-385-90002-3. Lexile 500. Grades K to 3.

A jealous witch attempts to get revenge on young Tsar Peter when he rejects her for the Little Sister of the Sun in this Russian folktale.

Storytelling World Award Honor Book.

Schur, Maxine Rose. *The Peddler's Gift.*
Kimberly Bulcken Root, illustrator. New York: Dial Books for Young Readers, 1999. 32 pages. ISBN 0-8037-1978-7. Grades K to 3.

A young boy learns lessons in strength, wisdom, and morality when

he tries to return a dreidel he stole from a simple peddler.
National Council for the Social Studies Notable Children's Trade Books in the Field of Social Studies.

Shepard, Aaron. *The Sea King's Daughter: A Russian Legend.*
Gennady Spirin, illustrator. New York: Atheneum Books for Young Readers, 1997. 40 pages. ISBN 0-689-80759-7 and 0-689-84259-7pbk. Lexile 670. Grades K to 3.

A poor musician called on to play at the Sea King's undersea palace encounters the Sea King's beautiful daughter, Volkhova, and wins her love.

Aesop Accolade, American Bookseller Pick of the Lists, American Library Association Notable Children's Books, Cincinnati Enquirer Best Illustrated Children's Books, National Council for the Social Studies Notable Children's Trade Books in the Field of Social Studies, New York Times Best Illustrated Book of the Year, and *Storytelling World Award Honor Book.*

Spirin, Gennady. *The Tale of the Firebird.*
New York: Penguin Putnam Books for Young Readers, 2002. 32 pages. ISBN 0-399-23584-1. Grades K to 3.

In his quest to obtain a firebird for his tsar father, a young prince enlists the help of a wolf as he completes several difficult tasks and rescues a beautiful princess.

Parent's Choice Silver Award.

Vagin, Vladimir. *The Enormous Carrot.*
New York: Scholastic, 1998. 32 pages. ISBN 0-590-45491-9. Lexile 470. Grades K to 3.

Farm animals come together in the effort to pull a gigantic carrot out of the ground and distribute it among themselves in this adaptation of a Russian folktale.

National Council for the Social Studies Notable Children's Trade Books in the Field of Social Studies.

Scottish

DeFelice, Cynthia. *Cold Feet.*
Andrew Parker, illustrator. New York: DK Publishing, 2000. 32 pages. ISBN 0-7894-2636-6. Lexile AD640. Grades 2 to 4.

The ghostly Scottish legend of a wandering bagpiper who takes a

pair of boots from a corpse, only to have the dead man return for them.
Boston Globe-Horn Book Picture Book Award.

Huck, Charlotte. *The Black Bull of Norroway: A Scottish Tale.*
Anita Lobel, illustrator. New York: Greenwillow Books, 2001. 40 pages.
ISBN 0-688-16901-5. Lexile AD700. Grades 2 to 4.

This Scottish folktale tells of three Norwegian sisters who hope for
good marriages. The first two receive wealth, while the bravery and
kindness of the third releases the Duke of Norway from an evil spell.

*American Library Association Notable Children's Books, National
Council for the Social Studies Notable Children's Trade Books in the
Field of Social Studies, National Council of Teachers of English Notable
Children's Books in the English Language Arts,* and *Parent's Choice
Silver Award.*

McNeil, Heather. *Celtic Breeze: Stories of the Otherworld from Scotland, Ireland, and Wales.*
Nancy Chien-Eriksen, illustrator. Englewood, CO: Libraries Unlimited,
2001. 200 pages. ISBN 1-56308-778-2 and 1-56308-961-0pbk.

Sixteen tales of the faery folk from Celtic lands is designed to be
read by older readers and adults.

Storytelling World Award Honor Book.

Philip, Neil. *Celtic Fairy Tales.*
Isabelle Brent, illustrator. New York: Viking, 1999. 144 pages. ISBN 0-
670-88387-5. Grades 3 to 6.

Twenty tales illustrated with ornate patterns of the Celts from the
traditions of Brittany, Cornwall, Ireland, Scotland, and Wales.

*National Council for the Social Studies Notable Children's Trade
Books in the Field of Social Studies.*

Walsh, Jill Paton. *Matthew and the Sea Singer.*
Alan Marks, illustrator. New York: Farrar, Straus & Giroux, 1993. 48
pages. ISBN 0-374-34869-3. Grades K to 4.

An orphaned boy with the gift of a beautiful voice is rescued by a
friend in this Scottish folktale.

Anne Izard Storytellers' Choice Award.

Williamson, Duncan. *Tales of the Seal People: Scottish Folk Tales.*
Chad McCail, illustrator. Northampton, MA: Interlink Publishing Group,
1998. 160 pages. ISBN 1-56656-101-9 and 0-940793-99-7pbk. Grades 3
to 7.

A collection of fourteen tales feature the silkies, seal people who take human shape, from the traditions of the Gaelic speaking people who live along Scotland's coastal areas.
Anne Izard Storytellers' Choice Award.

Yolen, Jane. *Greyling.*
David Ray, illustrator. New York: Putnam, 1991. 40 pages. ISBN 0-399-22262-6. Grades 1 to 5.

An old Scottish tale about a fisherman and his wife who adopt a seal pup that turns into a boy. During a terrible storm, Greyling reverts to his seal form and saves the fisherman from drowning in the sea.
Anne Izard Storytellers' Choice Award.

Slovakian

Martin, Rafe. *The Twelve Months.*
Toronto, Canada: Stoddart Kids, 2001. 32 pages. ISBN 0-7737-3249-7. Grades 1 to 4.

In this Cinderella tale from the former Czechoslovakia, a young girl is sent into the harsh winter by her cruel aunt and cousin to achieve impossible tasks. Her success is assisted by the twelve months of the year who appear in the form of twelve men.
Storytelling World Award Honor Book.

South American

DeSpain, Pleasant. *The Emerald Lizard: Fifteen Latin American Tales to Tell in English and Spanish.*
Don Bell, illustrator. Mario Lamo-Jimenez, translator. New York: August House, 1999. 192 pages. ISBN 0-87483-551-8 and 0-87483-552-6pbk. Grades 3 to 7.

Fifteen traditional Latin American folktales, legends, and myths collected from fifteen different countries are retold in both English and Spanish.
National Council for the Social Studies Notable Children's Trade Books in the Field of Social Studies.

Loya, Olga. *Momentos Magicos: Magic Moments.*
Carmen Lizardi-Rivera, translator. New York: August House, 1997. 160 pages. ISBN 0-87483-497-Xpbk. Grades 3 to 6.

Fifteen different Latin American folktales from the Caribbean, Central America, Mexico, and South America are presented bilingually and arranged into the four sections of scary stories, Trickster tales, strong women, and myths.

Aesop Accolade and *Storytelling World Award Honor Book.*

Maggi, Maria Elena, editor. *The Great Canoe: A Karina Legend.*
Gloria Calderon, illustrator. Elisa Amado, translator. Toronto, Canada: Groundwood Books, 2001. 32 pages. ISBN 0-88899-444-3. Grades K to 3.

A tale of the great flood by the indigenous Karina of eastern Venezuela.

The Bulletin of the Center for Children's Books Blue Ribbon Award and *Children's Literature Choices.*

McDermott, Gerald. *Jabuti the Tortoise: A Trickster Tale from the Amazon.*
San Diego, CA: Harcourt Children's Books, 2001. 32 pages. ISBN 0-15-200496-1. Grades K to 2.

A jealous vulture tricks a musically talented turtle into meeting the King of Heaven in this South American folktale from the Amazonian River Region.

International Reading Association Children's Choices.

Pitcher, Caroline. *Mariana and the Merchild: A Folk Tale from Chile.*
Jackie Morris, illustrator. Grand Rapids, MI: William B. Eerdmans Publishing Company, 2000. 32 pages. ISBN 0-8028-5204-1. Grades K to 3.

An infant mermaid is washed ashore in a seashell and raised by a lonely old woman who lives by the sea. The woman eventually returns the mermaid to the sea, but she returns often to bring gifts to the old woman.

National Council for the Social Studies Notable Children's Trade Books in the Field of Social Studies and *Storytelling World Award Honor Book.*

Thai

MacDonald, Margaret Read and Supaporn Vathanaprida. *The Girl Who Wore Too Much: A Folktale from Thailand.*
Yvonne Lebrun Davis, illustrator. New York: August House, 1998. 32 pages. ISBN 0-87483-503-8. Grades K to 3.

Illustrated with Pu-Thai silk colors, the young girl in this folktale finds that excesses can be unrewarding.

National Council for the Social Studies Notable Children's Trade Books in the Field of Social Studies.

Turkish

Walker, Barbara K. *The Art of the Turkish Tale, Vol. 2.*
Helen Siegel, illustrator. Lubbock, TX: Texas Tech University Press, 1993. 286 pages. ISBN 0-89672-265-1 and 0-89672-316-Xpbk. Grades 4 to 7.

Eighty tales translated from oral narratives in Turkey cover a wide variety of traditional folktales.

Anne Izard Storytellers' Choice Award.

Ukrainian

Kimmel, Eric A. *Sirko and the Wolf: A Ukrainian Tale.*
Robert Sauber, illustrator. New York: Holiday House, 1997. 32 pages. ISBN 0-8324-1257-1. (Out of print). Lexile AD350. Grades K to 4.

The friendship that exists between dogs and wolves is explained in this picture book story about a wolf that helps an abandoned sheepdog regain his place of honor.

Storytelling World Award Honor Book.

Vietnamese

Garland, Sherry. *Children of the Dragon: Selected Tales from Vietnam.*
Trina Schart Hyman, illustrator. San Diego, CA: Harcourt Children's Books, 2001. 58 pages. ISBN 0-15-224200-7. Lexile 1000. Grades 3 to 6.

These six Vietnamese folktales are illustrated with full color drawings in acrylic and ink.

Children's Literature Choices, International Reading Association Notable Books for a Global Society, and *Parent's Choice Award Recommended Book.*

Shepard, Aaron. *The Crystal Heart: A Vietnamese Legend.*
Joseph D. Fiedler, illustrator. New York: Simon & Schuster, 1998. 40 pages. ISBN 0-689-81551-4. Lexile 400. Grades 1 to 4.

An old fisherman dies of heartbreak after his encounter with the beautiful, privileged daughter of a mandarin. His heart turns to crystal, but it is released by the remorse of the young woman.

Storytelling World Award Honor Book.

Welsh

McNeil, Heather. *Celtic Breeze: Stories of the Otherworld from Scotland, Ireland, and Wales.*
Nancy Chien-Eriksen, illustrator. Englewood, CO: Libraries Unlimited, 2001. 200 pages. ISBN 1–56308-778-2 and 1-56308-961-0pbk.

Sixteen tales of the faery folk from Celtic lands is designed to be read by older readers and adults.

Storytelling World Award Honor Book.

Philip, Neil. *Celtic Fairy Tales.*
Isabelle Brent, illustrator. New York: Viking, 1999. 144 pages. ISBN 0-670-88387-5. Grades 3 to 6.

Twenty tales illustrated with ornate patterns of the Celts from the traditions of Brittany, Cornwall, Ireland, Scotland, and Wales.

National Council for the Social Studies Notable Children's Trade Books in the Field of Social Studies.

Multicultural

Adler, Naomi. *The Barefoot Book of Animal Tales from Around the World.*
Amanda Hall, illustrator. New York: Barefoot Books, 2003. 80 pages. ISBN 1-84148-941-7 and 1-84148-942-5pbk. Grades 2 to 4.

Nine animal-themed folktales from around the world are gathered from other storytellers and retold. This beautifully illustrated anthology

represents such diverse cultures such as Brazil, Canada, China, Kenya, and the United States.
Smithsonian Magazine Notable Books for Children.

Adler, Naomi. *Play Me a Story: Nine Tales About Musical Instruments.*
Greta Cencetti, illustrator. Brookfield, CT: Millbrook Press, 1998. 80 pages. ISBN 0-7613-0401-0. Lexile 910. Grades 3 to 6.

Nine tales from different cultures feature native instruments that reveal the transforming power of music.
National Council for the Social Studies Notable Children's Trade Books in the Field of Social Studies.

Baltuck, Naomi. *Apples from Heaven: Multicultural Folk Tales About Stories and Storytellers.*
North Haven, CT: Linnet Books, 1995. 144 pages. ISBN 0-208-02434-4. Grades 5 to 8.

Each traditional tale opens with a quote or proverb in this multicultural collection.
Anne Izard Storytellers' Choice Award.

Barchers, Suzanne I. *Wise Women: Folk and Fairy Tales from Around the World.*
Leann Mulineaux, illustrator. Englewood, CO: Libraries Unlimited, 1997. 324 pages. ISBN 0-87287-816-3 and 1-56308-592-5pbk.

This anthology of sixty multicultural tales that portray wise and capable women of all ages is designed to be read by older readers or retold to young children.
Storytelling World Award Honor Book.

Batt, Tanya Robyn. *The Fabrics of Fairytale: Stories Spun from Far and Wide.*
Rachel Griffin, illustrator. New York: Barefoot Books, 2000. 80 pages. ISBN 1-84148-061-4. Grades 3 to 6.

Seven multicultural tales focus on the use of textiles for their themes.
Storytelling World Award Honor Book.

Bierhorst, John, editor. *The Dancing Fox: Arctic Folktales.*
Mary K. Okheena, illustrator. New York: Morrow, 1997. 192 pages. ISBN 0-688-14406-3. Grades 4 to 6.

Eighteen stories that are filled with universal human experiences in troduce the Inuit cultures of Alaska, Canada, and Greenland.

National Council for the Social Studies Notable Children's Trade Books in the Field of Social Studies.

Caduto, Michael J. *Earth Tales from Around the World.*
Adelaide Murphy Tyrol, illustrator. Golden, CO: Fulcrum Publishing, 1997. 208 pages. ISBN 1-55591-968-5pbk. Grades 5 to 8.

Forty-eight traditional tales from around the world are logically arranged into ten themes that explore the earth and humankind's relationship to it.

Aesop Prize.

Climo, Shirley. *A Treasury of Mermaids: Mermaid Tales from Around the World.*
Jean Tseng and Mou-Sien Tseng, illustrators. New York: HarperCollins Children's Book Group, 1997. 80 pages. ISBN 0-06-023876-3. Grades 3 to 6.

Eight folktales from diverse cultures are filled with fantasy and mystery in their description of mermaids and mermen.

Storytelling World Award Honor Book.

Creeden, Sharon. *Fair Is Fair: World Folktales of Justice.*
New York: August House, 1997. 190 pages. ISBN 0-87483-400-7 and 0-87483-4775-5pbk. Grades 4 to Adult.

A professional lawyer presents thirty international folktales from China, Germany, Greece, Ireland, and Morocco that illustrate fairness under the law.

Aesop Prize and *Storytelling World Award Honor Book.*

Datlow, Ellen and Terri Windling, editors. *The Green Man: Tales from the Mythic Forest.*
Charles Vess, illustrator. New York: Viking Penguin, 2002. 400 pages. ISBN 0-670-03526-2. Grades 7 to 12.

A literary collection by various authors of short stories and poems that focus on the theme of the Green Man—the untamed nature spirit.

American Library Association Best Books for Young Adults.

DeSpain, Pleasant. *Fifteen Latin American Tales to Tell in English and Spanish.*
Don Bell, illustrator. Mario Lamo-Jimenez, translator. New York: August House, 1999. 192 pages. ISBN 0-87483-551-8 and 0-87483-552-6pbk. Grades 3 to 7.

Fifteen traditional Latin American folktales, legends, and myths collected from fifteen different countries are retold in both English and Spanish.
National Council for the Social Studies Notable Children's Trade Books in the Field of Social Studies.

Dundas, Marjorie. *Riddling Tales from Around the World.*
Jackson, MS: University Press of Mississippi, 2002. 224 pages. ISBN 1-57806-372-8 and 1-57806-373-6pbk.
Eighty-five culturally diverse tales represent thirteen major themes where a riddle is posed, and the tale constitutes the answer.
Storytelling World Award Honor Book.

Evetts-Secker, Josephine. *The Barefoot Book of Mother and Son Tales.*
Helen Cann, illustrator. New York: Barefoot Books, 1999. 80 pages. ISBN 1-902283-3058. Lexile 930. Grades 3 to 6.
Ten folktales from around the world are based on the mother-son relationship.
National Council for the Social Studies Notable Children's Trade Books in the Field of Social Studies.

Evetts-Secker, Josephine. *Father and Daughter Tales.*
Helen Cann, illustrator. New York: Abbeville, 1998. 80 pages. ISBN 0-7892-0392-8. Lexile 980. Grades 3 to 6.
An anthology of ten multicultural tales focuses on the relationship of father figures with their adventurous daughters.
Storytelling World Award Honor Book.

Forest, Heather. *Wisdom Tales from Around the World: Fifty Gems of Story and Wisdom from World Folklore.*
New York: August House, 1996. 156 pages. ISBN 0-87483-478-3 and 0-87483-479-1pbk. Grades 4 to 8.
Fifty brief tales reflect the wisdom of such cultures as African, Buddhist, Christian, Jewish, Native American, Sufi, Taoist, and Zen.
Storytelling World Award.

Forest, Heather. *Wonder Tales from Around the World.*
David Boston, illustrator. New York: August House, 1995. 155 pages. ISBN 0-87483-421-X and 0-87483-472-8pbk.
New York: August House audio, 1995. ISBN 0-87483-427-9.
Grades 4 to 6.
A professional storyteller relates twenty-seven folktales from around

the world. The tales are accompanied by full page pen and ink drawings. *Storytelling World Award.*

Garrity, Linda K. *The Tale Spinner: Folktales, Themes, and Activities.* Emilia Markovich, illustrator. Golden, CO: Fulcrum Publishing, 1999. 192 pages. ISBN 1-55591-970-7. Grades 3 to 6.

Included with this theme-oriented anthology of multicultural folktales are teaching suggestions, related books, and reproducibles to be used by elementary teachers, homeschoolers, and media specialists. *Youth Storytelling Pegasus Award.*

Goode, Diane. *Diane Goode's Book of Giants and Little People.* New York: Dutton Children's Books, 1997. 64 pages. ISBN 0-525-45660-0. Grades K to 3.

An anthology of nine stories and eight poems about characters that are either very small or extremely large such as fairies, elves, and giants. *Storytelling World Award Honor Book.*

Grindley, Sally. *Breaking the Spell.* Susan Field, illustrator. New York: Kingfisher, 1996. 80 pages. ISBN 0-7534-5002-X and 1-85697-35-4pbk. Grades 3 to 5.

Seven multicultural tales about enchantment take place in several different countries. *Storytelling World Award Honor Book.*

Hamilton, Martha and Mitch Weiss. *How and Why Stories: World Tales Kids Can Read.* Carol Lyon, illustrator. New York: August House, 1999. 112 pages. ISBN 0-87483-562-3 and 0-87483-561-5pbk. New York: August House abridged audio, 2000. ISBN 0-87483-594-1. Grades 3 to 6.

Twenty-five multicultural folktales explain how and why things are the way they are in nature and the world. Following each tale is a short scientific note explaining the natural phenomenon. *Youth Storytelling Pegasus Award.*

Hamilton, Martha and Mitch Weiss. *Noodlehead Stories: World Tales Kids Can Read.* Ariane Elsammak, illustrator. New York: August House, 2000. 96 pages. ISBN 0-87483-584-4 and 0-87483-585-2pbk. Grades 3 to 5.

Twenty-three very short international tales that young storytellers

can also perform.
National Council for the Social Studies Notable Children's Trade Books in the Field of Social Studies

Hamilton, Martha and Mitch Weiss. *Stories in My Pocket: Tales Kids Can Tell.*
Golden, CO: Fulcrum Publishing, 1997. 192 pages. ISBN 1-5559-957-Xpbk. Grades 4 to 7.
Thirty stories for beginning storytellers originate from folk literature and are arranged according to their level of difficulty.
Youth Storytelling Pegasus Award.

Hamilton, Martha and Mitch Weiss. *Through the Grapevine: World Tales Kids Can Read and Tell.*
Carol B. Lyon, illustrator. New York: August House, 2001. 128 pages. ISBN 0-87483-625-5 and 0-87483-624-7pbk. Grades 3 to 6.
An anthology of thirty-one short multicultural stories contain background information and tips for telling each tale.
Storytelling World Award Honor Book.

Hearne, Betsy. *Beauties and Beasts.*
Joanne Caroselli, illustrator. Westport, CT: Greenwood Publishing Group, 1993. 192 pages. ISBN 0-89774-29-1pbk. Grades 3 to 7.
Over two dozen multicultural folktales deal with the theme of a lonely beast who is transformed by love.
Anne Izard Storytellers' Choice Award.

Holt, David and Bill Mooney, editors. *More Ready-to-Tell Tales: From Around the World.*
New York: August House, 2000. 256 pages. ISBN 0-87483-592-5 and 0-87483-583-6pbk.
Forty-five multicultural tales are contributed by experienced storytellers and followed by tips for telling the stories. This anthology is designed for use by older readers and adults
Storytelling World Award Honor Book and *Youth Storytelling Pegasus Award.*

Holt, David and Bill Mooney, editors. *Sure-Fire Stories from America's Favorite Storytellers.*
New York: August House, 1994. 224 pages. ISBN 0-87483-380-9 and 0-87483-381-7pbk.
Forty popular storytellers share multicultural tales and tips for the

telling in this anthology designed for use by older readers and adults.
Storytelling World Award.

Jaffe, Nina and Steve Zeitlin. *The Cow of No Color: Riddle Stories and Justice Tales from World Traditions.*
Whitney Sherman, illustrator. New York: Henry Holt & Co., 1998. 128 pages. ISBN 0-8050-3736-5. Grades 3 to 8.
This multicultural collection of folktales deals with themes of fairness and justice and includes suggestions on how to enhance the storytelling experience for young people.
National Council for the Social Studies Notable Children's Trade Books in the Field of Social Studies.

Lottridge, Celia Barker. *Ten Small Tales: Stories from Around the World.*
Joanne Fitzgerald, illustrator. Toronto, Canada: Groundwood Books, 2001. 64 pages. ISBN 0-88899-156-8. Grades Preschool to 2.
Ten multicultural tales drawn from folktales, nursery rhymes, and fingerplays.
Anne Izard Storytellers' Choice Award.

Lupton, Hugh. *The Story Tree: Tales to Read Aloud.*
Sophie Fatus, illustrator. New York: Barefoot Books, 2001. 64 pages. ISBN 1-84148-312-5.
New York: Barefoot Books unabridged audio, 2001. ISBN 1-84148-417-2cd. Grades 1 to 6.
Seven popular folktales from around the world that are meant to be read aloud.
National Council for the Social Studies Notable Children's Trade Books in the Field of Social Studies.

MacDonald, Margaret Read. *Shake-It-Up Tales! Stories to Sing, Dance, Drum, and Act Out.*
New York: August House, 1999. 192 pages. ISBN 0-87483-590-9.
This adult resource features twenty multicultural tales that inspire the participation of elementary-aged children.
Storytelling World Award Honor Book.

McCaughrean, Geraldine. *The Bronze Cauldron: Myths and Legends of the World.*
New York: Margaret K. McElderry Books, 1998. 144 pages. ISBN 0-689-81758-4.

Hampton, NY: Chivers Children's Audio Books unabridged audio, 2000. ISBN 0-7450-5162-5. Grades 5 to 8.

Twenty-seven myths and legends from around the world tell of ordinary people who are changed by a mystery or great deed.

National Council for the Social Studies Notable Children's Trade Books in the Field of Social Studies and *Storytelling World Award Honor Book.*

Medlicott, Mary. *The King with Dirty Feet: And Other Stories from Around the World.*
Sue Williams, illustrator. New York: Kingfisher, 1998. 40 pages. ISBN 0-7534-516-4pbk. Grades 3 to 6.

A multicultural collection of tales from several locations.

Storytelling World Award Honor Book.

Milord, Susan. *Bird Tales from Near and Far.*
Linda S. Wingerter, illustrator. Charlotte, VT: Williamson, 1998. 96 pages. ISBN 1-885593-18-X. Grades 3 to 6.

Six multicultural folktales that focus on birds are linked with scientific facts and supported by projects and activities.

Storytelling World Award Honor Book.

Muten, Burleigh. *Grandmothers' Stories: Wise Woman Tales from Many Cultures.*
Sian Bailey, illustrator. New York: Barefoot Books, 1999. 80 pages. ISBN 1-902283-24-4.
New York: Barefoot Books unabridged audio, 2001. ISBN 1-84148-419-9cd. Grades 1 to 5.

A grandmother sharing stories at bedtime retells eight folktales from a variety of cultures.

National Council for the Social Studies Notable Children's Trade Books in the Field of Social Studies.

Muten, Burleigh. *The Lady of Ten Thousand Names: Goddess Stories from Many Cultures.*
Helen Cann, illustrator. New York: Barefoot Books, 2001. 80 pages. ISBN 1-84148-048-7. Grades 4 to 7.

Eight different goddesses from different cultures are portrayed in these myths and folktales.

National Council for the Social Studies Notable Children's Trade Books in the Field of Social Studies.

Norman, Howard. *The Girl Who Dreamed Only Geese: And Other Tales of the Far North.*
Diane and Leo Dillon, illustrators. San Diego, CA: Harcourt Children's Books, 1997. 164 pages. ISBN 0-15-230979-9. Lexile 600. Grades 3 to 6.
Ten Inuit tales from Siberia, Alaska, the Canadian Arctic, and Greenland.
Aesop Accolade and *Anne Izard Storytellers' Choice Award.*

Philip, Neil. *Celtic Fairy Tales.*
Isabelle Brent, illustrator. New York: Viking, 1999. 144 pages. ISBN 0-670-88387-5. Grades 3 to 6.
Twenty tales illustrated with the ornate patterns of the Celts from the traditions of Brittany, Cornwall, Ireland, Scotland, and Wales.
National Council for the Social Studies Notable Children's Trade Books in the Field of Social Studies.

Philip, Neil. *Illustrated Book of Fairy Tales.*
Nilesh Mistry, illustrator. New York: DK Publishing, 1998. 160 pages. ISBN 0-7894-2794-X. Grades K to 6.
This collection of new and traditional fairy tales from around the world includes notes about the culture in which each was created.
National Council for the Social Studies Notable Children's Trade Books in the Field of Social Studies.

Sierra, Judy. *Can You Guess My Name? Traditional Tales Around the World.*
Stefano Vitale, illustrator. New York: Clarion Books, 2002. 128 pages. ISBN 0-618-13328-3. Grades 3 to 6.
Fifteen folktales grouped into five categories that resemble "The Three Pigs," "The Bremen Town Musicians," "Rumpelstiltskin," "The Frog Prince," and "Hansel and Gretel."
Aesop Prize, International Reading Association Notable Books for a Global Society, National Council for the Social Studies Notable Social Studies Trade Books for Young People, and *Smithsonian Magazine Notable Books for Children.*

Sierra, Judy. *Nursery Tales Around the World.*
Stefano Vitale, illustrator. New York: Clarion Books, 1996. 114 pages. ISBN 0-395-67894-3. Lexile AD950. Grades K to 4.
Eighteen international tales are grouped into six categories and illustrated with colorful borders.

Aesop Prize, American Library Association Notable Children's Books, Horn Book Fanfare Honor List Blue Ribbon Winner, and *Publishers Weekly Best Books of the Year.*

Sockin, Brian Scott and Eileen L. Wong, editors. *Treasury of Children's Folklore.*
New York: Berkley Publishing Group, 1995. 208 pages. ISBN 0-425-14977-3. (Out of print). Grades 3 to 6.
This anthology of traditional folktales from around the world was written for the fiftieth anniversary of the relief organization CARE.
Storytelling World Award Honor Book.

Walker, Paul Robert. *Giants! Stories from Around the World.*
James Bernardin, illustrator. San Diego, CA: Harcourt Children's Books, 1995. 73 pages. ISBN 0-15-200883-7. Grades 3 to 6.
Seven classic giant stories originating from such diverse places as Africa, Europe, Hawaii, the Middle East, and the Pacific Northwest.
Aesop Accolade.

Walker, Paul Robert. *Little Folk: Stories from Around the World.*
San Diego, CA: Harcourt Children's Books, 1997. 80 pages. ISBN 0-15-200327-4. (Out of print). Grades 3 to 6.
Little folk who possess mysterious and magical powers are the focus of these eight multicultural tales.
Storytelling World Award Honor Book.

Yolen, Jane. *Gray Heroes: Elder Tales from Around the World.*
New York: Penguin Putnam, 1999. 256 pages. ISBN 0-14-027618-1. Grades 3 to 7.
Seventy-five multicultural folktales celebrate adventurous elderly women and men.
Anne Izard Storytellers' Choice Award.

Yolen, Jane. *Not One Damsel in Distress: World Folktales for Strong Girls.*
Susan Guevara, illustrator. San Diego, CA: Harcourt Children's Books, 2000. 116 pages. ISBN 0-15-202047-0. Grades 3 to 6.
Thirteen international legends that feature intelligent, courageous heroines.
National Council for the Social Studies Notable Children's Trade Books in the Field of Social Studies and *Storytelling World Award Honor Book.*

Appendix A

A Guide to the Awards

ABC Children's Booksellers Choices Award
This annual award honors the current year's best books for children and young adults. The books are selected by the bookseller members of the Association of Booksellers for Children.

Aesop Accolade
Aesop Prize
Given by the Children's Folklore Section of the American Folklore Society. Awarded to the most outstanding book or books incorporating folklore and published in English for children or young adults. The Aesop Prize committee also compiles the Aesop Accolade List, an annual roster of exceptional books from among Aesop Prize nominees.

AIM Children's Book Award
Sponsored by the New Zealand Government Printer, the Children's Book of the Year Award began in 1982 and continued as the AIM Children's Book Award when AIM Toothpaste took over sponsorship in 1990. The *New Zealand Post* became sponsors in 1997, and the award is now known as the New Zealand Post Children's Book Awards.

Alex Award
Funded by the Margaret Alexander Awards Trust and announced in conjunction with National Library Week, the Alex Award honors the top ten adult books enjoyed by young adults aged twelve through eighteen and published during that calendar year. The award is given in honor of

the late Margaret Alexander Edwards, Young Adult Specialist at the Enoch Pratt Free Library in Baltimore, Maryland.

American Association of University Women Award for Juvenile Literature
The North Carolina Division of the American Association of University Women, a national organization that promotes education and equity for all women and girls, presents this award.

American Book Award
The American Book Award was established in 1978 by the Before Columbus Foundation to recognize outstanding literary achievement by contemporary American authors without restriction to race, sex, ethnic background, or genre. The purpose of the award is to acknowledge the excellence and multicultural diversity of American writing.

American Bookseller Pick of the Lists
The monthly magazine *American Bookseller* includes semiannual "Pick of the Lists" of forthcoming children's books that booksellers predict will sell well in their bookstores.

American Booksellers Book of the Year Award (ABBY)
This award was established in 1991 to celebrate the books the members of the American Booksellers Association most enjoyed reading and recommending to their customers. It was renamed the Book Sense Book of the Year Award in 2000.

American Booksellers Choices
Presented each year to the book voted by members of the American Booksellers Association as the one they most enjoy recommending.

American Library Association Best Books for Middle Readers

American Library Association Best Books for Reluctant Young Readers

American Library Association Best Books for Young Adults

American Library Association 100 Best Books for Teens

American Library Association Quick Picks for Reluctant Young Adult Readers

American Library Association Recommended Books for Reluctant Young Adult Readers

American Library Association Top Ten Best Books for Young Adults

The Young Adult Library Services Association (YALSA) publishes two important lists annually that are available in pamphlet form: "Best Books for the Reluctant Young Reader" and "Best Books for Young Adults." In addition, other specialized lists are published which highlight the best books for teens and young adults.

American Library Association Notable Children's Books

The Notable Children's Books are selected from the different publishing houses during the calendar year. The Committee reads extensively throughout the year and, at the Midwinter Meeting of the Association for Library Service to Children, selects those titles they believe to be exceptional for a variety of reasons. The list is intended to be used by children to assist them in selecting books to read and to encourage children to seek out the few books that are considered outstanding among the many available in bookstores and libraries. Selections include books of especially commendable quality; books that exhibit venturesome creativity; and books of fiction, information, poetry, and pictures for all age levels (through age fourteen) that reflect and encourage children's interests. The lists are produced for young readers, middle readers, and older readers.

American Library Association Top Ten Historical Fiction for Youth

A yearly list of books that successfully balances compelling portrayals of historical times with thoughtfully conceived characters and solid storytelling.

Americas Award for Children's and Young Adult Literature

This award is given to literary works which authentically portray Latinos in the United States and is sponsored by the Consortium of Latin American Studies Program.

Anne Izard Storytellers' Choice Award

The Westchester Library System in New York honors noted librarian and storyteller Anne Izard with this award that was established after her death in 1990. It is given every two years to titles published in the field of storytelling.

Association of Jewish Libraries Award

The Jewish Librarians Association and the Jewish Library Association merged in 1965 to become the Association of Jewish Libraries. The Association encourages excellence in Jewish book publishing by sponsoring several book awards.

Australia's Children's Book of the Year Award

The Children's Book Council of Australia began presenting this annual award in 1946 to authors of books for older readers, books for younger readers, information books, and picture books.

Bay Area Book Reviewers Association Award (BABRA)

This San Francisco, California, awards program is designed to honor outstanding contributions to books and literature by writers living and working in the Bay Area.

Beehive Award

The Children's Literature Association of Utah (CLAU) sponsors book awards in five categories of picture book, fiction, children's informational book, young adult, and poetry. Winners are chosen from nominated books voted on by the children of Utah. The Award changed its title to "Beehive Award" in the year 2003.

Belgian Book Prize

Information was unavailable at the time of publication.

Bisto Awards

The Bisto Awards began in 1990 by the Irish Children's Book Trust to acknowledge excellence in illustration and written text in Irish children's literature. Renamed the Bisto Awards, they are presented in association with Children's Books Ireland to books published in the calendar year by authors or illustrators born or currently living in Ireland.

Booklinks Best Book of the Year

Booklinks: Connecting Books, Libraries and Classrooms is a journal published by Booklist Publications. Designed to connect children with high quality books, it features many articles about using books in the school curriculum and occasional articles that highlight award winning books.

Booklist Editors' Choice
Booklist Reviewer's Choice
Booklist Starred Review
Booklist Top Ten Folklore Books for Youth
Booklist Top Ten Historical Fiction for Youth

Booklist is a periodical published twice a month by the American Library Association. It reviews children's and young adult books and regularly publishes special-interest lists. Especially noteworthy titles are given stars; "Editors' Choice" is an annual list of the most outstanding books in several different categories.

Book Sense Book of the Year Award

Previously called the American Booksellers Book of the Year Award (ABBY Award), this commendation is given by independent booksellers to represent their favorite books of the year in several different categories. The award is announced at the annual Book Expo America Convention.

Boston Globe-Horn Book Award
Boston Globe-Horn Book Award Honor Book
Boston Globe-Horn Book Picture Book Award

Award winners and Honor Books are announced each fall at the New England Library Association conference. Differing from the Newbery and Caldecott lists, books published in the United States but written by non-Americans are eligible. Although the award was first presented in 1967, this award for excellence in literature for children and young adults has also included a category for nonfiction since 1976. Currently, a committee of three children's literature professionals evaluates books in the three categories of picture books, fiction and poetry, and nonfiction.

Boy's Club of America Award

An award administered by the Boy's and Girl's Club of America that is obsolete.

The Bulletin of the Center for Children's Books Blue Ribbon Award (BCCB Blue Ribbon Award)

Blue Ribbons are chosen annually by the *Bulletin* staff to represent what they believe to be the best of the previous year's literature for youth. Lists include a broad range of genres and age groups.

The Bulletin of the Center for Children's Books Children's Book Award

A journal that reviews children's books for public and school librarians. An annual award is presented by the staff of the *Bulletin* to the best of the previous year's literature for youth.

Buxtehude Bulla Prize

A German award for outstanding children's books that promote peace.

Caldecott Honor Book
Caldecott Medal

Sponsored by the American Library Association and the Association for Library Service to Children, this award established in 1938 honors 19th century English illustrator Randolph J. Caldecott. A medal is presented annually to the illustrator of the most distinguished American picture book for children published in the United States during the preceding year. The recipient must be a citizen or resident of the United States.

California Children's Book, Video, and Software Award

Information was unavailable at the time of publication.

Canada Council Children's Literature Prize

The Canada Council for the Arts established this prize for the best books by Canadian writers and illustrators in 1975. In 1987, this award became the Governor General's Award for Children's Literature.

Canadian Library Association Book of the Year for Children Award
Canadian Library Association Notable Book

Established in 1947, this medal sponsored by the National Book Service is presented annually to the author of the best children's book published during the previous year in Canada. The author must be a citizen or resident of Canada. The award is administered by the Canadian Association of Children's Librarians.

Canadian Library Association Young Adult Canadian Book Award

Established in 1980 by the Young Adult Caucus of the Saskatchewan Library Association, this award is presented annually to a single Canadian author who writes an outstanding book that appeals to young adults between the ages of thirteen and eighteen. The award is administered by the Young Adult Services Interest Group of the Canadian Library Association.

Carl Sandburg Award

In memory of Carl Sandburg, a longtime International Platform Association member and former editor of *Talent* magazine, this award is given to the poet of an outstanding literary work.

Carnegie Medal
Carnegie Medal Commendation

Andrew Carnegie made his fortune in the United States steel industry and subsequently set up more than twenty-eight hundred libraries across the English speaking world. One of Britain's oldest literary awards, the Carnegie Medal is sponsored by The Chartered Institute of Library and Information Professionals (CILIP) and is administered by librarians. The award is given annually to an outstanding children's book written in English.

Carter G. Woodson Book Award

Carter G. Woodson, Ph.D., was a distinguished African American historian and educator who wrote books for young people and adults and founded the Association for the Study of Negro Life and History. The National Council for the Social Studies established this award in 1974 to encourage the writing and publishing of exemplary social science books for young people. These books sensitively depict ethnicity and ethnic minorities in the United States.

Charlotte Zolotow Award
Charlotte Zolotow Award Highly Commended Book

This award is given in honor of Charlotte Zolotow, a distinguished book editor for thirty-eight years at Harper Junior Books and author of more than sixty-five picture books. The Cooperative Children's Book Center, a library at the University of Wisconsin-Madison School of Education, gives the award to the author of the text of an outstanding picture book published in the United States during the preceding year.

Children's Book Committee at the Bank Street College of Education Award
Child Study Children's Book Committee Children's Book of the Year
Child Study Committee Children's Book Award

Includes three awards: the Josette Frank Award (formerly the Child

Study Committee Children's Book Award and renamed in 1998) for fiction; the Flora Stieglitz Straus Award for nonfiction; and the Claudia Lewis Award for poetry. It is presented to works for children or young people that "deal realistically and in a positive way with problems in their world."

Children's Literature Choices

This national book award recognizes one hundred fifty outstanding children's books for creative storytelling and factual accuracy and gives them awards in six different categories. Children's literature reviewers include book authors, librarians, writers, editors, teachers, children's literature specialists, and physicians.

Children's Literature Council of Southern California Book Award

An award given to authors and illustrators living in Southern California. Categories for the awards vary from year to year, but all books are published in the previous year.

Christopher Award

Father James Keller, M.M., founded the Christophers in 1945 on the principle that one person can make a difference and change the world for the better. (The name "Christopher" comes from the Greek word for Christbearer.) Since 1949, awards in the category of Books for Young People are presented each February to works "which affirm the highest values of the human spirit."

Cincinnati Enquirer Best Illustrated Children's Books

Information was unavailable at the time of publication.

Commonwealth Club of California Book Award

An annual awards program given by the Commonwealth Club of California that honors books with "exceptional literary merit" in several categories. Authors must have been legal residents of California at the time the manuscript was submitted for publication, and the book must be published during the year the award is being considered. Awards are designated by gold and silver medals.

Cooperative Children's Book Center Children's Book of the Year

Established in 1963, the Cooperative Children's Book Center (CCBC) is located in the School of Education at the University of Wisconsin–Madison and serves as a research library for adults with an interest in children's and young adult literature. In addition to its review of trade books, it also recommends books through its publication of selected awards and distinction lists.

Coretta Scott King Award
Coretta Scott King Award Honor Book
Coretta Scott King Illustrator Award

Sponsored by the American Library Association (Social Responsibilities Round Table). Established in 1969, it is designed to commemorate the life and work of the late Dr. Martin Luther King, Jr., and to honor his wife for her courage and determination in continuing to work for peace and world brotherhood. The award is presented annually to an African American author for an outstandingly inspirational and educational contribution published during the previous year. A separate award for African American illustrators was added in 1979.

Coretta Scott King/John Steptoe Award for New Talent

Named in honor of the prolific African American picture book artist, John Steptoe, this award is administered by the American Library Association and given to an African American author or illustrator for an outstanding book produced at the beginning of his or her career.

The Council on Interracial Books for Children

Information was unavailable at the time of publication.

Dorothy Canfield Fisher Award

Established in 1957 and co-sponsored by the Vermont Department of Libraries and the Vermont Congress of Parents and Teachers, this award is given to the book on the masterlist that is most recommended by children. The award is named in memory of the late Vermont author.

Edgar Award

The Mystery Writers of America present the award named for Edgar Allen Poe to honor the best in mystery literature in fiction and nonfiction that was published or produced during the previous year.

Esther Glen Award

Recognizes the most distinguished contribution to children's literature by an author who is a citizen or resident of New Zealand. This award is sponsored by the Library and Information Association of New Zealand Aotearoa.

Friends of American Writers Juvenile Book Merit Award

The Friends of American Writers was established in 1922 to encourage high standards among the writers of American literature. In 1960, this Chicago-based organization started giving the Juvenile Book Merit Award to books that have a Midwestern setting or are written by authors from Midwestern states. In 2003, the award was discontinued.

Friends of Children and Literature Award (FOCAL)

A support group of the Central Los Angeles Public Library, its annual award is for the author or illustrator of a creative book that has enriched a child's appreciation for and knowledge of California. There are no restrictions as to the publication years of the books considered for the award.

Geoffrey Bilson Award for Historical Fiction for Young People

Established in honor of an author who was also a professor of history, this award is given to an outstanding work of historical fiction for young people published during the previous calendar year and written by a Canadian author. A jury selected by the Canadian Children's Book Centre judges the books eligible for the award.

George C. Stone Center for Children's Books Recognition of Merit Award

The George C. Stone Center for Children's Books is part of the Claremont Graduate University located in Claremont, California. The Recognition of Merit Award is an annual award that was first presented in 1965. It is given to an author or illustrator of a children's book "for its power to please and heighten the awareness of children and teachers as they have shared the book(s) in their classrooms." The winner is invited to accept the award at the Claremont Reading Conference in March.

Georgia Children's Book Award
Georgia Children's Picture Storybook Award

The College of Education at the University of Georgia grants these awards to an author living in North America who has been published during the last five years. The list of nominated books is voted on by children attending school in Georgia.

Golden Kite Award
Golden Kite Award Honor Book

The only award presented to children's book authors and artists by their fellows. Four Golden Kite statuettes are awarded each year for fiction, nonfiction, picture book text, and picture illustration to the most outstanding children's books published during that year and written or illustrated by members of the Society of Children's Book Writers and Illustrators.

Governor General's Award for Children's Literature

The Canada Council for the Arts established this prize for the best books by Canadian writers and illustrators in 1975 and called it the Canada Council Children's Literature Prizes. In 1987, this award became the Governor General's Award for Children's Literature.

Grand Prize of the Salon de L'Enfance

Information was unavailable at the time of publication.

Guardian Fiction Prize
Guardian First Book Award

Originally the Guardian Fiction Prize, this award was renamed the Guardian First Book Award in 1999. It is given annually for an outstanding work of fiction by a British or Commonwealth author that was first published in the United Kingdom during the preceding year. Books are nominated by reading groups organized by the Borders bookstore chain. Picture books and books by previous winners are excluded from consideration.

Gyldendal Prize for Best Scandinavian Children's Book

Information was unavailable at the time of publication.

Horn Book Children's Classics

In 1947, Boston Public Library librarian Alice Jordan compiled the first list of classics drawn from lists of notable books for children. These books are favorites among generations of children and are used to develop a guideline for home library use. The list falls into the main categories of For the Very Young; Stories; Echoes of Times Past; Myths, Legends, and Folklore; and Nonfiction.

Horn Book Fanfare Honor List
Horn Book Fanfare Honor List Blue Ribbon Winner

A highly selective annual list of recommended books that appears in issues of the *Horn Book* magazine, a periodical that reviews recommended children's and young adult titles.

International Board on Books for Young People (IBBY)

Books selected for the biennial Honor List are published within a given period before the year they are selected. The books are considered representative of the best in children's literature from each country and are recommended as worthy of publication throughout the world. The objective of the International Board on Books is to encourage international understanding through children's literature.

International Reading Association Children's Book Award

Two awards, fiction and nonfiction, are presented to authors who have published a first or second book. Books from any country and in any language are grouped into the categories of primary, intermediate, and young adult and must be published in the calendar year they are considered for the award.

International Reading Association Children's Choices
International Reading Association Teachers' Choices
International Reading Association Young Adults' Choices

The prize program of the International Reading Association honors new international talents in children's literature. Publishers are invited to submit candidates whose early written work suggests unusual promise for successful careers in creating books for children. Co-sponsored by the Children's Book Council, three book lists are published annually: Children's Choices, Teachers' Choices, and Young Adults' Choices.

International Reading Association Notable Books for a Global Society

Twenty-five fiction, nonfiction, and poetry books written for students in Grades K to 12 and used to enhance cultural awareness and understanding are listed annually by the Notable Books for a Global Society Committee, part of the International Reading Association Children's Literature and Reading Special Interest Group.

Irish Children's Book Trust Book of the Year

The Bisto Awards began in 1990 by the Irish Children's Book Trust to acknowledge excellence in illustration and written text in Irish children's literature. Renamed the Bisto Awards, they are presented in association with Children's Books Ireland to books published in the calendar year by authors or illustrators born or currently living in Ireland.

Jane Addams Children's Book Award
Jane Addams Children's Book Award Honor Citation
Jane Addams was the first American woman to win the Nobel Peace Prize. The award named for her has been presented annually since 1953 by the Women's International League for Peace and Freedom and the Jane Addams Peace Association. It is given to the children's book of the preceding year that most effectively promotes the causes of peace, social justice, and world community.

Jefferson Cup Award
Jefferson Cup Award Honor Book
This annual award is named for the famous Virginian and third president of the United States, Thomas Jefferson, whose personal library provided the nucleus for the Library of Congress. Administered by the Children's and Young Adult Round Table of the Virginia Library Association, the award is given to a distinguished book for young people published during the previous year in the fields of American history, biography, or historical fiction.

Jewish Book Council Children's Book Award
The Jewish Book Council sponsors this award that focuses on distinguished Jewish authors from the United States or Canada who write children's literature.

Joan G. Sugarman Children's Book Award
Information was unavailable at the time of publication.

John and Patricia Beatty Award
An annual award given by the California Library Association that honors the author of a book that best promotes an awareness of California and its people. John Beatty served as a professor of English History and Humanities, and he and his wife Patricia wrote eleven books of fiction for young readers.

Josette Frank Award
An annual award given by the Children's Book Committee at the Bank Street College of Education, it honors works of outstanding fiction in which children deal positively with personal difficulties and grow emotionally and morally. Josette Frank was the director of children's books at the Child Study Association as well as a distinguished author and editor.

Judy Lopez Children's Book Award
Judy Lopez Children's Book Award Certificate of Merit
Sponsored by the Women's National Book Association, this award honors the memory of one of its founding members who was active in the publishing and bookselling professions and had a strong interest in literacy development. Eligible titles are "works of literary excellence for nine to twelve year olds, written by a citizen or resident of the United States." Winning books are published in the year preceding the award.

Junior Library Guild Selection
Junior Literary Guild Selection
The Junior Literary Guild began in 1929 as a book club that distributed selected current books to children. In 1988, the name was changed to the Junior Library Guild in order to reflect the change of market to school and public libraries. The main criteria for book selection for the nine children's age groups is that they provide a satisfying reading experience. The Junior Library Guild list includes fiction, nonfiction, poetry, biography, historical fiction, humor, and mystery.

Land of Enchantment Children's Book Award (LECBA)
Sponsored by the New Mexico Library Association and the New Mexico Reading Association, this award is chosen from a master list by children in Grades 4 to 8 who reside in New Mexico. The copyright of the award winning book must be within five years prior to the award date and the author must live in the United States.

Laura Ingalls Wilder Award
Sponsored by the Association for Library Service to Children (American Library Association). Named for the American author, it honors an author or illustrator whose books are published in the United States and have made a substantial and lasting contribution to literature for children. The bronze medal was presented every five years between 1960 and 1980, but it is now given every three years.

Lesbian and Gay Children's/Young Adult Award
Established in 1971 by the American Library Association Social Responsibilities Round Table's Gay, Lesbian, and Bisexual Task Force, this award is presented annually to authors of books of exceptional merit published during the prior calendar year that examine the lesbian, gay, and/or bisexual experience.

Lester and Orpen Dennys Award

A fiction book award established by the Canadian publishing firm, Lester and Orpen Dennys, prior to the 1991 departure of one of its publishers, Louise Dennys, to the Knopf/Random House publishing firm.

Lewis Carroll Shelf Award

Currently inactive, the society based on the author of *Alice in Wonderland* gave an annual literary award until 1979.

Lupine Award

Presented annually by the Children's and Young Adults' Services Section of the Maine Library Association. Designed to honor a living author or illustrator who is a resident of Maine or who has created an outstanding work with a focus on Maine. The book must be published within the preceding year and be appropriate for readers up to seventeen years of age.

Margaret A. Edwards Award

Sponsored by the Young Adult Library Services Association (American Library Association) and awarded to an author for lifetime achievement in writing for teenagers. It is given to an author whose work helps teenagers to better understand themselves and their world. The award honors Margaret A. Edwards, a librarian who was passionate about services for young adults and believed strongly that young adults move beyond themselves into the larger world through literature.

Marion Bannett Ridgway Award

Information was unavailable at the time of publication.

Michael L. Printz Award

Celebrates outstanding literature for young adults and honors the late Topeka, Kansas school librarian.

Middle East Book Award

The Middle East Outreach Council established the Middle East Book Award in 1999 to recognize books for children and young adults that contribute to an understanding of the Middle East. Books are judged on their appeal, characterization, plot, and authenticity of their portrayal of a Middle Eastern subject.

Mildred L. Batchelder Award
Mildred L. Batchelder Award Honor Book

Sponsored by the American Library Association and awarded to outstanding translated books for children. The award goes to the United States publisher responsible for the English language edition of the work. The award honors a former executive director of the Association for Library Service to Children who encouraged and promoted translated versions of the world's best literature for children.

Minnesota Book Awards

The Minnesota Humanities Commission sponsors this annual awards program that recognizes, honors, and celebrates Minnesota's literary culture. Winners are presented in the ten different categories of Anthology & Collections, Autobiography & Memoir, Children, Fine Press, History & Biography, Nature & Minnesota, Novel & Short Story, Poetry, Popular Fiction, and Youth Literature.

National Book Award For Children's Literature
National Book Award For Young People's Literature

Presented each year in November to recognize an outstanding contribution to children's literature. It carries a $10,000 cash prize. The award committee emphasizes literary merit and considers books of all genres written for children and young adults by American writers.

National Council for the Social Studies Notable Children's Trade Books in the Field of Social Studies
National Council for the Social Studies Notable Social Studies Trade Books for Young People

The books that appear in these annotated book lists are evaluated and selected by a Book Review Committee appointed by the National Council for the Social Studies (NCSS) in cooperation with the Children's Book Council (CBC). NCSS and CBC have cooperated on this annual bibliography since 1972. Books selected are written primarily for children in Grades K to 8 and are published during the previous year. The selection committee looks for books that emphasize human relations while representing a diversity of groups. Books that are sensitive to a broad range of cultural experiences; present an original theme or a fresh slant on a traditional topic; are easily readable and of high literary quality; or have a pleasing format with illustrations that enrich the text are also sought. Several reviewers read each book, and books are included on the list by committee assent.

National Council of Teachers of English Notable Trade Books in the Language Arts
National Council of Teachers of English Recommended Books

The National Council of Teachers of English (NCTE) works in conjunction with the Children's Literature Assembly to publish booklists of recommended titles for children and young adults. Thirty children's trade books selected annually for their outstanding ability to enhance language awareness for children in Grades K to 8 receive the designation "Notable Book."

National Jewish Book Award

The Jewish Book Council sponsors this award that focuses on distinguished Jewish authors from the United States or Canada who write in the areas of fiction, nonfiction, and children's literature.

Newbery Honor Book
Newbery Medal

Sponsored by the American Library Association and the Association for Library Service to Children, it was established in 1922 in honor of the 18th century British bookseller, John Newbery. The medal is presented annually to the author of the most distinguished contribution to American literature for children published in the United States during the preceding year. The recipient must be a citizen or resident of the United States. There is no limit to the number of Newbery Medal Honor Books selected, and none need be named, but two or three Honor Books are usually chosen each year in addition to the Newbery Medal winner.

New York City School District Best Books for Teens

Information was unavailable at the time of publication.

New York Herald Tribune Award

A literary award given to books judged to be the best by the staff of the obsolete *New York Herald Tribune.*

New York Public Library Books for the Teen Age
New York Public Library Children's Books
New York Public Library 100 Favorite Children's Books

A well-established and prestigious annual listing of books for children and young adults compiled by the staff of the New York Public Library. The bibliography, "100 Favorite Children's Books," has selections that are considered to be some of the best children's books in many different genres, regardless of their original date of publication.

New York Times Best Illustrated Book of the Year
New York Times Notable Books of the Year
New York Times Outstanding Children's Books
New York Times Ten Best Picture Books of the Year

The "national newspaper of record" reviews children's books regularly and makes selective choices of outstanding children's books. A list of notable books is published each December in the categories of children's and young adult literature.

New Zealand Post Children's Book Awards

Sponsored by the New Zealand Government Printer, the Children's Book of the Year Award began in 1982 and continued as the AIM Children's Book Award when AIM Toothpaste took over sponsorship in 1990. The *New Zealand Post* became sponsors in 1997, and the award is now known as the New Zealand Post Children's Book Awards.

Oklahoma Book Award

Sponsored by the Oklahoma Center for the Book in the Department of Libraries, this award celebrates books published in the previous year written about Oklahoma or by Oklahomans.

Outstanding Science Trade Books for Children
Outstanding Science Trade Books for Students K-12

The National Science Teachers Association (NSTA) and the Children's Book Council (CBC) formed a review panel in 1973 and began cooperating on a bibliography that selected outstanding children's science trade books. The books selected target Grades K to 8. Beginning in 2002, the list has been expanded to include high school as well.

Parenting Magazine Best Book
Parenting Magazine Ten Best

Information was unavailable at the time of publication.

Parent's Choice Award
Parent's Choice Storybook Honor Award

Given to those books, toys, videos, computer programs, magazines, audio recordings, and television programs that are judged (by groups of parents, children, and other experts) to be the highest quality and most appealing products in their genre. Criteria for judgments include the highest production standards, universal human values, and a unique quality that pushes the product a notch above the others. Award levels of commendation include Gold, Silver, Recommended, and Approved.

Phoenix Award
Phoenix Award Honor Book
Established in 1985 and awarded annually by the Children's Literature Association to a book originally published in English twenty years previously that did not receive a major award at the time of its publication. The Children's Literature Association is an organization of scholars, teachers, librarians, writers, illustrators, and parents who are interested in developing the serious study of children's literature.

Publishers Weekly Best Books of the Year
Publishers Weekly Best Children's Books
Publishers Weekly "Critic's Choice"
Publishers Weekly Editor's Choice
Publishers Weekly Select Children's Books
Publishers Weekly Starred Review
A weekly periodical that reviews forthcoming books and puts together a list of books that booksellers choose as their favorites.

Pulitzer Prize
The Pulitzer Prize is awarded annually in April by the Pulitzer Prize board of Columbia University for distinguished achievement in journalism, literature, drama, and music. The 1904 will of Joseph Pulitzer, one of the greatest American newspaper publishers in history, established the prizes as an incentive to excellence.

Pura Belpre Award
Given biennially by the Association of Library Services for Children, a division of the American Library Association, this award is presented to a Latino writer or illustrator whose work best represents the Latino cultural experience in an outstanding work of literature for children and youth. Pura Belpre was the first Latina librarian in the New York Public Library.

Reading Rainbow Review Book
This educational program is designed to encourage children to read good books and motivate them to visit their local libraries through the use of television. The criteria for book selection for this program are literary and artistic excellence; adaptability to television; appropriate theme and length; and cultural diversity.

Riverbank Review Children's Books of Distinction Award

An annual award presented by *Riverbank Review*, a quarterly magazine about children's literature. The award honors titles in the categories of picture books, fiction, nonfiction, and poetry published in the year of consideration. Books are examined for outstanding quality in text and illustration; appeal to children and adults; and lasting literary value. Award winning titles are featured in the magazine's Spring issue.

Ruth Schwartz Children's Book Award

In memory of the late Toronto bookseller, this award is given annually by the Canadian Bookseller's Association to a writer of Canadian citizenship who produced an outstanding book of children's literature.

School Library Journal Best Book
School Library Journal Best Book of the Year
School Library Journal "Best of the Best" Children's Books
School Library Journal Starred Review

Published monthly, this journal reviews nearly all new children's and young adult books, stars those of special merit, and includes an annual "Best Books" feature in its December issue.

Scott O'Dell Award for Historical Fiction

This annual award was established by the author Scott O'Dell in 1982 to encourage new authors to focus on historical fiction. The award is presented for a work of historical fiction published by an American publisher and set in the New World.

Sequoyah Children's Book Award
Young Adult Sequoyah Award

Honors the Native American Sequoyah (ca. 1760 to 1843) for his achievement in creating the Cherokee syllabary. Award winning titles on the masterlists are deemed to be of literary excellence and are published at least three years prior to the award year. This award is sponsored by the Oklahoma Library Association and is considered a "student's choice" award.

Sheila A. Egoff Prize

Honoring retired professor of librarianship and children's literature specialist, Sheila A. Egoff, the prize is given to a children's book published anywhere in the world and written by an author who has lived in British Columbia for three of the previous five years. The award was established in 1987 and is presented annually to the best book written for children ages sixteen and younger. Books are judged on text or illustration and originality.

Smithsonian Magazine Notable Books for Children

An annual selection by the staff of the *Smithsonian Magazine* to represent the best of that year's literature for children. Published by the Smithsonian Institution, the *Smithsonian Magazine* regularly covers topics on American and natural history, art, music, and contemporary society. The books on the list reflect that emphasis.

Society of Illustrators Medal

A jury of outstanding illustrators, art directors, and editors in the field of children's book publishing choose gold and silver medal recipients from the Children's Illustrated Book entries during the Society's annual "Original Art" exhibition. Eligible books include picture books, illustrated chapter books, and illustrated young adult books that have been published in the United States during the current or previous year. The Society of Illustrators is based at the New York Museum of American Illustration.

Society of Midlands Authors Award

An award program that includes children's fiction and nonfiction categories. The authors and/or subject matter of books receiving the award have a connection to the twelve-state American Midlands (Midwest). A Midlands author is one who resides in the Midlands, who grew up there, or whose book has a Midlands setting.

Society of School Librarians International Book Award (SSLI)

The Society of School Librarians recognizes excellence in children's publications in the areas of language arts, science, and social studies by giving an award to the author of the most distinguished literary work for young people published in the preceding year.

Southern California Council on Literature for Children

An award given to authors and illustrators living in Southern California. Categories for the awards vary from year to year, but all books are published in the previous year.

Storytelling World Award
Storytelling World Award Honor Book

Sponsored by East Tennessee State University and *Storytelling World Magazine*, fifty highly qualified judges from a variety of professional backgrounds spend several months examining resources published or recorded during the previous three years and choosing awards that apply to seven different categories.

Sydney Taylor Book Award
Sydney Taylor Book Award Honor Book
Awarded annually by the Association of Jewish Libraries to outstanding children's literature with a positive Jewish theme that is published during the preceding year. The award honors the author of the classic *All-Of-A-Kind Family*.

USA Through Children's Books
A featured bibliography published in *Booklist*, May 1, 1986.

Utah Children's Book Award
The Children's Literature Association of Utah (CLAU) sponsors book awards in five categories of picture book, fiction, children's informational book, young adult, and poetry. Winners are chosen from nominated books voted on by the children of Utah. The Award changed its title to "Beehive Award" in the year 2003.

Volunteer State Book Award
Volunteer State Book Award Masterlist
Children read a minimum of three of the twenty nominated titles on the masterlist and then vote for their favorite in this annual award sponsored by the Tennessee Library Association and the Tennessee Association of School Librarians. Titles are chosen for the masterlist by professional librarians and educators who work with students in Grades K to 12.

Western Heritage Award
Given annually by the National Cowboy Hall of Fame and Western Heritage Center to a juvenile book that best portrays the authentic American West. The award honors winners in fifteen different categories of literature, film, television, and music.

Western Writers of America Spur Award
Given annually for distinguished writing about the American West. When the Western Writers of America established the gold and silver awards in 1953, western fiction was a staple of the American publishing industry. The awards have been broadened to include the genres of nonfiction, biographies, and film.

Whitbread Book Award
Whitbread Book of the Year

This annual award is given in the four categories of novel, first novel, poetry, and biography to authors who reside for three or more years in Great Britain or Ireland. Books that win the Whitbread Book Award are eligible to become the Whitbread Book of the Year, which is announced two weeks later.

Writer's Guild of Alberta Awards for Excellence

The Writers Guild of Alberta and the Book Publishers Association of Alberta unite to present twenty-three awards to authors and publishers in Canada.

Yorkshire Post Book Award

The Yorkshire Post Book Award was first established in 1972 and is selected annually by a panel of judges headed by the *Yorkshire Post* Literary Editor. Eligibility is limited to British authors.

Young People's Awards

Presented for excellence in a series.

Youth Storytelling Pegasus Award

A panel comprised of a combination of professional teachers, youth storytelling coaches, and experienced youth storytellers award publications for excellence in promoting youth storytelling. The awards are given in nine different categories.

Appendix B

Sources

Bibliography

Adamson, Lynda G. *Literature Connections to American History K-6.* Englewood, CO: Libraries Unlimited, 1998.

Adamson, Lynda G. *Literature Connections to American History 7-12.* Englewood, CO: Libraries Unlimited, 1998.

Adamson, Lynda G. *Literature Connections to World History K-6.* Englewood, CO: Libraries Unlimited, 1998.

Adamson, Lynda G. *Literature Connections to World History 7-12.* Englewood, CO: Libraries Unlimited, 1998.

Association for Library Service to Children. *The Newbery and Caldecott Awards, 1999 ed.* Chicago, IL: American Library Association, 1999.

Books in Print. New York: R.R. Bowker, 2002.

Mahmoud, Lisa, ed. *Children's Books: Awards and Prizes.* New York: Children's Book Council, 1996.

Webography

"ABC Children's Booksellers Choices Awards." *Association of Booksellers for Children* 2002 [5 Aug. 2002].
www.abfc.com/choices_award.html

"Aesop Prize and Aesop Accolades." *Aesop Prize of the Children's Folklore Section of the American Folklore Society* 2002 [12 July 2003].
http://afsnet.org/sections/children/aesop.htm

"AIM Children's Book Award." *New Zealand Books* 2002
    [26 Aug. 2002].
    www.nzbooks.com/nzbooks/static/aim.asp
"American Book Award." *Stanford University* 2000 [7 July 2002].
    www.stanford.edu/~rickford/award.html
"American Bookseller's Book of the Year Award." *The Children's Lit-
    erature Web Guide* 1998 [7 July 2002].
    www.acs.ucalgary.ca/~dkbrown
"American Bookseller's Pick of the Lists, 1999." *American Booksellers
    Association* 2002 [7 July 2002].
    www.ambook.org/news/features/2447.html
"American Book Sense Book of the Year Award." *American Booksellers
    Asssociation* 2002 [7 July 2002].
    www.bookweb.org/news/awards/3433.html
"Americas Award for Children's and Young Adult Literature." *Center
    for Latin American and Caribbean Studies, University of Wisconsin-
    Milwaukee* 2003 [12 July 2003].
    www.uwm.edu/Dept/CLACS/outreach_americas.html
"Anne Izard Storytellers' Choice Award." *Online Westchester Library
    System* 2003 [12 July 2003].
    www.westchesterlibraries.org/owls/izard.html
"Awards and Scholarships." *The Association of Jewish Libraries* 2003
    [12 July 2003].
    www.jewishlibraries.org/ajlweb/awardsscholarships.htm
"Beehive Awards." *Children's Literature Association of Utah* 2003
    [5 Aug. 2003].
    www.clau.org/
"Best Books." *School Library Journal* 2003 [12 July 2003].
    http://slj.reviewsnews.com/index.asp?layout=bestBooks
"Best Books for Young Adults." *American Library Association* 2002
    [17 Apr. 2002].
    www.ala.org/yalsa/booklists/bbya
"Bisto Awards 2001." *Rollercoaster.ie* 2002 [26 Aug. 2002].
    www.rollercoaster.ie/books/bisto_shortlist_2001.asp
"Bisto Book of the Year Award 2003." *Children's Books of Ireland* 2003
    [12 July 2003].
    www.childrensbooksireland.com/bisto_book_awards/winners_shortli
    st_2003.shtml
"Booklinks." *American Library Association* 2002 [5 Aug. 2002].
    www.ala.org/Booklinks/

"Booklist Editors' Choice." *American Library Association* 2002
    [7 July 2002].
    www.ala.org/booklist/v98/edch-yo.html
"Booklist Editors' Choice." *American Library Association* 2003
    [12 July 2003].
    http://staging.ala.org/Content/NavigationMenu/Products_and_Public
    ations/Periodicals/Booklist/Editors_Choice/2002/Editors_Choice,_20
    02__Books_for_Youth.htm
"Booklist Editors' Choice for Young Adults." *American Library Asso-
    ciation* 2003 [12 July 2003].
    http://staging.ala.org/Content/NavigationMenu/Products_and_Public
    ations/Periodicals/Booklist/Editors_Choice/2002/Editors_Choice,_20
    02__Adult_Books_for_Young_Adults.htm
"Book of the Year for Children Award." *Canadian Library Association*
    2003 [12 July 2003].
    www.cla.ca/awards/boyc.htm
"Book Sense Book of the Year Award." *American Booksellers Associa-
    tion* 2003 [12 July 2003].
    www.ala.org/booklist/v98/cdch-yo.html
"Books for the Teen Age 2003." *New York Public Library* 2002 [12 July
    2003].
    www.nypl.org/home/branch/teen/bta1.html
"Books in Print." *R.R. Bowker* 2002 [20 Apr. 2002].
    www.booksinprint.com
"Boston Globe-Horn Book Awards." *Horn Book, Inc.* 2003 [12 July
    2003].
    www.hbook.com/bghb.shtml
"The Bulletin of the Center for Children's Books: 2002 Blue Ribbons."
    The Bulletin of the Center for Children's Books 2003 [12 July 2003].
    www.lis.uiuc.edu/puboff/bccb/blue02.html
"The Carnegie Medal." *Children's Literature Web Guide* 1998 [7 July
    2002].
    www.ucalgary.ca/~dkbrown/carnegie.html
"The Carnegie Medal." *The CLIP Carnegie and Kate Greenway Chil-
    dren's Book Awards* 2002 [7 July 2002].
    www.carnegiegreenaway.org.uk/carnegie/carn.html
"Carter G. Woodson Book Awards." *National Council for the Social
    Studies* 2003 [12 July 2003].
    www.ncss.org/awards/writing.shtml
"The Charlotte Zolotow Award." *Cooperative Children's Book Center*
    2003 [7 July 2003].
    www.education.wisc.edu/ccbc/zolotow.htm

"Children's Book Awards." *International Reading Association* 2002 [5 Aug. 2002].
www.reading.org/awards/children.html

"Children's Book of the Year Awards." *Victorian Network* 2001 [15 Sep. 2002].
http://home.vicnet.net.au/~ozlit/cbawards.html

"Children's Classics." *The Horn Book, Inc.* 2002 [5 Aug. 2002].
www.hbook.com/childclass1.shtml

"The Children's Literature Association 2002 Phoenix Award." *Children's Literature Associaton* 2002 [17 Apr. 2002].
http://ebbs.english.vt.edu/chla/Phoenix.html

"The Children's Literature Association 2003 Phoenix Award." *Children's Literature Associaton* 2003 [12 July 2003].
http://ebbs.english.vt.edu/chla/Phoenix.html

"Children's Literature Choice List 2003." *Children's Literature Choices* 2003 [12 July 2003].
www.childrenlit.com/clc03.html

"Children's Literature Council of Southern California Awards." *Children's Literature Council of Southern* California 2002 [17 Apr. 2002].
www.childrensliteraturecouncil.org/book

"Child Study Committee Children's Book and Bank Street College Award." *Bank Street College of Education* 2002 [17 Apr. 2002].
www.bnkst.edu/bookcommittee/awards.html

"Choices Booklists." *International Reading Association* 2002 [17 Apr. 2002].
www.reading.org/choices

"Christopher Award Winners." *The Christophers* 2003 [12 July 2003].
www.christophers.org/awards2.html

"The Coretta Scott King Award." *American Library Association* 2002 [7 July 2002].
www.ala.org/srrt/csking/index.html

"The Coretta Scott King Award." *American Library Association* 2003 [12 July 2003].
www.ala.org/Template.cfm?Section=Winners

"Edgar Allen Poe Award." *Mystery Writers of America* 2003 [12 July 2003].
www.mysterywriters.org/

"Esther Glen Award." *New Zealand Book Council* 2002 [5 Aug. 2002].
www.vuw.ac.nz/nzbookcouncil/awards/estherglen.htm

"Father James Keller, M.M., Man of Hope." *The Christophers* 2002
[7 July 2002].
www.christophers.org

"Focal Award Winners." *Los Angeles Public Library* 2002
[17 Apr. 2002].
www.lapl.org/kidspath/booklist/focal_award.htm

"Friends of American Writers Juvenile Book Merit Award." *Friends of American Writers* 2002 [5 Aug. 2002].
home.columbus.rr.com/tspaul/pages/bio/faw.htm

"Geoffrey Bilson Award." *Canadian Children's Book Centre* 2002
[4 Apr. 2002].
www.bookcentre.ca/bilson/2002.htm

"Georgia Children's Literature Book Awards." *College of Education, University of Georgia* 2002 [7 July 2002].
www.coe.uga.edu/gachildlit/awards/winners.html

"GLBT Book Award Winners." *American Library Association* 2002
[8 July 2002].
http://calvin.usc.edu/~trimmer/ala_hp.html

"The Golden Kite Award." *Society of Children's Book Writers and Illustrators* 2003 [12 July 2003].
www.scbwi.org/awards.htm

"Governor General's Awards for Children's Literature." *Children's Literature Web Guide* 2002 [5 Aug. 2002].
www.ucalgary.ca/~dkbrown/gg_award.html

"Guardian First Book Award." *Christchurch City Libraries* 2003
[12 July 2003].
http://library.christchurch.org.nz/Guides/LiteraryPrizes/Guardian_fir
st.asp

Hall, H.R. "The Scott O'Dell Award for Historical Fiction." *Scott O'Dell* 2003 [12 July 2003].
www.scottodell.com/sosoaward.html

"IBBY Honour List." *International Board on Books for Young People* 2003 [7 July 2003].
www.ibby.org/Seiten/04_honour.htm

"International Platform Association Awards." *International Platform Association* 2002 [7 July 2002].
www.internationalplatform.com/Awards.htm.

"Jane Addams Children's Book Award." *Cooperative Children's Book Center, University of Wisconsin-Madison* 2003 [16 June 2003].
www.soemadison.wisc.edu/ccbc/addams/list.htm

"Jefferson Cup Award." *Virginia Library Association* 2002
    [7 July 2002].
    www.shentel.net/handleylibrary/jefferson.htm
"Jefferson Cup Award." *Virginia Library Association* 2003
    [12 July 2003].
    http://www.vla.org/cyart/jefferson_cup/jeffersoncup_index.htm
"John and Patricia Beatty Award." *California Library Association* 2002
    [29 Mar. 2002].
    www.cla-net.org/groups/beatty/beatty.html
"The John Newbery Medal." *American Library Association* 2003
    [15 July 2003].
    www.ala.org/alsc/newbery.html
"John Steptoe Award for New Talent." *American Library Association*
    2002 [17 Apr. 2002].
    www.ala.org/srrt/csking/new_talent.html
"John Steptoe Award for New Talent." *American Library Association*
    2003 [12 July 2003].
    http://www.ala.org/Template.cfm?Section=New_Talent_Award
"Josette Frank Award." *Bank Street College of Education* 2001
    [17 Apr. 2002].
    www.bnkst.edu/bookcommittee/awards.html
"Josette Frank Award." *Bank Street College of Education* 2003
    [12 July 2003].
    www.bankstreet.edu:8080/news/stories/storyReader$66
"Judy Lopez Memorial Award for Children's Literature." *Children's Literature Council of Southern California* 2002 [3 May 2002].
    www.childrensliteraturecouncil.org/other_org.htm
"Junior Library Guild History." *Junior Library Guild* 2002
    [5 Aug. 2002].
    www.juniorlibraryguild.com/jlghistory.htm
"Land of Enchantment Book Award Winners." *New Mexico Library Association* 2003 [13 July 2003].
    www.nmla.org/enchantment.htm
"Laura Ingalls Wilder Medal." *American Library Association* 2001
    [14 Apr. 2002].
    www.ala.org/alsc/wilder.html
"Louise Dennys." *National Library of Canada* 2002 [5 Aug. 2002].
    www.nlc-bnc.ca/2/12/h12-283-e.html
"The Lupine Award." *Windham Public Library* 2003 [15 July 2003].
    www.windham.lib.me.us/lupine.htm

"The Margaret A. Edwards Award." *American Library Association* 2002 [15 Apr. 2002].
www.ala.org/yalsa/edwards/

"The Michael L. Printz Award for Excellence in Young Adult Literature." *American Library Association* 2002 [17 Apr. 2002].
www.ala.org/yalsa/printz/index.html

"The Michael L. Printz Award for Excellence in Young Adult Literature." *American Library Association* 2003 [12 July 2003].
www.ala.org/Content/NavigationMenu/YALSA/Booklists_and_Boo k_Awards/Michael_L__Printz_Award/Printz,_Michael_L__Award.h tm

"Middle East Outreach Council MEOC Announces Middle East Book Awards 2001." *Middle East Outreach Council* 2002 [5 Aug. 2002].
http://inic.utexas.edu/menic/meoc/

"The Mildred L. Batchelder Award." *American Library Association* 2002 [17 Apr. 2002].
www.ala.org/alsc/batch.html

"The Mildred L. Batchelder Award." *American Library Association* 2003 [12 July 2003].
www.ala.org/Content/NavigationMenu/ALSC/Awards_and_Scholars hips1/Literary_and_Related_Awards/Batchelder_Award/Batchelder_ Award_Current_Winner2/Batchelder_Award_Current_Winner.htm

"Minnesota Book Awards." *The Minnesota Humanities Commission* 2003 [5 June 2003].
www.minnesotahumanities.org/Book/awards.htm

"More Information about the CCBC." *University of Wisconsin-Madison* 2002 [5 Aug. 2002].
www.soemadison.wisc.edu/ccbc/more.htm

"National Book Awards." *American Booksellers Association* 2002 [17 Apr. 2002].
www.bookweb.org//news/awards/1289.html

"National Book Awards." *American Booksellers Association* 2003 [17 July 2003].
www.nationalbook.org/nbathisyear.html

"National Jewish Book Awards." *Oberlin Online* 2002 [5 Aug. 2002].
www.oberlin.edu/~jsluk/jewish.htm

"National Jewish Book Awards." *My Jewish Books* 2003 [16 July 2003].
www.myjewishbooks.com/awards01.html

"New York Times Notable Books of the Year." *Adbooks* 2003 [12 July 2003].
www.geocities.com/adbooks/nytimes.html

"New York Times Outstanding Children's Books of the Year." *New York Times* 2003 [12 July 2003].
     http://query.nytimes.com/full-page?res=9DOOEFDF1338F93BA357
     5CIA96C8B

"North Carolina Office of Archives and History." *North Carolina Literary and Historical Association* 2002 [5 Aug. 2002].
     www.ah.dcr.state.nc.us/affiliates/lit-hist/lit-hist.htm

"Notable Books for a Global Society." *Children's Literature and Reading Special Interest Group of the International Reading Association* 2002 [5 Aug. 2002].
     www.csulb.edu/org/childrenslit/Projects/Notable_Books_for_a_Glob
     al_Soc/notable_books

"Notable Books for a Global Society." *Children's Literature and Reading Special Interest Group of the International Reading Association* 2003 [12 July 2003].
     www.csulb.edu/org/childrens-lit/proj/nbgs/intro-nbgs.html

"Notable Social Studies Books for Young People." *National Council for the Social Studies* 2003 [8 July 2003].
     www.socialstudies.org/resources/notable/

"Outstanding Science Trade Books for Students K-12." *National Science Teachers Association* 2003 [5 July 2003].
     www.nsta.org/ostbc

"The Parent's Choice Awards." *Parent's Choice Foundation* 2003 [15 July 2003].
     www.parents-choice.org/get_direct.cfm?cat=p_boo

"Pulitzer Prize." *Oberlin Online* 2002 [5 Aug. 2002].
     www.oberlin.edu/~jsluk/pulitzer.htm.

"The Pura Belpre Award." *The American Library Association* 2002 [17 Apr. 2002].
     www.ala.org/alsc/belpre.html

"Quick Picks for Young Adult Readers." *American Library Association* 2002 [3 May 2002].
     www.ala.org/yalsa/booklists/quickpicks

"Quick Picks for Young Adult Readers." *American Library Association* 2003 [12 July 2003].
     www.ala.org/Content/NavigationMenu/YALSA/Booklists_and_Boo
     k_Awards/Quick_Picks_for_Reluctant_Young_Adult_Readers/2003
     _Quick_Picks_for_Reluctant_Young_Adult_Readers.htm

"The Randolph Caldecott Medal." *American Library Association* 2002 [17 Apr. 2002].
     www.ala.org/alsc/caldecott.html

"The Randolph Caldecott Medal." *American Library Association* 2003
    [12 July 2003].
    www.ala.org/Content/NavigationMenu/ALSC/Awards_and_Scholars
    hips1/Literary_and_Related_Awards/Caldecott_Medal/Caldecott_M
    edal.htm
"Reading Rainbow." *Reading Rainbow Program Overview* 2002
    [5 Aug. 2002].
    www.canlearn.com/READINGR/rrdescrip.html
"Riverbank Review Children's Books of Distinction." *Riverbank Review*
    2002 [5 Aug. 2002].
    www.riverbankreview.com/bod02fic.html
"Riverbank Review Children's Books of Distinction." *Riverbank Review*
    2003 [12 July 2003].
    www.riverbankreview.com/bod03.html
"Ruth Schwartz Children's Book Award." *National Book Service* 2003
    [12 July 2003].
    www.nbs.com/choiceawd.htm#Schwartz
"Sequoyah Book Awards." *Oklahoma Library Association* 2003
    [23 Apr. 2003].
    www.bartlesville.lib.ok.us/sequoyah/
"71st Annual California Book Award Winners." *The Commonwealth
    Club of California* 2003 [7 July 2003].
    www.commonwealthclub.org/bookawards.html
"Sheila Egoff Children's Prize." *B.C. Book Prizes* 2002 [16 Mar. 2002].
    www.harbour.sfu.ca/bcbook/index.html
"Smithsonian Magazine Notable Books for Children." *Smithsonian
    Magazine* 2002 [12 July 2003].
    www.smithsonianmag.si.edu/smithsonian/issues01/nov01/book_revi
    ew.html
"The Society of Illustrators Original Art 2002." *The Society of Illustra-
    tors* 2002 [5 Aug. 2002].
    www.societyillustrators.org/exhibition_competition/OAcall_2002.ht
    ml
"Society of Midlands Authors Award." *Society of Midlands Authors*
    2003 [8 July 2003].
    www.midlandauthors.com/index.htm
"Society of School Librarians International Book Award." *Society of
    School Librarians International* 2002 [17 Apr. 2002].
    http://falcon.jmu.edu/~ramseyil/ssli.htm
"The Spur Awards." *Western Writers of America* 2002 [17 Apr. 2002].
    www.westernwriters.org/spur_awards.htm

"Storytelling World Annual Awards." *Storytelling World* 2002
    [14 June 2002].
    http://pages.preferred.com/~hjoy/events/awards/index.html
"Storytelling World Annual Awards." *Storytelling World* 2003
    [14 July 2003].
    http://pages.preferred.com/~hjoy/events/awards/2003win.htm
"The Sydney Taylor Book Awards." *Association of Jewish Libraries*
    2003 [15 July 2003].
    www.jewishlibraries.org
"21st Annual BABRA Awards." *Bay Area Book Reviewers Association*
    2002 [15 Apr. 2002].
    www.poetryflash.org/02BABRA.html
"22nd Annual BABRA Awards." *Bay Area Book Reviewers Association*
    2003 [15 July 2003].
    www.poetryflash.org/BABRA.03.html#ChildsLit
"The 2001 Alex Awards." *American Library Association* 2002
    [1 Apr. 2002].
    www.ala.org/yalsa/booklists/alex/2002alextxt.html
 "The 2001 Cuffies." *Publishers Weekly/Reed Business Information* 2002
    [8 July 2002].
    http://publishersweekly.reviewsnews.com
"2001 Notable Children's Books." *American Library Association* 2002
    [17 Apr. 2002].
    www.ala.org/alsc/nbook02.html
"2001 Notable Children's Books in the Language Arts." *Language Arts:
    Vol. 79, No. 4. The National Council of Teachers of English* 2002
    [15 Apr. 2002].
    www.ncte.org/pdfs/subscribers-only/la/0794mar02/LA0794Notable.
    pdf
"2002 Notable Children's Books." *American Library Association* 2002
    [17 Apr. 2002].
    www.ala.org/alsc/nbook02.html
"2002 Oklahoma Book Award Winner." *Oklahoma Center for the Book*
    2002 [5 Aug. 2002].
    www.odl.state.ok.us/obc/02win.htm
"2002 to 2003 Dorothy Canfield Fisher Books." *Montpelier School Dis-
    trict* 2002 [7 July 2002].
    http://mps.k12.vt.us/msms/dcf/dcf.html
"The 2003 Alex Awards." *American Library Association* 2003.
    [12 July 2003].
    www.ala.org/Content/NavigationMenu/YALSA/Booklists_and_Boo
    k_Awards/Alex_Awards/2003_Alex_Awards.htm

"2003 Notable Children's Books." *American Library Association* 2003 [17 July 2003].
www.ala.org/Content/NavigationMenu/ALSC/Awards_and_Scholars hips1/Childrens_Notable_Lists/2003_Childrens_Notable_Books/200 3_Childrens_Notable_Books.htm

"2003 Oklahoma Book Award Winner." *Oklahoma Center for the Book* 2003 [15 July 2002].
http://www.odl.state.ok.us/ocb/03win.htm

"Utah Children's Book Awards." *Children's Literature Association of Utah* 2002 [5 Aug. 2002].
www.clau.org/

"Volunteer State Book Award." *The Tennessee Association of School Librarians* 2002 [5 Aug. 2002].
www.korrnet.org/tasl/vsba.htm

"Western Heritage Awards." *National Cowboy and Western Heritage Museum* 2001 [17 Apr. 2002].
www.cowboyhalloffame.org/e_awar_winn.html

"Whitbread Book Award." *Oberlin Online* 2002 [5 Aug. 2002].
www.oberlin.edu/~jsluk/whitbread.htm

"Winners of Alberta Book Awards Gala." *Writers Guild of Alberta* 2002 [5 Aug. 2002].
www.writersguild.ab.ca/awards.htm

"The Yorkshire Post Book Award." *British Literary Prizes* 2002 [24 Nov. 2002].
www.unca.edu/`moseley/yorkshire.html

"Youth Storytelling Pegasus Award." *Voices Across America Youth Storytelling* 2003 [13 July 2003].
www.youthstorytelling.com/vaa/pegawards.htm

Author/Title Index

Subject Index

About the Author

Beth Bartleson Zarian received her master's degree in library and information science from the University of Wisconsin in 1989, specializing in reference. In addition to memberships in the American Library Association and the American Folklore Society, she recently concluded a three-year appointment to the curriculum committee of School District 67 in Lake Forest, Illinois. She resides with her husband and four sons in Boulder, Colorado.